Zodiac P.I.

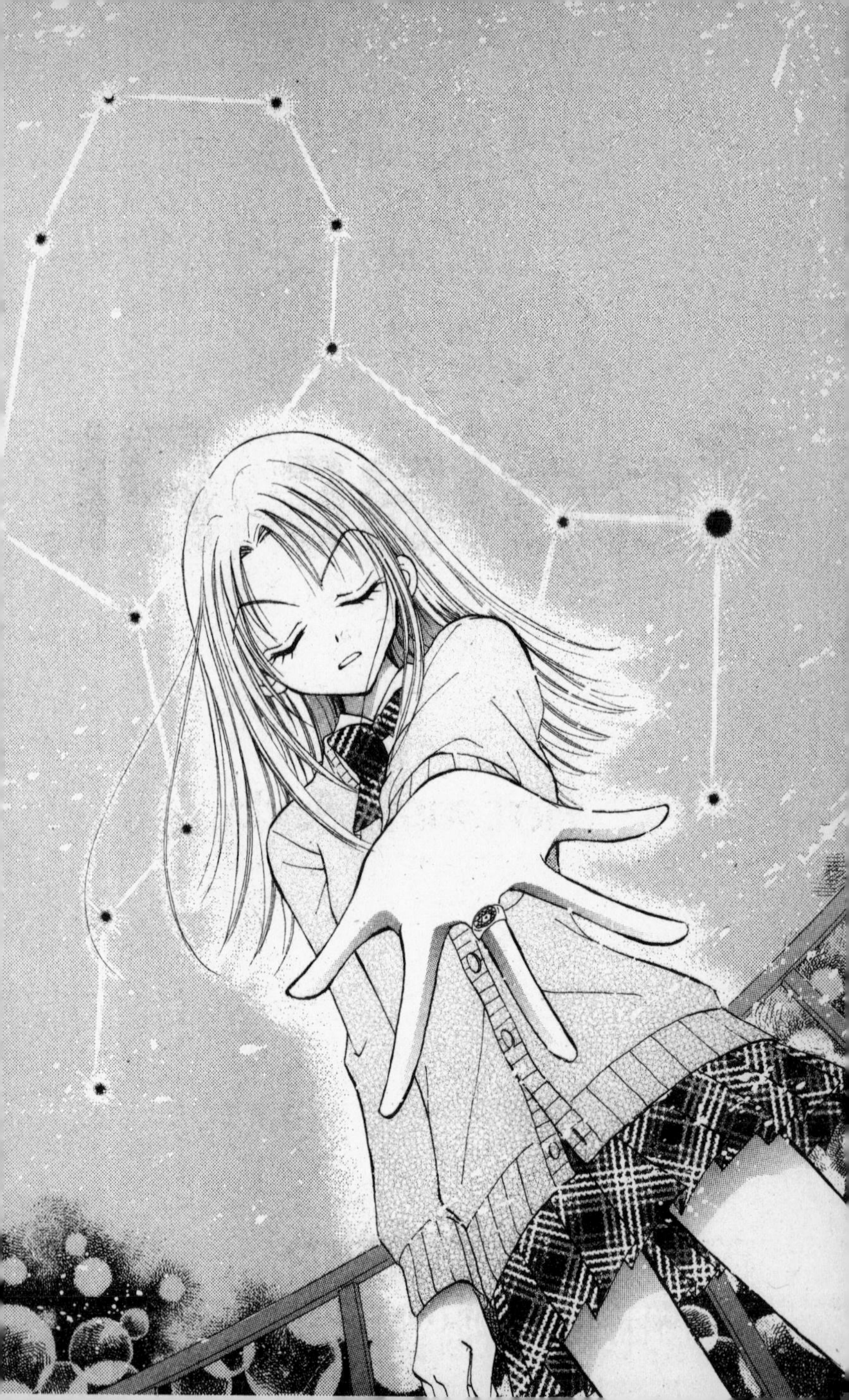

Zodiac P.I.

Vol. 1
Natsumi Ando

HAMBURG // LONDON // LOS ANGELES // TOKYO

Zodiac P.I. Vol. 1
Created by Natsumi Ando

Translation - Takae Brewer
English Adaptation - Chris Poole
Associate Editor - Jodi Bryson
Retouch and Lettering - Karen Taylor
Production Artist - Camellia Cox
Graphic Designer - Monalisa de Asis
Cover Design - Raymond Makowski

Editor - Julie Taylor
Digital Imaging Manager - Chris Buford
Production Manager - Jennifer Miller
Managing Editor - Lindsey Johnston
Editor-in-Chief - Rob Tokar
VP of Production - Ron Klamert
Publisher - Mike Kiley
President and C.O.O. - John Parker
C.E.O. and Chief Creative Officer - Stuart Levy

A  Manga

TOKYOPOP Inc.
5900 Wilshire Blvd. Suite 2000
Los Angeles, CA 90036

E-mail: info@TOKYOPOP.com
Come visit us online at www.TOKYOPOP.com

ISBN: 1-59182-383-8

First TOKYOPOP printing: July 2003

10 9 8 7 6 5 4 3

Printed in the USA

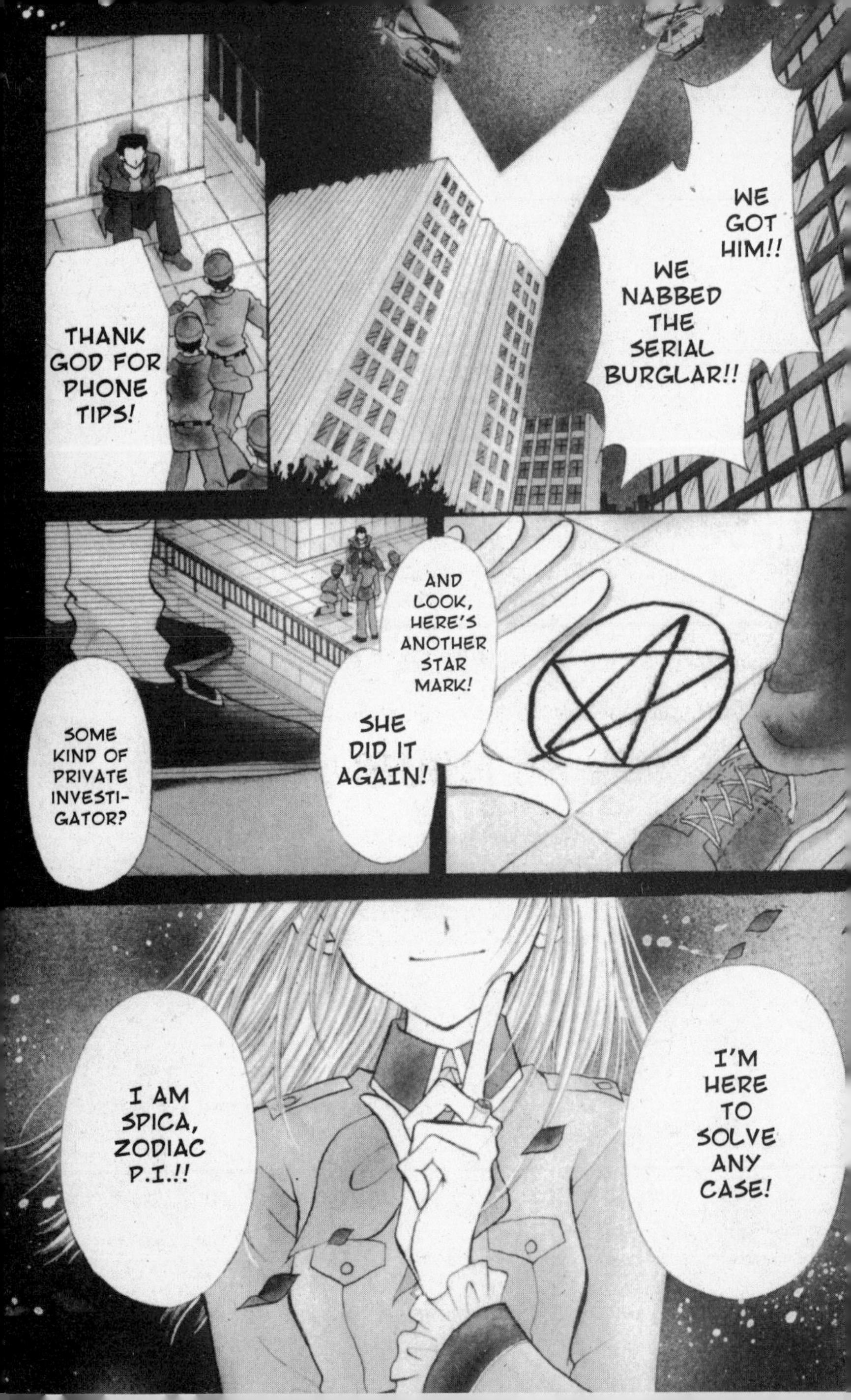
WE GOT HIM!!
WE NABBED THE SERIAL BURGLAR!!
THANK GOD FOR PHONE TIPS!
AND LOOK, HERE'S ANOTHER STAR MARK!
SHE DID IT AGAIN!
SOME KIND OF PRIVATE INVESTI-GATOR?
I'M HERE TO SOLVE ANY CASE!
I AM SPICA, ZODIAC P.I.!!

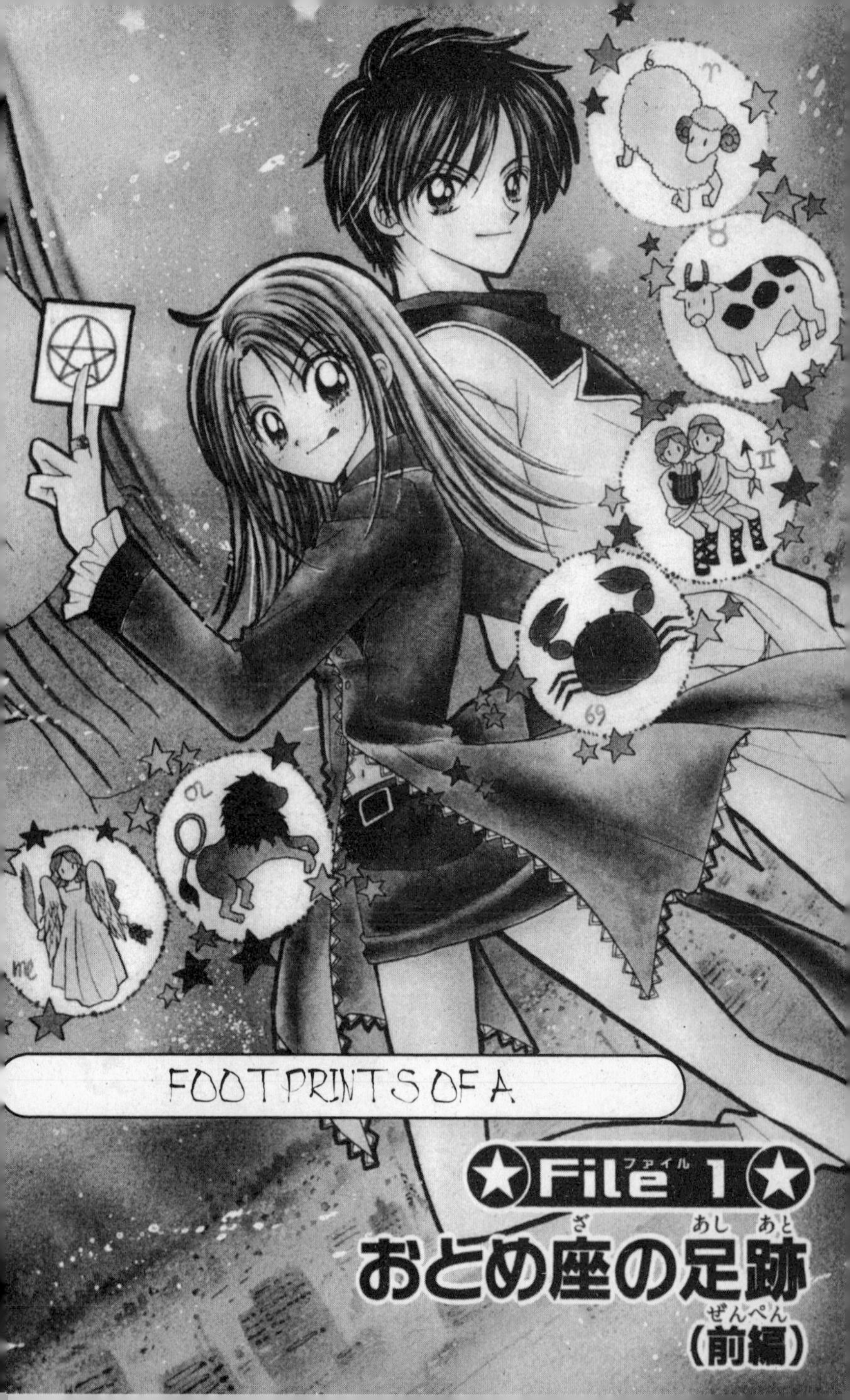
FOOT PRINTS OF A
★File 1★
ファイル
おとめ座の足跡
ざ あしあと
(前編)
ぜんぺん

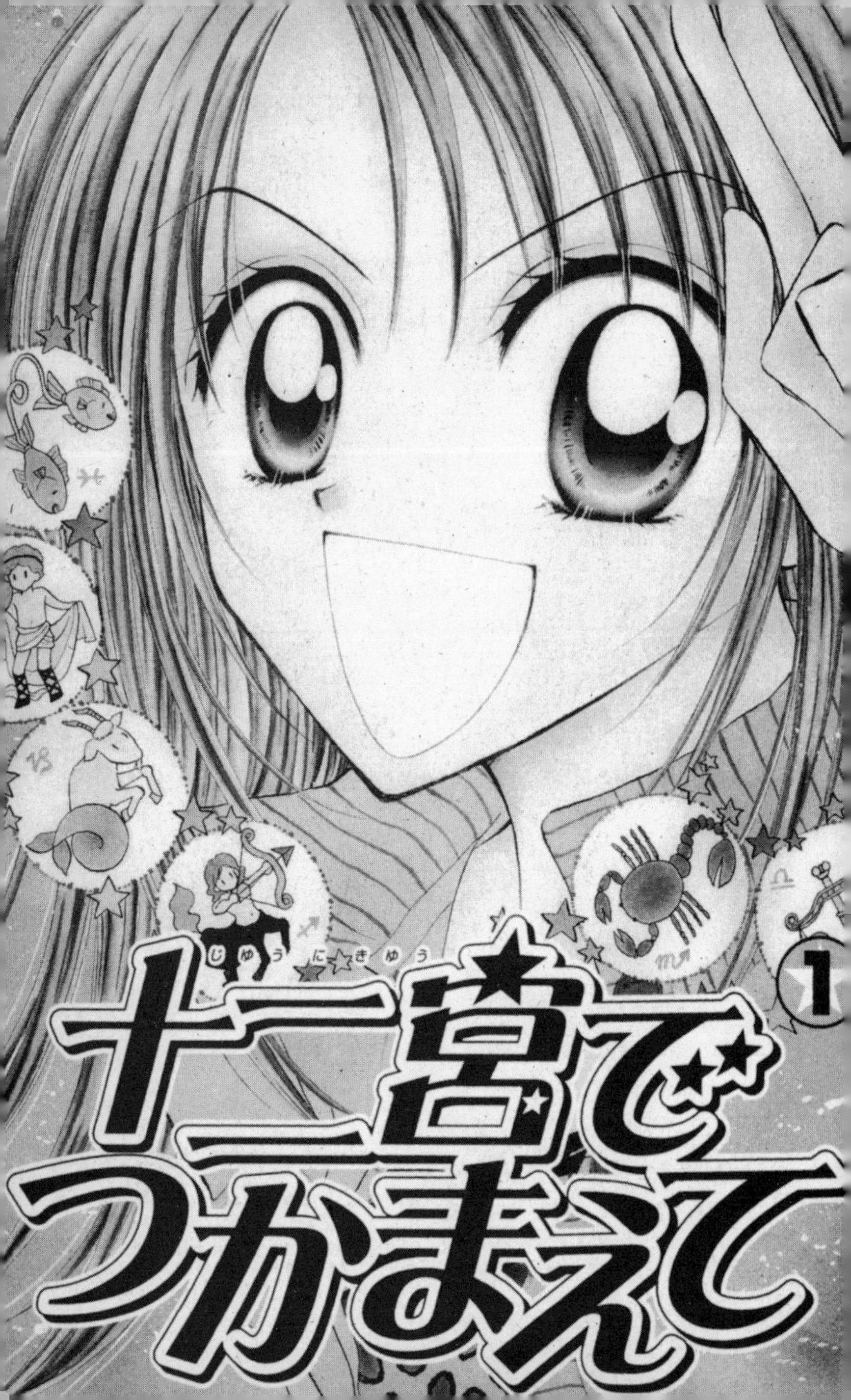
じゅうにきゅう
十二宮でつかまえて
1

GREETINGS FROM THE AUTHOR

HELLO! IT'S BEEN QUITE A WHILE SINCE I WROTE THE LAST SERIES. I BET YOU WONDER WHAT THIS NEW SERIES IS ALL ABOUT. THE TITLE *ZODIAC P.I.* DOESN'T GIVE YOU MUCH OF A CLUE REGARDING WHAT KIND OF STORY IT IS, DOES IT? IN A NUTSHELL, IT'S A DETECTIVE STORY. SOME READERS ASK ME WHAT "ZODIAC" MEANS. IT MEANS THE SIGNS OF THE ZODIAC, AS IN THE DAILY HOROSCOPES IN THE NEWSPAPER. I HOPE YOU ENJOY THE SERIES IN TERMS OF BOTH MYSTERIES AND ASTROLOGY. I AM ON A 4-WEEK VACATION AND COMPLETELY RELAXED. DURING THE VACATION, I DECIDED TO DO MY ROOM OVER AND WORKED PRETTY HARD. I HAVE A MUSCLE ACHE ALL OVER NOW. I HAVE A TERRIBLE BACK PAIN ALSO. I AM SO SHORT ON PHYSICAL STRENGTH...

I'VE BEEN WORKING AT NIGHT FOR THE PAST COUPLE OF YEARS, LIVING IN A WORLD WHERE DAY AND NIGHT ARE REVERSED. MY BIOLOGICAL RHYTHM IS SO MESSED UP THAT I DON'T GET SLEEPY UNTIL DAWN!! I'VE GOT TO FIX THIS.

I AM SO LAZY...

I SHOULD LOOK AT THE BRIGHT SIDE.
THE NIGHT LIFE IS A LOT OF FUN.

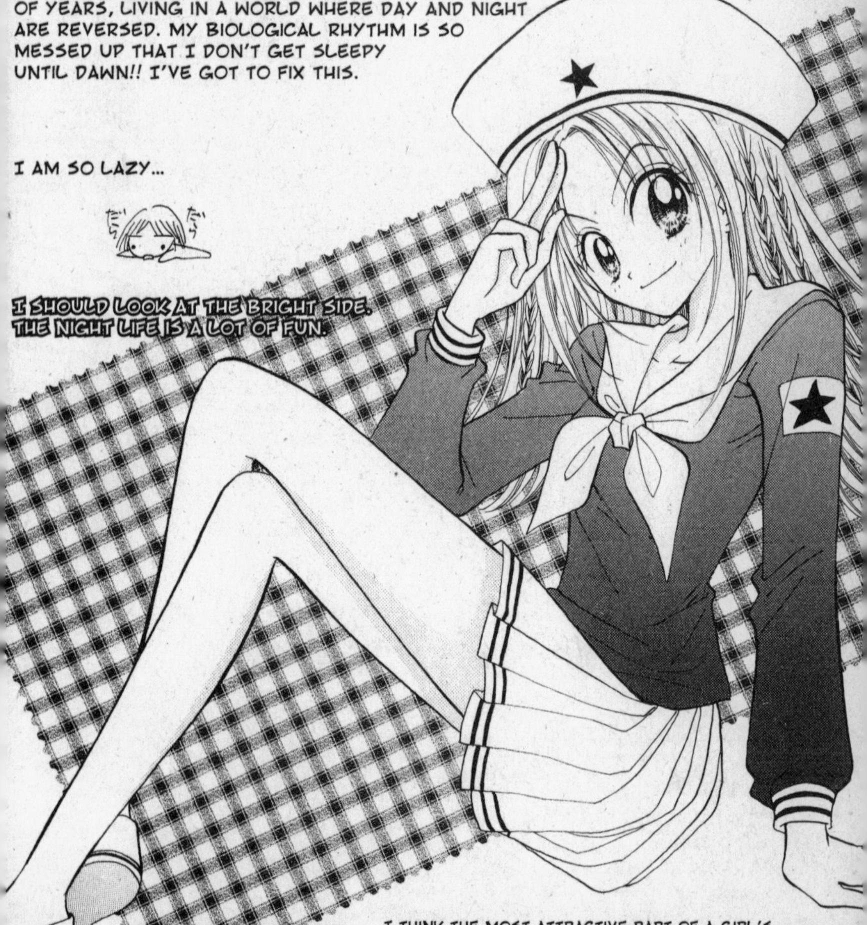

I THINK THE MOST ATTRACTIVE PART OF A GIRL'S BODY IS HER LEGS! AM I WEIRD? THAT'S WHY I TEND TO MAKE MY CHARACTERS WEAR MINISKIRTS.

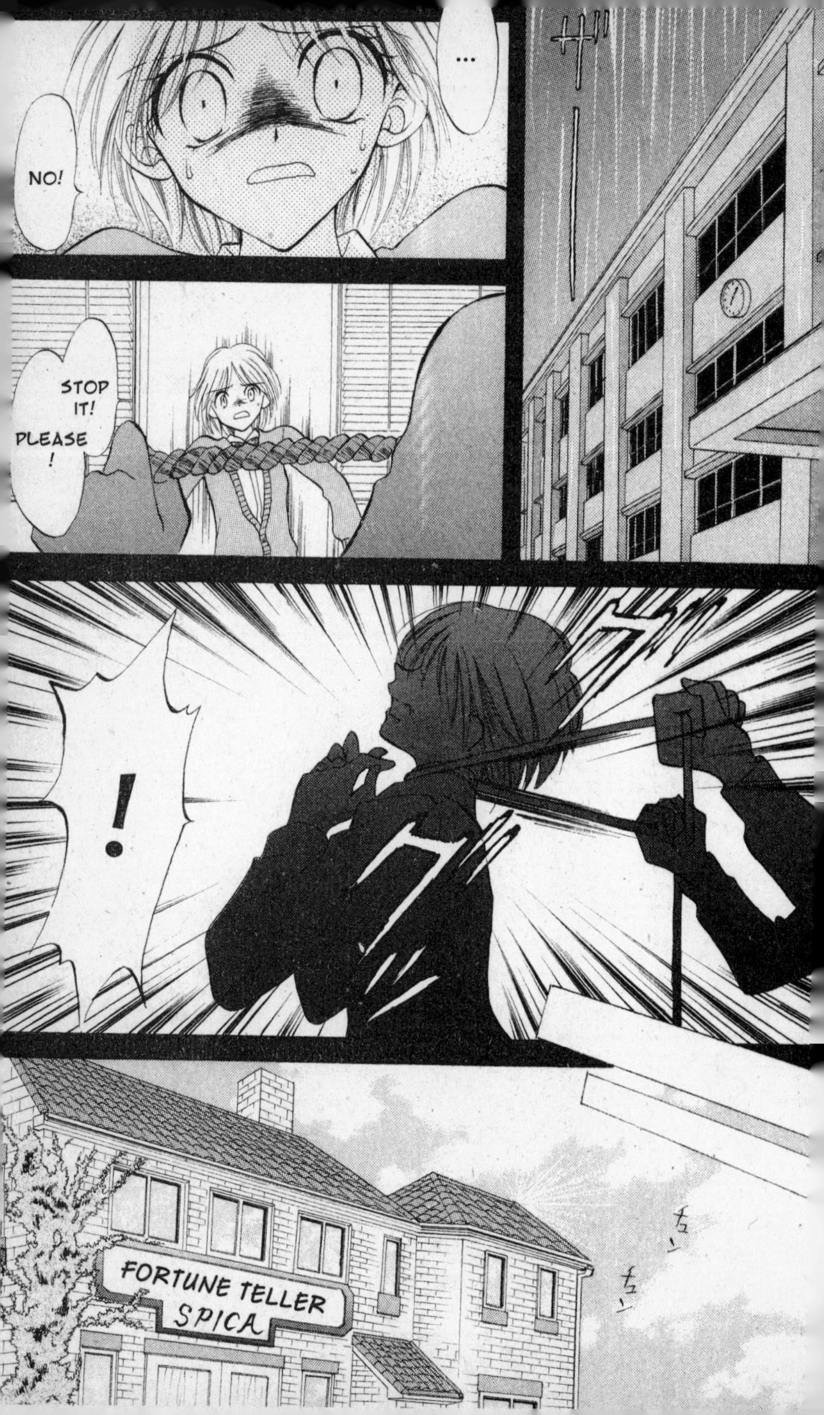
...
NO!
STOP IT! PLEASE!
!
FORTUNE TELLER SPICA

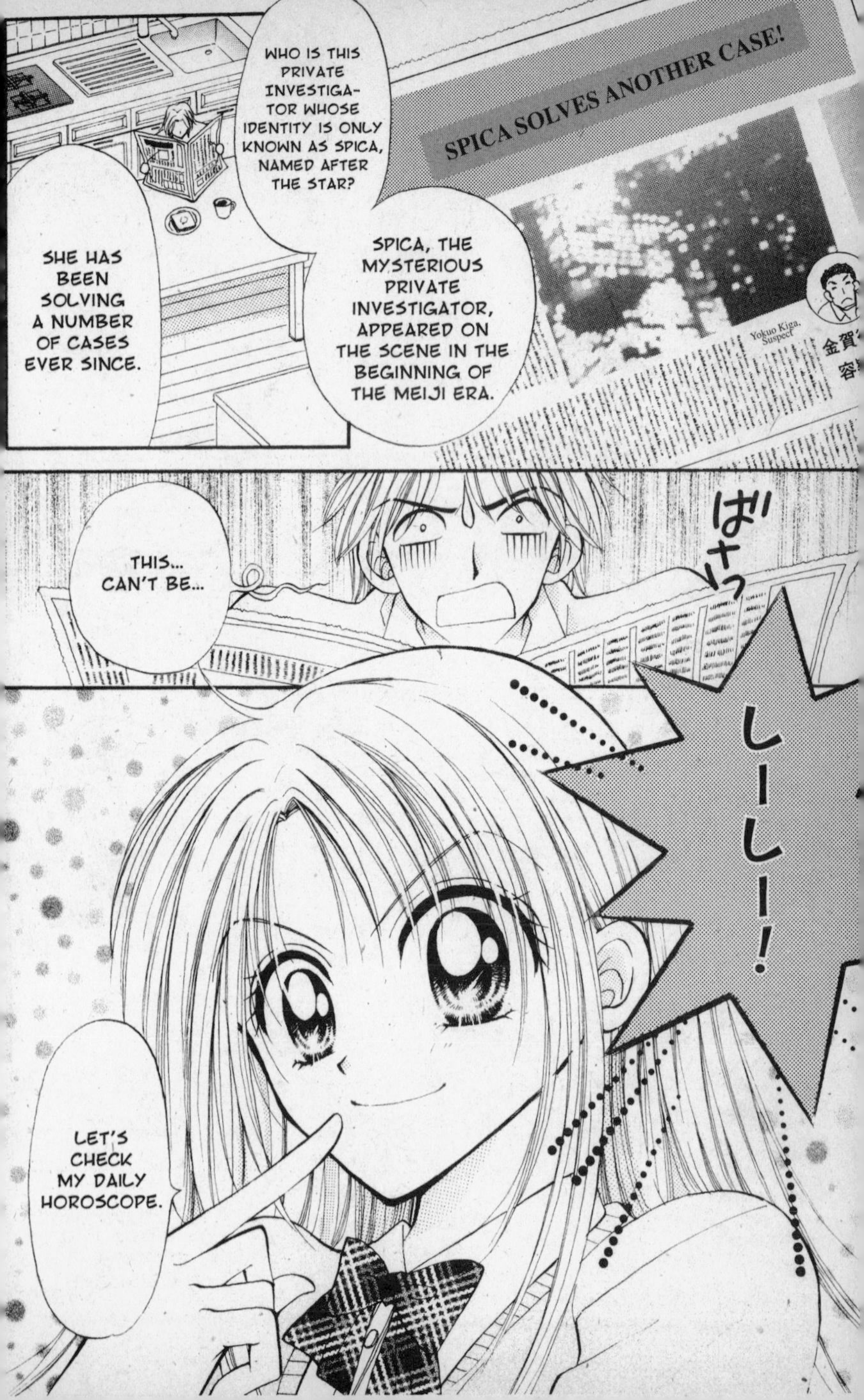
SPICA SOLVES ANOTHER CASE!
Yokuo Kiga, Suspect
金賀
容
WHO IS THIS PRIVATE INVESTIGATOR WHOSE IDENTITY IS ONLY KNOWN AS SPICA, NAMED AFTER THE STAR?
SPICA, THE MYSTERIOUS PRIVATE INVESTIGATOR, APPEARED ON THE SCENE IN THE BEGINNING OF THE MEIJI ERA.
SHE HAS BEEN SOLVING A NUMBER OF CASES EVER SINCE.
ぱさっ
THIS... CAN'T BE...
しーしー!
LET'S CHECK MY DAILY HOROSCOPE.

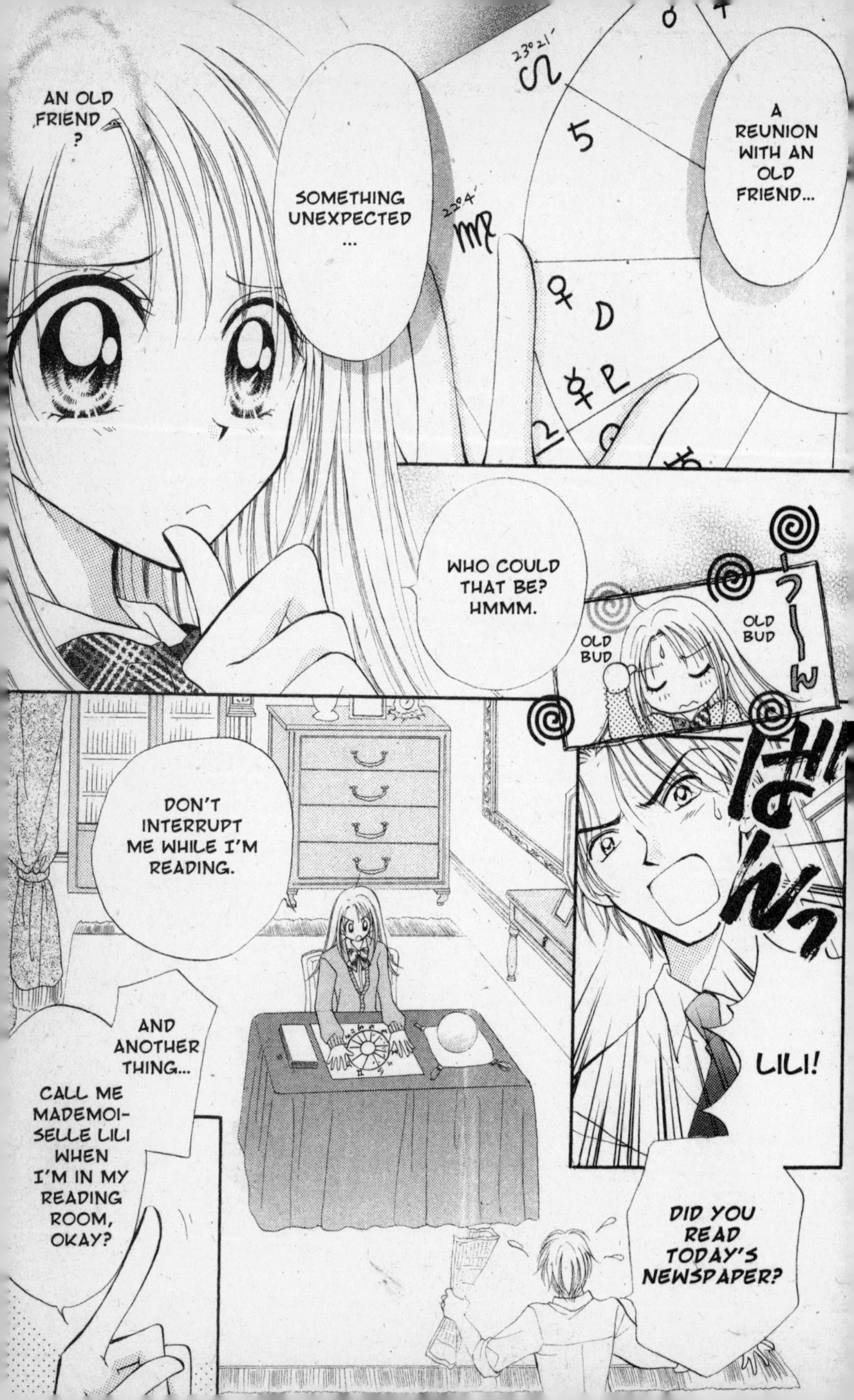

A REUNION WITH AN OLD FRIEND...
SOMETHING UNEXPECTED ...
AN OLD FRIEND ?
WHO COULD THAT BE? HMMM.
OLD BUD
OLD BUD
うーん
ぱんっ
LILI!
DID YOU READ TODAY'S NEWSPAPER?
DON'T INTERRUPT ME WHILE I'M READING.
AND ANOTHER THING...
CALL ME MADEMOISELLE LILI WHEN I'M IN MY READING ROOM, OKAY?

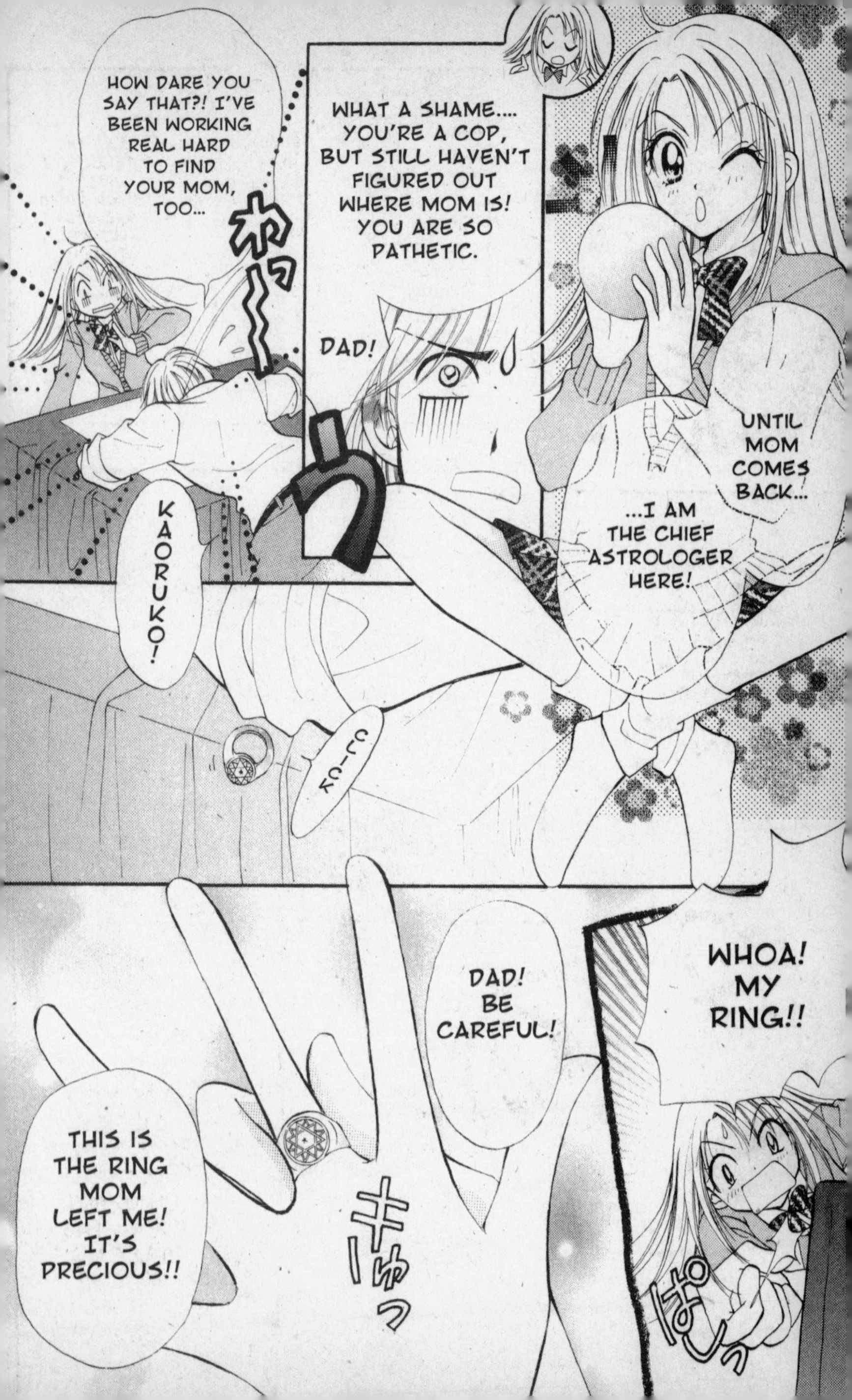
UNTIL MOM COMES BACK...
...I AM THE CHIEF ASTROLOGER HERE!
WHAT A SHAME.... YOU'RE A COP, BUT STILL HAVEN'T FIGURED OUT WHERE MOM IS! YOU ARE SO PATHETIC.
DAD!
HOW DARE YOU SAY THAT?! I'VE BEEN WORKING REAL HARD TO FIND YOUR MOM, TOO...
わーっ
KAORUKO!
CLICK
WHOA! MY RING!!
ぱしっ
DAD! BE CAREFUL!
THIS IS THE RING MOM LEFT ME! IT'S PRECIOUS!!
キュッ

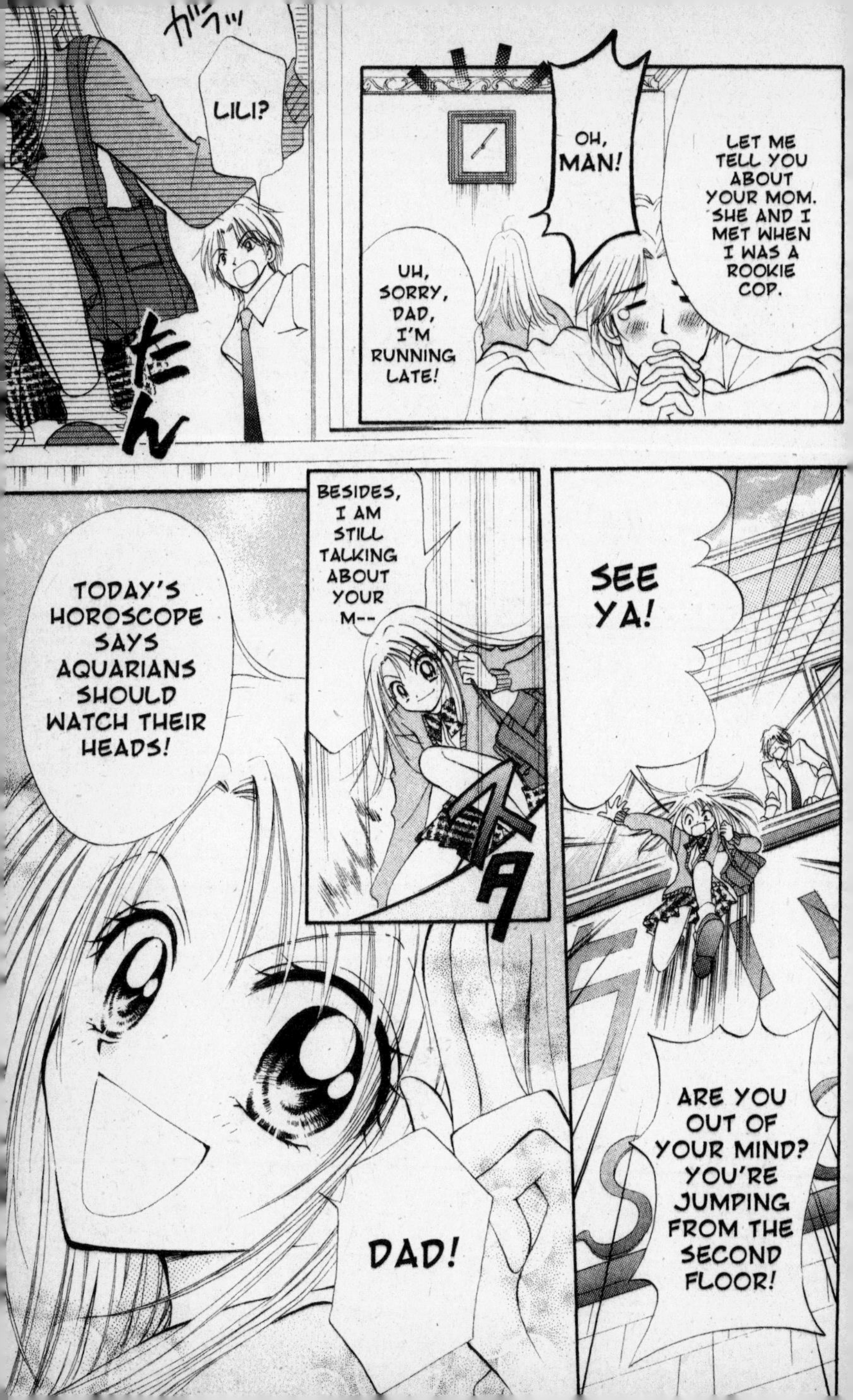
LET ME TELL YOU ABOUT YOUR MOM. SHE AND I MET WHEN I WAS A ROOKIE COP.
OH, MAN!
UH, SORRY, DAD, I'M RUNNING LATE!
ガラッ
LILI?
たん
SEE YA!
ARE YOU OUT OF YOUR MIND? YOU'RE JUMPING FROM THE SECOND FLOOR!
BESIDES, I AM STILL TALKING ABOUT YOUR M--
TODAY'S HOROSCOPE SAYS AQUARIANS SHOULD WATCH THEIR HEADS!
DAD!

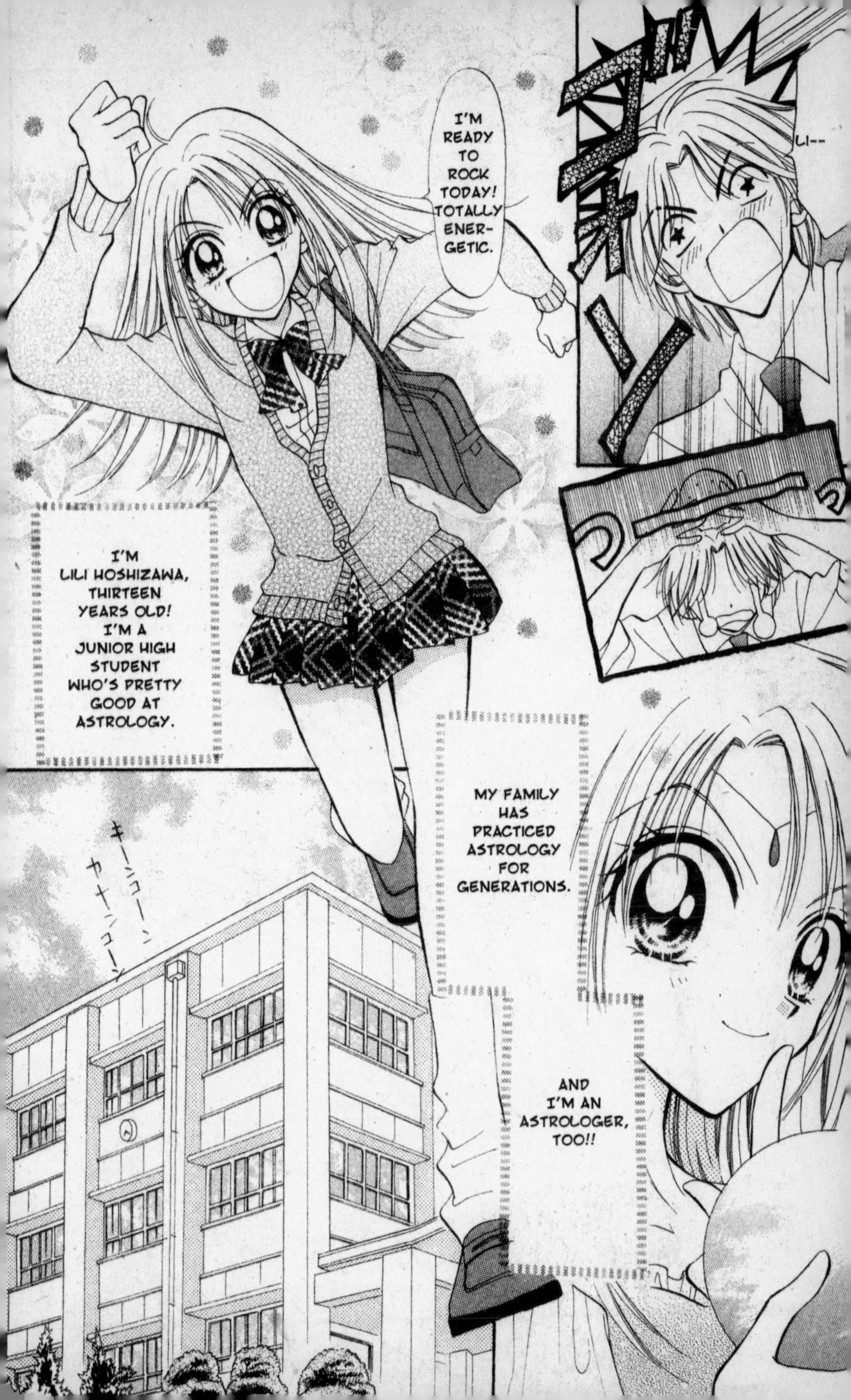
LI--
I'M READY TO ROCK TODAY! TOTALLY ENERGETIC.
I'M LILI HOSHIZAWA, THIRTEEN YEARS OLD! I'M A JUNIOR HIGH STUDENT WHO'S PRETTY GOOD AT ASTROLOGY.
MY FAMILY HAS PRACTICED ASTROLOGY FOR GENERATIONS.
AND I'M AN ASTROLOGER, TOO!!
キーンコーン
カーンコーン

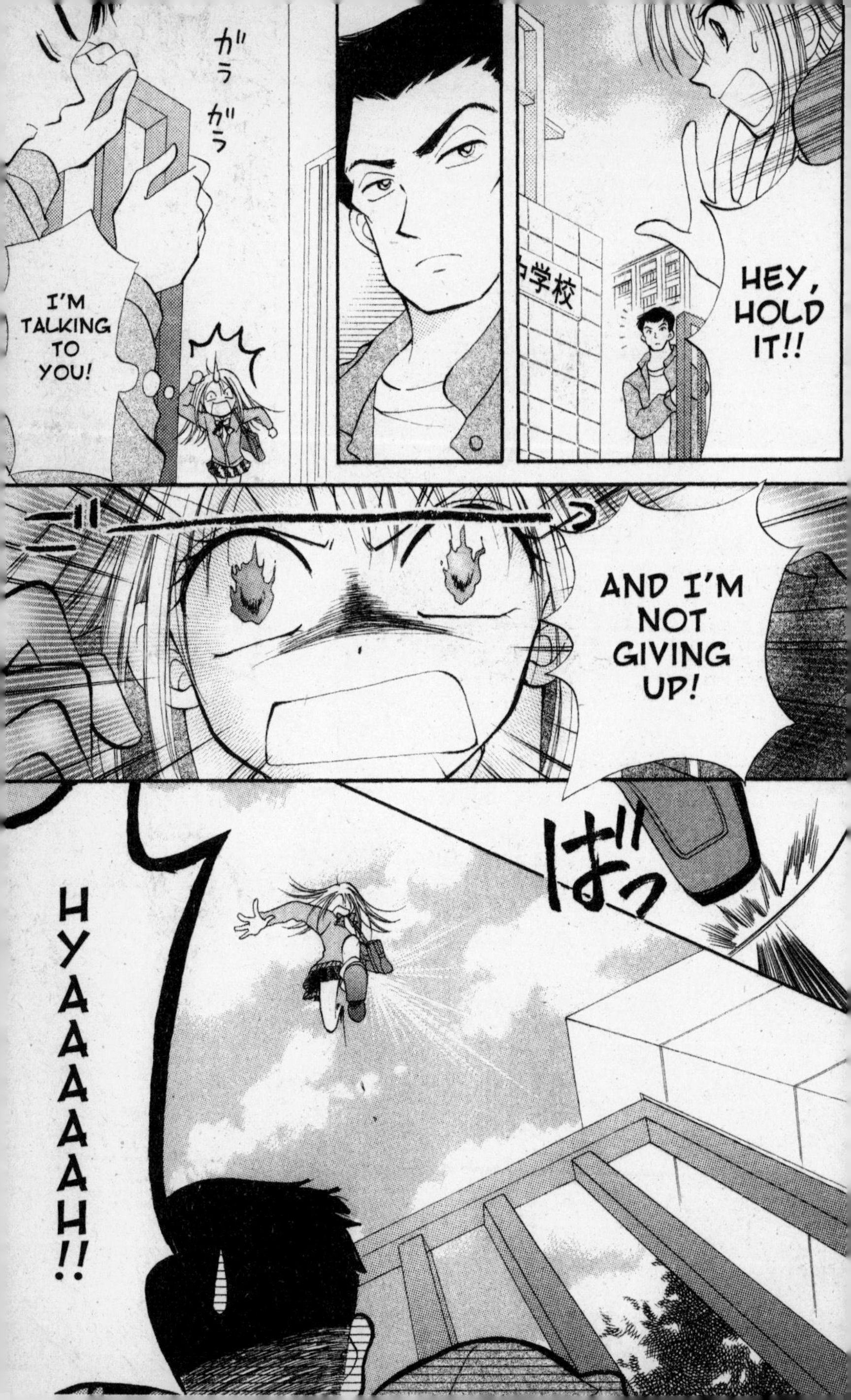
HEY, HOLD IT!!
学校
ガラ ガラ
I'M TALKING TO YOU!
AND I'M NOT GIVING UP!
ぱっ
HYAAAAAAH!!

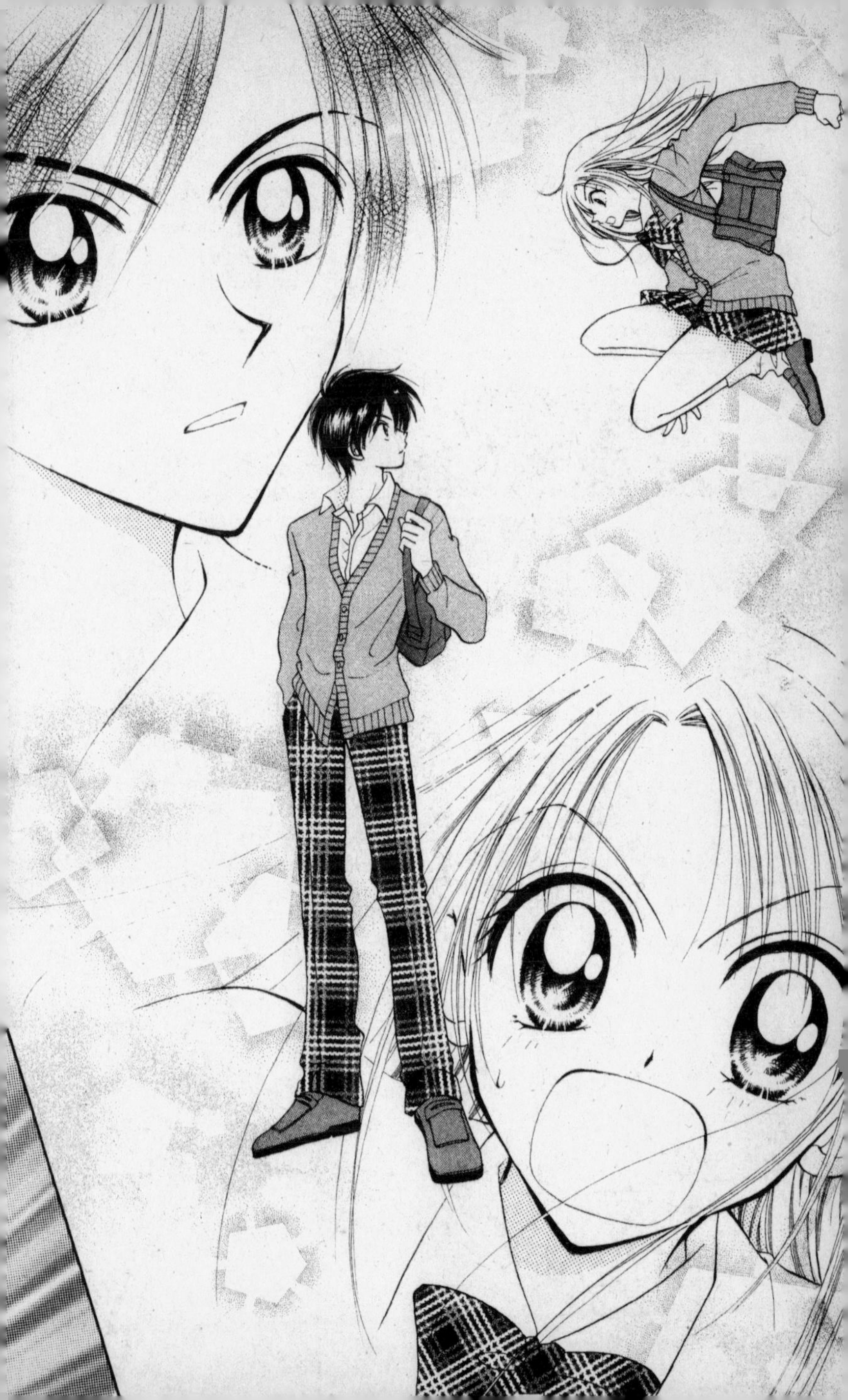

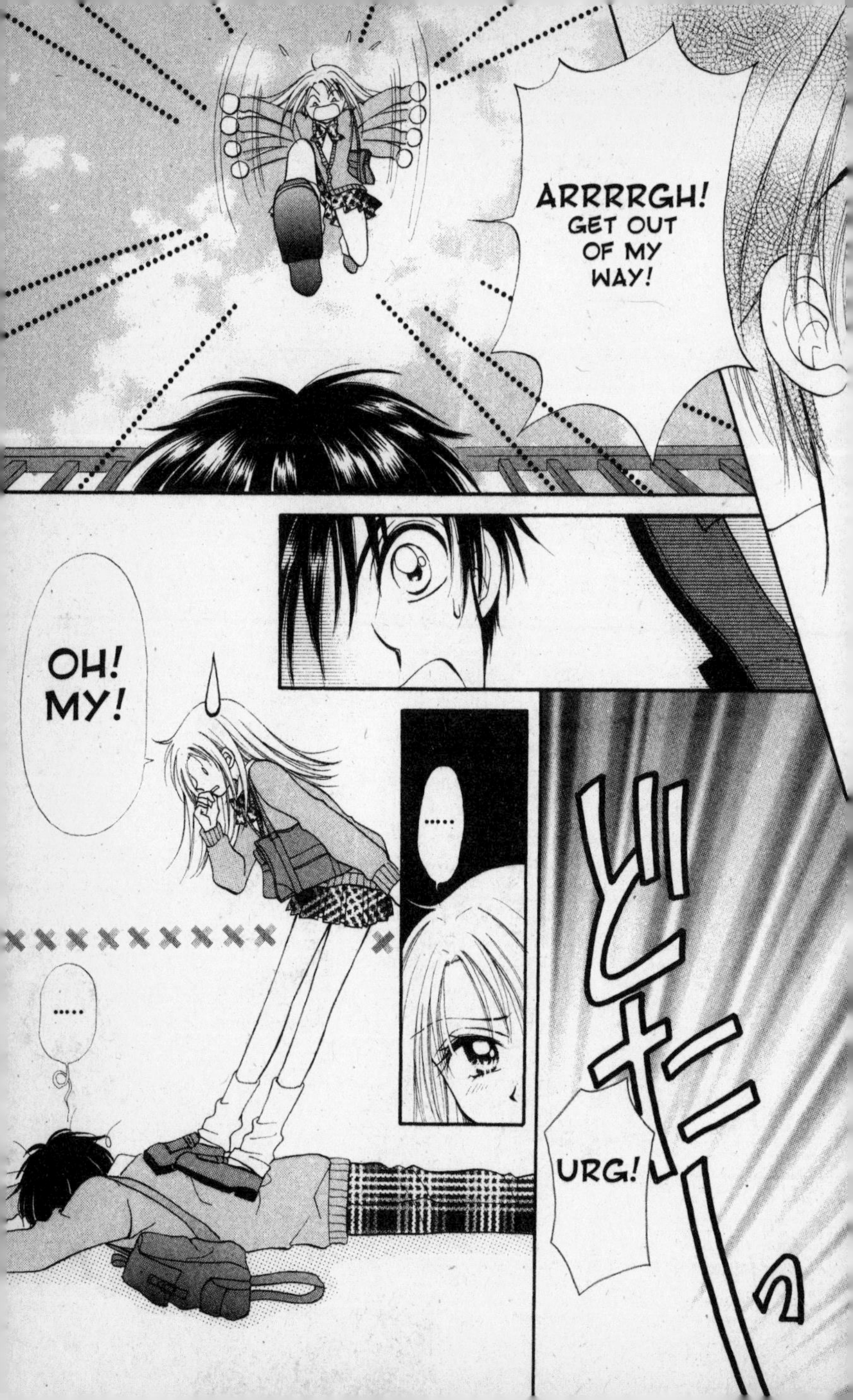
ARRRRGH! GET OUT OF MY WAY!
URG!
......
OH! MY!
......

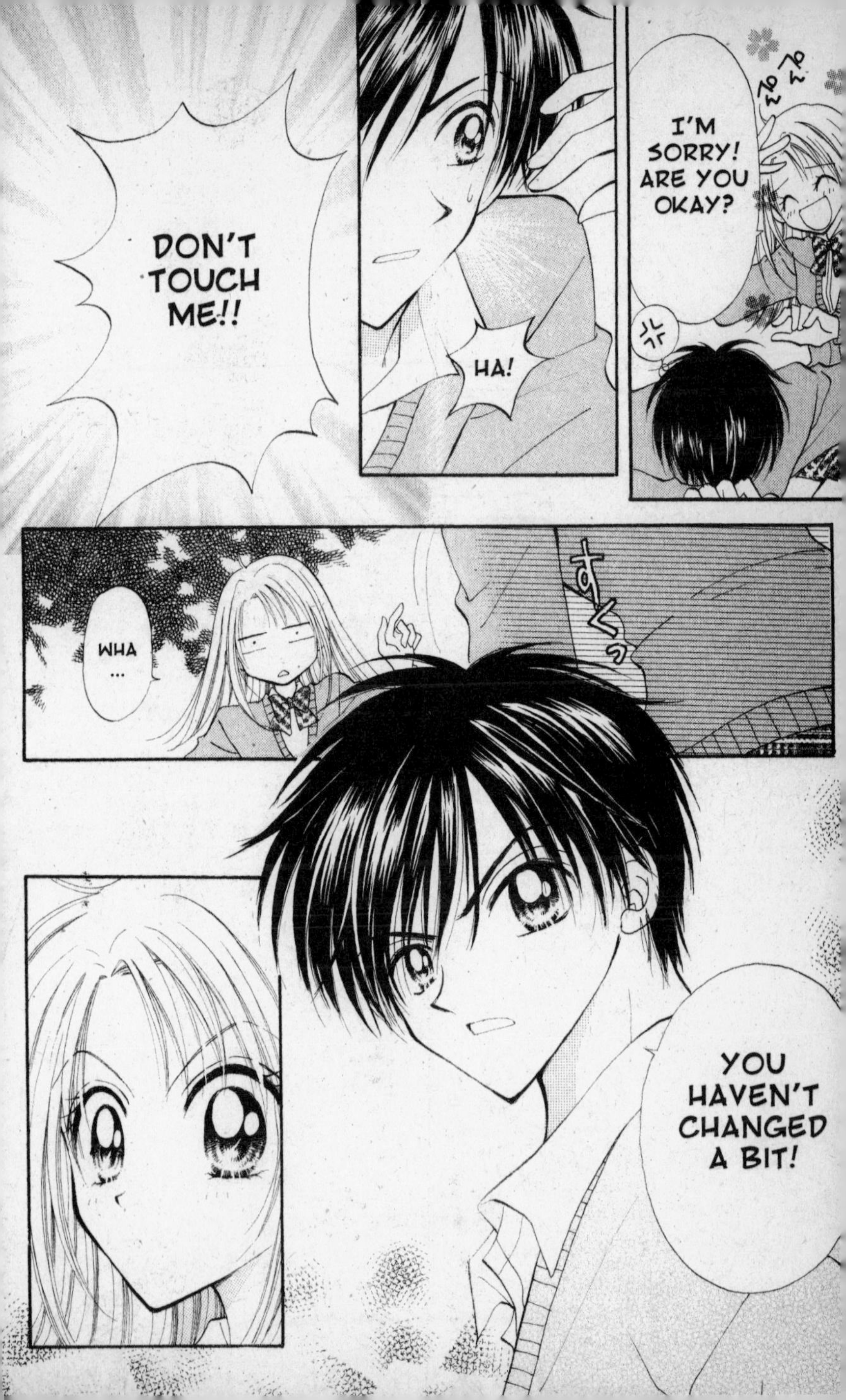
I'M SORRY! ARE YOU OKAY?
HA!
DON'T TOUCH ME!!
すくっ
WHA ...
YOU HAVEN'T CHANGED A BIT!

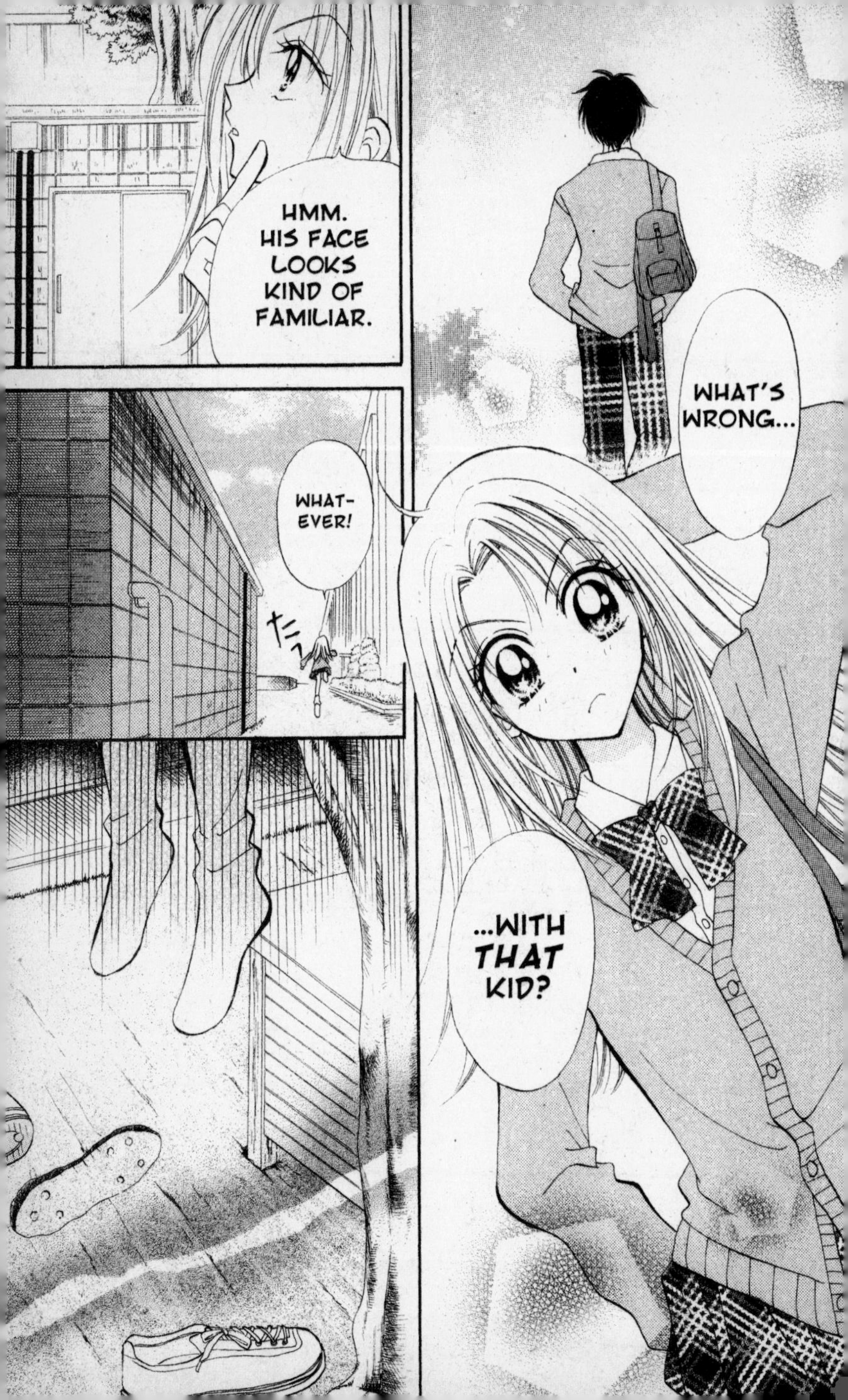
WHAT'S WRONG...
...WITH THAT KID?
HMM. HIS FACE LOOKS KIND OF FAMILIAR.
WHAT-EVER!

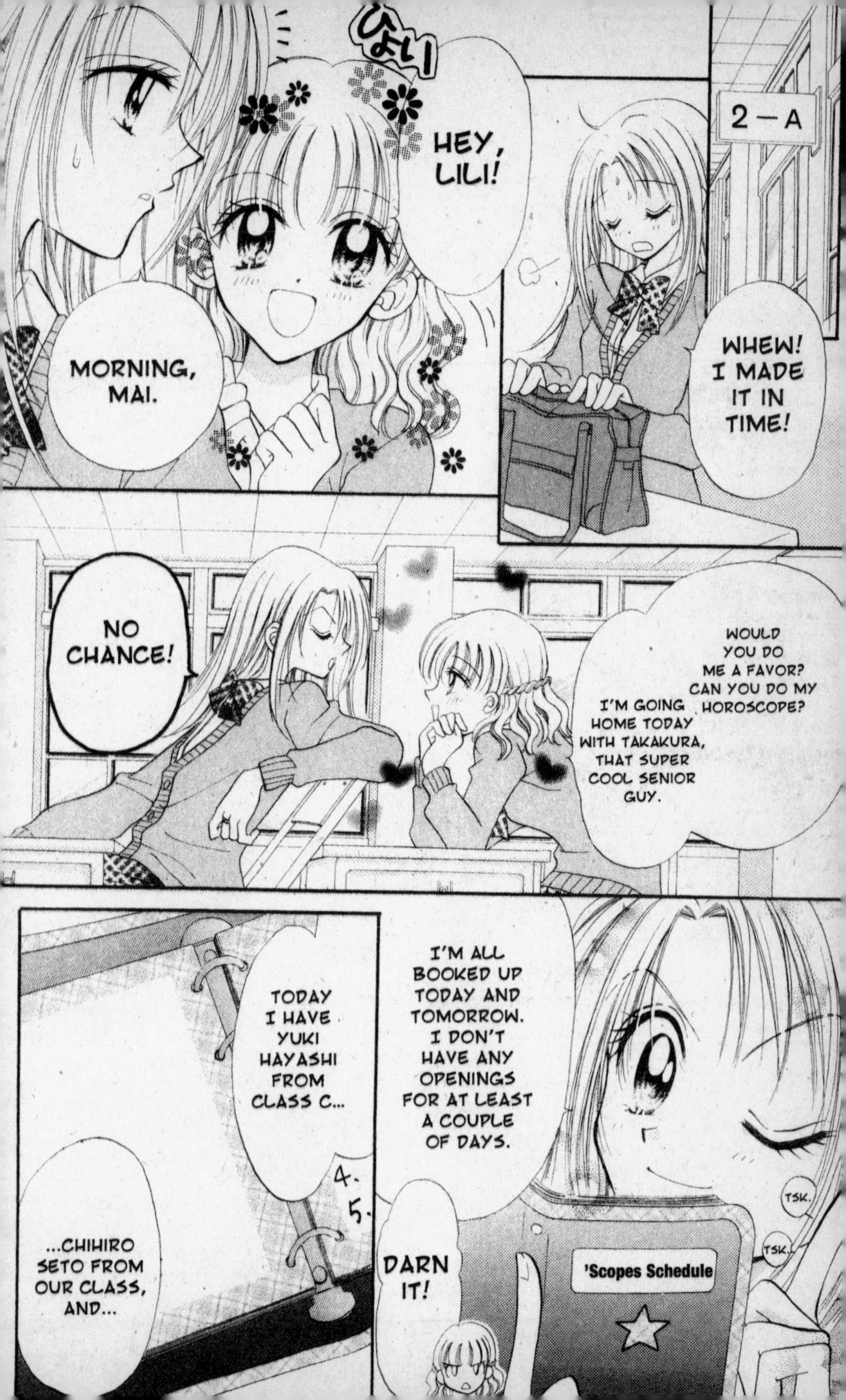
2-A
WHEW! I MADE IT IN TIME!
ひょい
HEY, LILI!
MORNING, MAI.
I'M GOING HOME TODAY WITH TAKAKURA, THAT SUPER COOL SENIOR GUY.
WOULD YOU DO ME A FAVOR? CAN YOU DO MY HOROSCOPE?
NO CHANCE!
I'M ALL BOOKED UP TODAY AND TOMORROW. I DON'T HAVE ANY OPENINGS FOR AT LEAST A COUPLE OF DAYS.
TSK.
TSK.
'Scopes Schedule
DARN IT!
TODAY I HAVE YUKI HAYASHI FROM CLASS C...
4.
5.
...CHIHIRO SETO FROM OUR CLASS, AND...

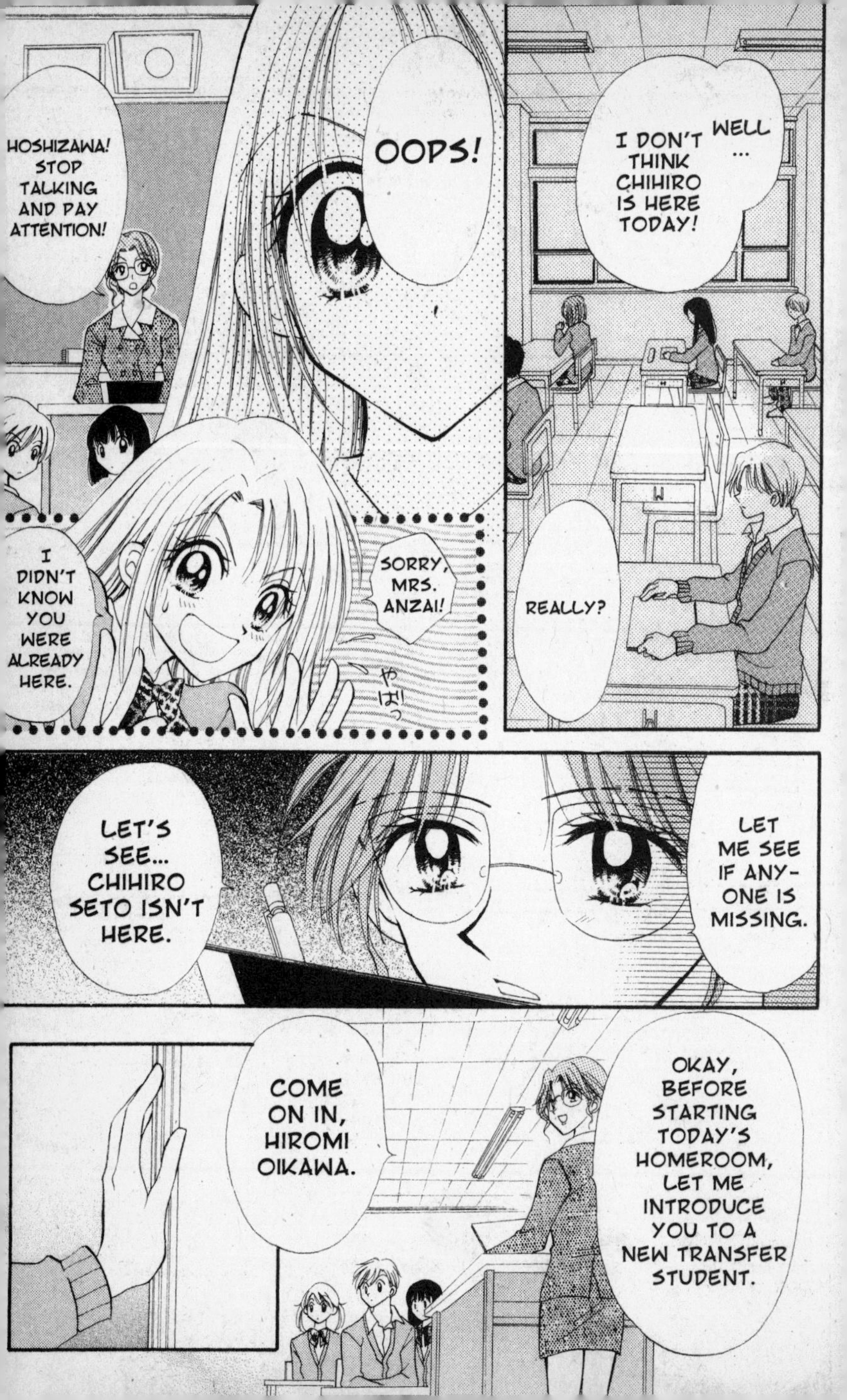
WELL...
I DON'T THINK CHIHIRO IS HERE TODAY!
REALLY?
HOSHIZAWA! STOP TALKING AND PAY ATTENTION!
OOPS!
SORRY, MRS. ANZAI!
I DIDN'T KNOW YOU WERE ALREADY HERE.
やばっ
LET ME SEE IF ANY-ONE IS MISSING.
LET'S SEE... CHIHIRO SETO ISN'T HERE.
OKAY, BEFORE STARTING TODAY'S HOMEROOM, LET ME INTRODUCE YOU TO A NEW TRANSFER STUDENT.
COME ON IN, HIROMI OIKAWA.

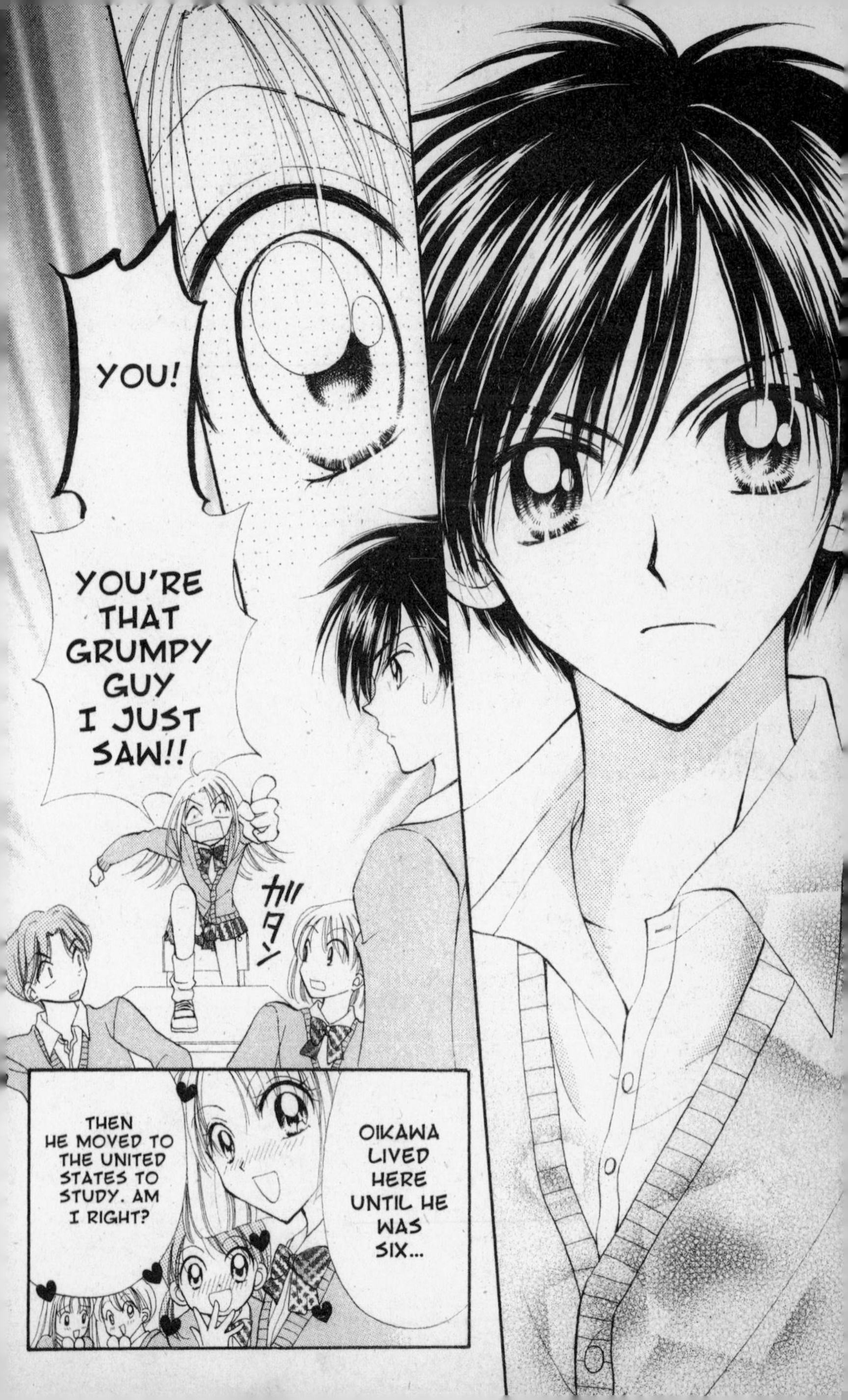
YOU!
YOU'RE THAT GRUMPY GUY I JUST SAW!!
ガタン
OIKAWA LIVED HERE UNTIL HE WAS SIX...
THEN HE MOVED TO THE UNITED STATES TO STUDY. AM I RIGHT?

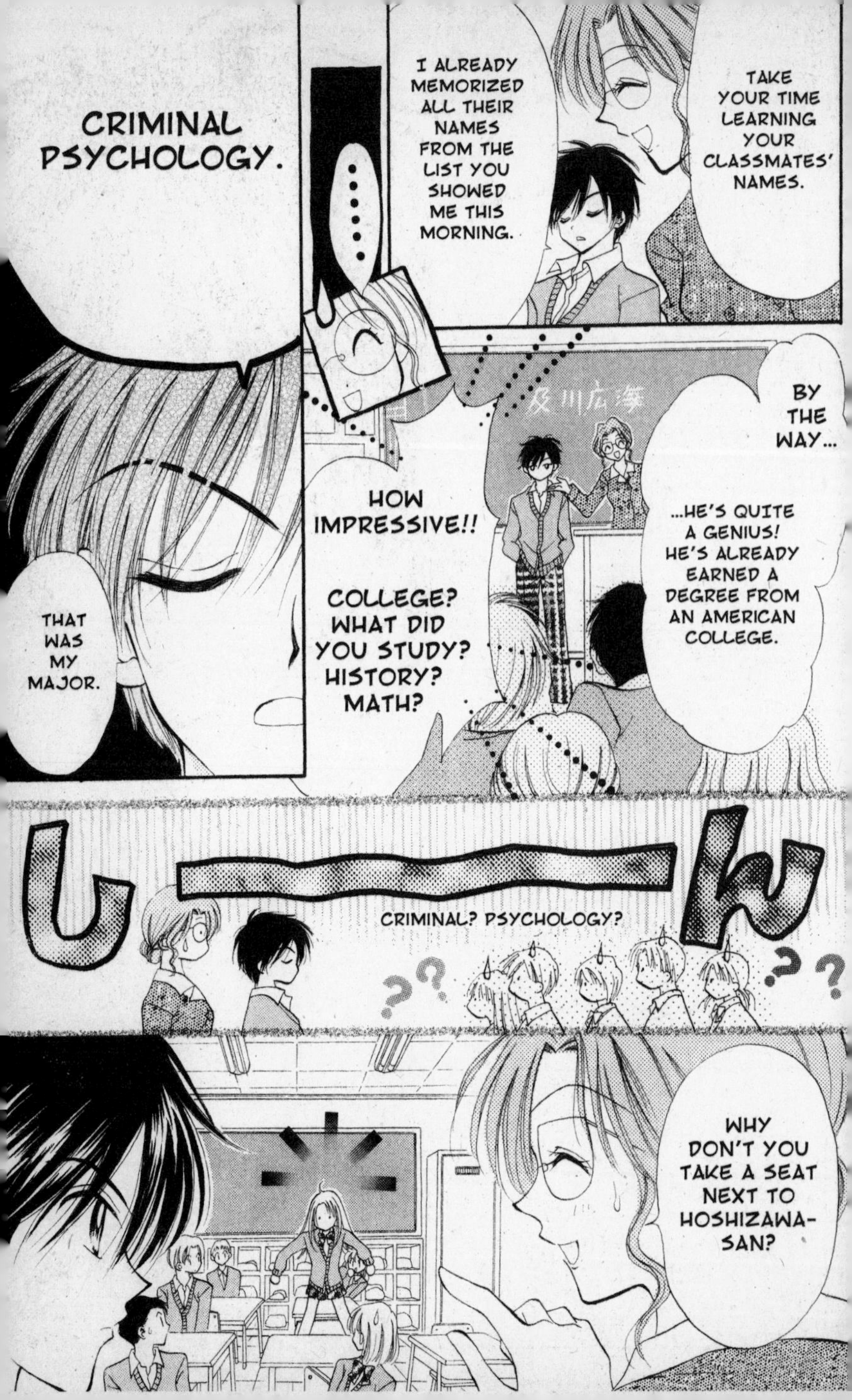
TAKE YOUR TIME LEARNING YOUR CLASSMATES' NAMES.
I ALREADY MEMORIZED ALL THEIR NAMES FROM THE LIST YOU SHOWED ME THIS MORNING.
......
及川広海
BY THE WAY...
...HE'S QUITE A GENIUS! HE'S ALREADY EARNED A DEGREE FROM AN AMERICAN COLLEGE.
HOW IMPRESSIVE!!
COLLEGE? WHAT DID YOU STUDY? HISTORY? MATH?
CRIMINAL PSYCHOLOGY.
THAT WAS MY MAJOR.
U———N
CRIMINAL? PSYCHOLOGY?
??
??
WHY DON'T YOU TAKE A SEAT NEXT TO HOSHIZAWA-SAN?

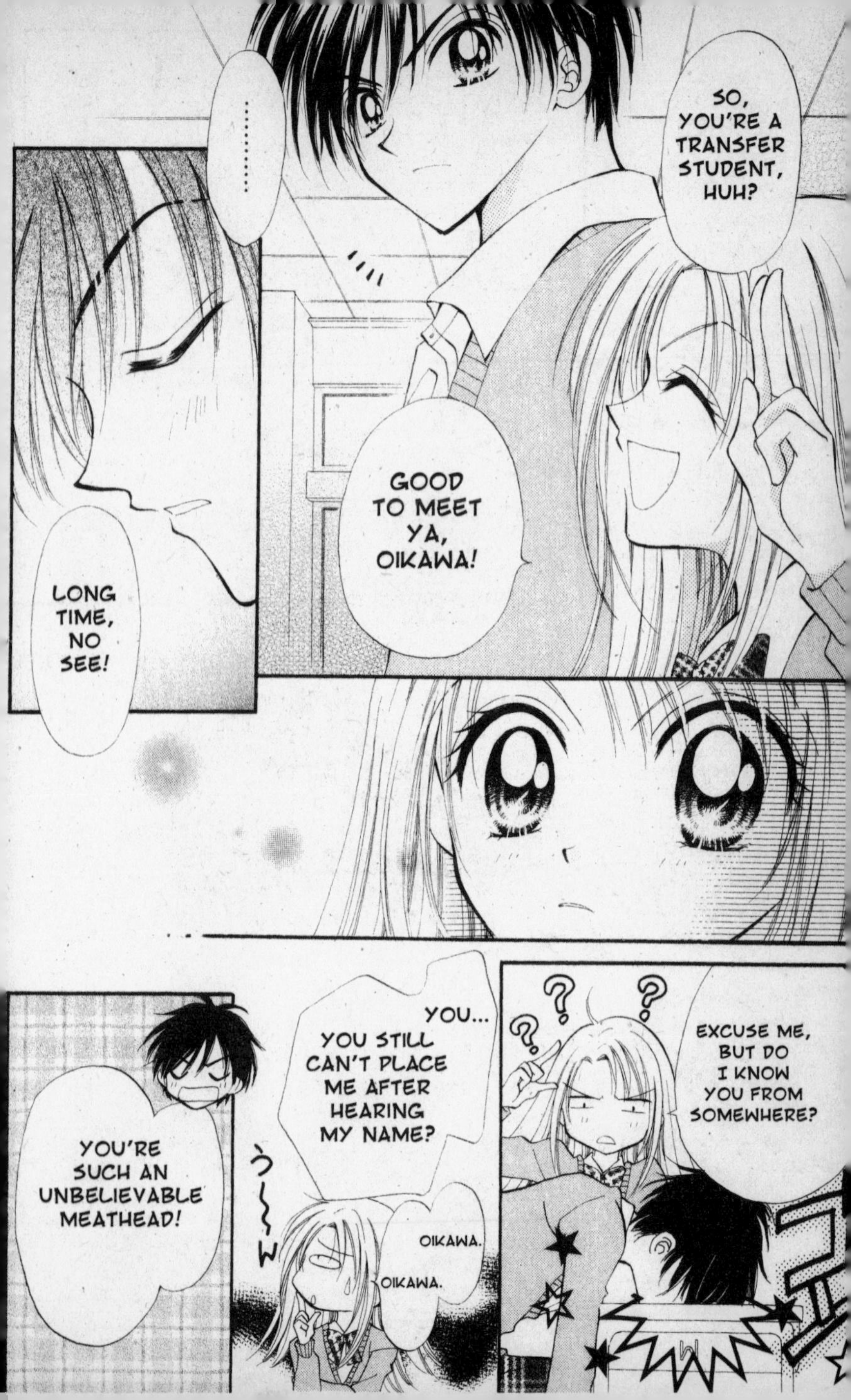
SO, YOU'RE A TRANSFER STUDENT, HUH?
......
GOOD TO MEET YA, OIKAWA!
LONG TIME, NO SEE!
EXCUSE ME, BUT DO I KNOW YOU FROM SOMEWHERE?
YOU... YOU STILL CAN'T PLACE ME AFTER HEARING MY NAME?
OIKAWA.
OIKAWA.
YOU'RE SUCH AN UNBELIEVABLE MEATHEAD!

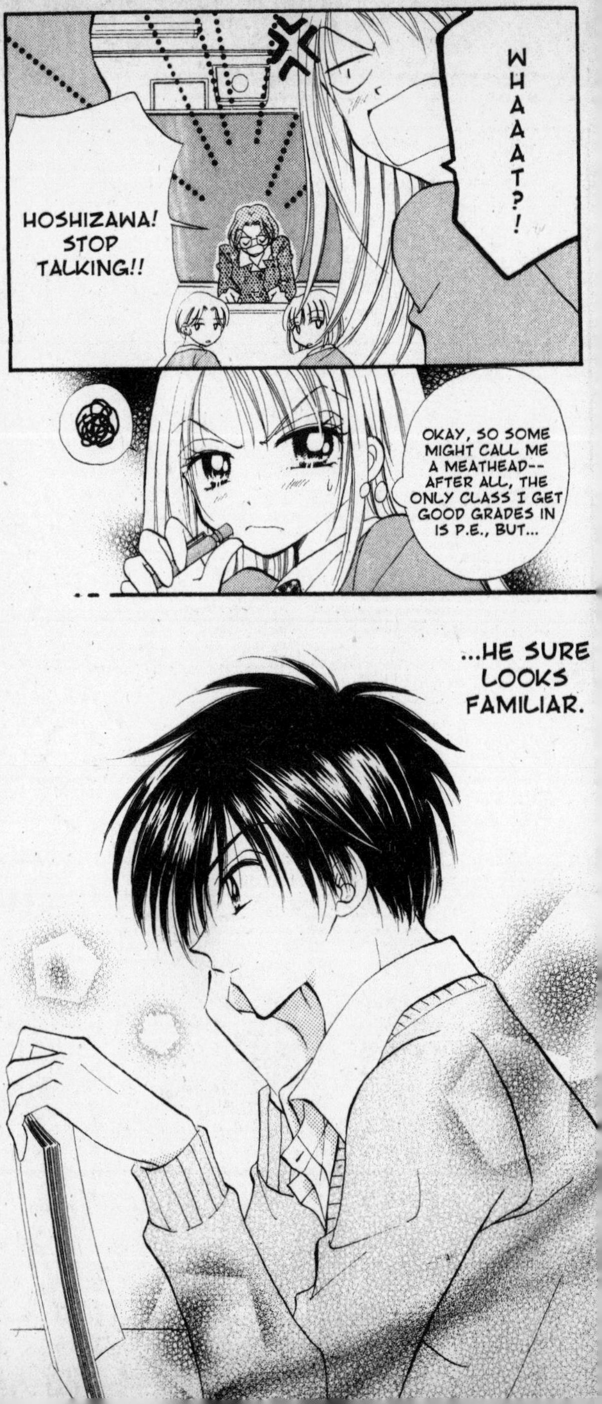
WHAAAT?!
HOSHIZAWA! STOP TALKING!!
OKAY, SO SOME MIGHT CALL ME A MEATHEAD--AFTER ALL, THE ONLY CLASS I GET GOOD GRADES IN IS P.E., BUT...
...HE SURE LOOKS FAMILIAR.

Profile

I wrote my profile for KC before, but let me give you the updated one.

Name: Natsumi Ando (Not my real name!)

DOB: January 27th

Sign: Aquarius

Skills: I'm the ultimate multitasker. I can listen to the radio, watch TV, eat and read a book all at the same time! (Am I just lazy or what? Hee hee hee!!)

Favorite celebrities: It depends. Right now I'm a big fan of Morning Musume.

Favorite color: Primary colors like red and yellow.

Additional skills: Fast writing with not-so-great penmanship.

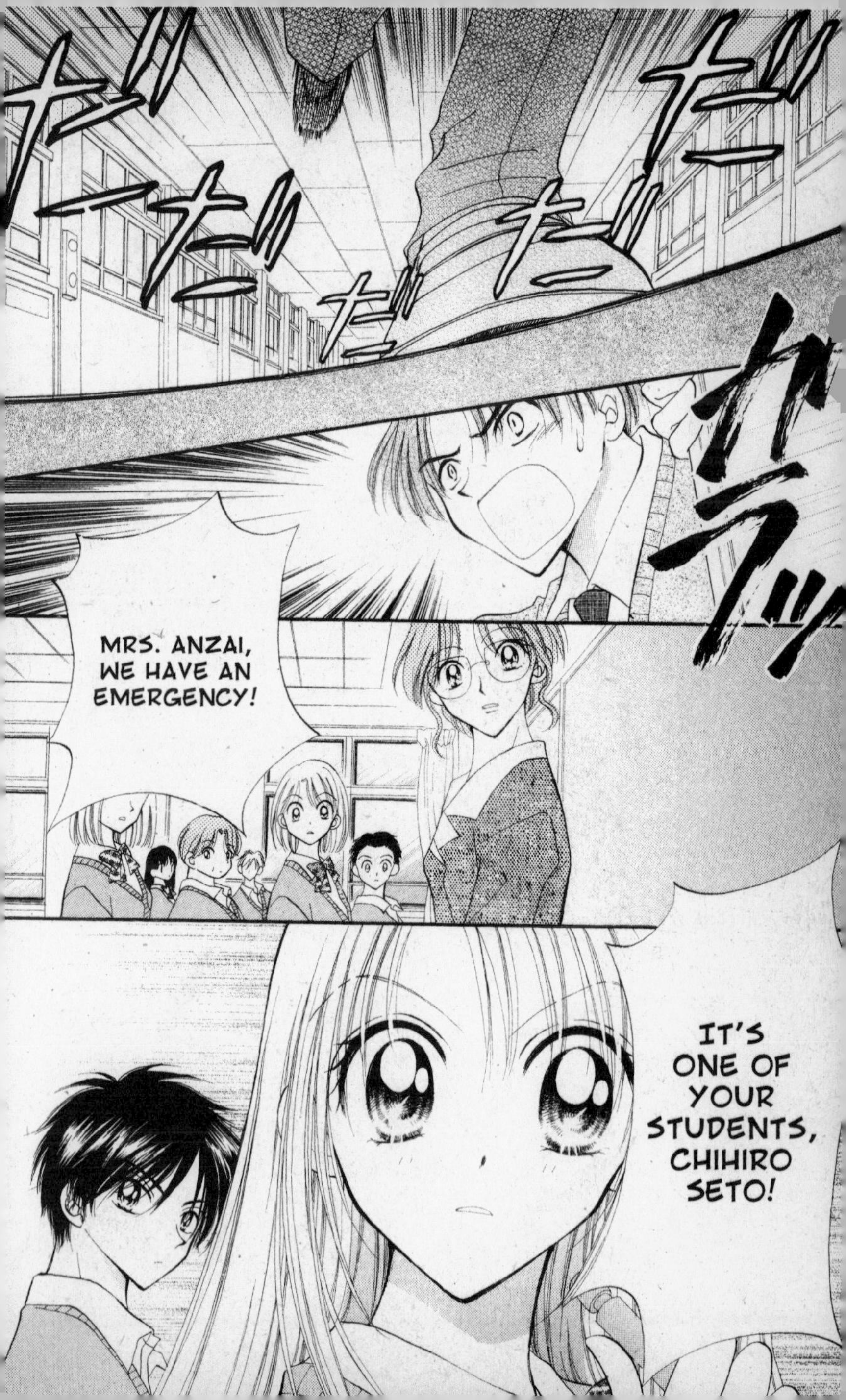
MRS. ANZAI, WE HAVE AN EMERGENCY!
IT'S ONE OF YOUR STUDENTS, CHIHIRO SETO!

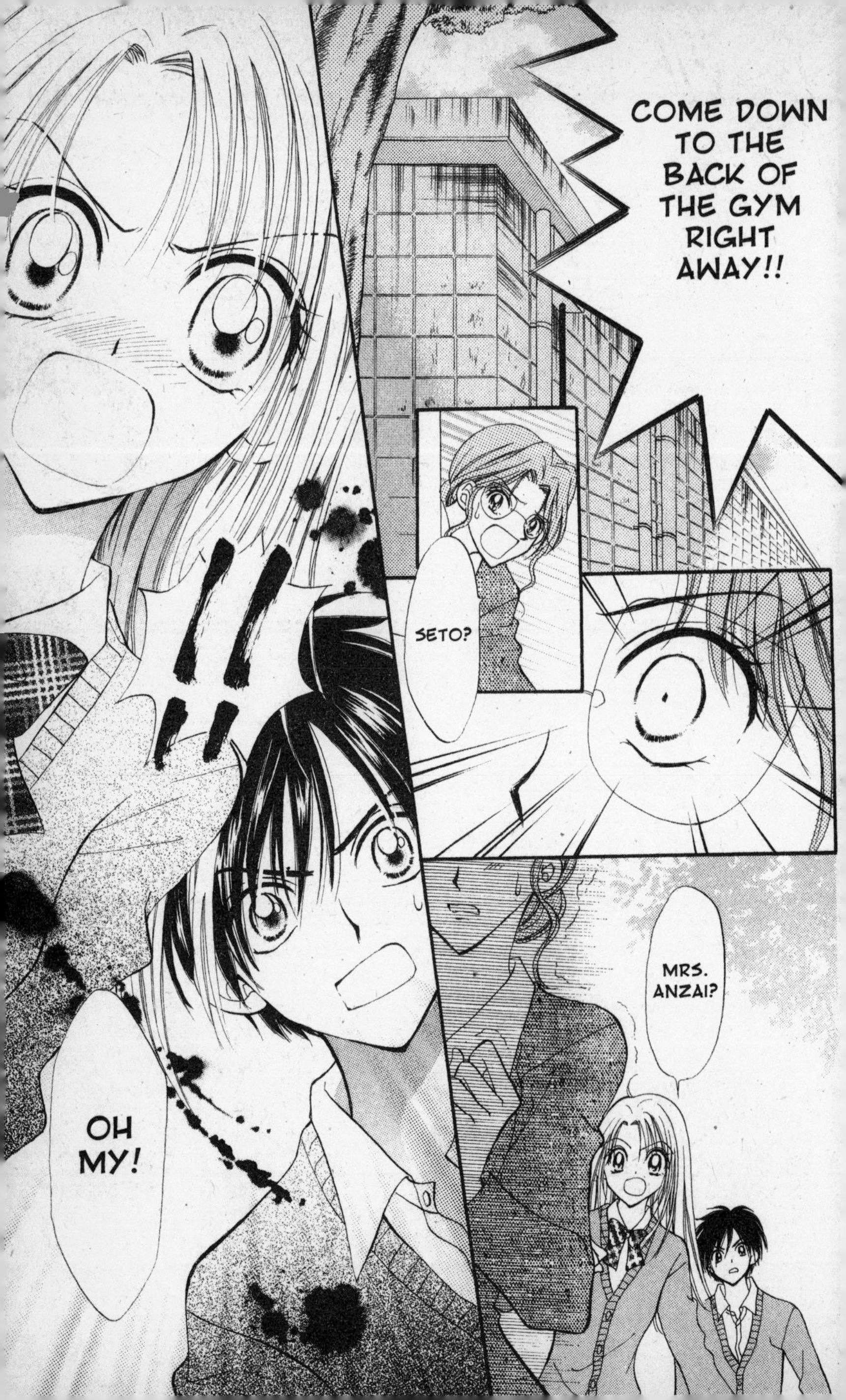
COME DOWN TO THE BACK OF THE GYM RIGHT AWAY!!
SETO?
MRS. ANZAI?
!!
OH MY!

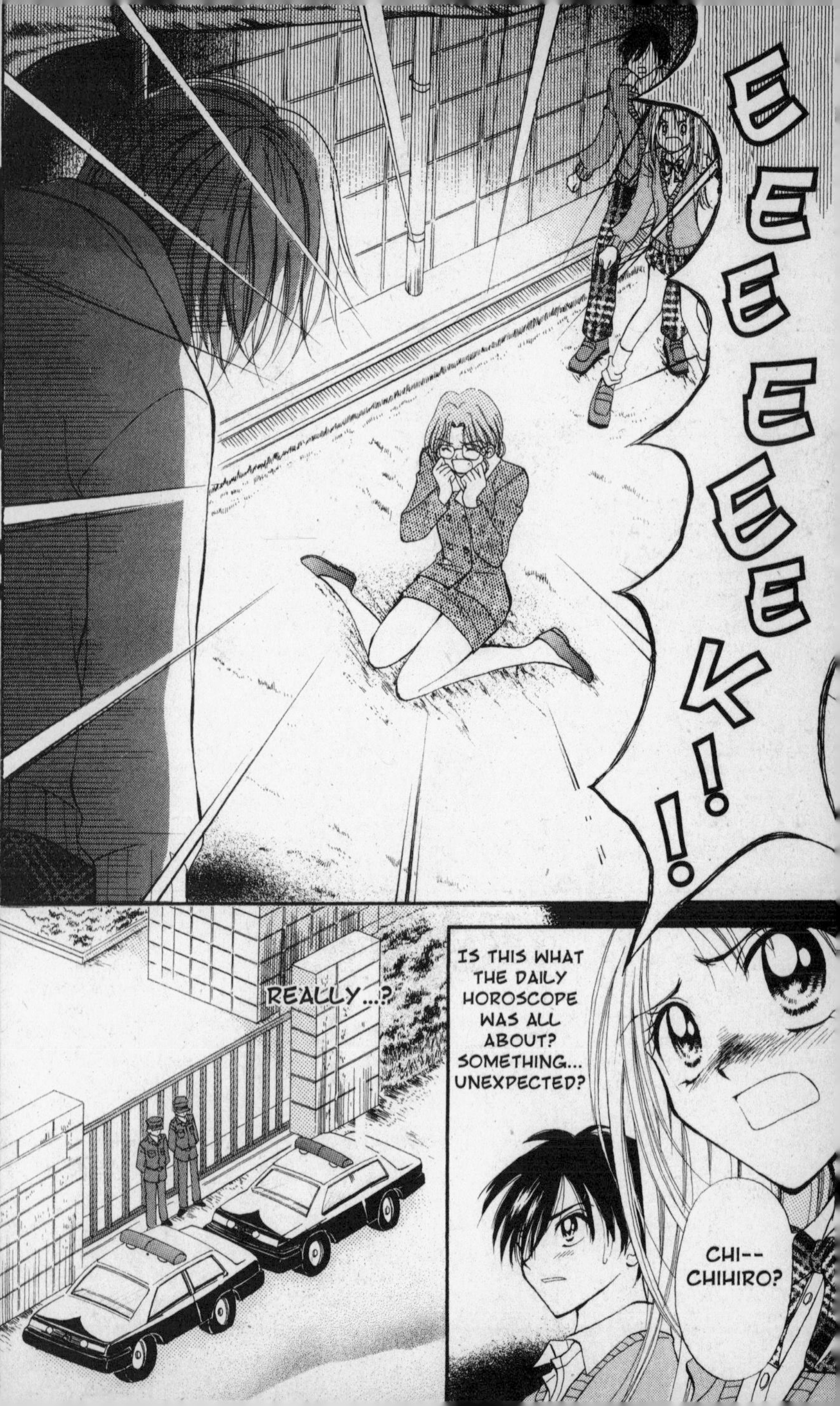
EEEEEEK!!
IS THIS WHAT THE DAILY HOROSCOPE WAS ALL ABOUT? SOMETHING... UNEXPECTED?
CHI-- CHIHIRO?
REALLY...?

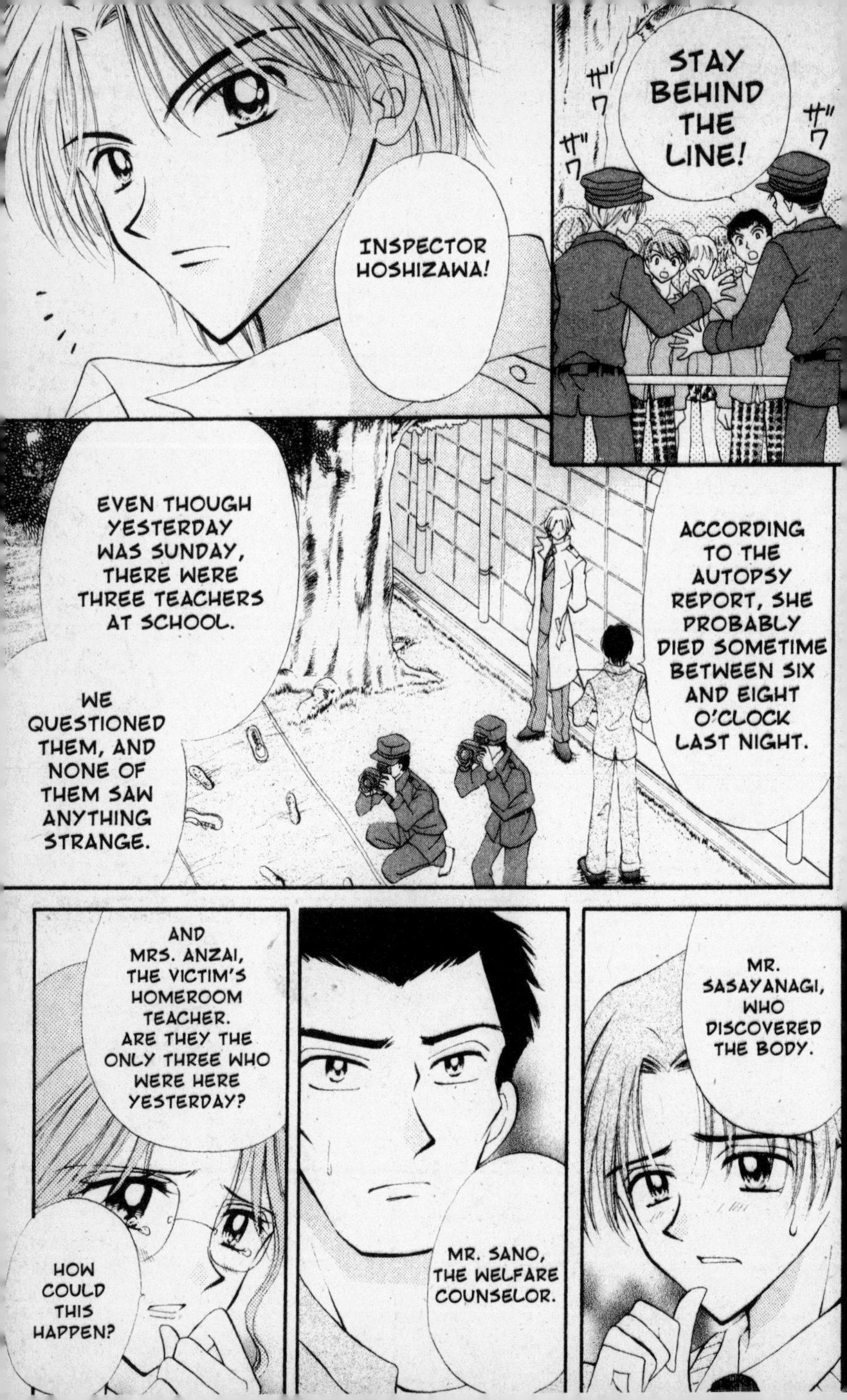
ザワ
ザワ
ザワ
STAY BEHIND THE LINE!
INSPECTOR HOSHIZAWA!
ACCORDING TO THE AUTOPSY REPORT, SHE PROBABLY DIED SOMETIME BETWEEN SIX AND EIGHT O'CLOCK LAST NIGHT.
EVEN THOUGH YESTERDAY WAS SUNDAY, THERE WERE THREE TEACHERS AT SCHOOL.
WE QUESTIONED THEM, AND NONE OF THEM SAW ANYTHING STRANGE.
MR. SASAYANAGI, WHO DISCOVERED THE BODY.
MR. SANO, THE WELFARE COUNSELOR.
AND MRS. ANZAI, THE VICTIM'S HOMEROOM TEACHER. ARE THEY THE ONLY THREE WHO WERE HERE YESTERDAY?
HOW COULD THIS HAPPEN?

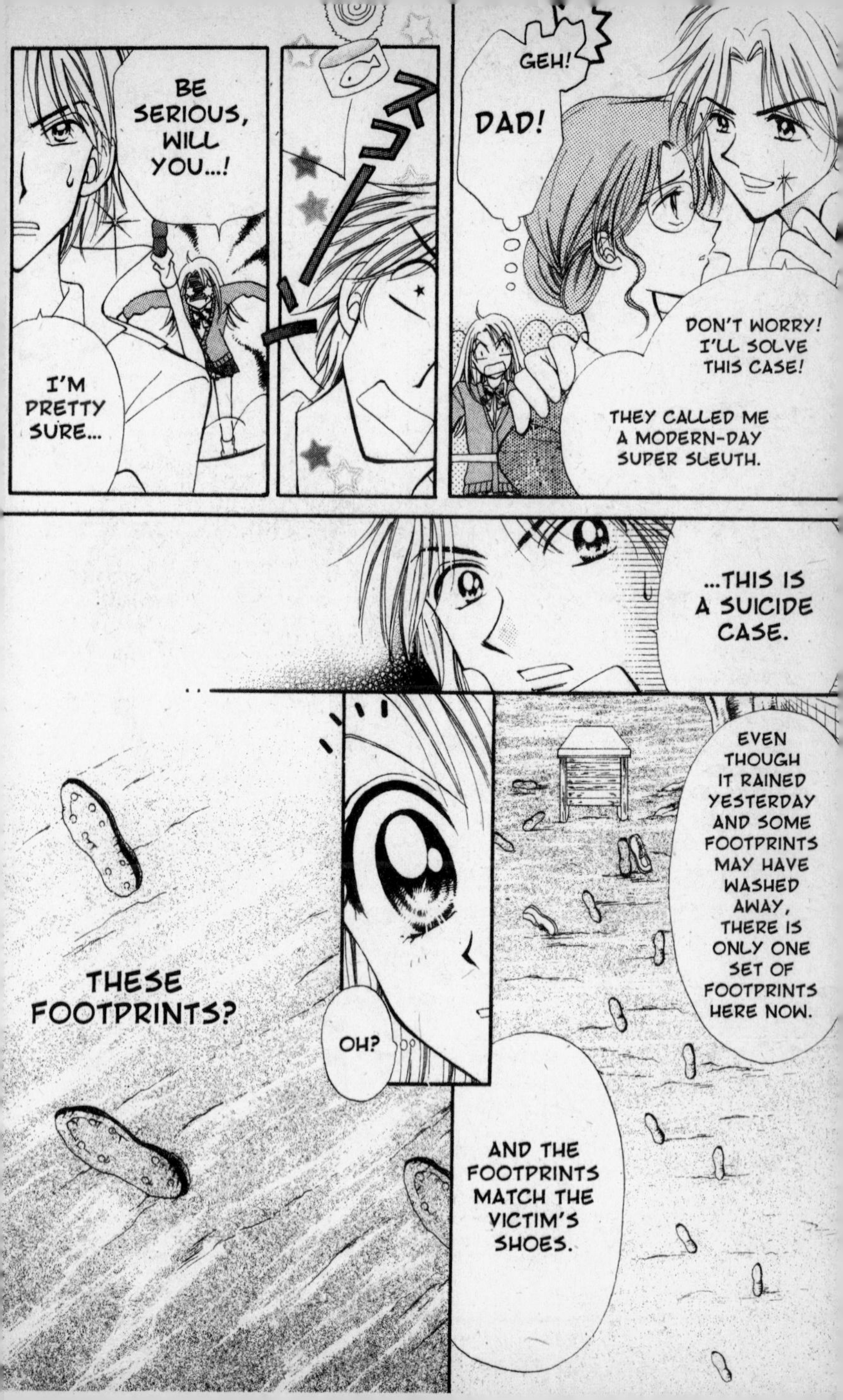
GEH!
DAD!
DON'T WORRY! I'LL SOLVE THIS CASE!
THEY CALLED ME A MODERN-DAY SUPER SLEUTH.
BE SERIOUS, WILL YOU...!
I'M PRETTY SURE...
...THIS IS A SUICIDE CASE.
EVEN THOUGH IT RAINED YESTERDAY AND SOME FOOTPRINTS MAY HAVE WASHED AWAY, THERE IS ONLY ONE SET OF FOOTPRINTS HERE NOW.
AND THE FOOTPRINTS MATCH THE VICTIM'S SHOES.
OH?
THESE FOOTPRINTS?

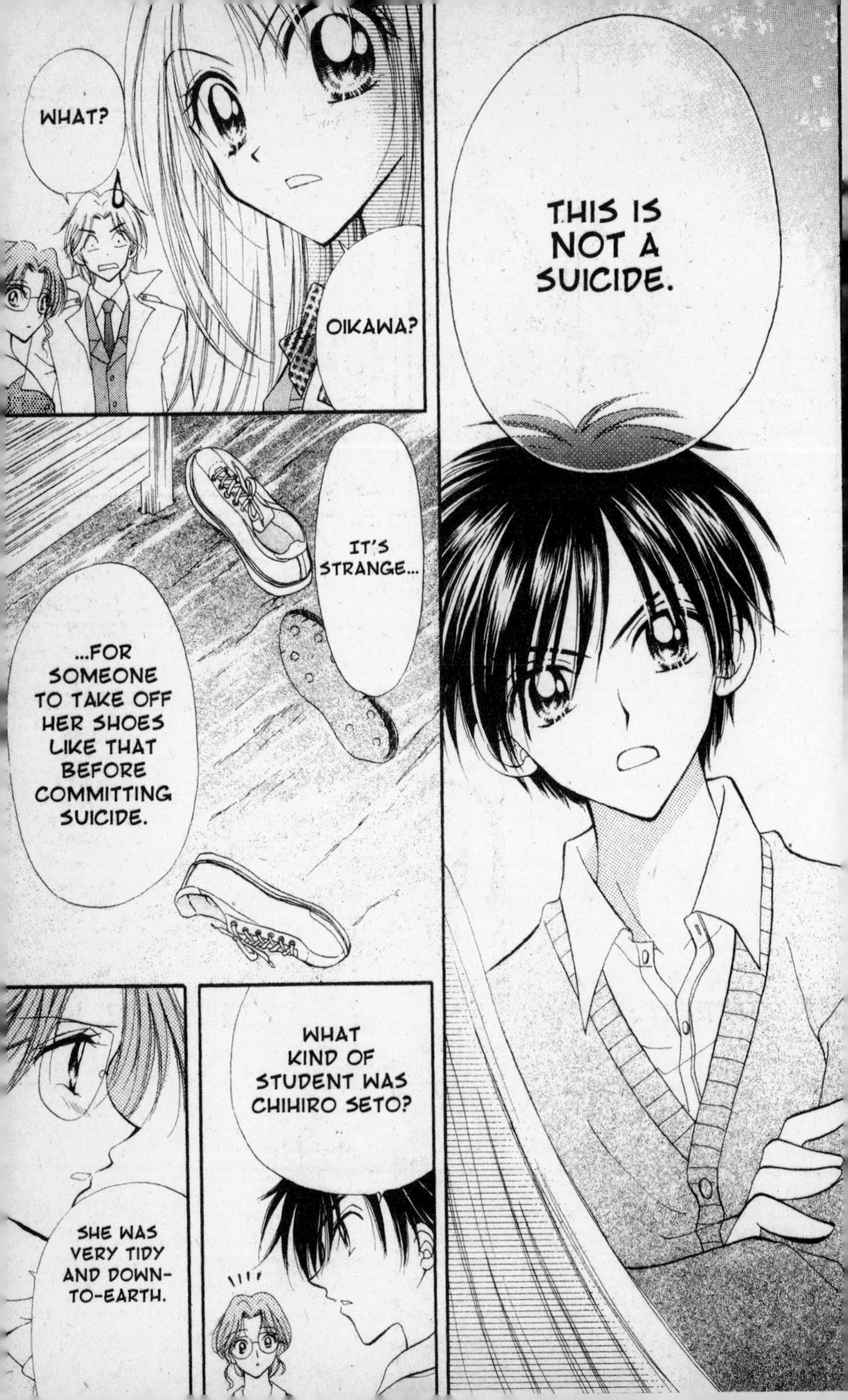
THIS IS NOT A SUICIDE.
OIKAWA?
WHAT?
IT'S STRANGE...
...FOR SOMEONE TO TAKE OFF HER SHOES LIKE THAT BEFORE COMMITTING SUICIDE.
WHAT KIND OF STUDENT WAS CHIHIRO SETO?
SHE WAS VERY TIDY AND DOWN-TO-EARTH.

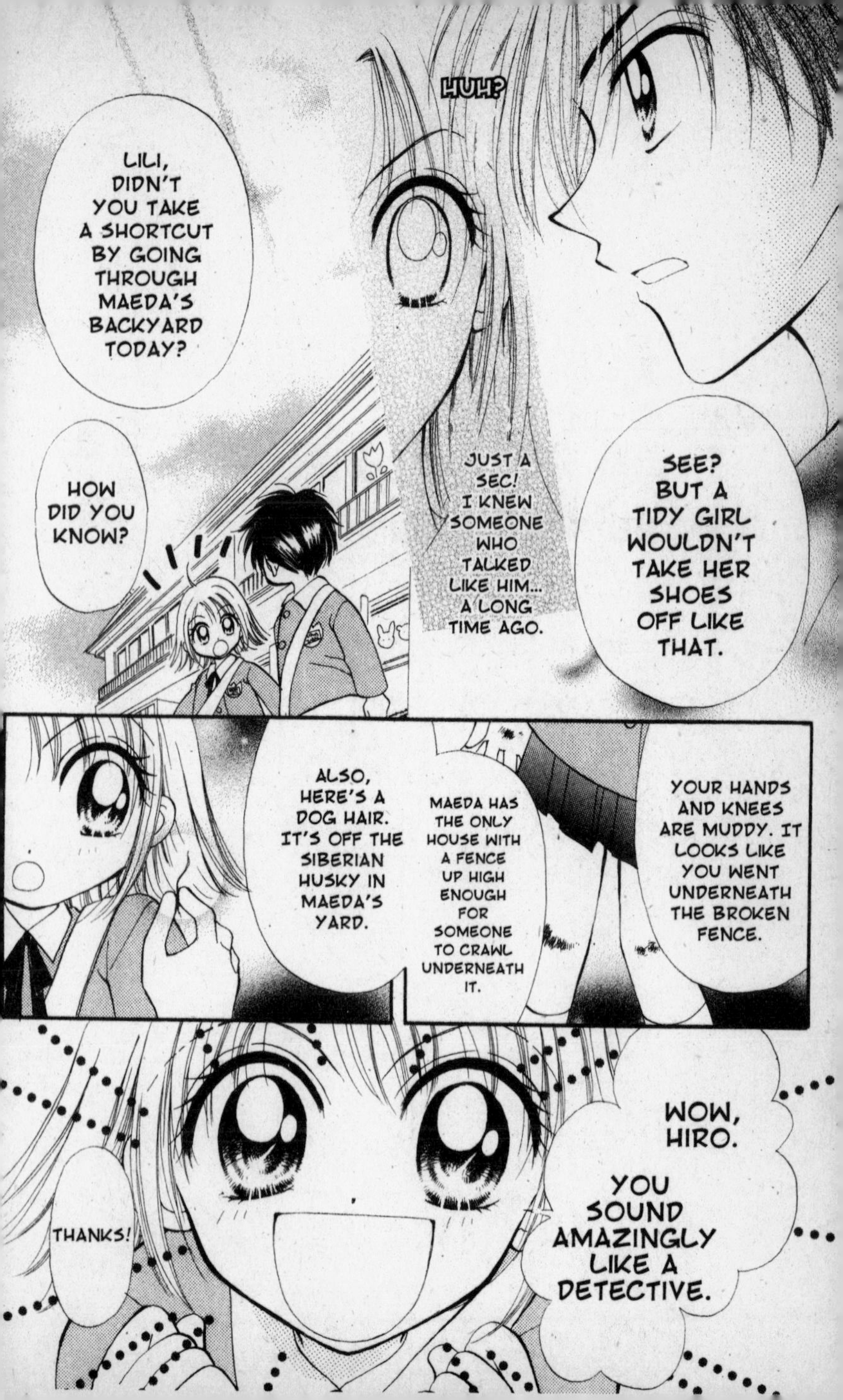
HUH?
LILI, DIDN'T YOU TAKE A SHORTCUT BY GOING THROUGH MAEDA'S BACKYARD TODAY?
HOW DID YOU KNOW?
SEE? BUT A TIDY GIRL WOULDN'T TAKE HER SHOES OFF LIKE THAT.
JUST A SEC! I KNEW SOMEONE WHO TALKED LIKE HIM... A LONG TIME AGO.
YOUR HANDS AND KNEES ARE MUDDY. IT LOOKS LIKE YOU WENT UNDERNEATH THE BROKEN FENCE.
MAEDA HAS THE ONLY HOUSE WITH A FENCE UP HIGH ENOUGH FOR SOMEONE TO CRAWL UNDERNEATH IT.
ALSO, HERE'S A DOG HAIR. IT'S OFF THE SIBERIAN HUSKY IN MAEDA'S YARD.
WOW, HIRO.
YOU SOUND AMAZINGLY LIKE A DETECTIVE.
THANKS!

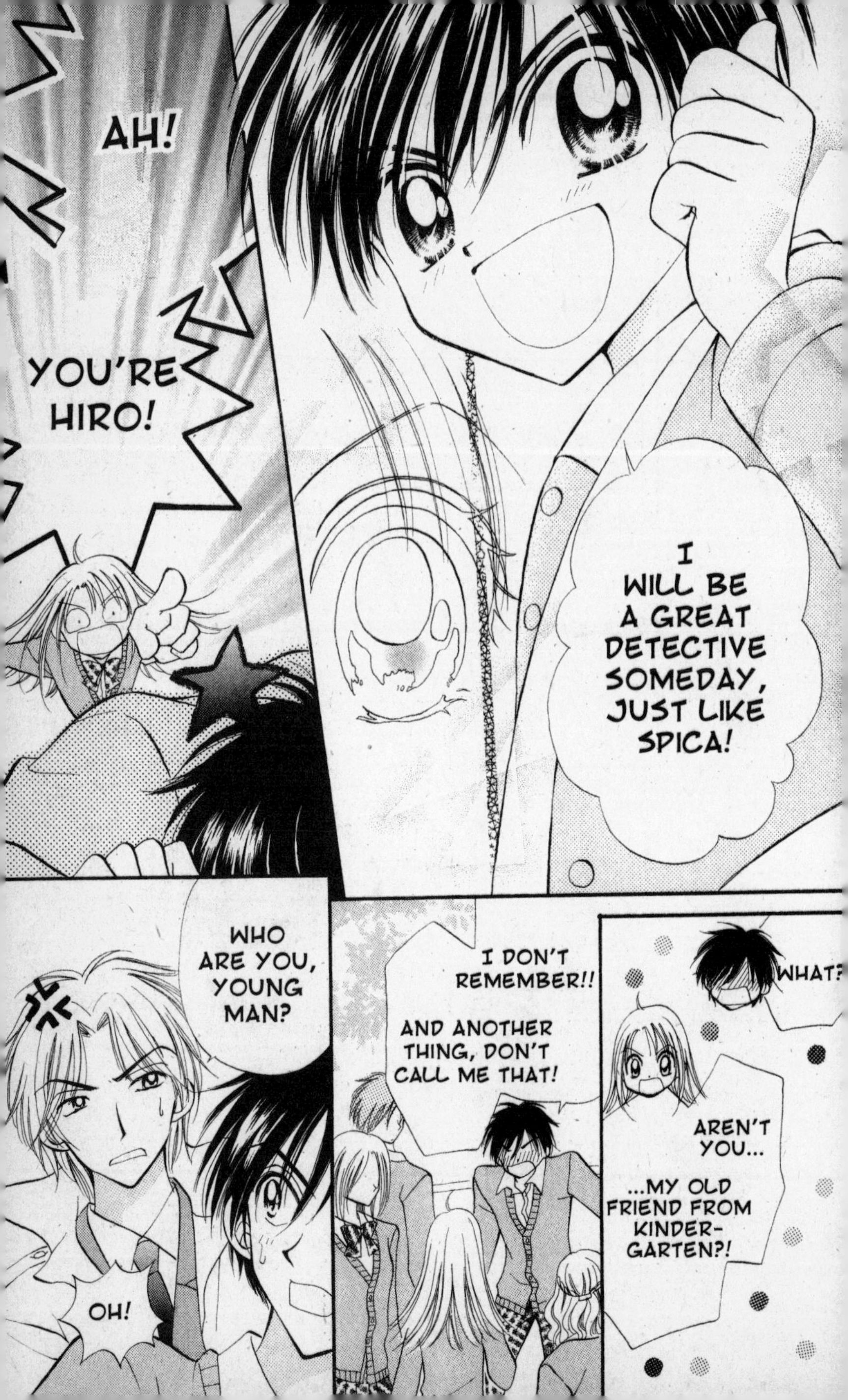
I WILL BE A GREAT DETECTIVE SOMEDAY, JUST LIKE SPICA!
AH!
YOU'RE HIRO!
WHAT?
AREN'T YOU...
...MY OLD FRIEND FROM KINDER-GARTEN?!
I DON'T REMEMBER!!
AND ANOTHER THING, DON'T CALL ME THAT!
WHO ARE YOU, YOUNG MAN?
OH!

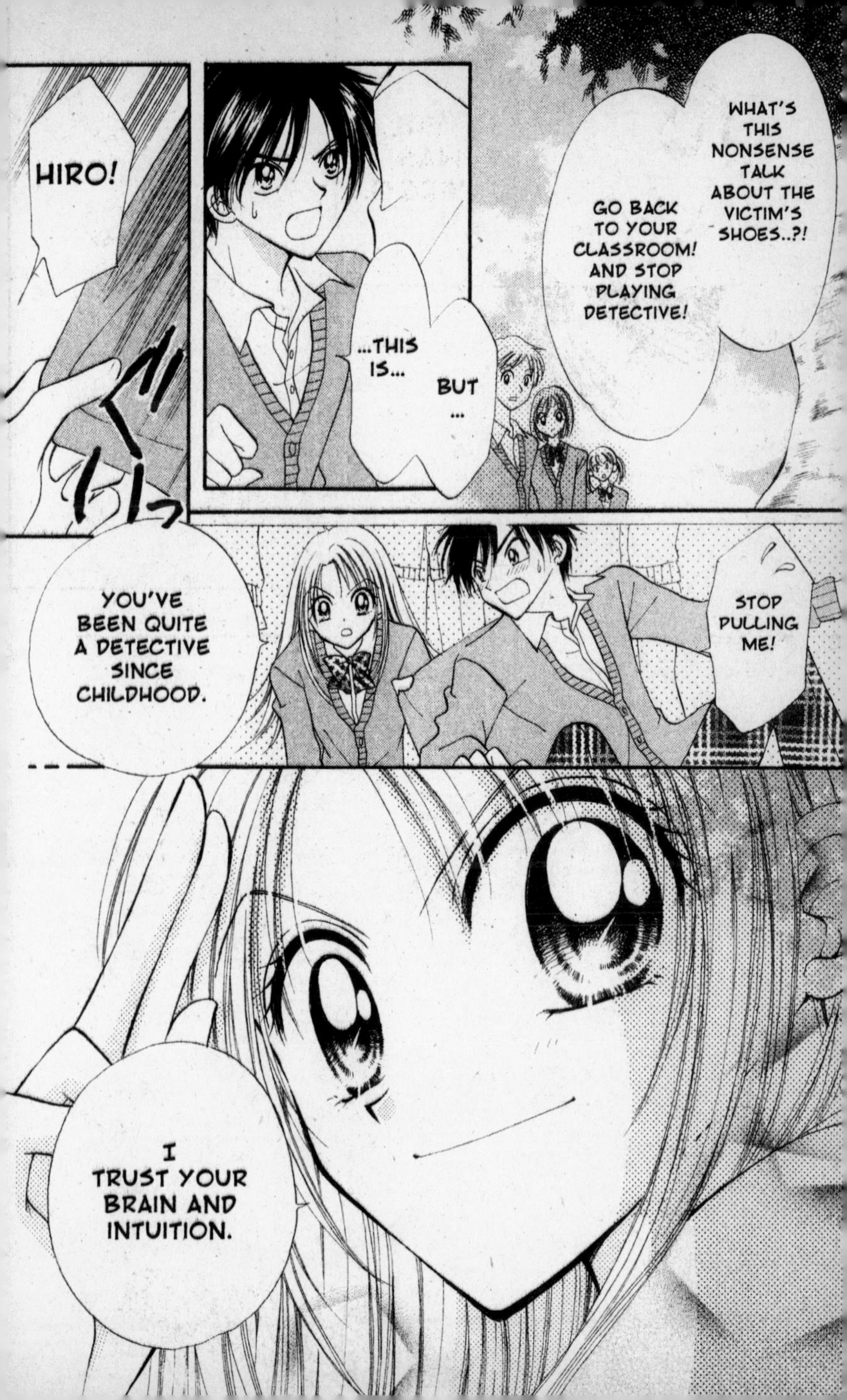
WHAT'S THIS NONSENSE TALK ABOUT THE VICTIM'S SHOES..?!
GO BACK TO YOUR CLASSROOM! AND STOP PLAYING DETECTIVE!
BUT ...
...THIS IS...
HIRO!
STOP PULLING ME!
YOU'VE BEEN QUITE A DETECTIVE SINCE CHILDHOOD.
I TRUST YOUR BRAIN AND INTUITION.

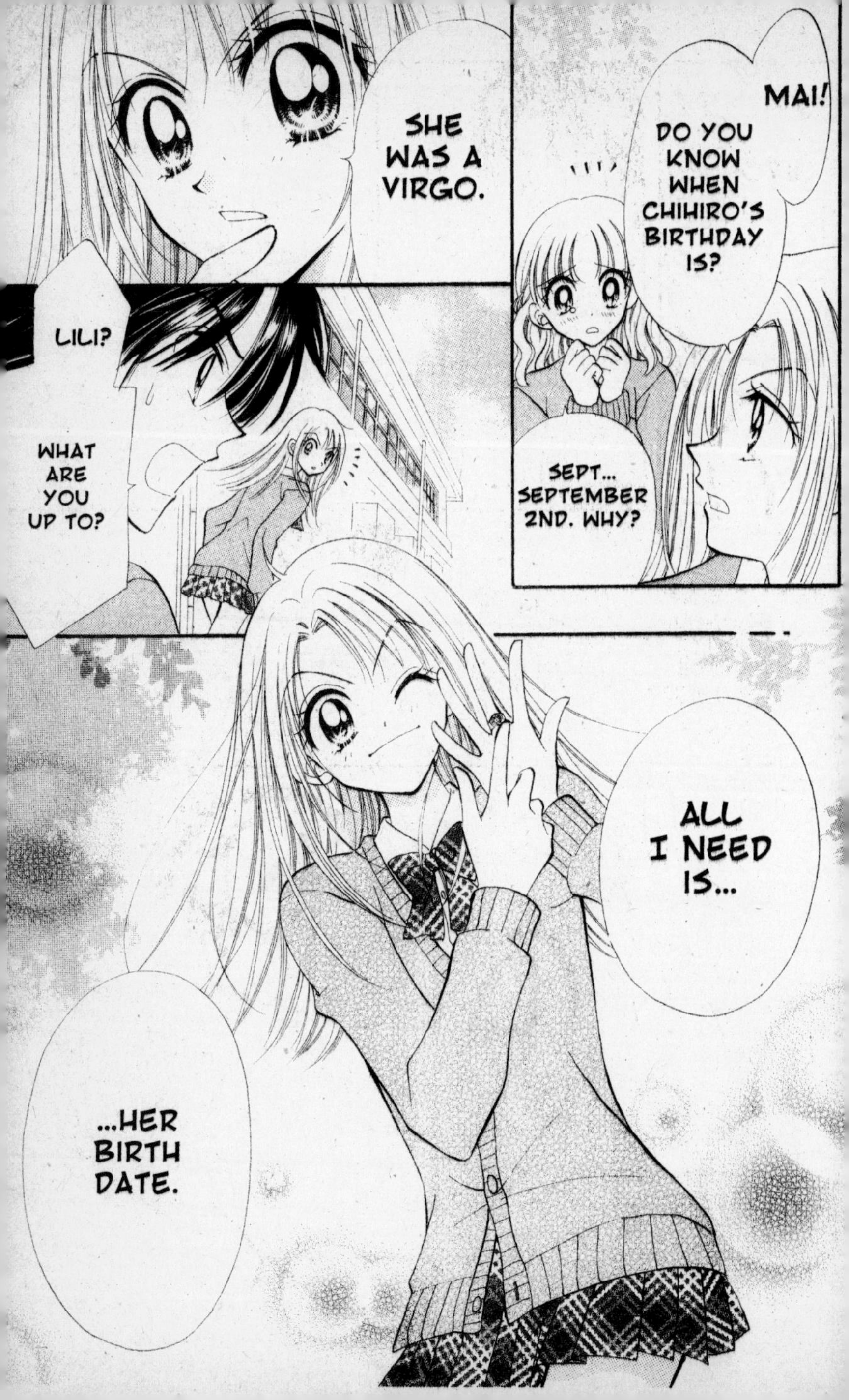
MAI! DO YOU KNOW WHEN CHIHIRO'S BIRTHDAY IS?
SEPT... SEPTEMBER 2ND. WHY?
SHE WAS A VIRGO.
LILI?
WHAT ARE YOU UP TO?
ALL I NEED IS...
...HER BIRTH DATE.

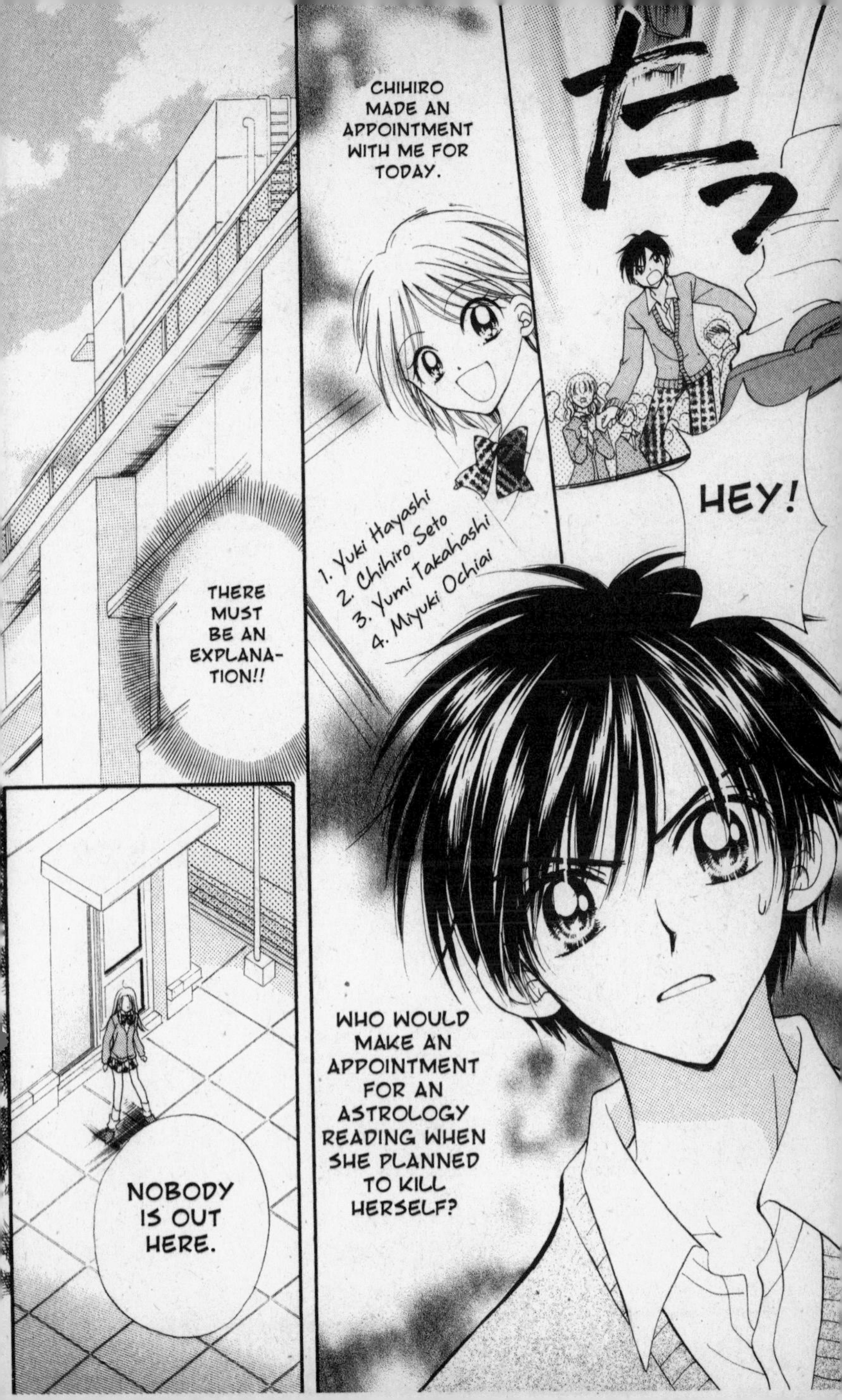
たーっ
HEY!
CHIHIRO MADE AN APPOINTMENT WITH ME FOR TODAY.
1. Yuki Hayashi
2. Chihiro Seto
3. Yumi Takahashi
4. Miyuki Ochiai
WHO WOULD MAKE AN APPOINTMENT FOR AN ASTROLOGY READING WHEN SHE PLANNED TO KILL HERSELF?
THERE MUST BE AN EXPLANATION!!
NOBODY IS OUT HERE.

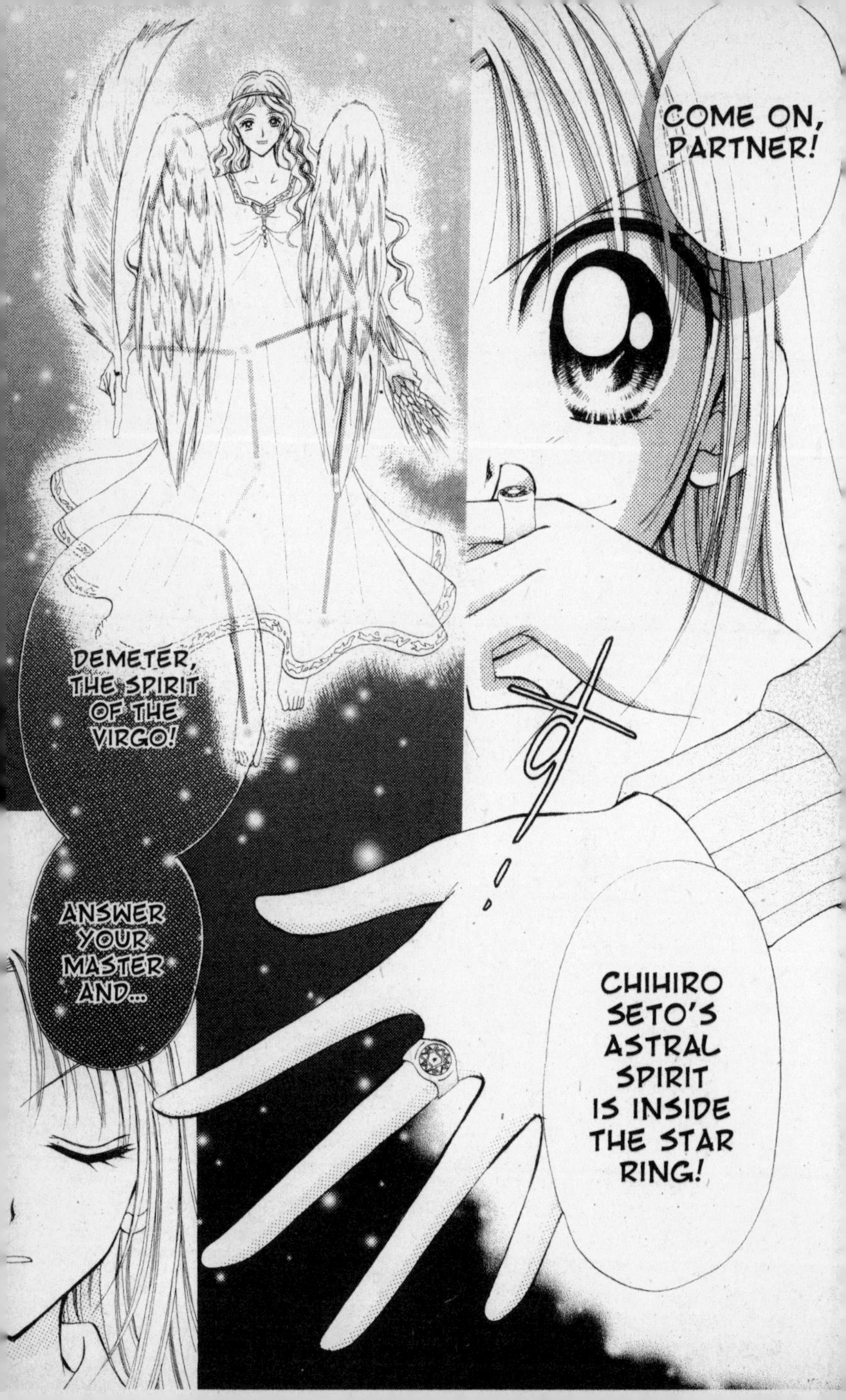
COME ON, PARTNER!
DEMETER, THE SPIRIT OF THE VIRGO!
CHIHIRO SETO'S ASTRAL SPIRIT IS INSIDE THE STAR RING!
ANSWER YOUR MASTER AND...

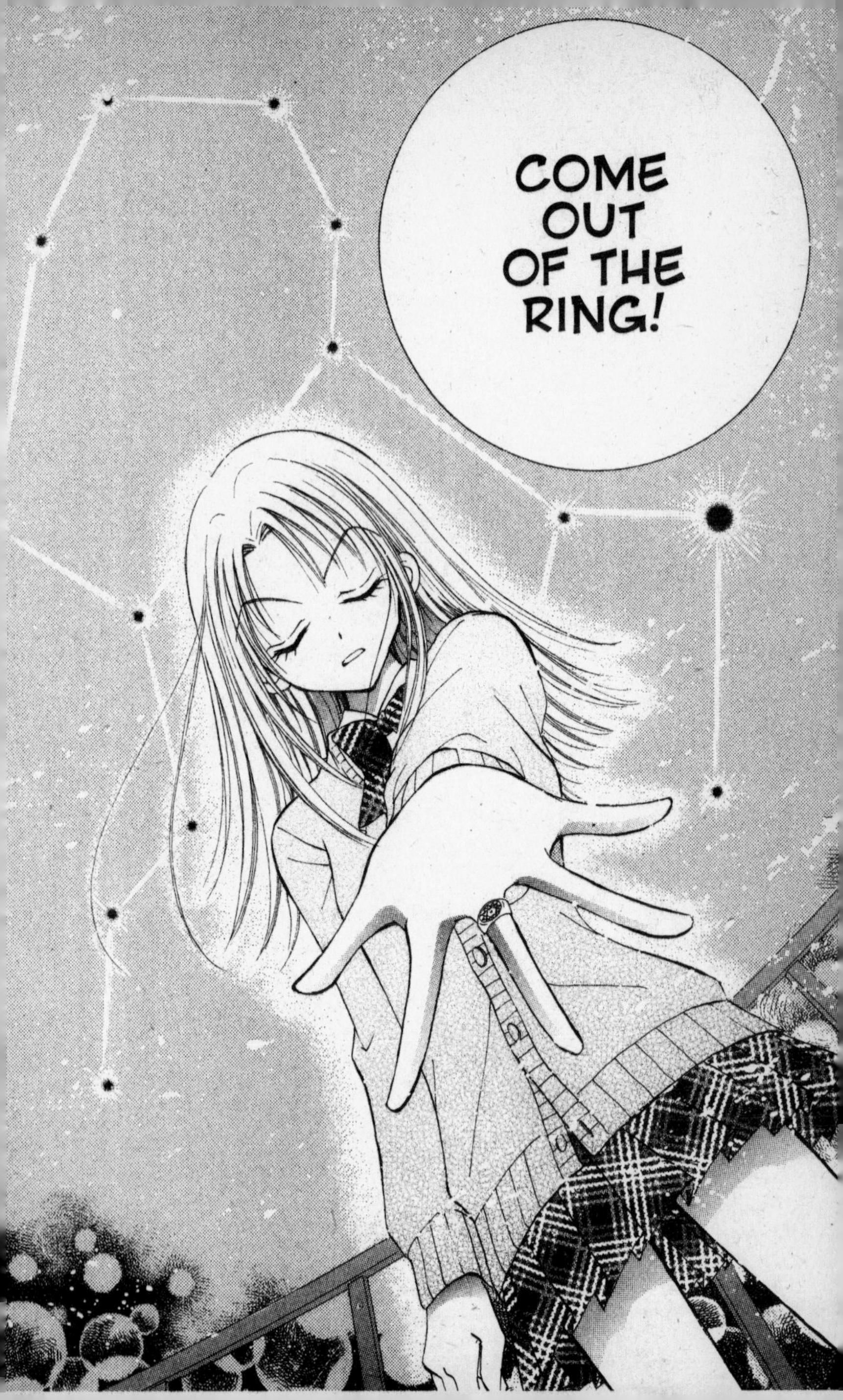
COME OUT OF THE RING!

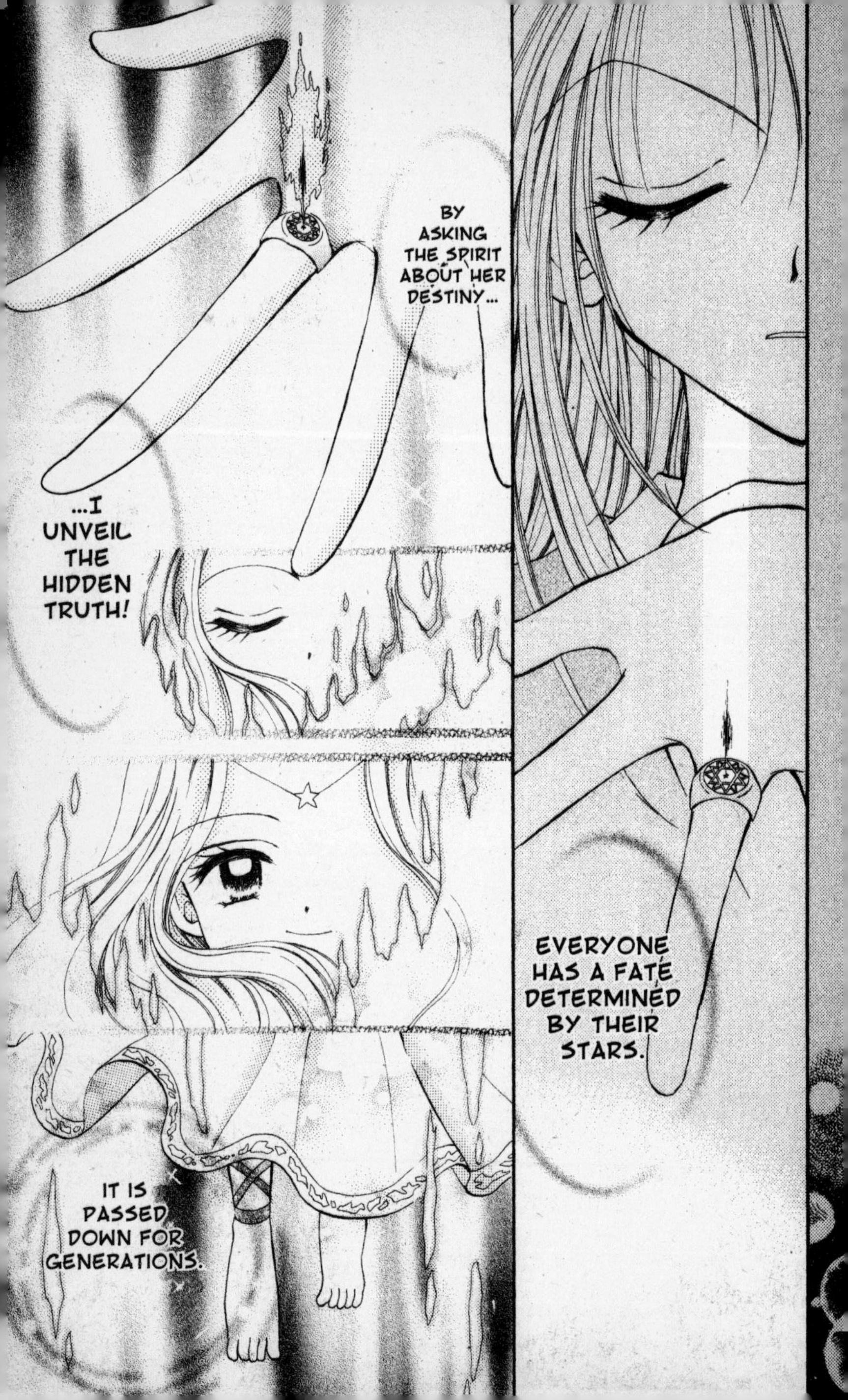
EVERYONE HAS A FATE DETERMINED BY THEIR STARS.
BY ASKING THE SPIRIT ABOUT HER DESTINY...
...I UNVEIL THE HIDDEN TRUTH!
IT IS PASSED DOWN FOR GENERATIONS.

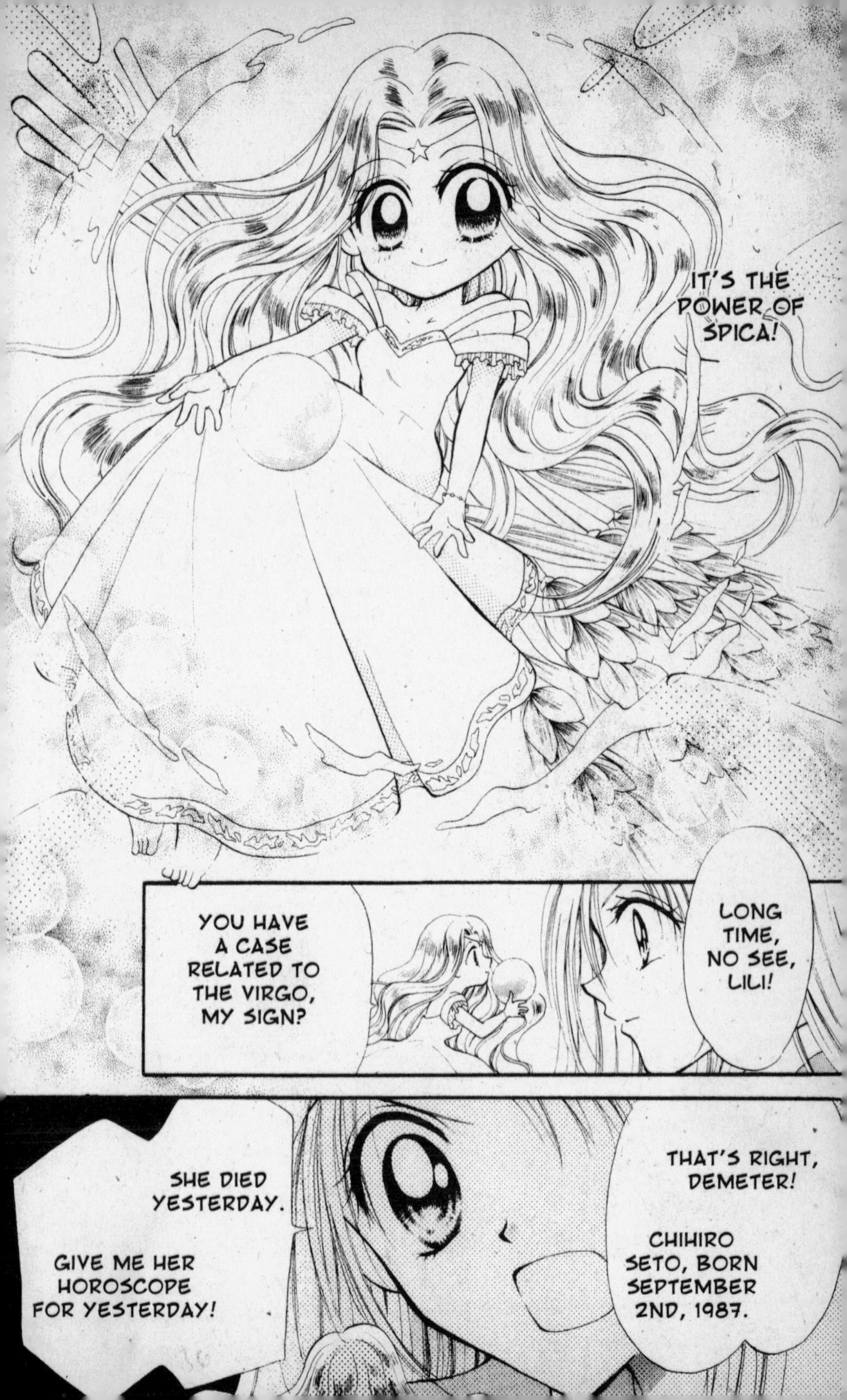
IT'S THE POWER OF SPICA!
LONG TIME, NO SEE, LILI!
YOU HAVE A CASE RELATED TO THE VIRGO, MY SIGN?
THAT'S RIGHT, DEMETER!
CHIHIRO SETO, BORN SEPTEMBER 2ND, 1987.
SHE DIED YESTERDAY.
GIVE ME HER HOROSCOPE FOR YESTERDAY!

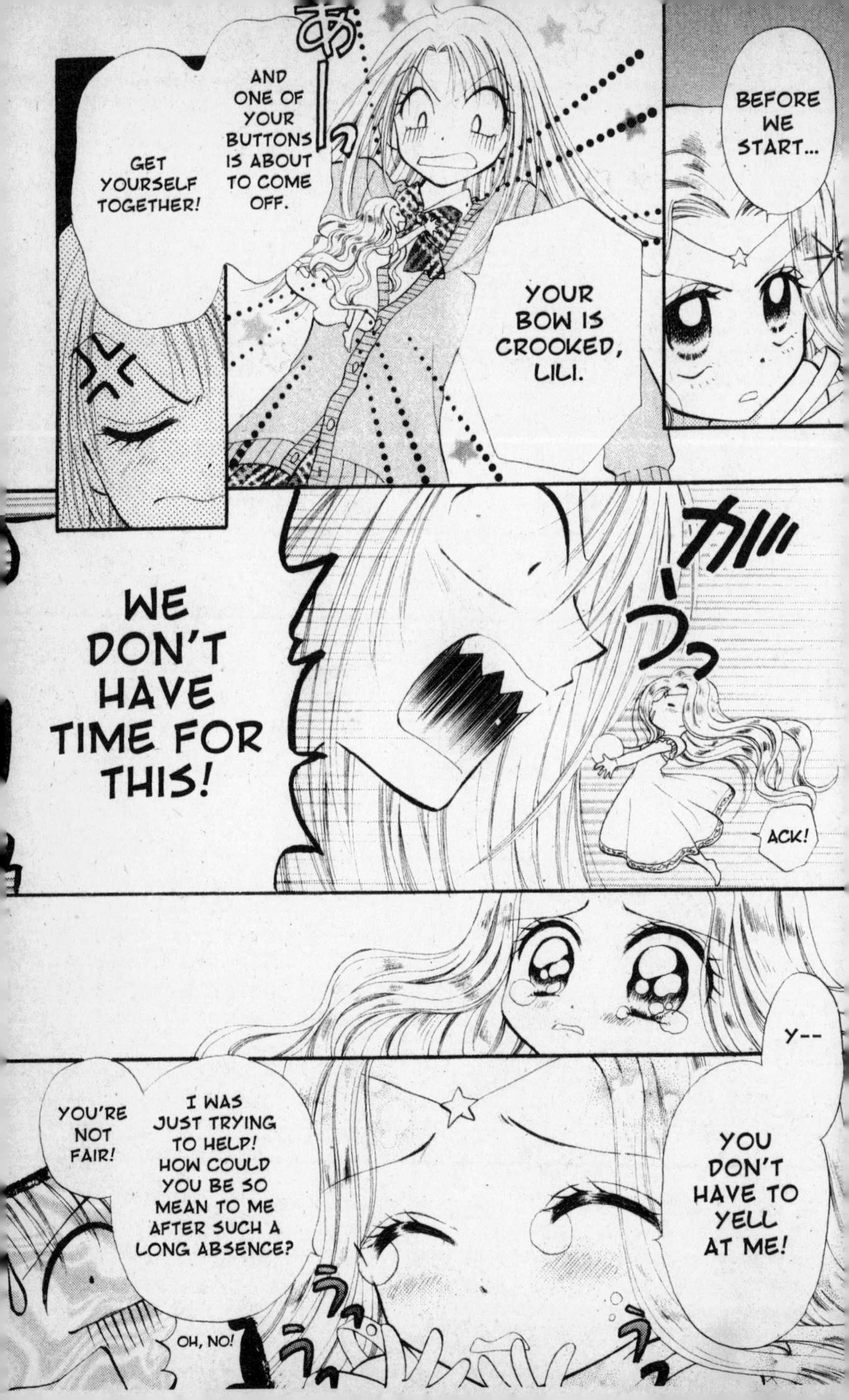
BEFORE WE START...
YOUR BOW IS CROOKED, LILI.
あーっ
AND ONE OF YOUR BUTTONS IS ABOUT TO COME OFF.
GET YOURSELF TOGETHER!
ACK!
WE DON'T HAVE TIME FOR THIS!
Y--
YOU DON'T HAVE TO YELL AT ME!
I WAS JUST TRYING TO HELP! HOW COULD YOU BE SO MEAN TO ME AFTER SUCH A LONG ABSENCE?
YOU'RE NOT FAIR!
OH, NO!

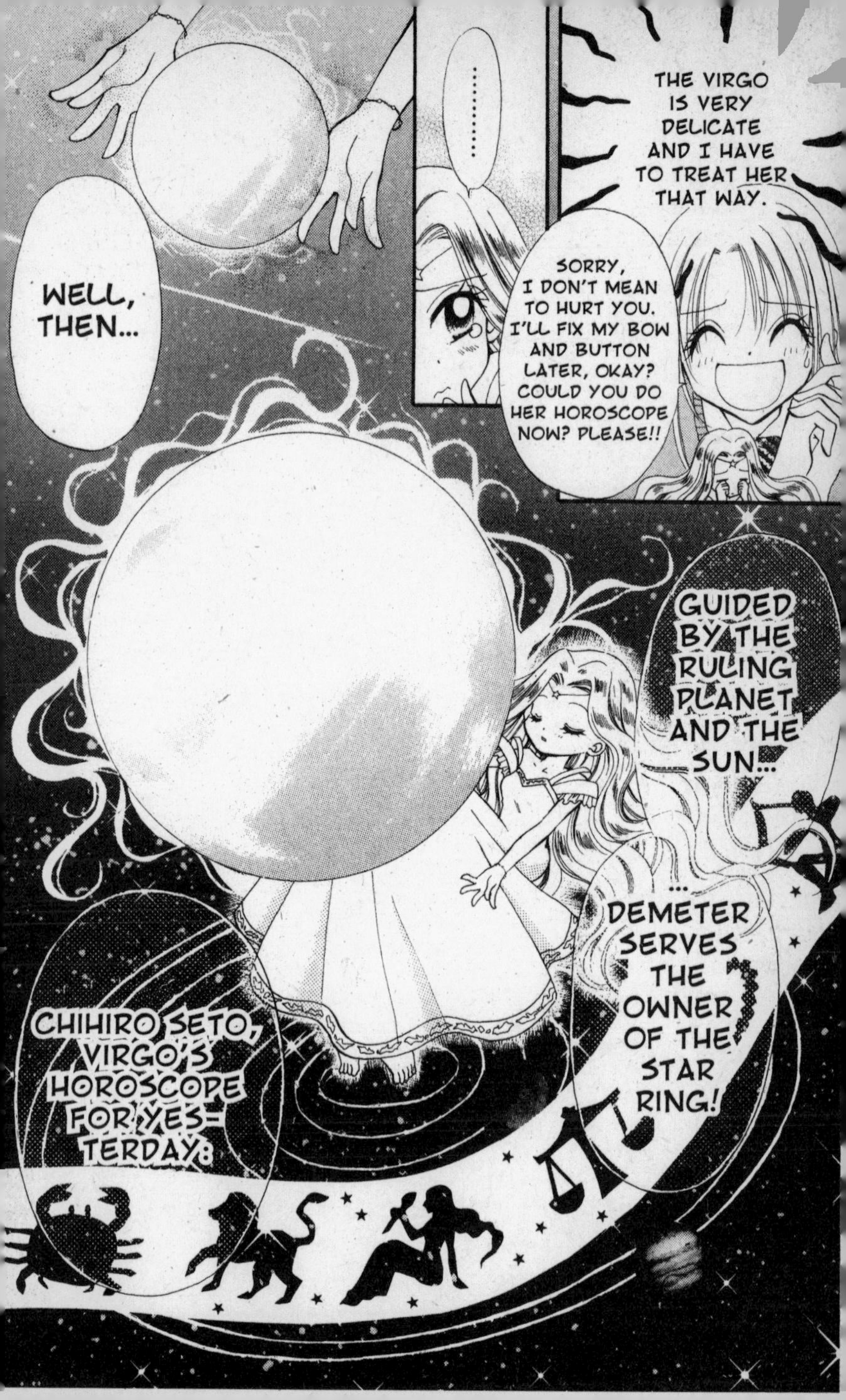
THE VIRGO IS VERY DELICATE AND I HAVE TO TREAT HER THAT WAY.
SORRY, I DON'T MEAN TO HURT YOU. I'LL FIX MY BOW AND BUTTON LATER, OKAY? COULD YOU DO HER HOROSCOPE NOW? PLEASE!!
......
WELL, THEN...
GUIDED BY THE RULING PLANET AND THE SUN...
...DEMETER SERVES THE OWNER OF THE STAR RING!
CHIHIRO SETO, VIRGO'S HOROSCOPE FOR YES-TERDAY:

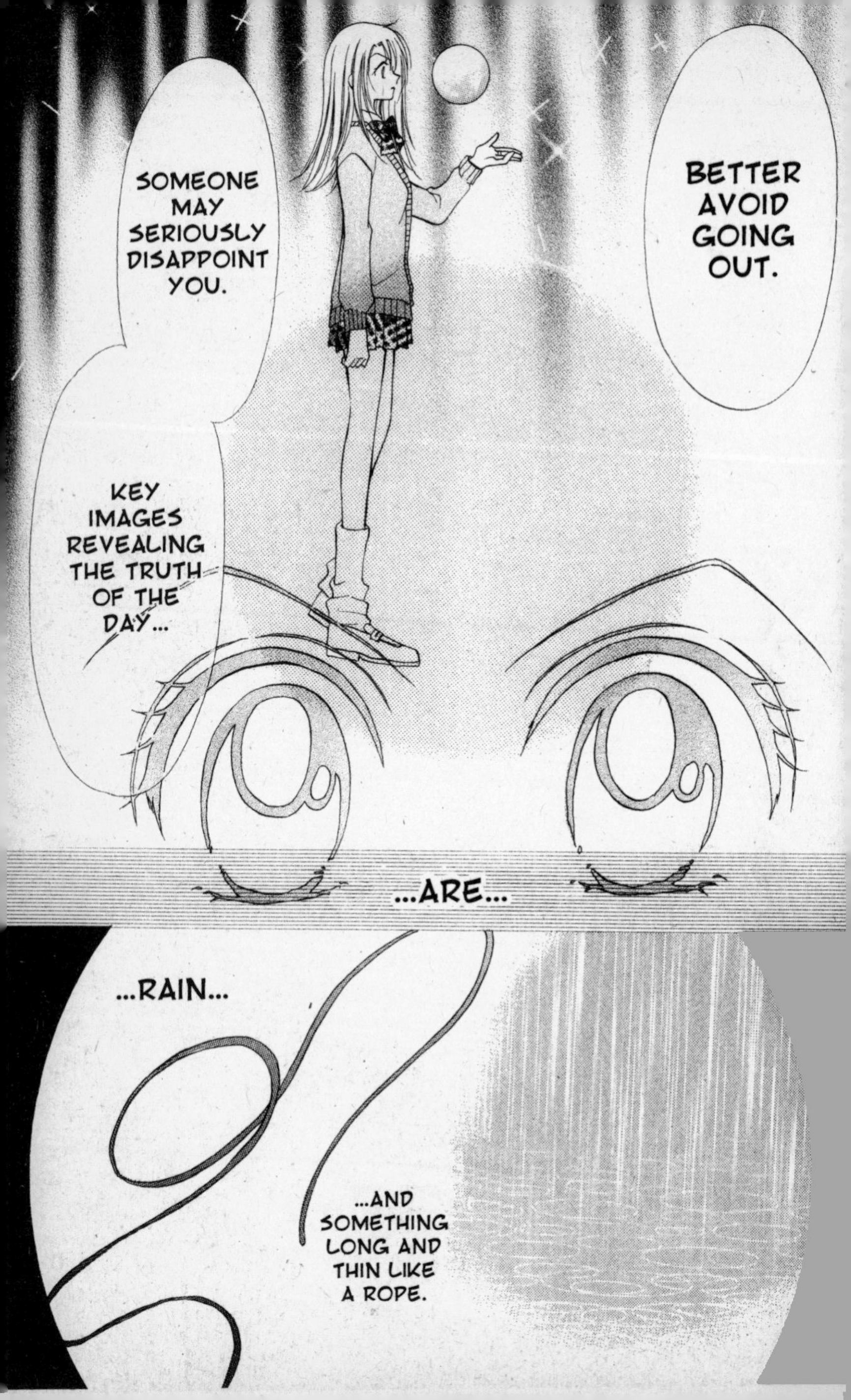
BETTER AVOID GOING OUT.
SOMEONE MAY SERIOUSLY DISAPPOINT YOU.
KEY IMAGES REVEALING THE TRUTH OF THE DAY...
...ARE...
...RAIN...
...AND SOMETHING LONG AND THIN LIKE A ROPE.

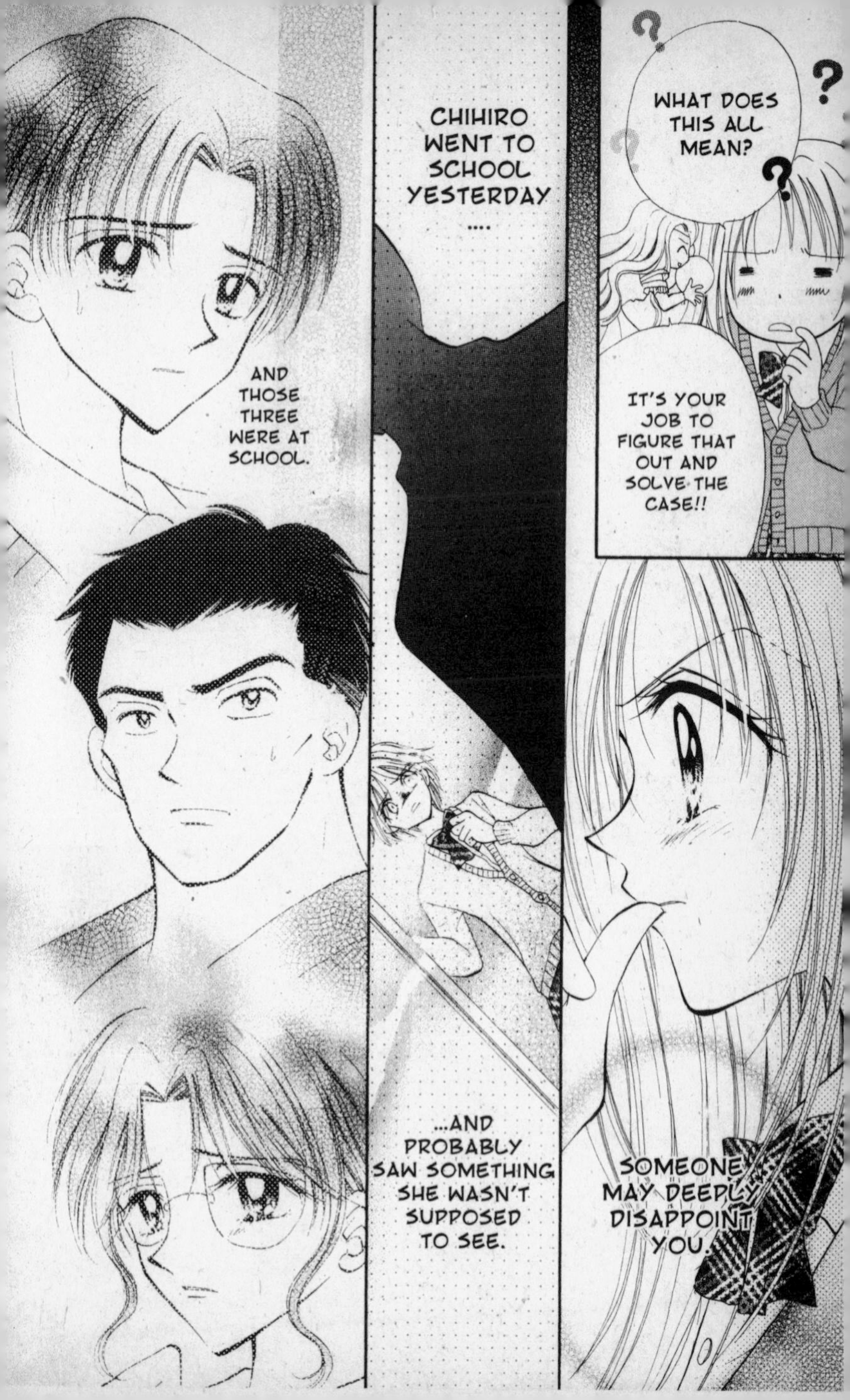

WHAT DOES THIS ALL MEAN?
IT'S YOUR JOB TO FIGURE THAT OUT AND SOLVE THE CASE!!
SOMEONE MAY DEEPLY DISAPPOINT YOU.
CHIHIRO WENT TO SCHOOL YESTERDAY ....
...AND PROBABLY SAW SOMETHING SHE WASN'T SUPPOSED TO SEE.
AND THOSE THREE WERE AT SCHOOL.

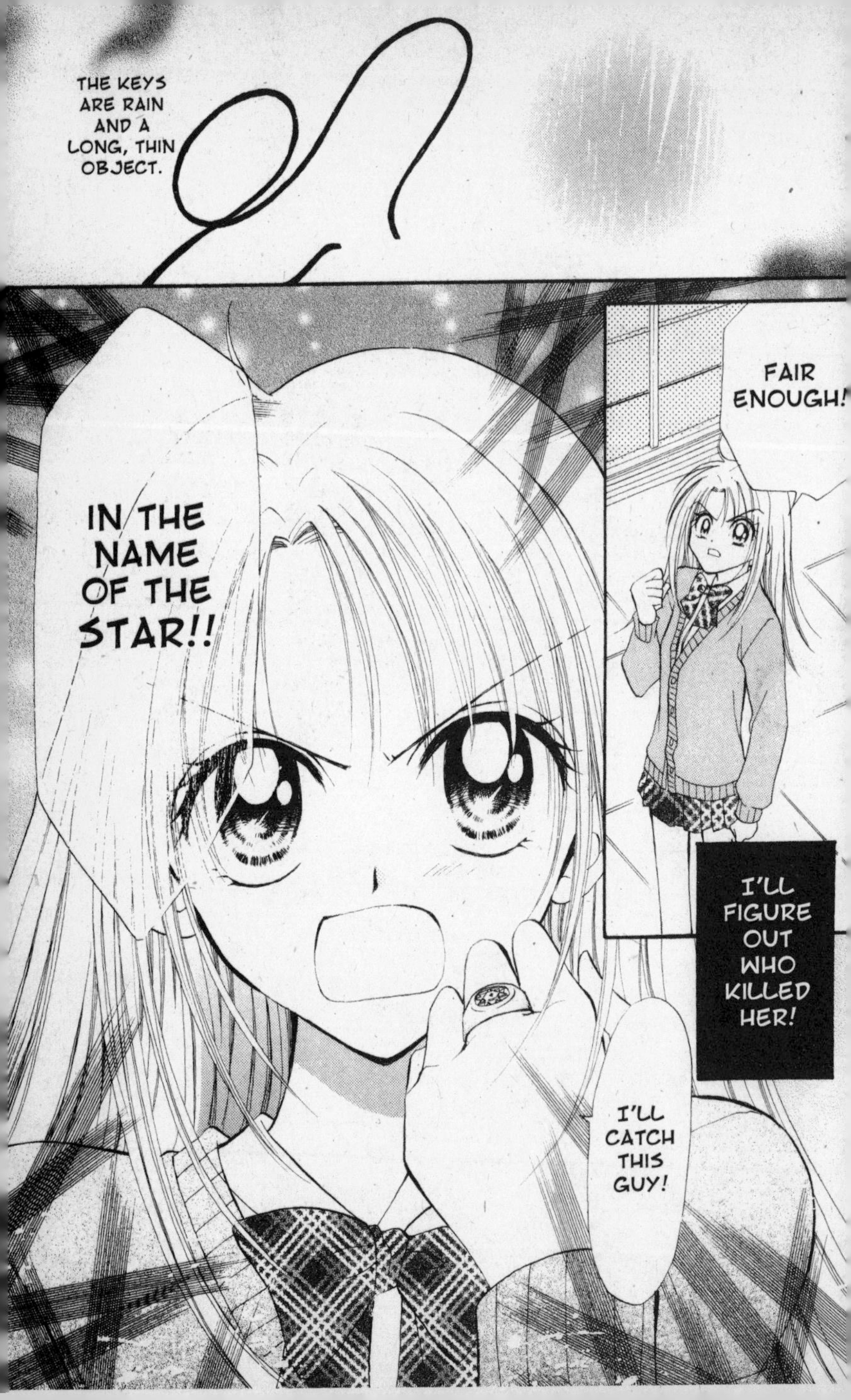
THE KEYS ARE RAIN AND A LONG, THIN OBJECT.
FAIR ENOUGH!
I'LL FIGURE OUT WHO KILLED HER!
I'LL CATCH THIS GUY!
IN THE NAME OF THE STAR!!

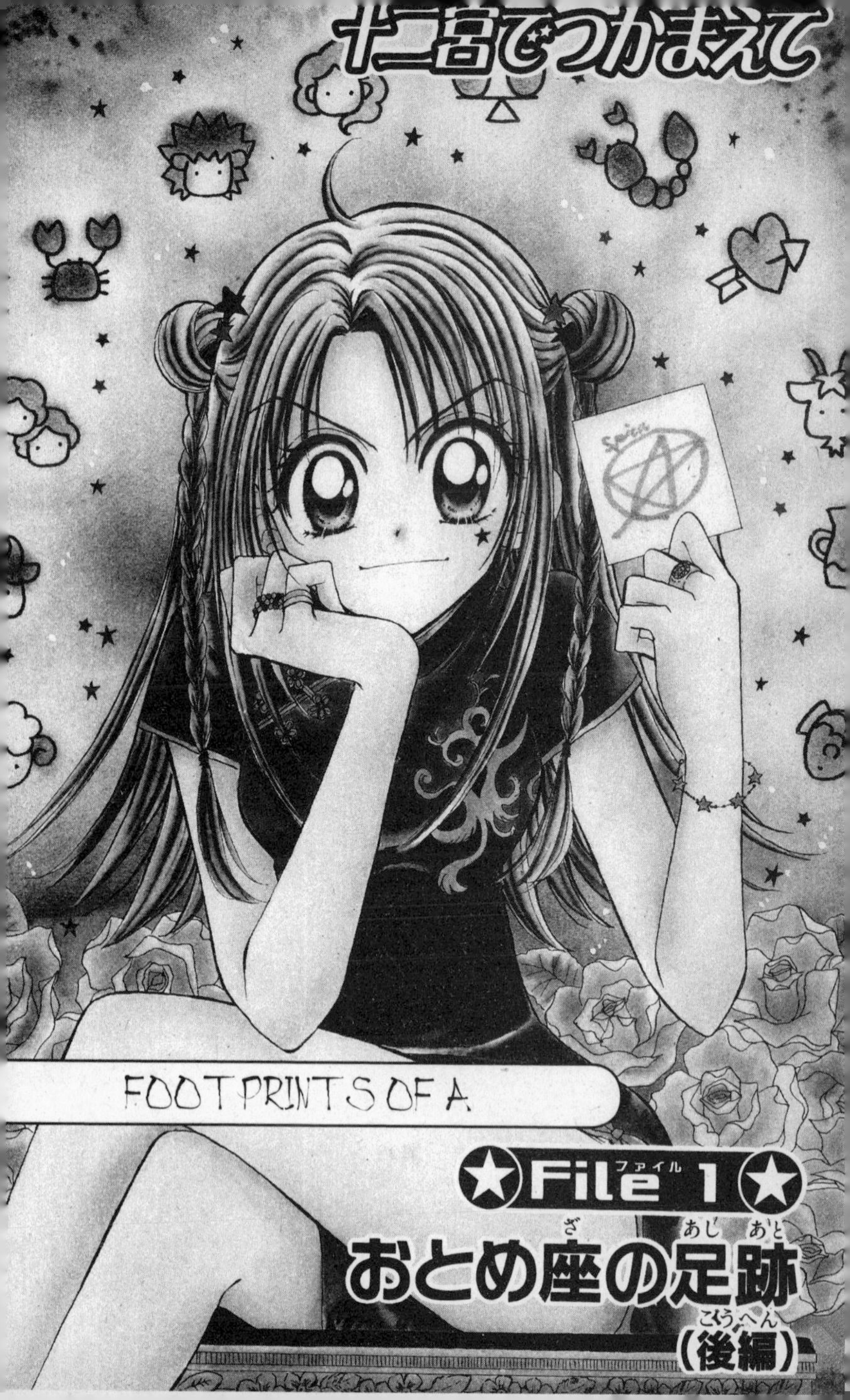

十二宮でつかまえて
FOOT PRINTS OF A
★File 1★
おとめ座の足跡
（後編）

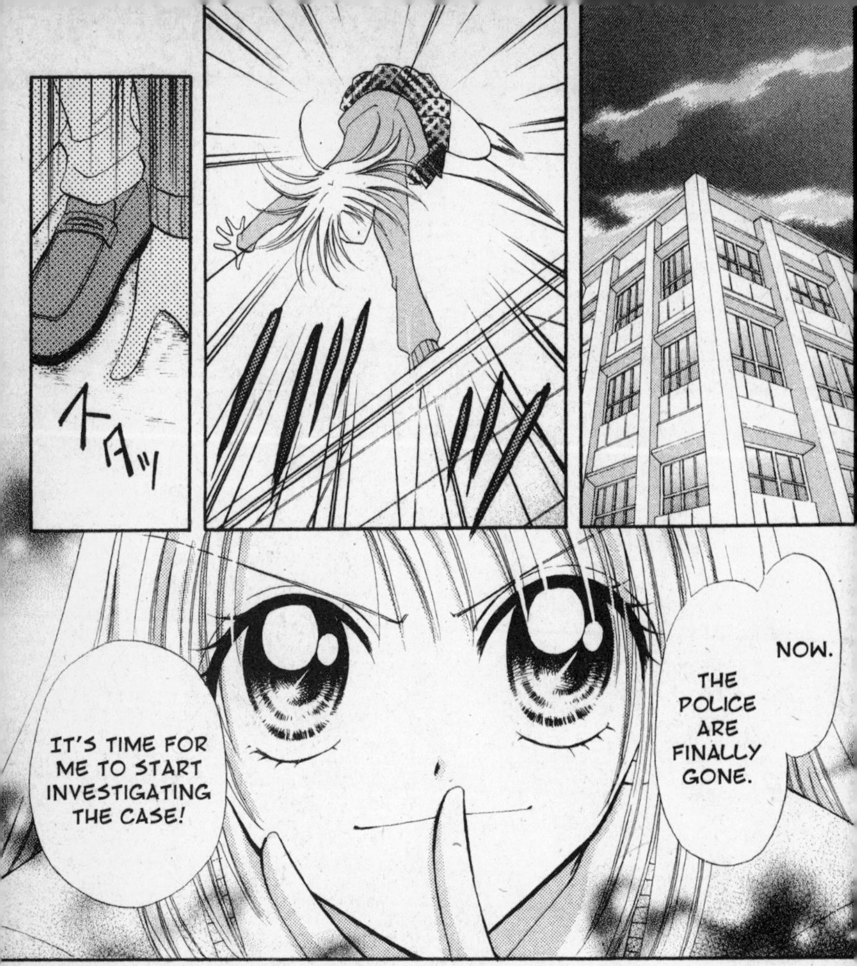
スタッ
THE POLICE ARE FINALLY GONE.
NOW.
IT'S TIME FOR ME TO START INVESTIGATING THE CASE!

Mademoiselle Lili's Astrology (1)

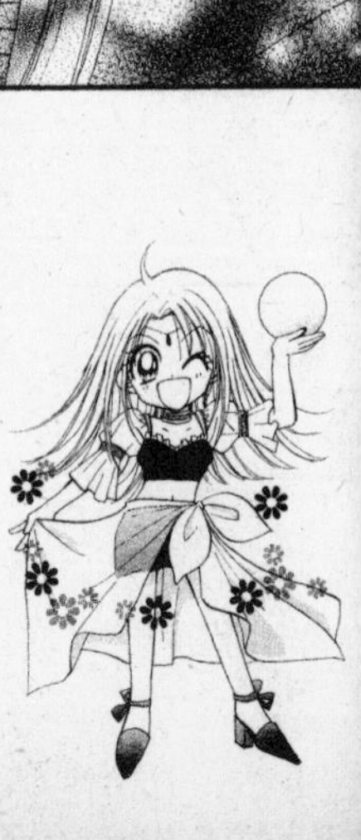

The most common horoscope, such as the one you read in the newspaper, is based on the sun signs of the zodiac. In common horoscopes, the movement of the sun is the only consideration. In a more detailed astrological analysis, the positions of ten planets and their relationships to each other are also considered. In other words, each person has up to 10 signs that will determine their character and destiny. I have six signs: Aquarius, Pisces, Taurus, Gemini, Libra, and Sagittarius. You might want to check what signs YOU have. Each sign has its own characteristics and it all can be very interesting.

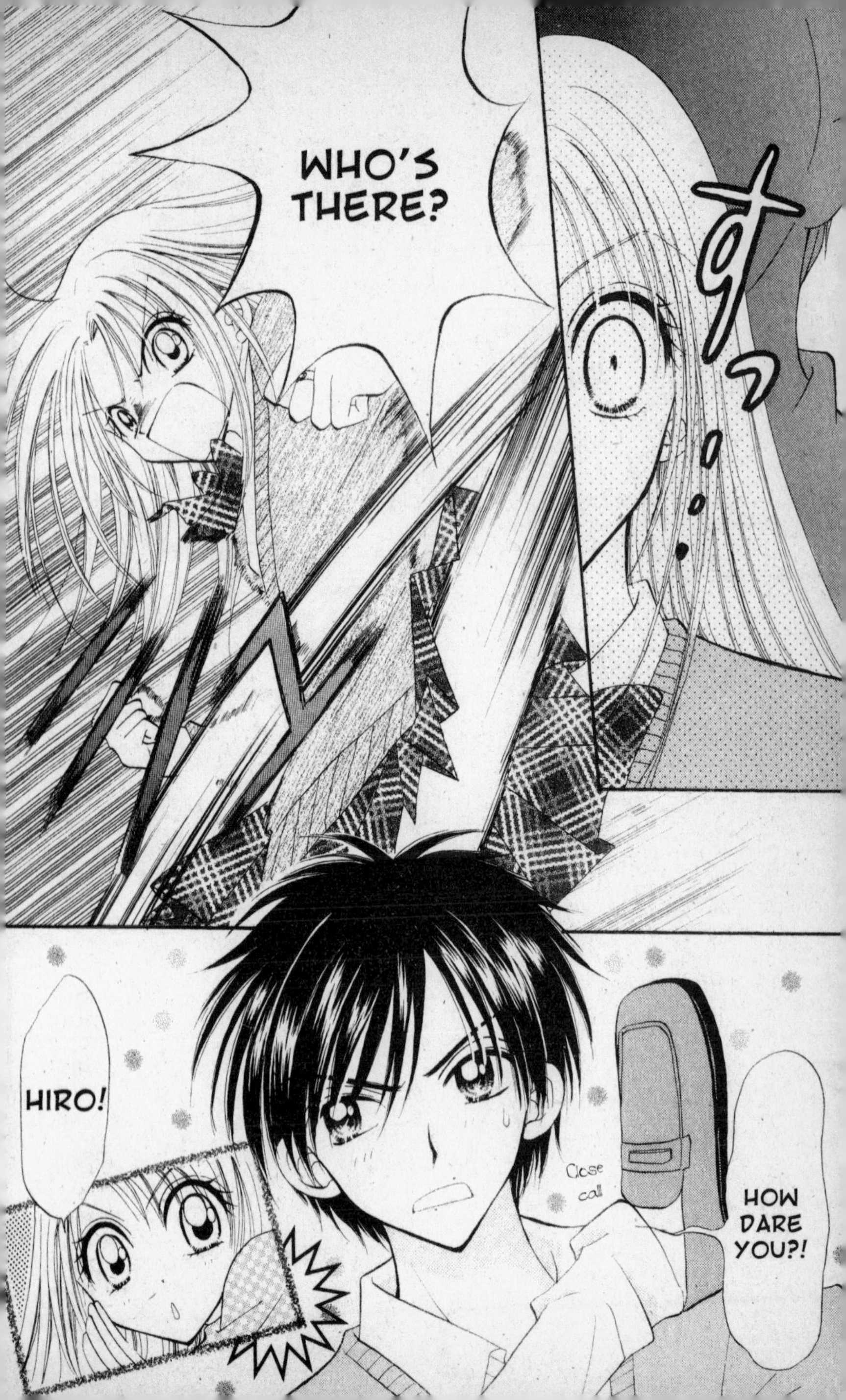
WHO'S THERE?
すっ
HOW DARE YOU?!
Close call
HIRO!

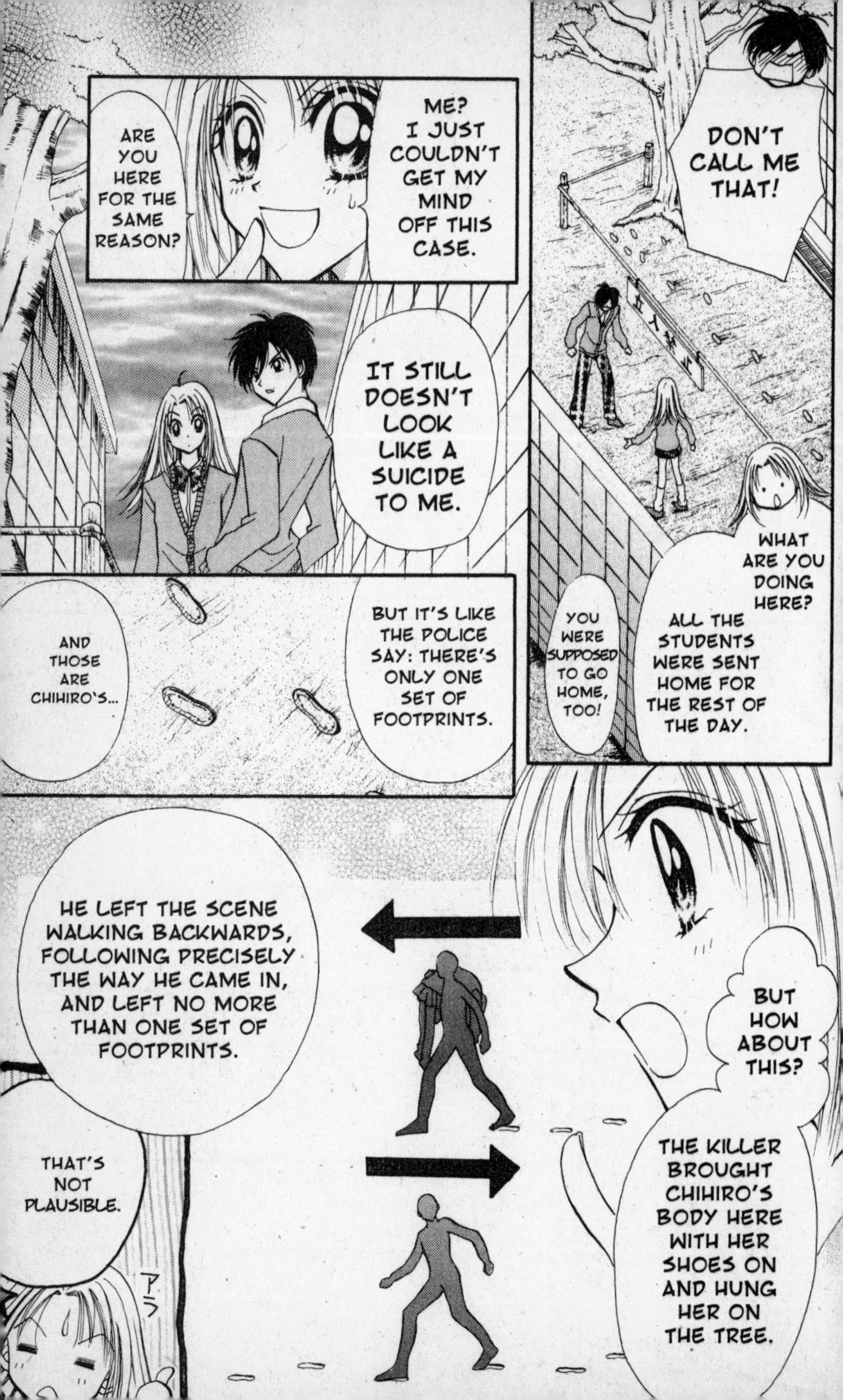
DON'T CALL ME THAT!
WHAT ARE YOU DOING HERE?
ALL THE STUDENTS WERE SENT HOME FOR THE REST OF THE DAY.
YOU WERE SUPPOSED TO GO HOME, TOO!
ME? I JUST COULDN'T GET MY MIND OFF THIS CASE.
ARE YOU HERE FOR THE SAME REASON?
IT STILL DOESN'T LOOK LIKE A SUICIDE TO ME.
BUT IT'S LIKE THE POLICE SAY: THERE'S ONLY ONE SET OF FOOTPRINTS.
AND THOSE ARE CHIHIRO'S...
BUT HOW ABOUT THIS?
THE KILLER BROUGHT CHIHIRO'S BODY HERE WITH HER SHOES ON AND HUNG HER ON THE TREE.
HE LEFT THE SCENE WALKING BACKWARDS, FOLLOWING PRECISELY THE WAY HE CAME IN, AND LEFT NO MORE THAN ONE SET OF FOOTPRINTS.
THAT'S NOT PLAUSIBLE.

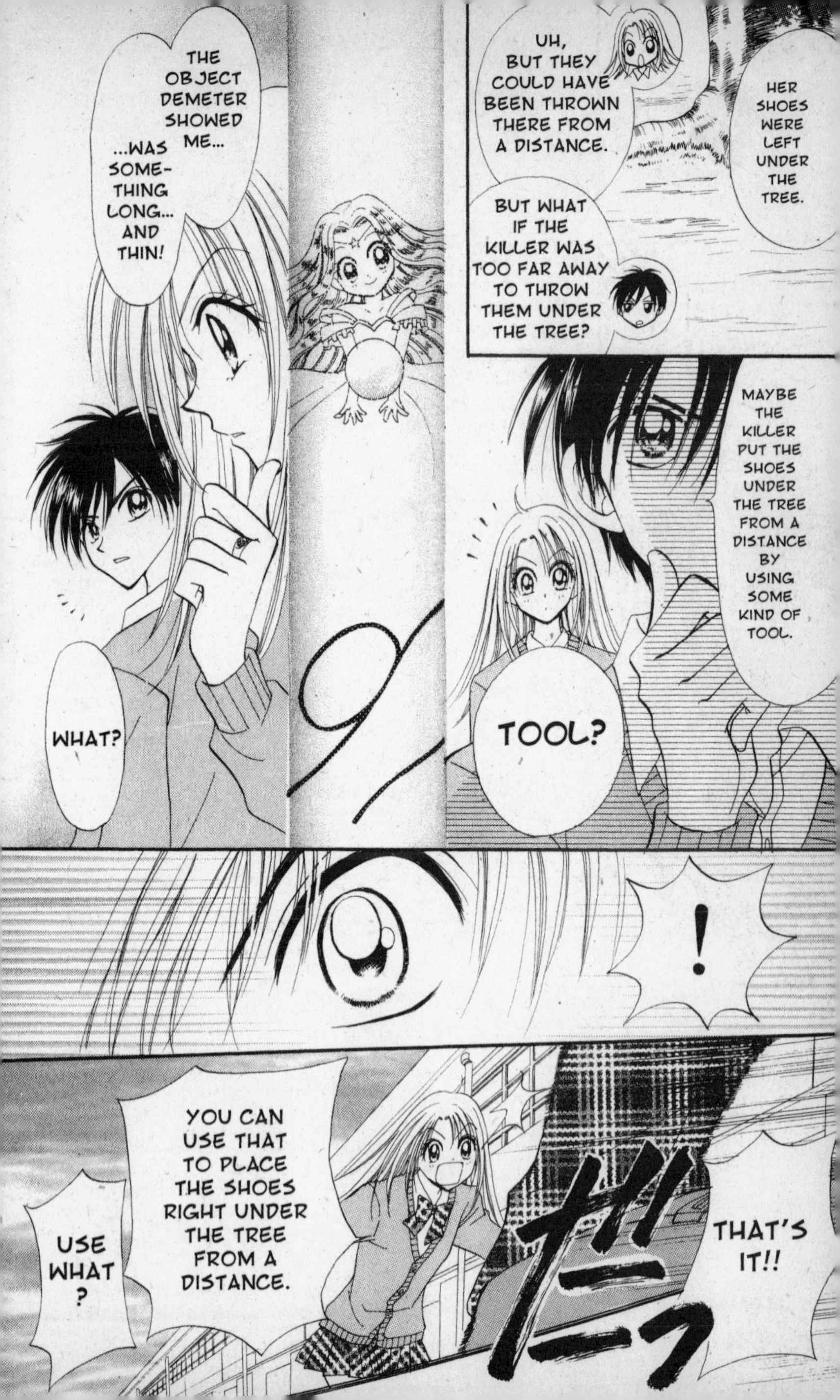
HER SHOES WERE LEFT UNDER THE TREE.
UH, BUT THEY COULD HAVE BEEN THROWN THERE FROM A DISTANCE.
BUT WHAT IF THE KILLER WAS TOO FAR AWAY TO THROW THEM UNDER THE TREE?
MAYBE THE KILLER PUT THE SHOES UNDER THE TREE FROM A DISTANCE BY USING SOME KIND OF TOOL.
TOOL?
THE OBJECT DEMETER SHOWED ME...
...WAS SOME-THING LONG... AND THIN!
WHAT?
!
THAT'S IT!!
YOU CAN USE THAT TO PLACE THE SHOES RIGHT UNDER THE TREE FROM A DISTANCE.
USE WHAT?

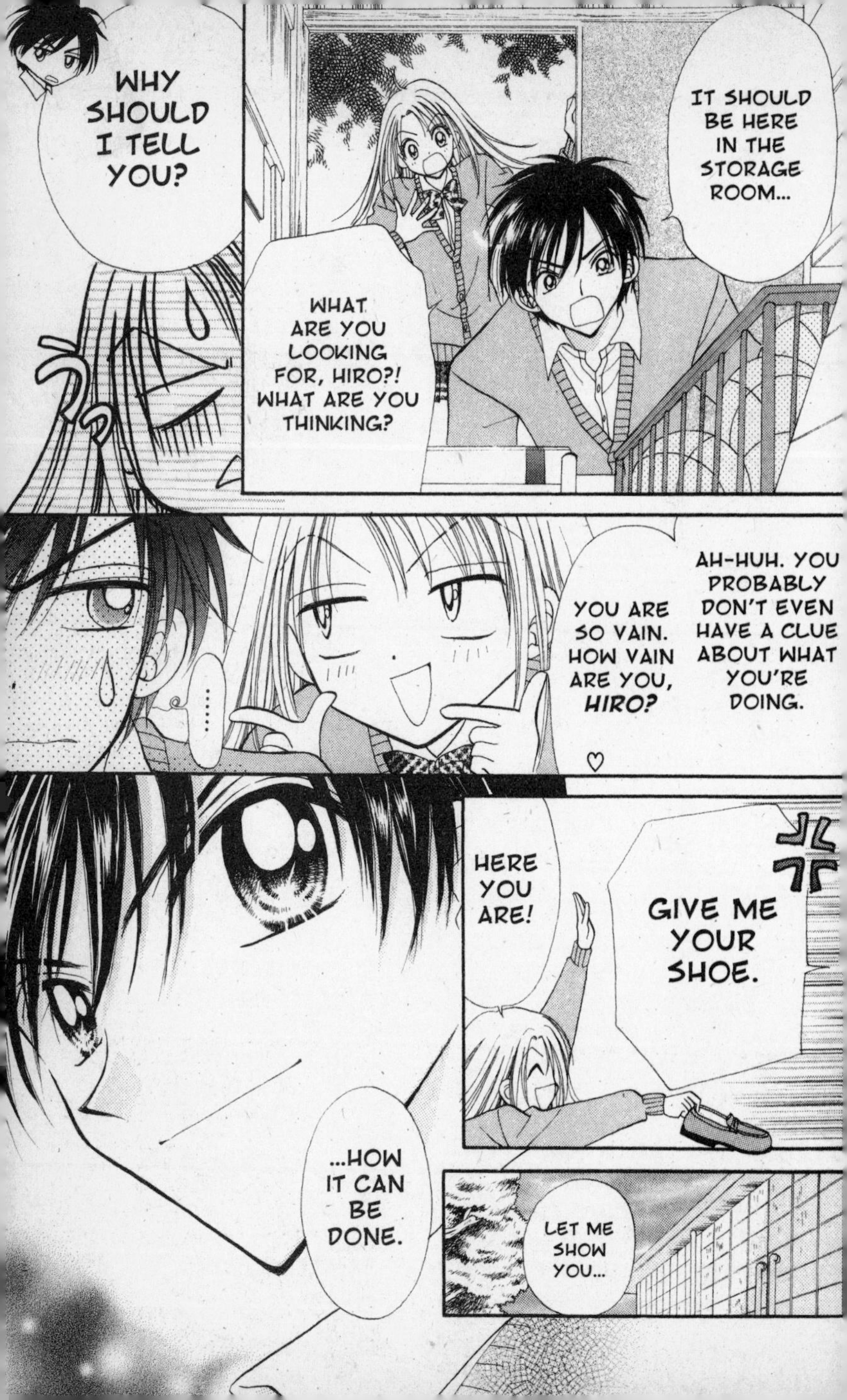
IT SHOULD BE HERE IN THE STORAGE ROOM...
WHAT ARE YOU LOOKING FOR, HIRO?! WHAT ARE YOU THINKING?
WHY SHOULD I TELL YOU?
AH-HUH. YOU PROBABLY DON'T EVEN HAVE A CLUE ABOUT WHAT YOU'RE DOING.
YOU ARE SO VAIN. HOW VAIN ARE YOU, HIRO? ♡
......
GIVE ME YOUR SHOE.
HERE YOU ARE!
LET ME SHOW YOU...
...HOW IT CAN BE DONE.

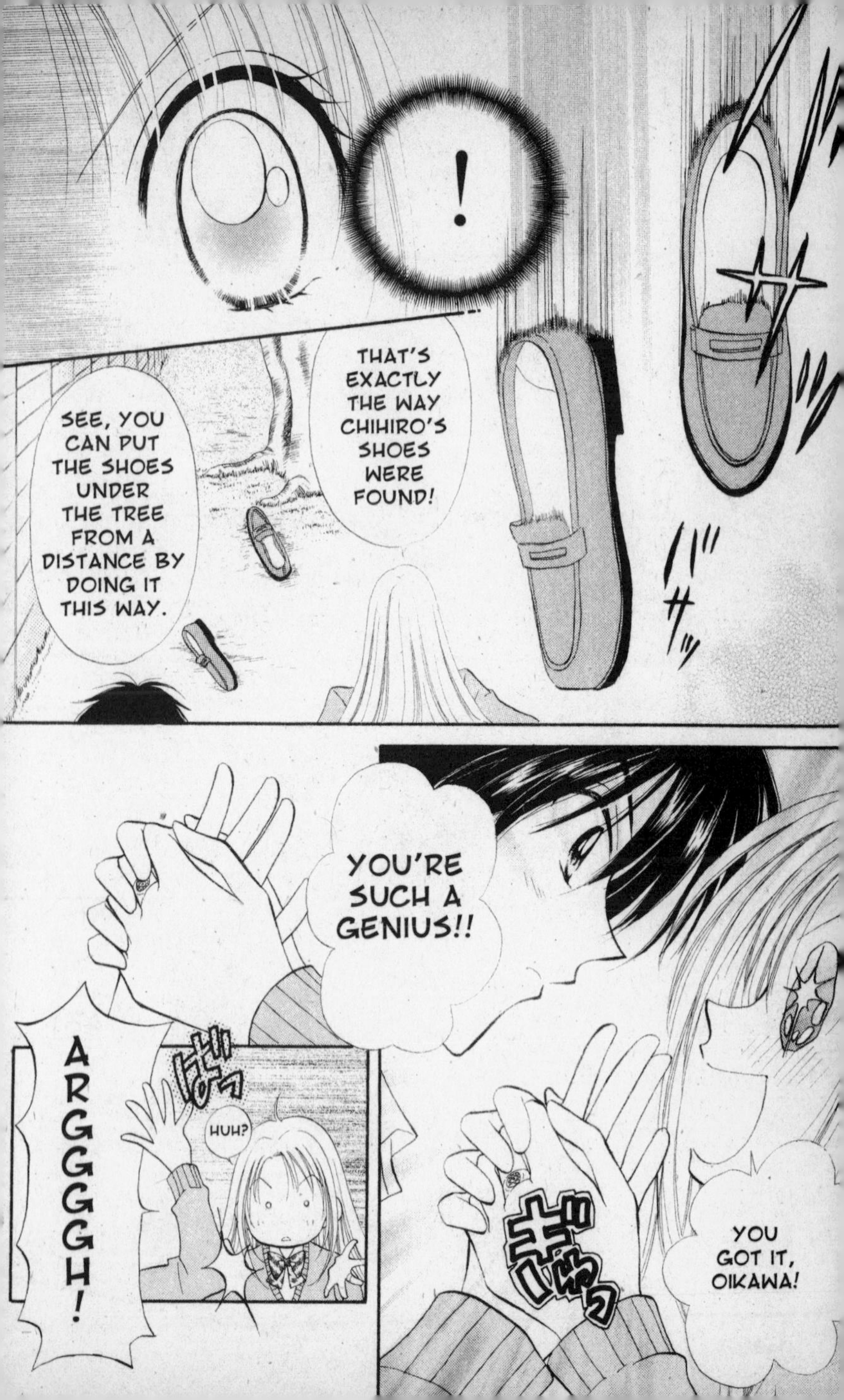
!
THAT'S EXACTLY THE WAY CHIHIRO'S SHOES WERE FOUND!
SEE, YOU CAN PUT THE SHOES UNDER THE TREE FROM A DISTANCE BY DOING IT THIS WAY.
YOU'RE SUCH A GENIUS!!
YOU GOT IT, OIKAWA!
ARGGGGH!
HUH?

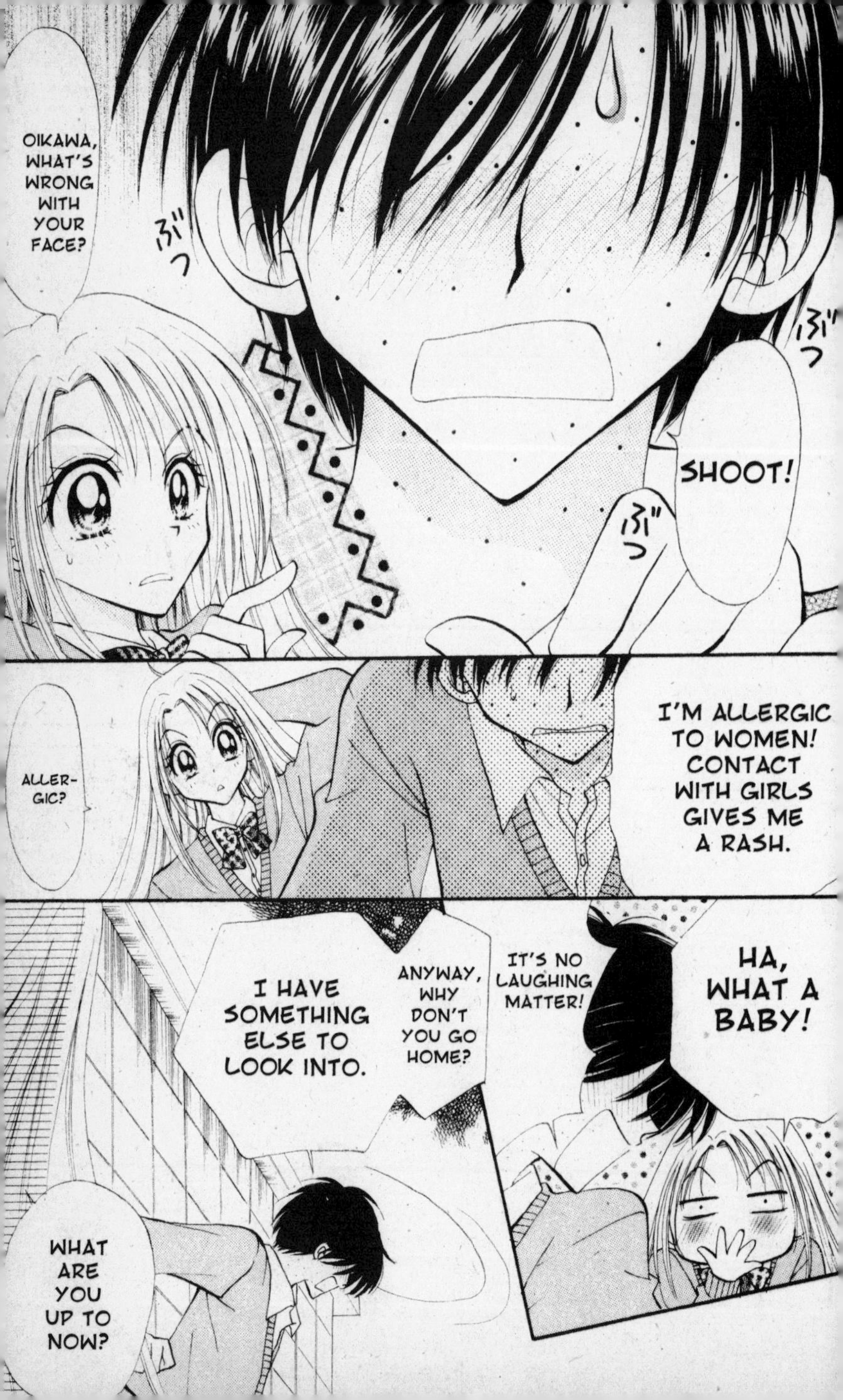
ぶつ
SHOOT!
ぶつ
ぶつ
OIKAWA, WHAT'S WRONG WITH YOUR FACE?
I'M ALLERGIC TO WOMEN! CONTACT WITH GIRLS GIVES ME A RASH.
ALLER-GIC?
HA, WHAT A BABY!
IT'S NO LAUGHING MATTER!
ANYWAY, WHY DON'T YOU GO HOME?
I HAVE SOMETHING ELSE TO LOOK INTO.
WHAT ARE YOU UP TO NOW?

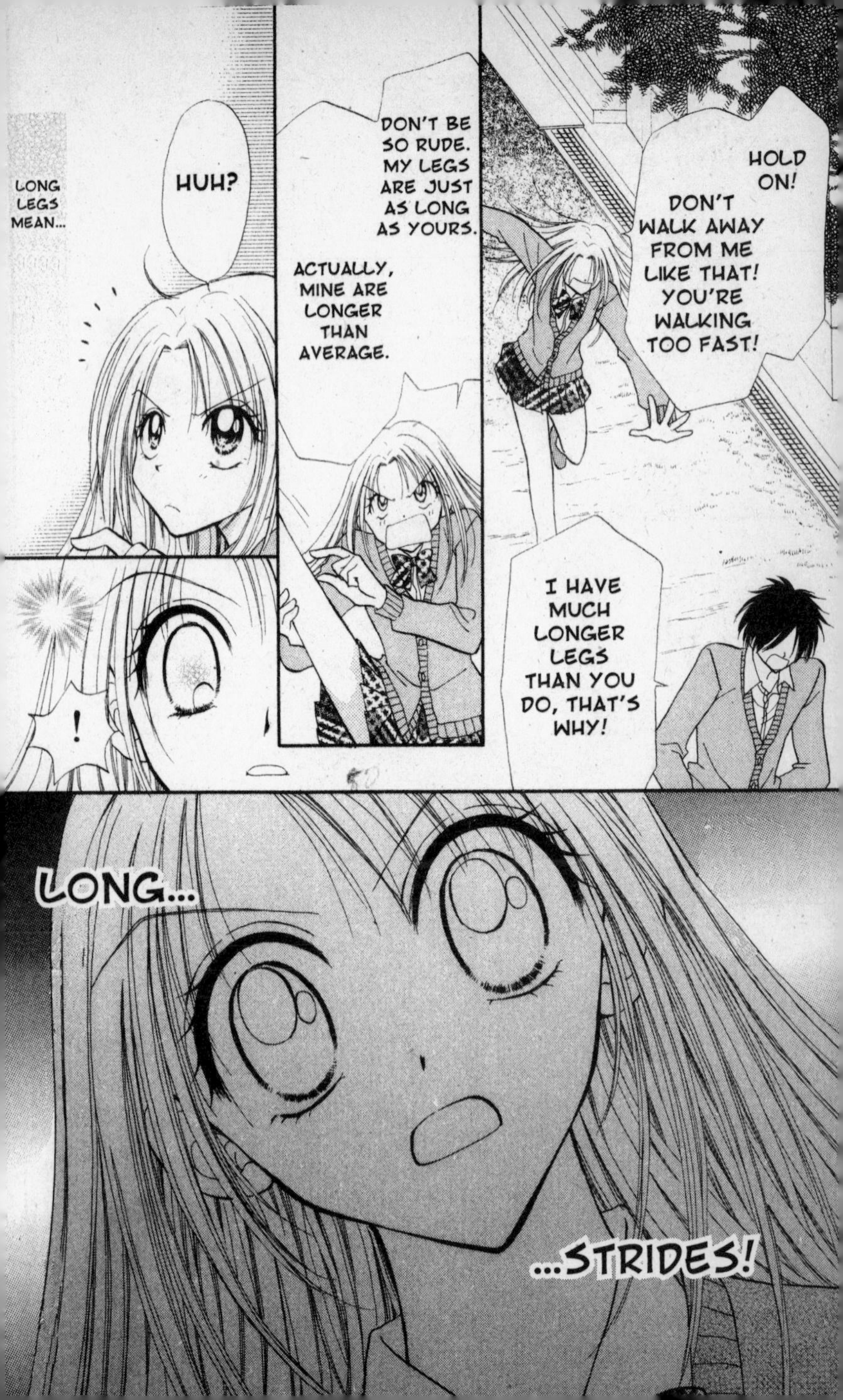
HOLD ON!
DON'T WALK AWAY FROM ME LIKE THAT! YOU'RE WALKING TOO FAST!
I HAVE MUCH LONGER LEGS THAN YOU DO, THAT'S WHY!
DON'T BE SO RUDE. MY LEGS ARE JUST AS LONG AS YOURS.
ACTUALLY, MINE ARE LONGER THAN AVERAGE.
HUH?
LONG LEGS MEAN...
!
LONG...
...STRIDES!

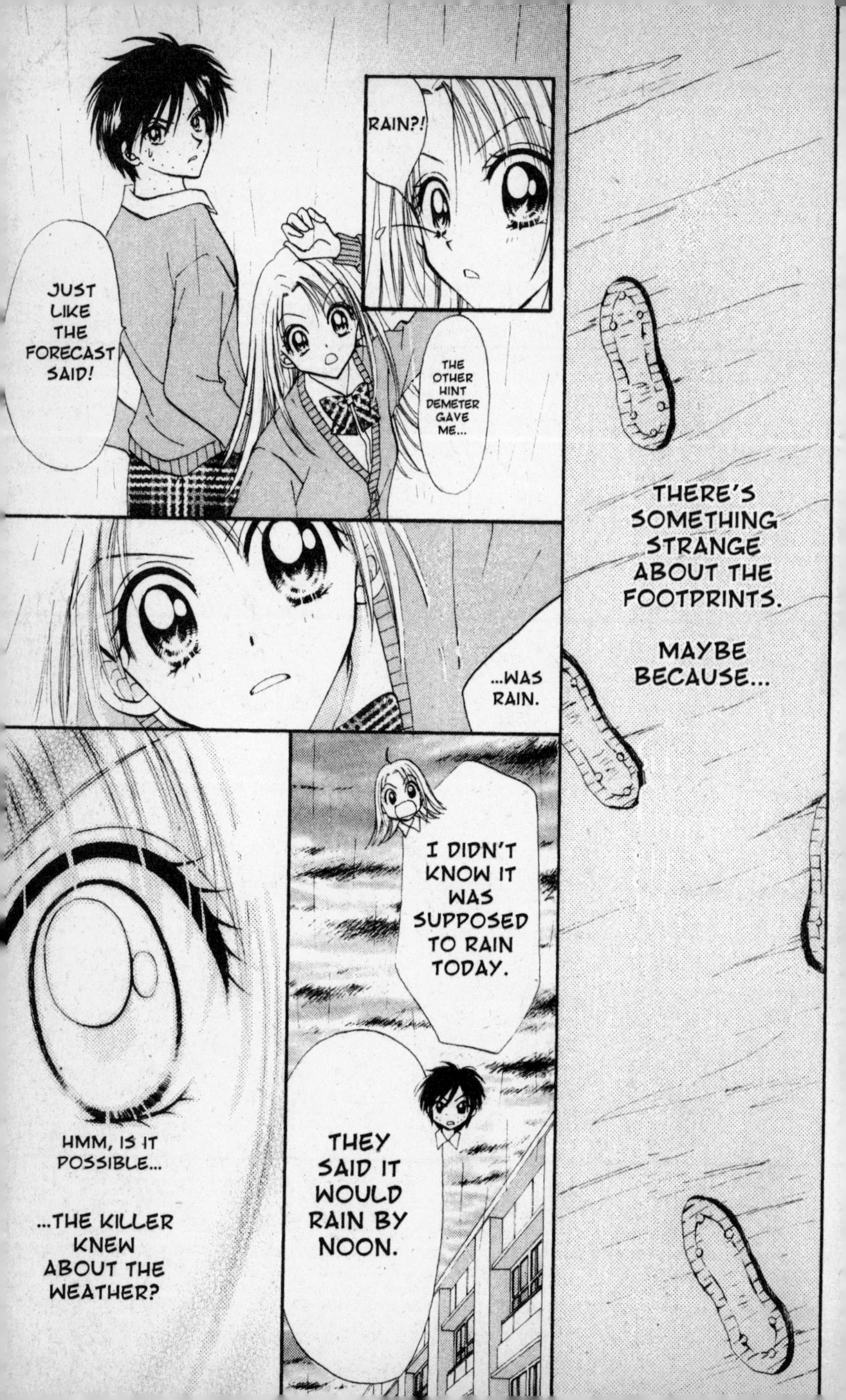
THERE'S SOMETHING STRANGE ABOUT THE FOOTPRINTS.
MAYBE BECAUSE...
RAIN?!
THE OTHER HINT DEMETER GAVE ME...
JUST LIKE THE FORECAST SAID!
...WAS RAIN.
I DIDN'T KNOW IT WAS SUPPOSED TO RAIN TODAY.
THEY SAID IT WOULD RAIN BY NOON.
HMM, IS IT POSSIBLE...
...THE KILLER KNEW ABOUT THE WEATHER?

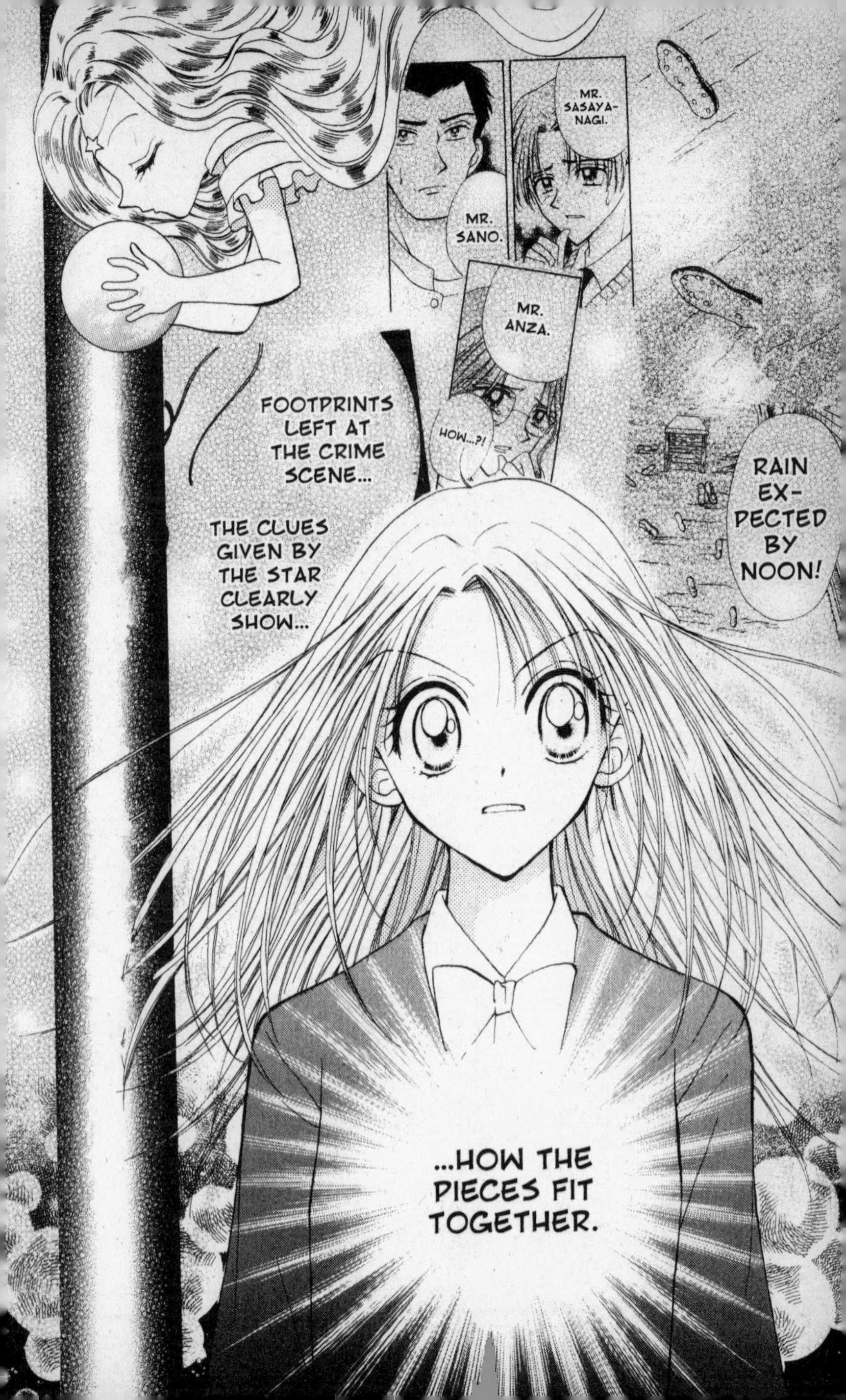
MR. SASAYANAGI.
MR. SANO.
MR. ANZA.
HOW...?!
RAIN EXPECTED BY NOON!
FOOTPRINTS LEFT AT THE CRIME SCENE...
THE CLUES GIVEN BY THE STAR CLEARLY SHOW...
...HOW THE PIECES FIT TOGETHER.

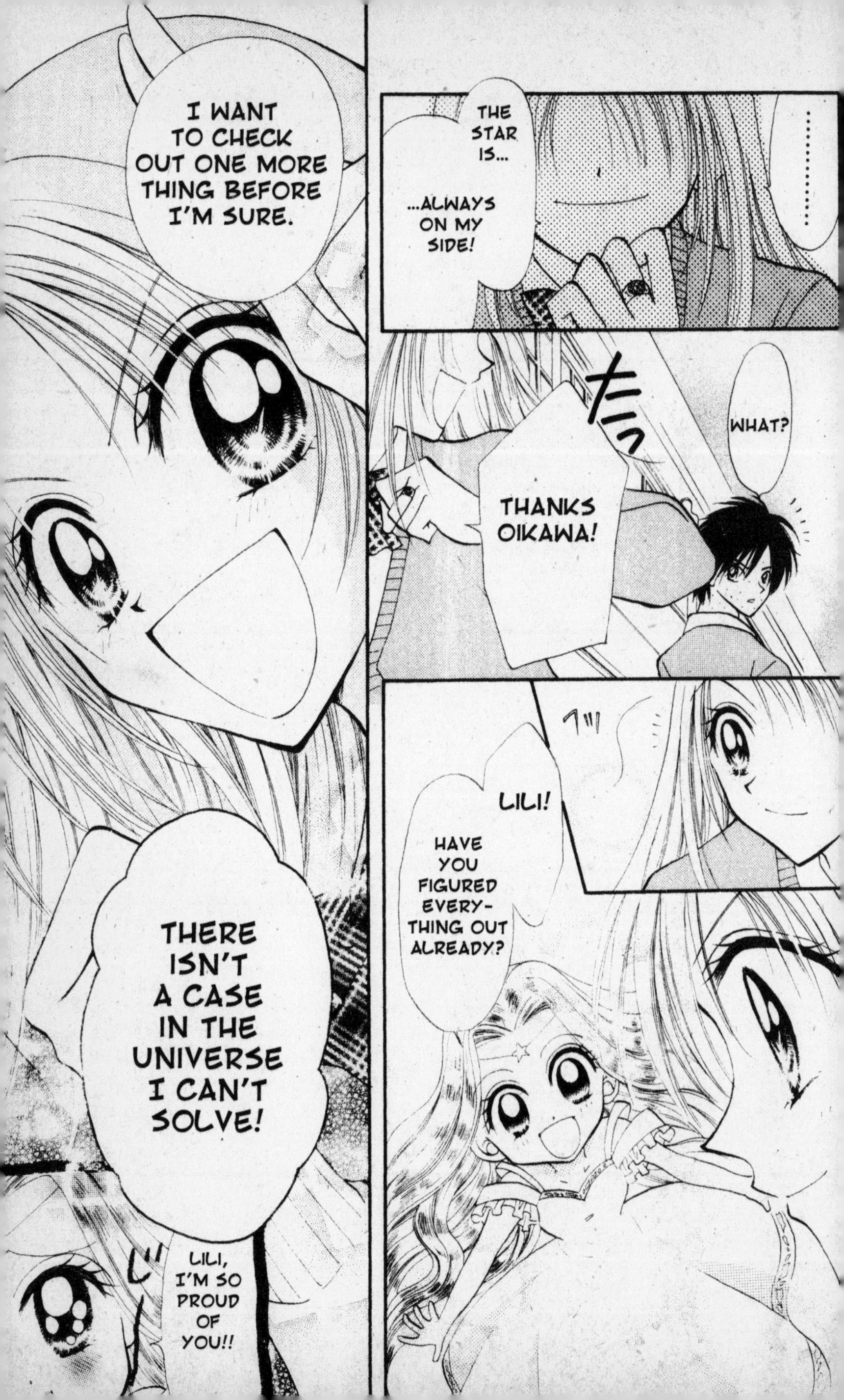
......
THE STAR IS...
...ALWAYS ON MY SIDE!
WHAT?
THANKS OIKAWA!
LILI!
HAVE YOU FIGURED EVERY-THING OUT ALREADY?
I WANT TO CHECK OUT ONE MORE THING BEFORE I'M SURE.
THERE ISN'T A CASE IN THE UNIVERSE I CAN'T SOLVE!
LILI, I'M SO PROUD OF YOU!!

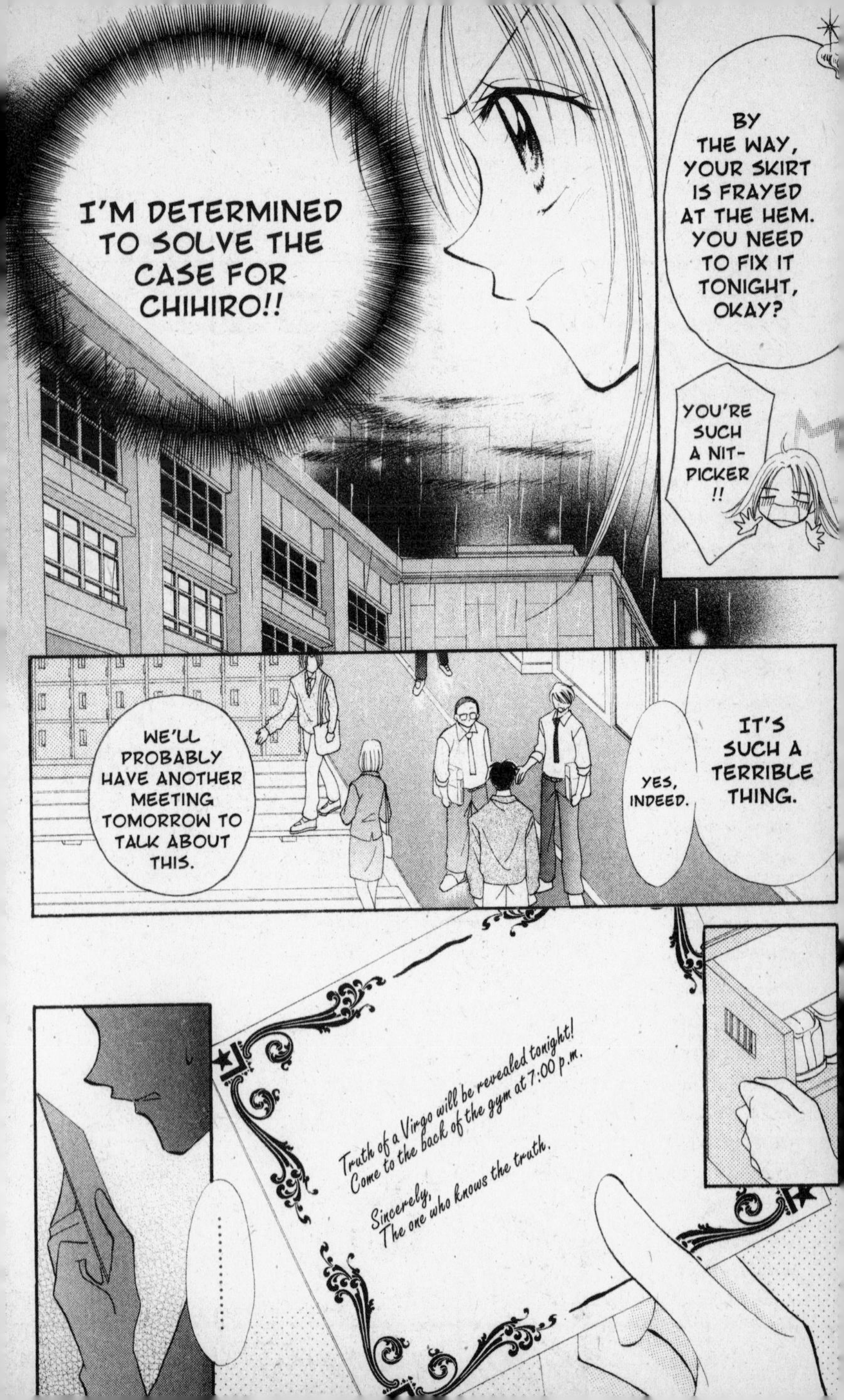
BY THE WAY, YOUR SKIRT IS FRAYED AT THE HEM. YOU NEED TO FIX IT TONIGHT, OKAY?
YOU'RE SUCH A NIT-PICKER!!
I'M DETERMINED TO SOLVE THE CASE FOR CHIHIRO!!
IT'S SUCH A TERRIBLE THING.
YES, INDEED.
WE'LL PROBABLY HAVE ANOTHER MEETING TOMORROW TO TALK ABOUT THIS.
Truth of a Virgo will be revealed tonight!
Come to the back of the gym at 7:00 p.m.
Sincerely,
The one who knows the truth.
……

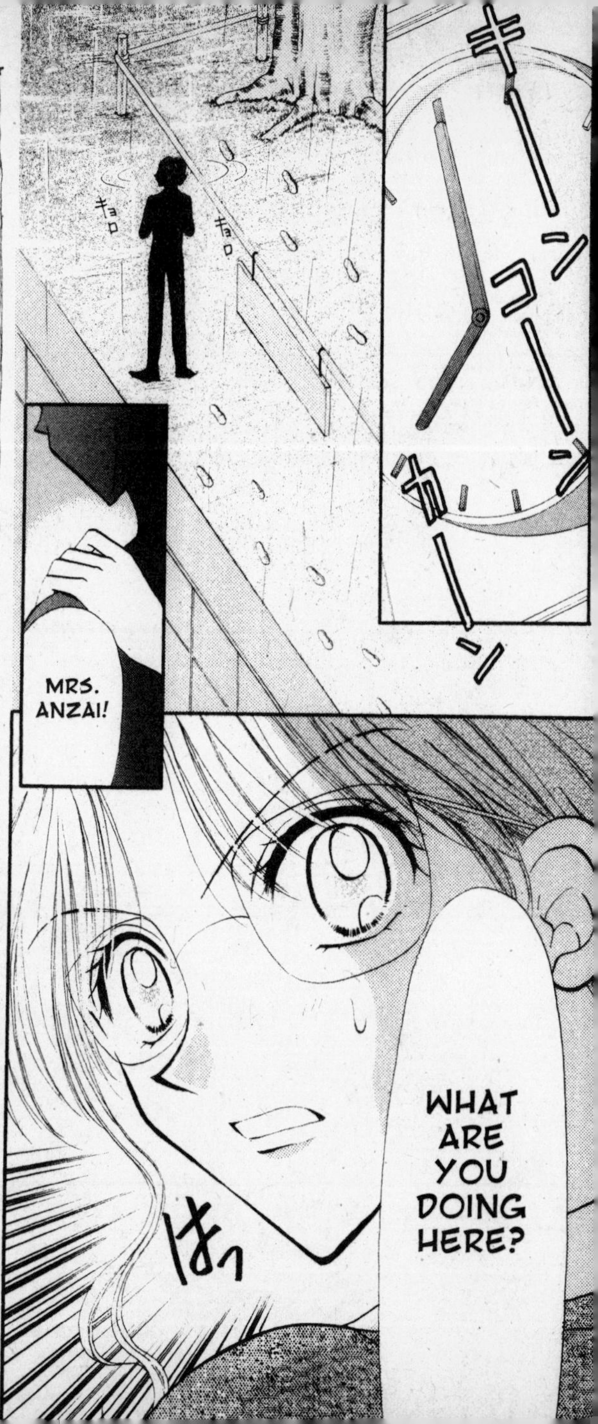
キョロ
キョロ
MRS. ANZAI!
WHAT ARE YOU DOING HERE?
はっ

2.

The Stars

When I was little, I loved looking at the starry sky. I even studied stars for my science project. I dreamed of becoming a curator who talks about stars and shows films at the planetarium. Unfortunately, I had no clue how to get a job like that. I also loved Greek mythology. Now that I'm grown, I feel differently about Zeus. After all, he's a womanizer!! I don't have a deep understanding of astrology, but I've been learning a lot by reading books about it. My staff and I often get a kick out of talking about signs and astrology during meetings.

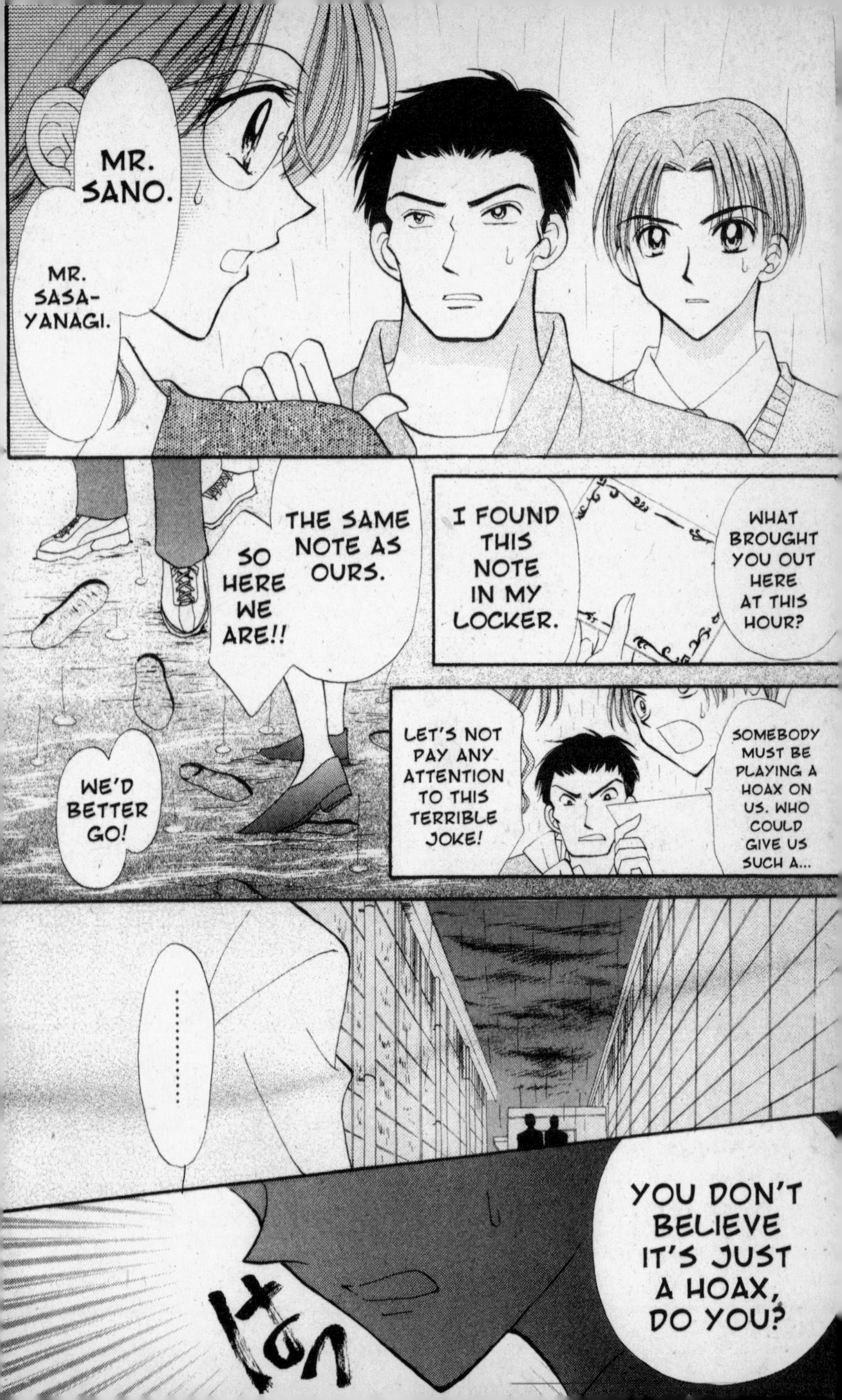
MR. SANO.
MR. SASA-YANAGI.
WHAT BROUGHT YOU OUT HERE AT THIS HOUR?
I FOUND THIS NOTE IN MY LOCKER.
SOMEBODY MUST BE PLAYING A HOAX ON US. WHO COULD GIVE US SUCH A...
LET'S NOT PAY ANY ATTENTION TO THIS TERRIBLE JOKE!
THE SAME NOTE AS OURS.
SO HERE WE ARE!!
WE'D BETTER GO!
......
YOU DON'T BELIEVE IT'S JUST A HOAX, DO YOU?

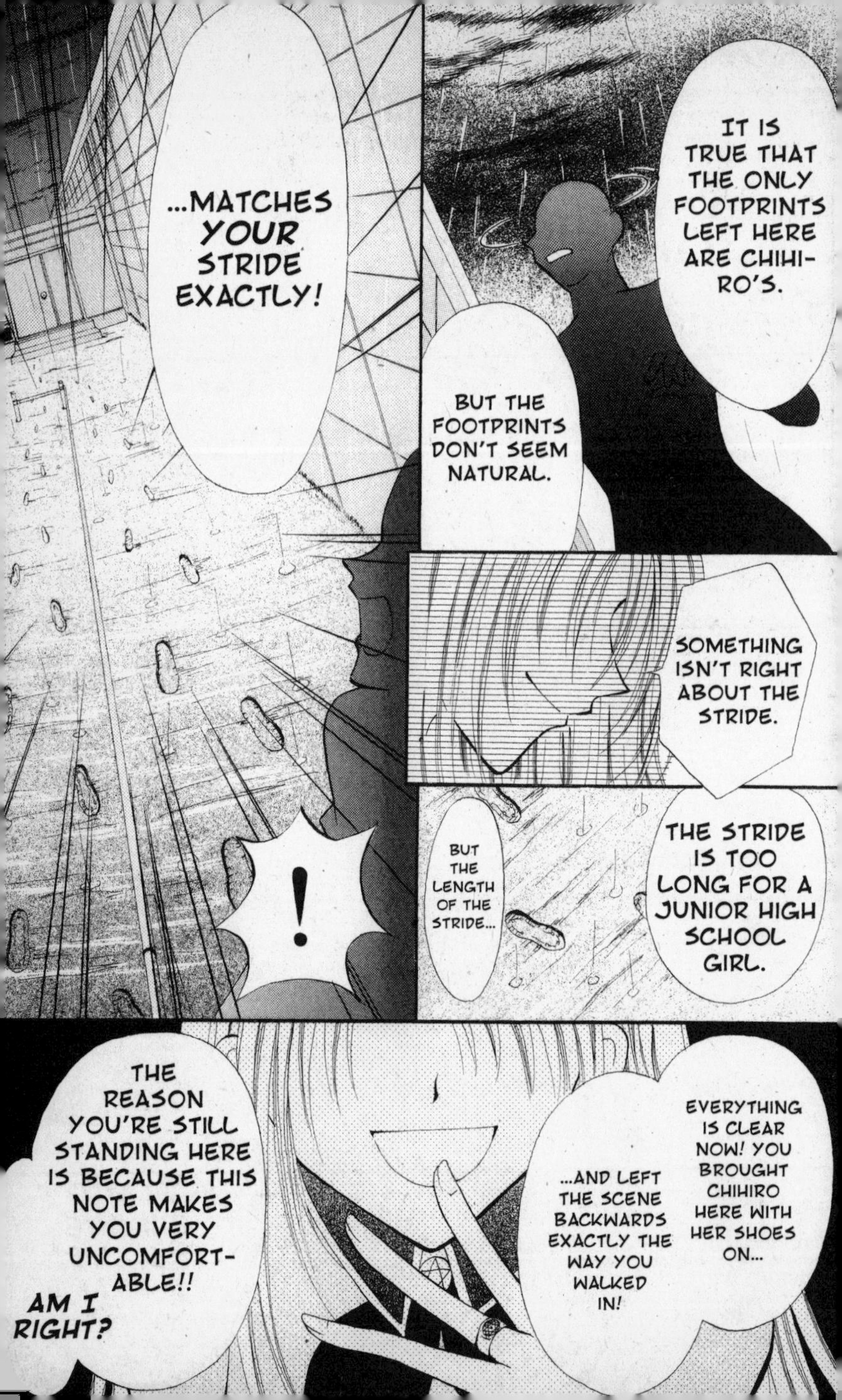

IT IS TRUE THAT THE ONLY FOOTPRINTS LEFT HERE ARE CHIHI-RO'S.
BUT THE FOOTPRINTS DON'T SEEM NATURAL.
SOMETHING ISN'T RIGHT ABOUT THE STRIDE.
THE STRIDE IS TOO LONG FOR A JUNIOR HIGH SCHOOL GIRL.
BUT THE LENGTH OF THE STRIDE...
...MATCHES YOUR STRIDE EXACTLY!
!
EVERYTHING IS CLEAR NOW! YOU BROUGHT CHIHIRO HERE WITH HER SHOES ON...
...AND LEFT THE SCENE BACKWARDS EXACTLY THE WAY YOU WALKED IN!
THE REASON YOU'RE STILL STANDING HERE IS BECAUSE THIS NOTE MAKES YOU VERY UNCOMFORT-ABLE!!
AM I RIGHT?

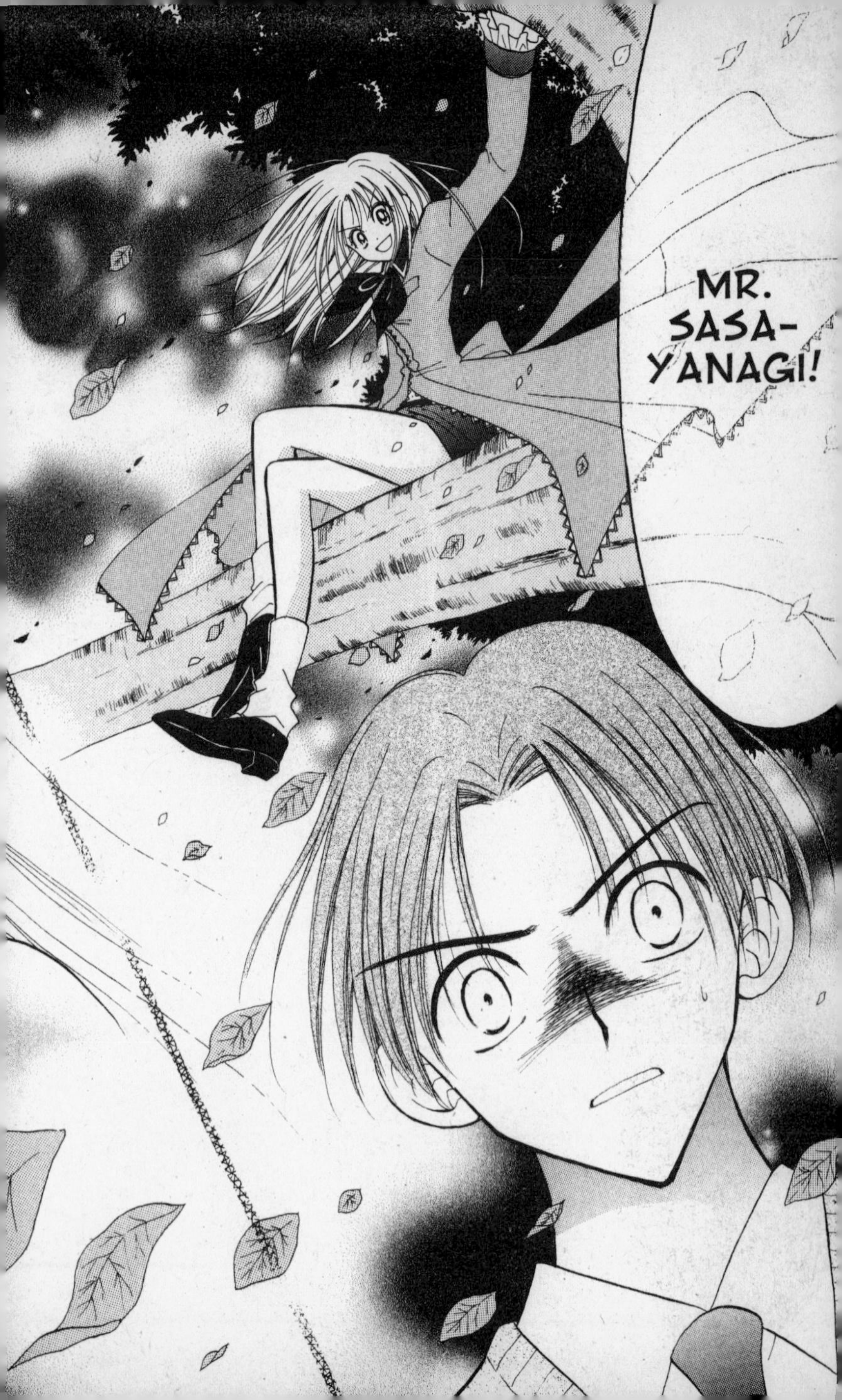
MR. SASA-YANAGI!

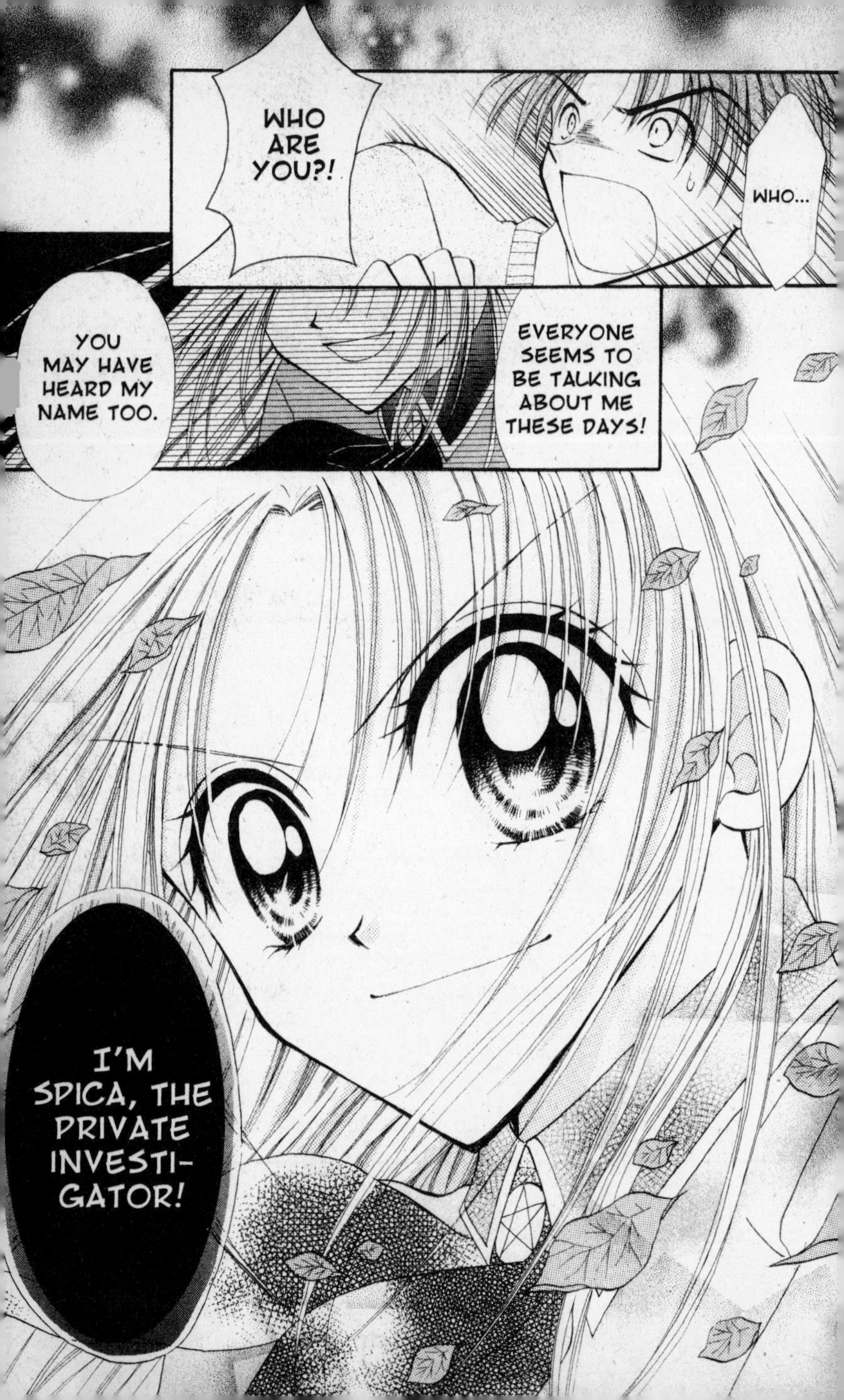
WHO...
WHO ARE YOU?!
EVERYONE SEEMS TO BE TALKING ABOUT ME THESE DAYS!
YOU MAY HAVE HEARD MY NAME TOO.
I'M SPICA, THE PRIVATE INVESTI-GATOR!

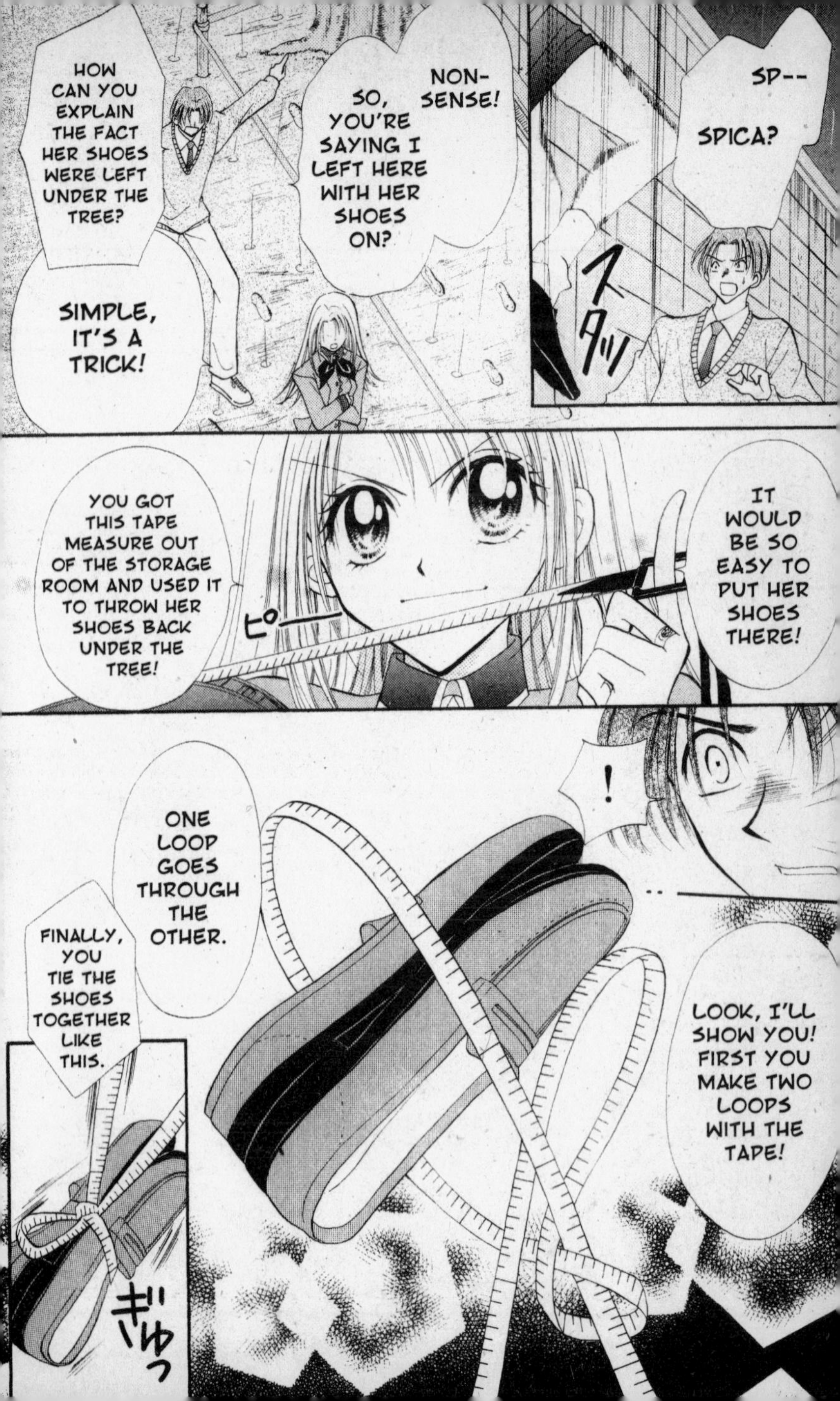
SP-- SPICA?
スタッ
NON-SENSE!
SO, YOU'RE SAYING I LEFT HERE WITH HER SHOES ON?
HOW CAN YOU EXPLAIN THE FACT HER SHOES WERE LEFT UNDER THE TREE?
SIMPLE, IT'S A TRICK!
IT WOULD BE SO EASY TO PUT HER SHOES THERE!
ピー
YOU GOT THIS TAPE MEASURE OUT OF THE STORAGE ROOM AND USED IT TO THROW HER SHOES BACK UNDER THE TREE!
!
..—
LOOK, I'LL SHOW YOU! FIRST YOU MAKE TWO LOOPS WITH THE TAPE!
ONE LOOP GOES THROUGH THE OTHER.
FINALLY, YOU TIE THE SHOES TOGETHER LIKE THIS.
ぎゅっ

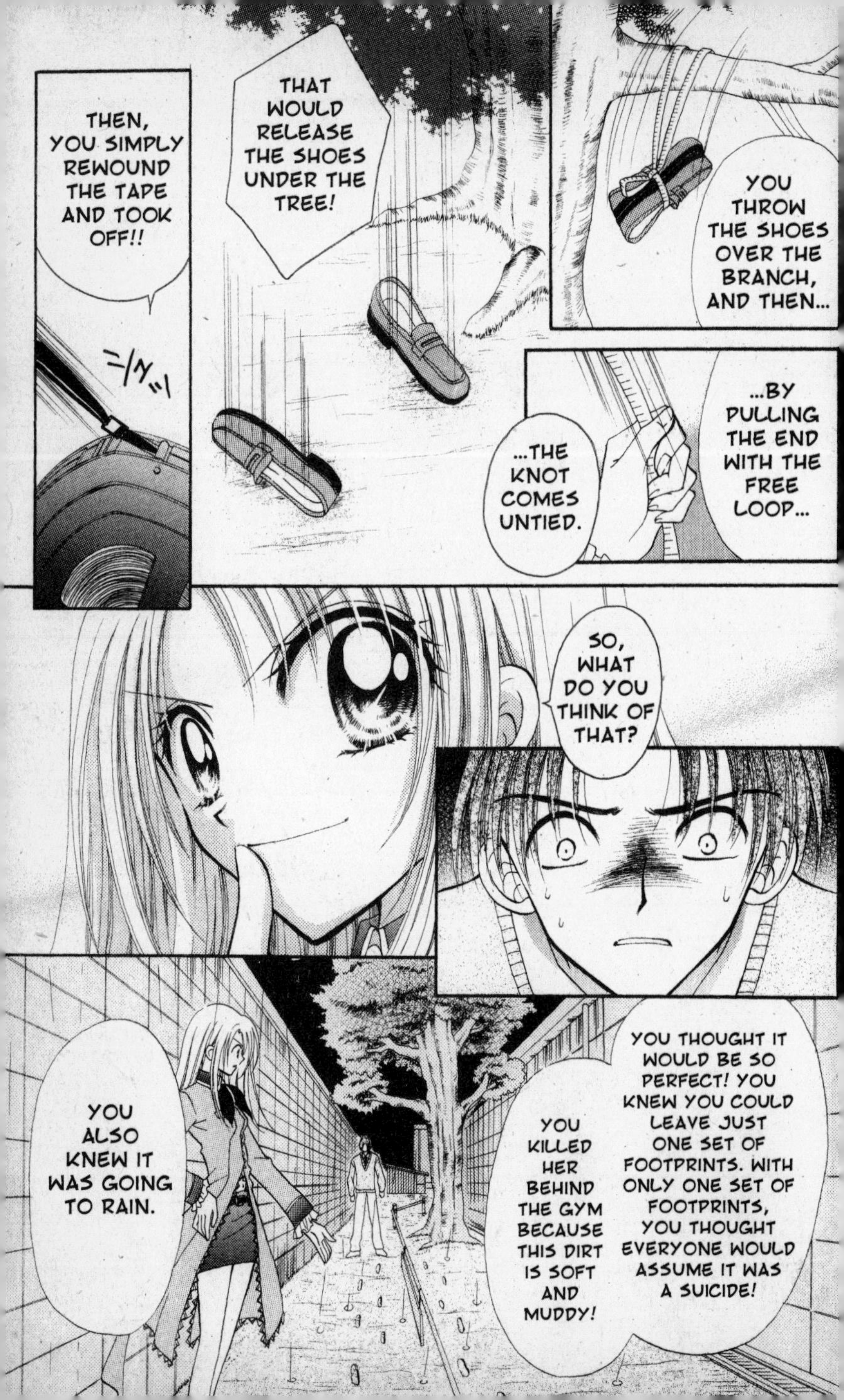
YOU THROW THE SHOES OVER THE BRANCH, AND THEN...
...BY PULLING THE END WITH THE FREE LOOP...
...THE KNOT COMES UNTIED.
THAT WOULD RELEASE THE SHOES UNDER THE TREE!
THEN, YOU SIMPLY REWOUND THE TAPE AND TOOK OFF!!
SO, WHAT DO YOU THINK OF THAT?
YOU THOUGHT IT WOULD BE SO PERFECT! YOU KNEW YOU COULD LEAVE JUST ONE SET OF FOOTPRINTS. WITH ONLY ONE SET OF FOOTPRINTS, YOU THOUGHT EVERYONE WOULD ASSUME IT WAS A SUICIDE!
YOU KILLED HER BEHIND THE GYM BECAUSE THIS DIRT IS SOFT AND MUDDY!
YOU ALSO KNEW IT WAS GOING TO RAIN.

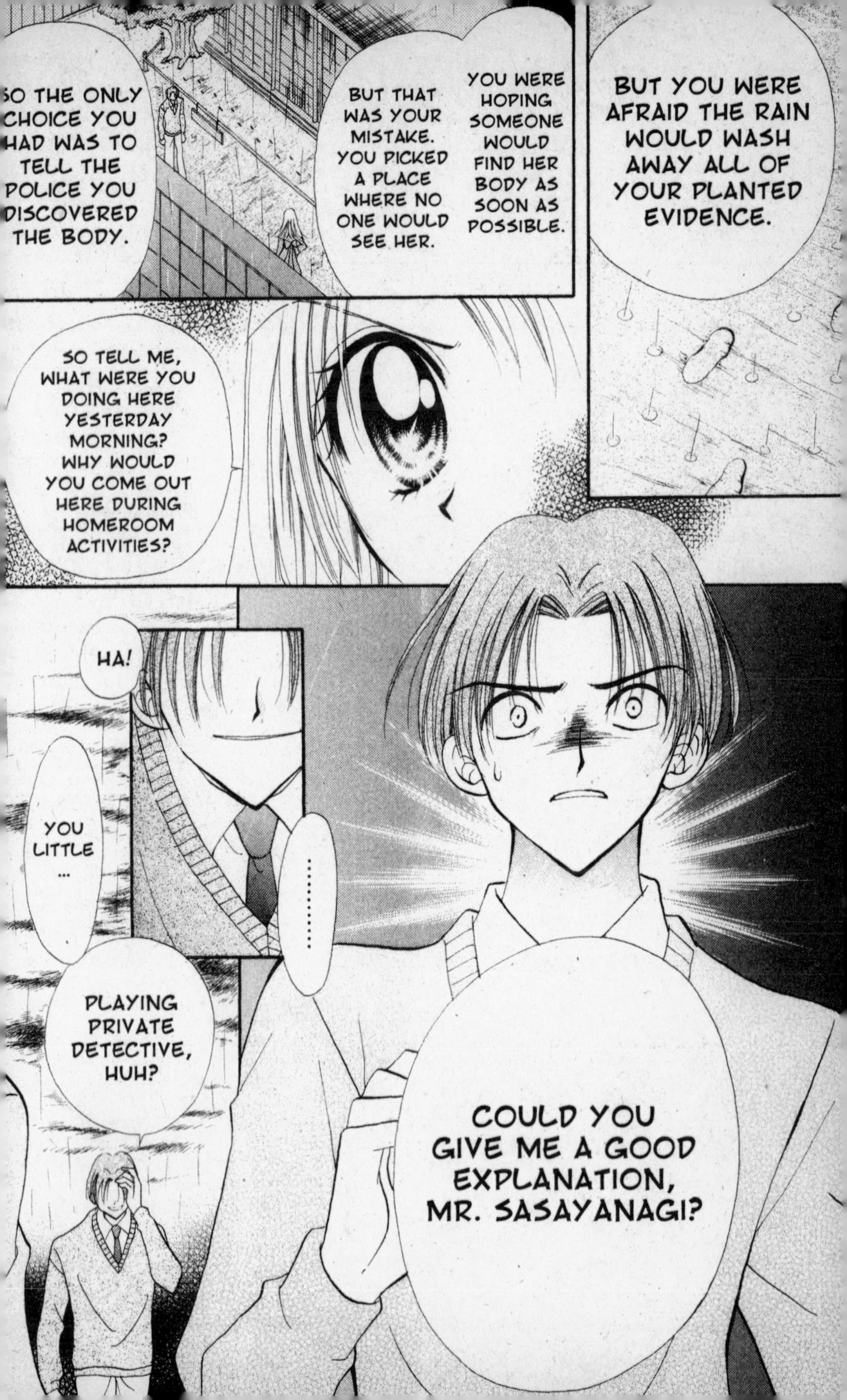
BUT YOU WERE AFRAID THE RAIN WOULD WASH AWAY ALL OF YOUR PLANTED EVIDENCE.
YOU WERE HOPING SOMEONE WOULD FIND HER BODY AS SOON AS POSSIBLE.
BUT THAT WAS YOUR MISTAKE. YOU PICKED A PLACE WHERE NO ONE WOULD SEE HER.
SO THE ONLY CHOICE YOU HAD WAS TO TELL THE POLICE YOU DISCOVERED THE BODY.
SO TELL ME, WHAT WERE YOU DOING HERE YESTERDAY MORNING? WHY WOULD YOU COME OUT HERE DURING HOMEROOM ACTIVITIES?
COULD YOU GIVE ME A GOOD EXPLANATION, MR. SASAYANAGI?
......
HA!
YOU LITTLE ...
PLAYING PRIVATE DETECTIVE, HUH?

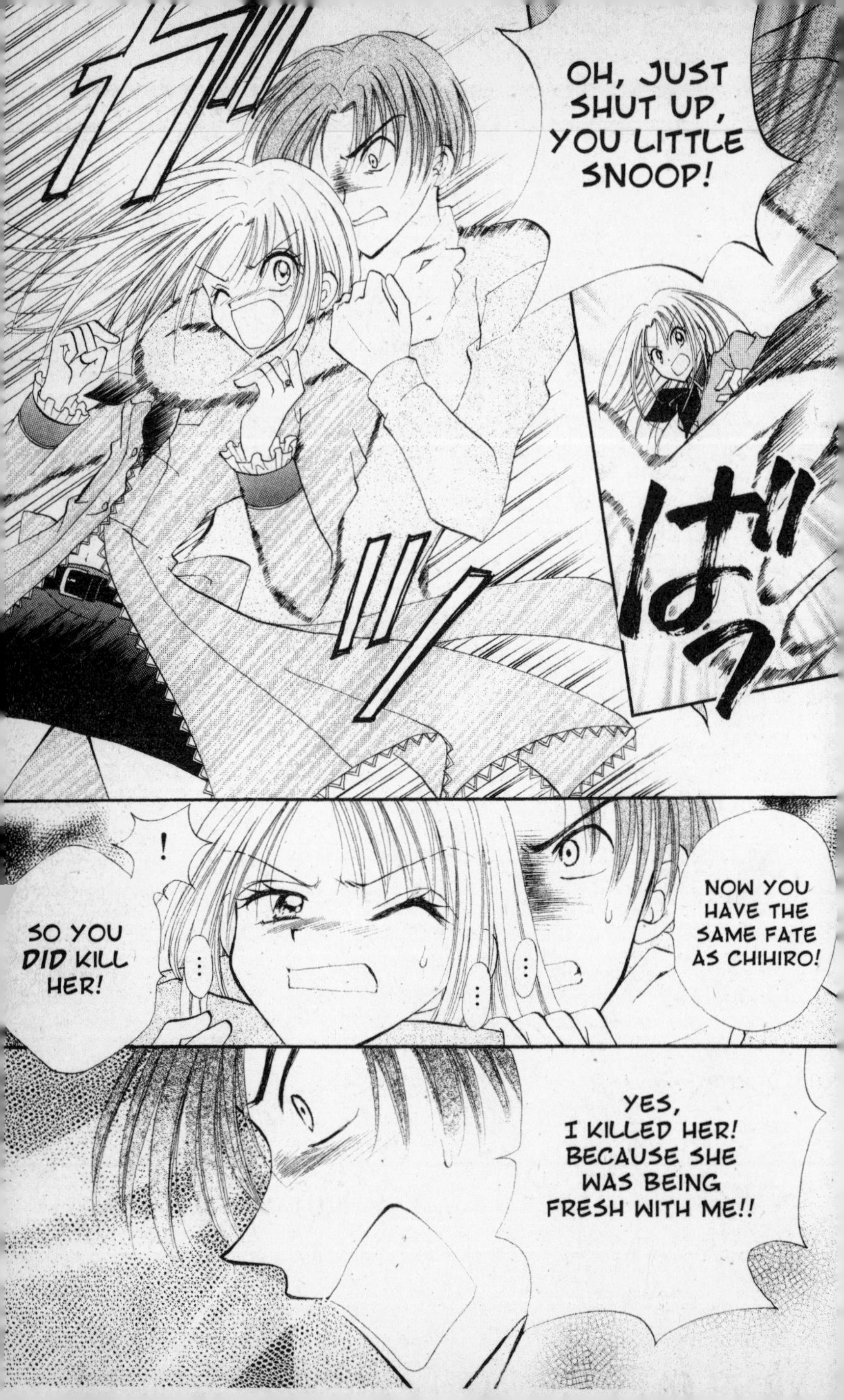
OH, JUST SHUT UP, YOU LITTLE SNOOP!
はっ
NOW YOU HAVE THE SAME FATE AS CHIHIRO!
...
...
!
SO YOU DID KILL HER!
YES, I KILLED HER! BECAUSE SHE WAS BEING FRESH WITH ME!!

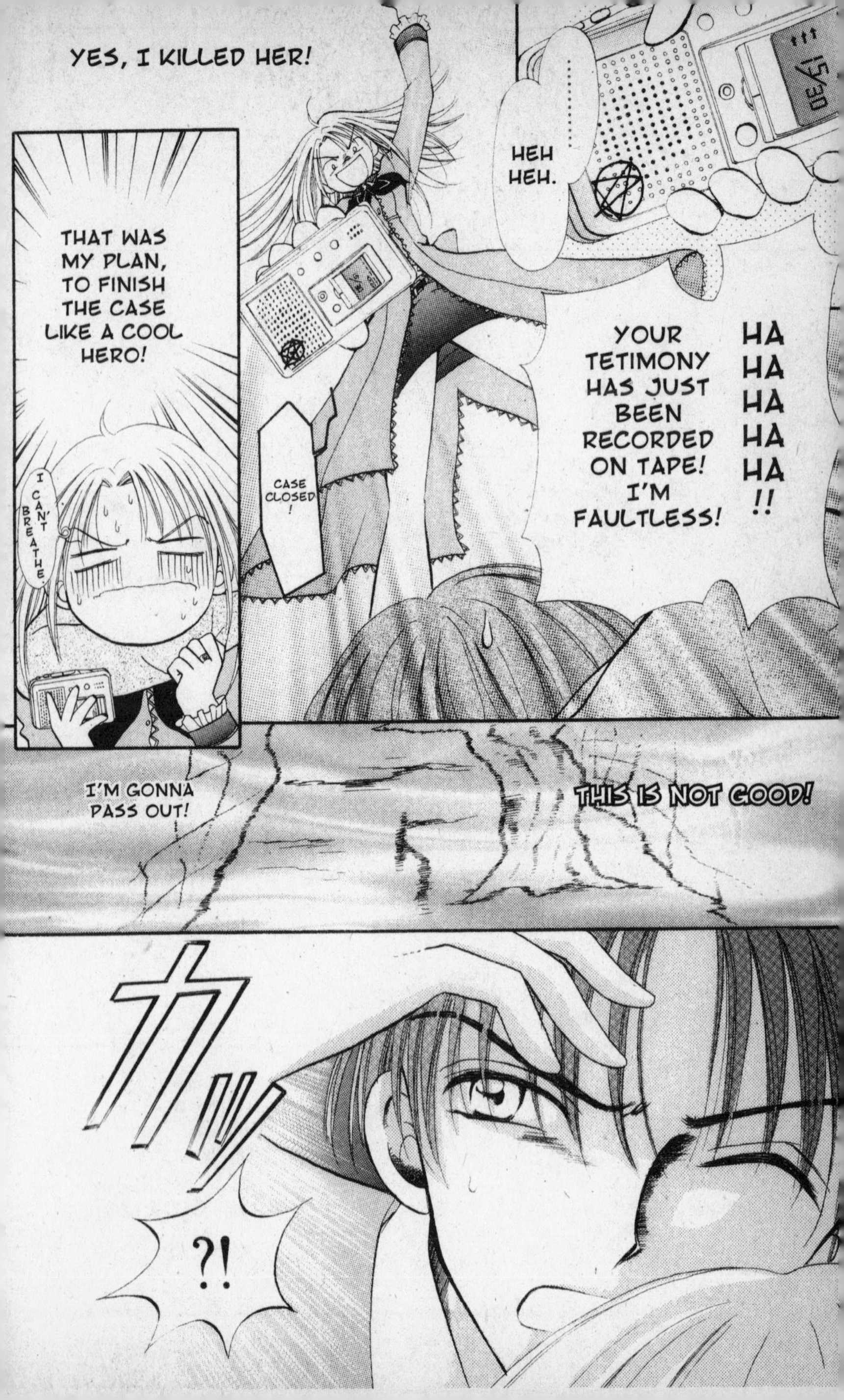
HEH HEH.
YES, I KILLED HER!
HA HA HA HA HA!!
YOUR TETIMONY HAS JUST BEEN RECORDED ON TAPE! I'M FAULTLESS!
CASE CLOSED!
THAT WAS MY PLAN, TO FINISH THE CASE LIKE A COOL HERO!
I CAN'T BREATHE.
THIS IS NOT GOOD!
I'M GONNA PASS OUT!
カッ
?!

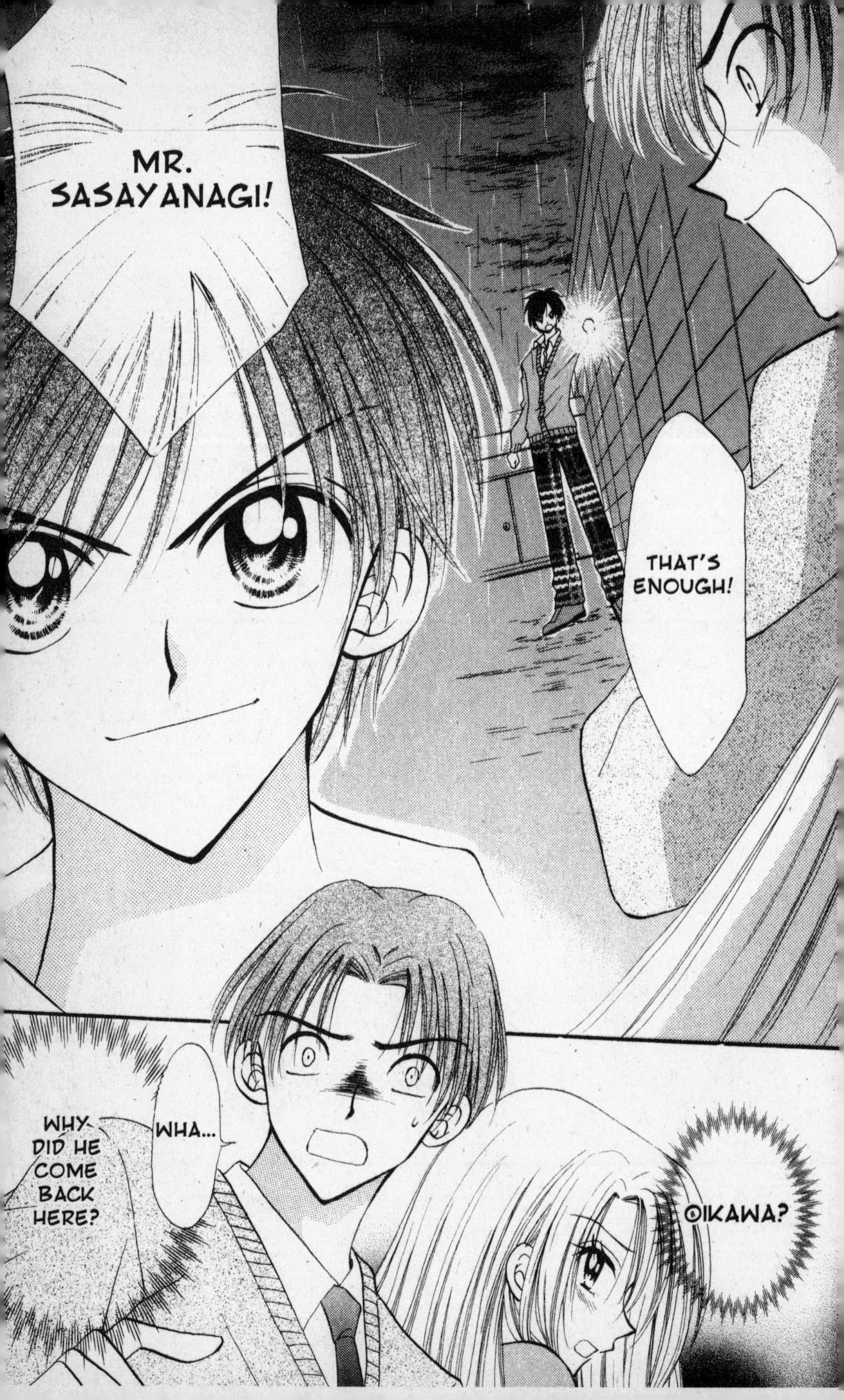
THAT'S ENOUGH!
MR. SASAYANAGI!
OIKAWA?
WHA...
WHY DID HE COME BACK HERE?

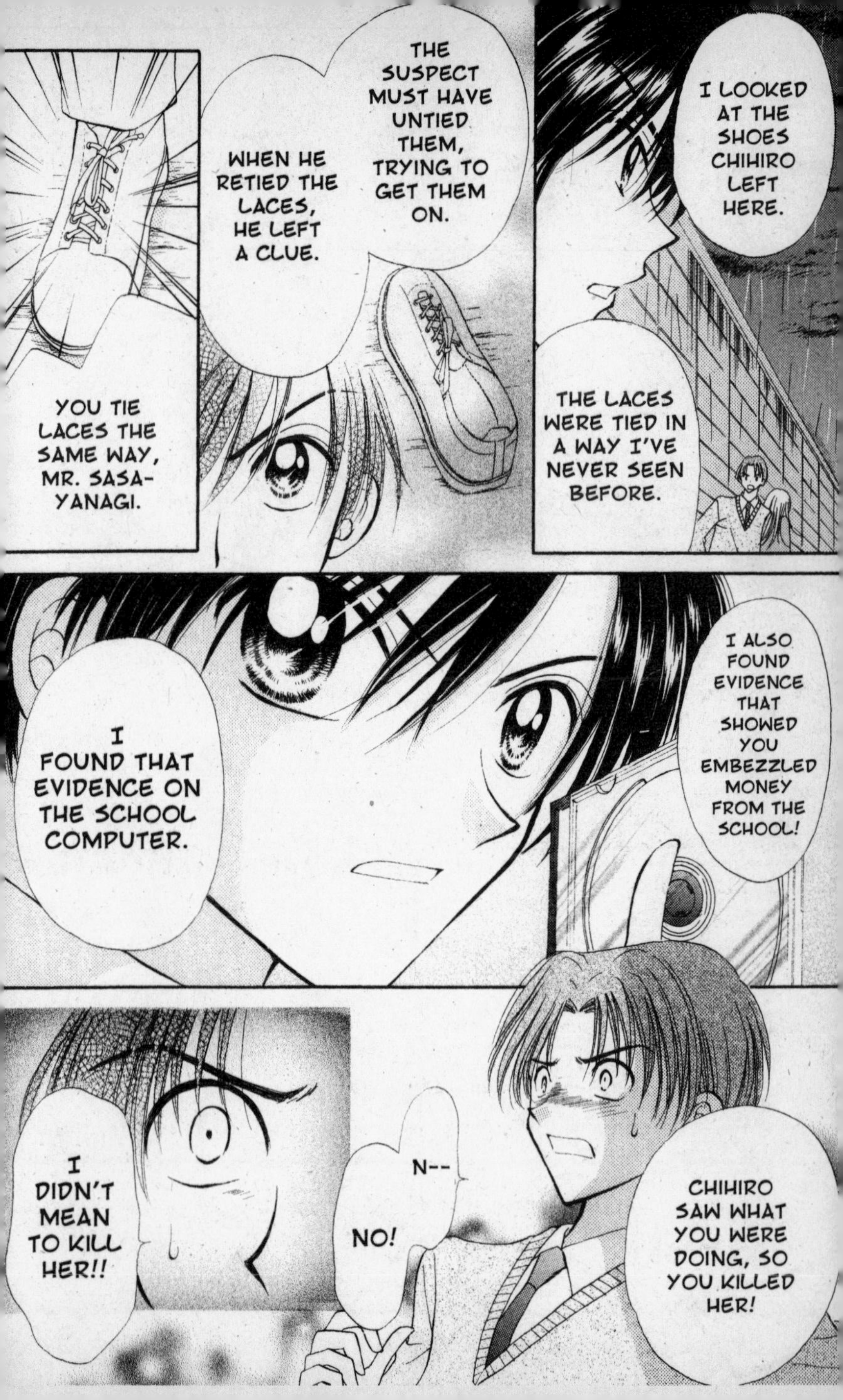
I LOOKED AT THE SHOES CHIHIRO LEFT HERE.
THE LACES WERE TIED IN A WAY I'VE NEVER SEEN BEFORE.
THE SUSPECT MUST HAVE UNTIED THEM, TRYING TO GET THEM ON.
WHEN HE RETIED THE LACES, HE LEFT A CLUE.
YOU TIE LACES THE SAME WAY, MR. SASA-YANAGI.
I ALSO FOUND EVIDENCE THAT SHOWED YOU EMBEZZLED MONEY FROM THE SCHOOL!
I FOUND THAT EVIDENCE ON THE SCHOOL COMPUTER.
CHIHIRO SAW WHAT YOU WERE DOING, SO YOU KILLED HER!
N--
NO!
I DIDN'T MEAN TO KILL HER!!

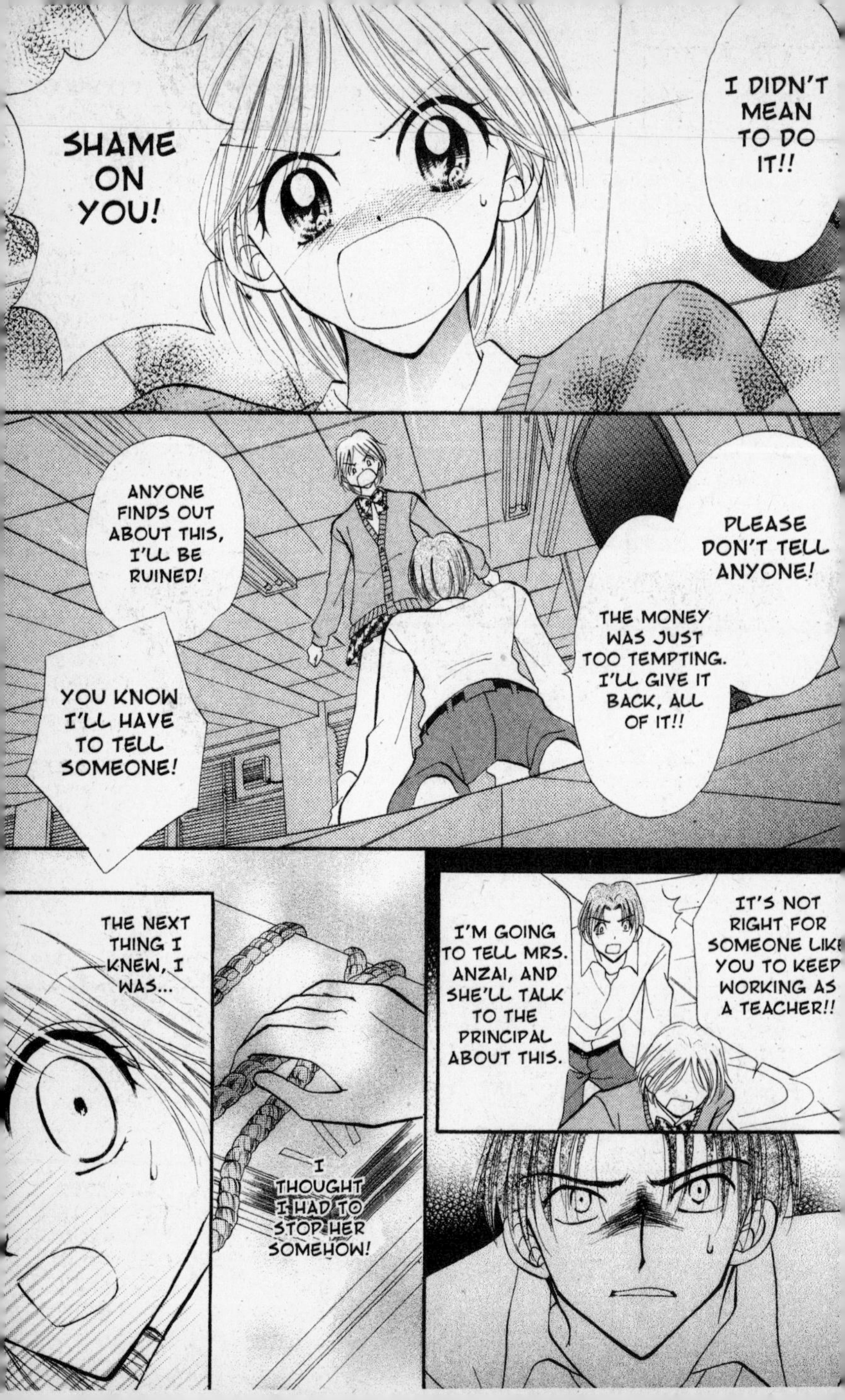
I DIDN'T MEAN TO DO IT!!
SHAME ON YOU!
PLEASE DON'T TELL ANYONE!
THE MONEY WAS JUST TOO TEMPTING. I'LL GIVE IT BACK, ALL OF IT!!
ANYONE FINDS OUT ABOUT THIS, I'LL BE RUINED!
YOU KNOW I'LL HAVE TO TELL SOMEONE!
IT'S NOT RIGHT FOR SOMEONE LIKE YOU TO KEEP WORKING AS A TEACHER!!
I'M GOING TO TELL MRS. ANZAI, AND SHE'LL TALK TO THE PRINCIPAL ABOUT THIS.
I THOUGHT I HAD TO STOP HER SOMEHOW!
THE NEXT THING I KNEW, I WAS...

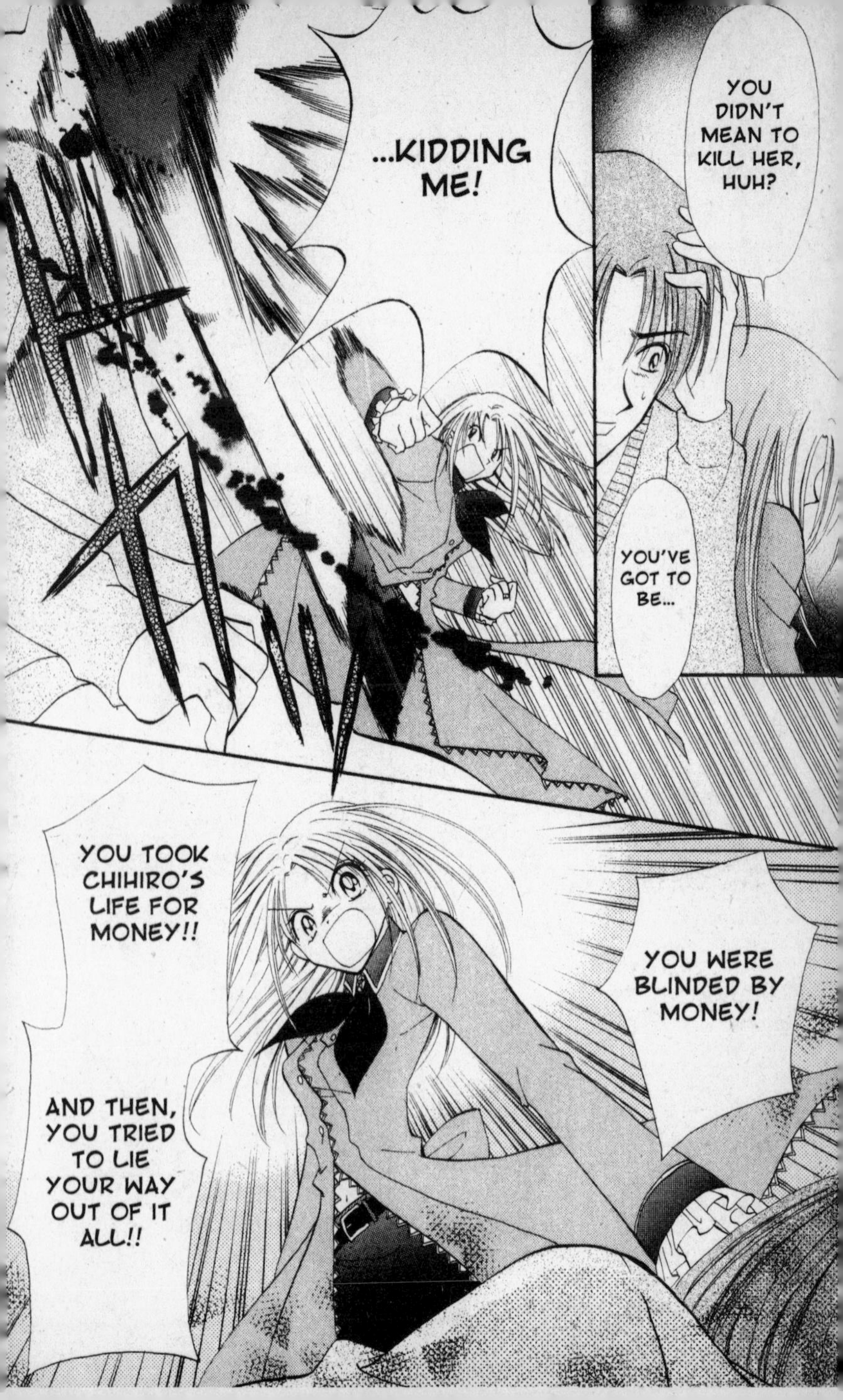
YOU DIDN'T MEAN TO KILL HER, HUH?
YOU'VE GOT TO BE...
...KIDDING ME!
YOU WERE BLINDED BY MONEY!
YOU TOOK CHIHIRO'S LIFE FOR MONEY!!
AND THEN, YOU TRIED TO LIE YOUR WAY OUT OF IT ALL!!

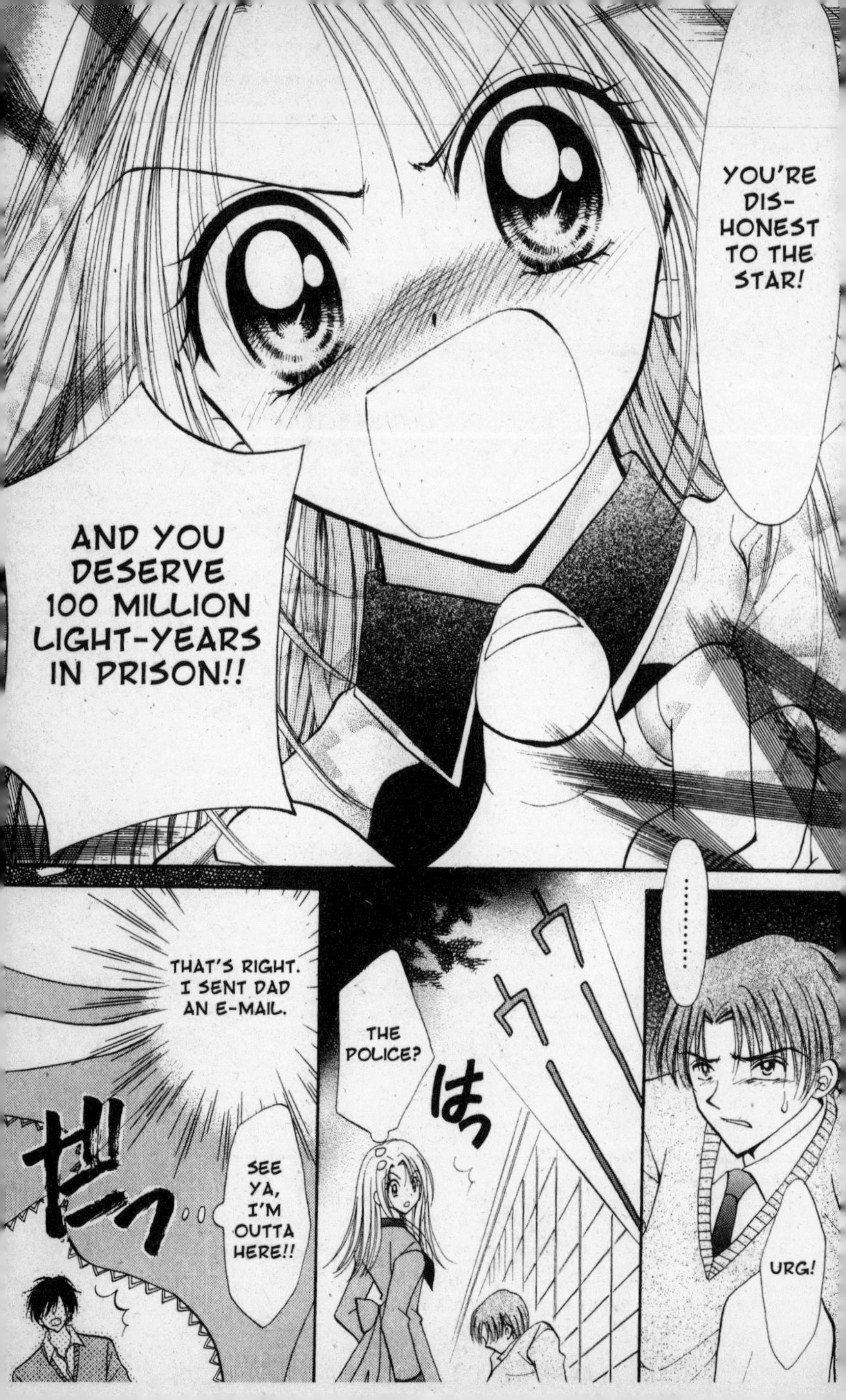
YOU'RE DIS-HONEST TO THE STAR!
AND YOU DESERVE 100 MILLION LIGHT-YEARS IN PRISON!!
......
URG!
THE POLICE?
はっ
THAT'S RIGHT. I SENT DAD AN E-MAIL.
SEE YA, I'M OUTTA HERE!!

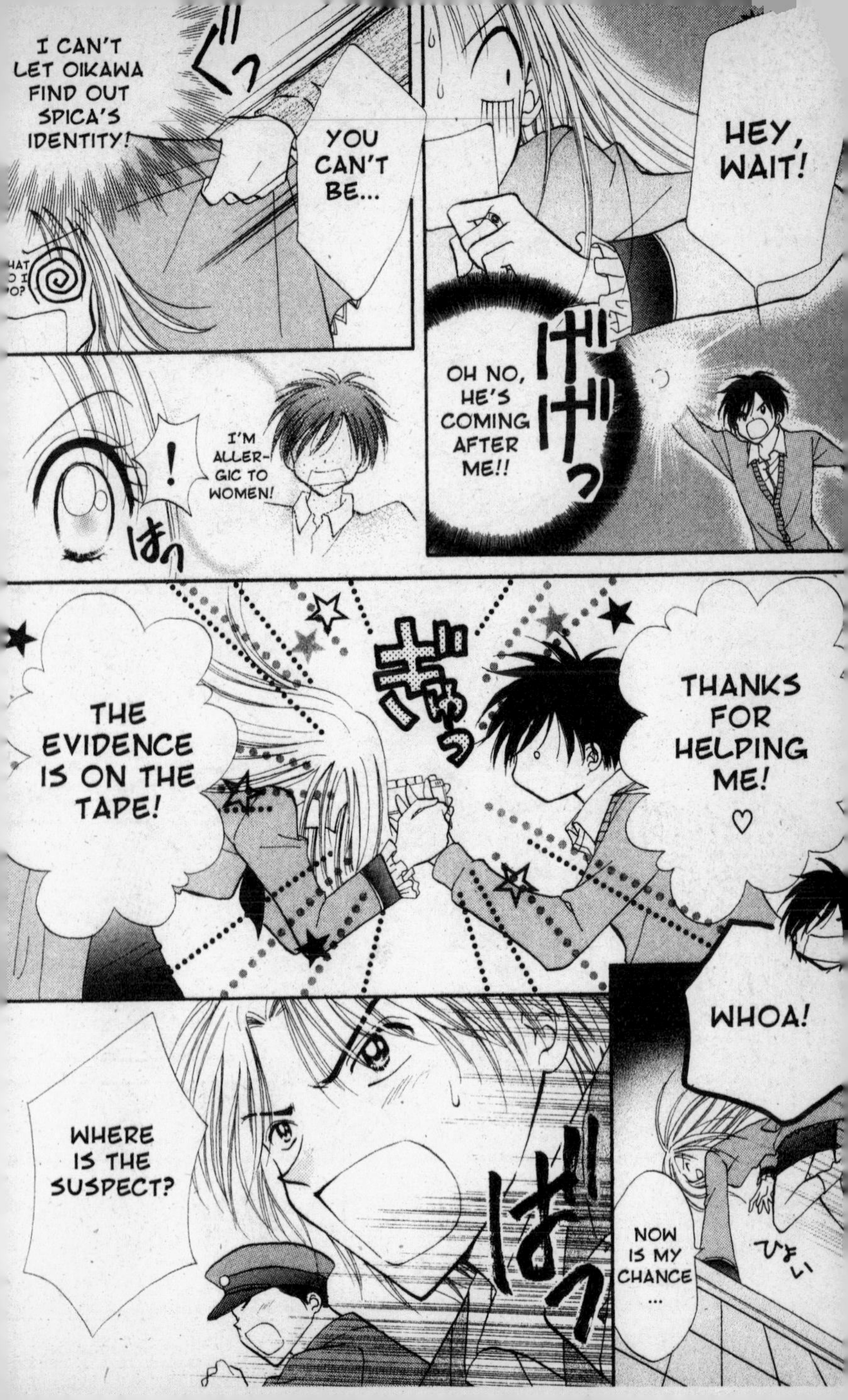
HEY, WAIT!
げげっ
OH NO, HE'S COMING AFTER ME!!
ぐっ
YOU CAN'T BE...
I CAN'T LET OIKAWA FIND OUT SPICA'S IDENTITY!
I'M ALLERGIC TO WOMEN!
!
はっ
THANKS FOR HELPING ME! ♡
ぎゅっ
THE EVIDENCE IS ON THE TAPE!
WHOA!
ぴょい
NOW IS MY CHANCE ...
ばっ
WHERE IS THE SUSPECT?

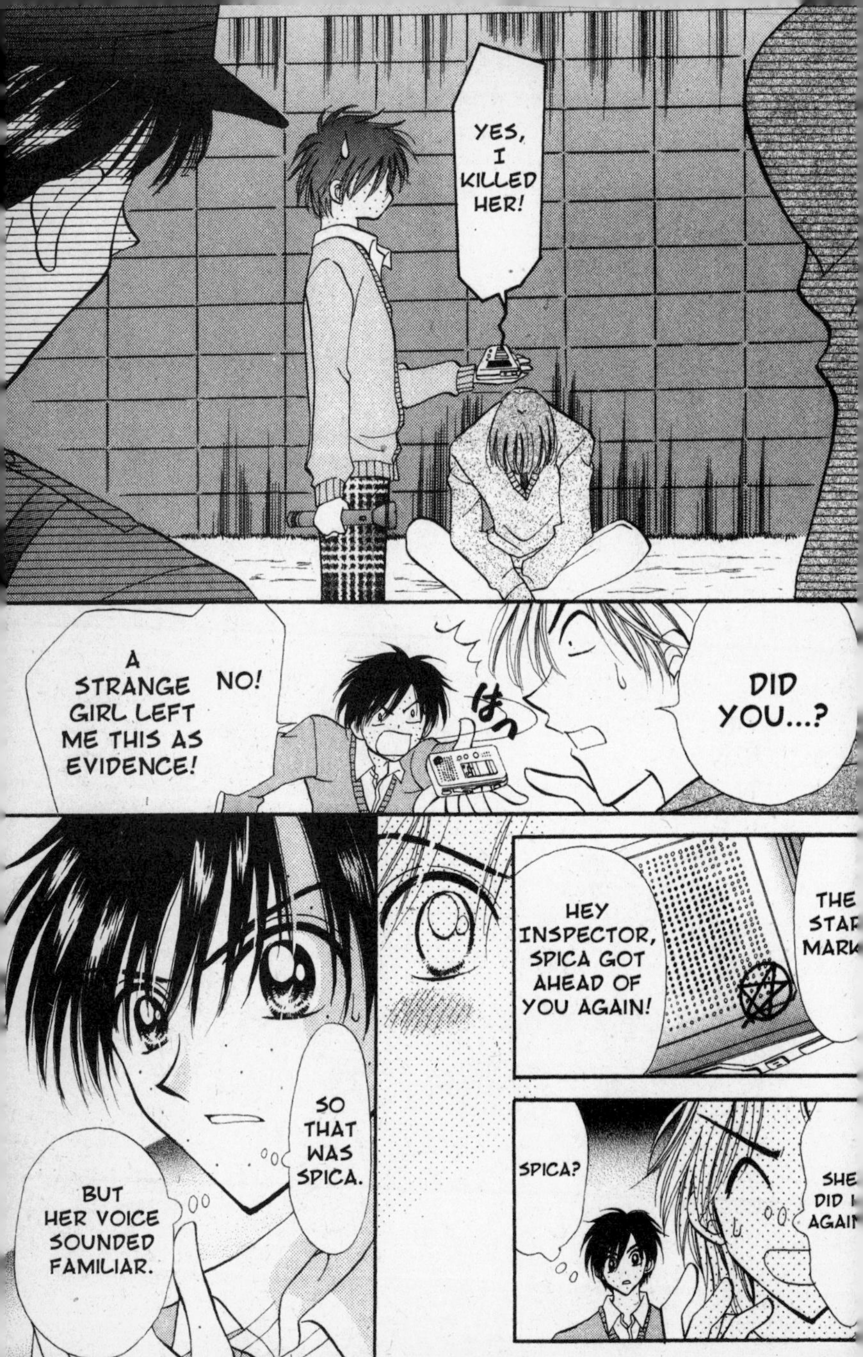
YES, I KILLED HER!
DID YOU...?
はっ
NO!
A STRANGE GIRL LEFT ME THIS AS EVIDENCE!
THE STAR MARK
HEY INSPECTOR, SPICA GOT AHEAD OF YOU AGAIN!
SHE DID IT AGAIN
SPICA?
SO THAT WAS SPICA.
BUT HER VOICE SOUNDED FAMILIAR.

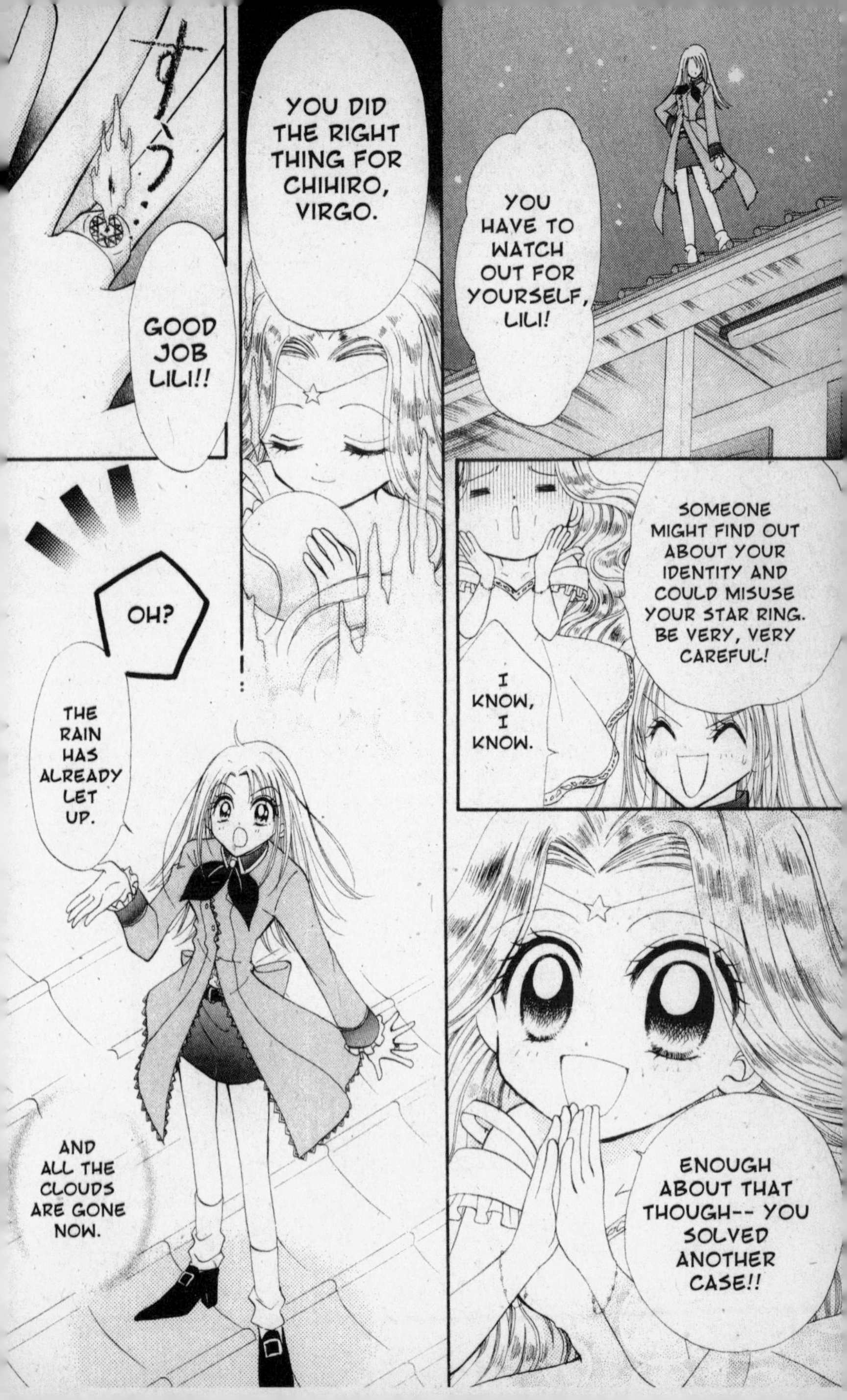
YOU HAVE TO WATCH OUT FOR YOURSELF, LILI!
SOMEONE MIGHT FIND OUT ABOUT YOUR IDENTITY AND COULD MISUSE YOUR STAR RING. BE VERY, VERY CAREFUL!
I KNOW, I KNOW.
ENOUGH ABOUT THAT THOUGH-- YOU SOLVED ANOTHER CASE!!
YOU DID THE RIGHT THING FOR CHIHIRO, VIRGO.
すぅ…
GOOD JOB LILI!!
OH?
THE RAIN HAS ALREADY LET UP.
AND ALL THE CLOUDS ARE GONE NOW.

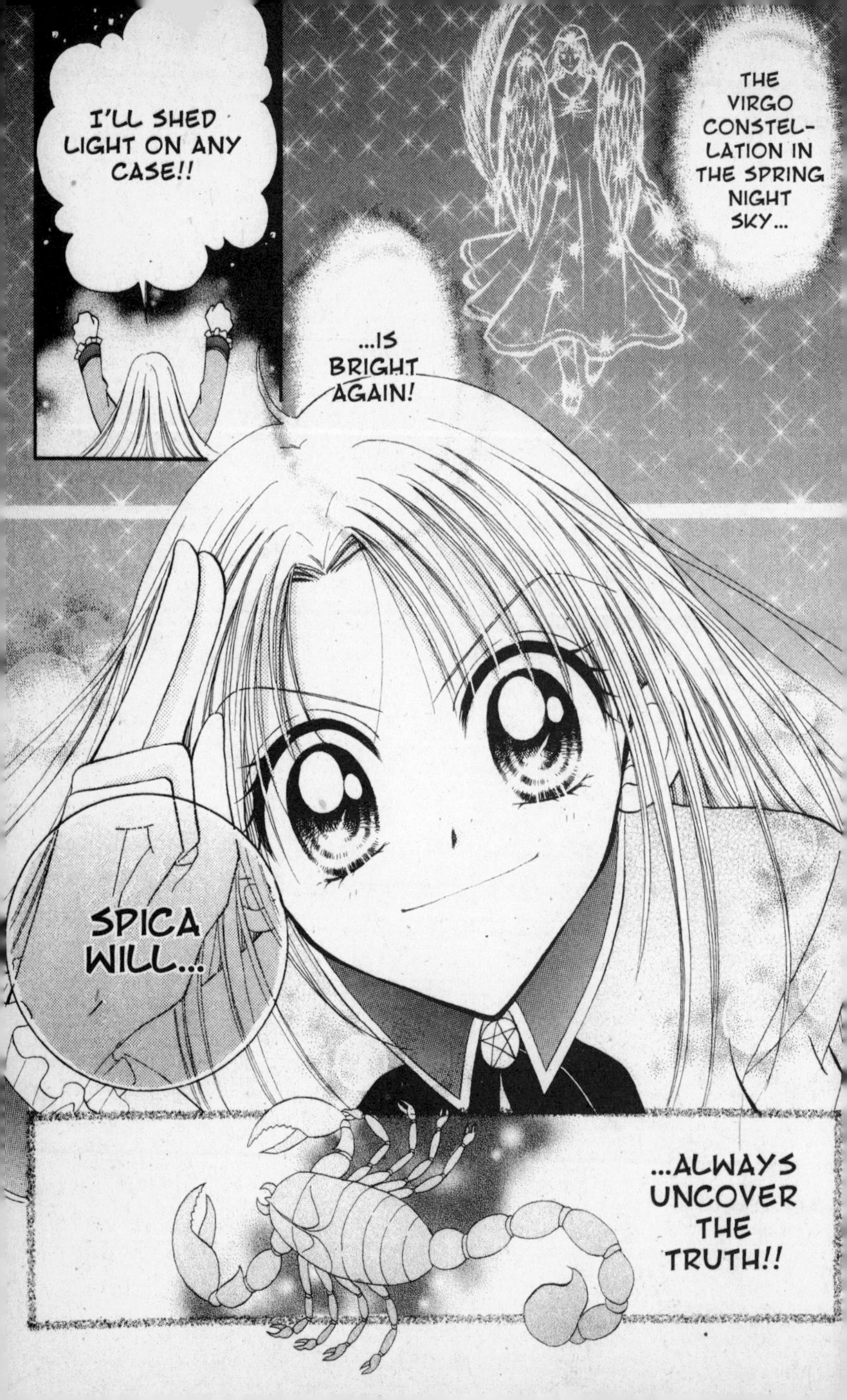
THE VIRGO CONSTEL-LATION IN THE SPRING NIGHT SKY...
...IS BRIGHT AGAIN!
I'LL SHED LIGHT ON ANY CASE!!
SPICA WILL...
...ALWAYS UNCOVER THE TRUTH!!

ばん
4コマ版

Zodiac P.J.

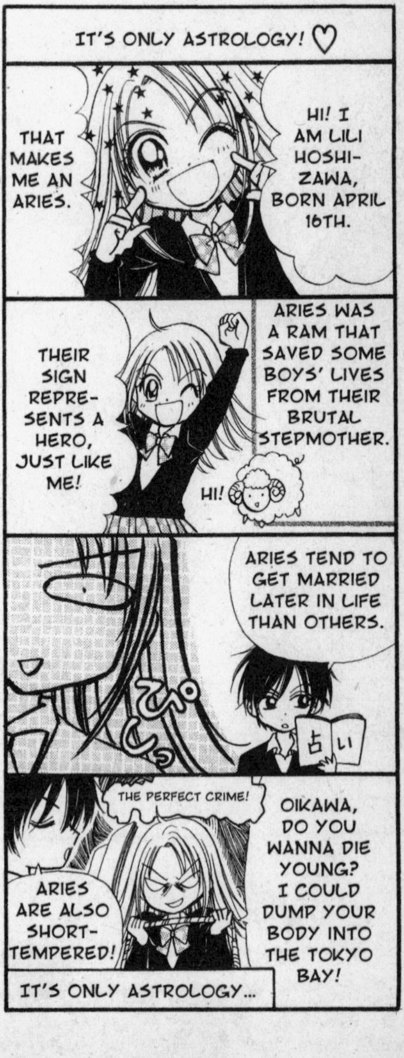
IT'S ONLY ASTROLOGY! ♡
HI! I AM LILI HOSHIZAWA, BORN APRIL 16TH.
THAT MAKES ME AN ARIES.
ARIES WAS A RAM THAT SAVED SOME BOYS' LIVES FROM THEIR BRUTAL STEPMOTHER.
THEIR SIGN REPRESENTS A HERO, JUST LIKE ME!
HI!
ARIES TEND TO GET MARRIED LATER IN LIFE THAN OTHERS.
ぴしっ
占い
OIKAWA, DO YOU WANNA DIE YOUNG? I COULD DUMP YOUR BODY INTO THE TOKYO BAY!
THE PERFECT CRIME!
ARIES ARE ALSO SHORT-TEMPERED!
IT'S ONLY ASTROLOGY...

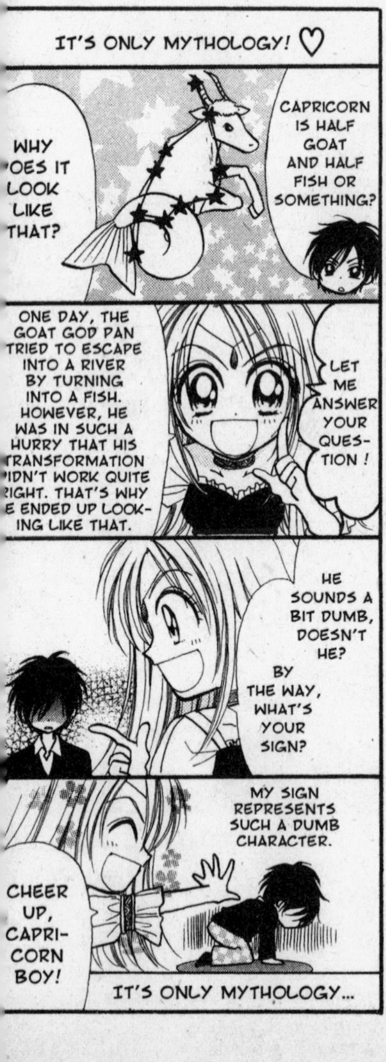
IT'S ONLY MYTHOLOGY! ♡
CAPRICORN IS HALF GOAT AND HALF FISH OR SOMETHING?
WHY DOES IT LOOK LIKE THAT?
LET ME ANSWER YOUR QUESTION!
ONE DAY, THE GOAT GOD PAN TRIED TO ESCAPE INTO A RIVER BY TURNING INTO A FISH. HOWEVER, HE WAS IN SUCH A HURRY THAT HIS TRANSFORMATION DIDN'T WORK QUITE RIGHT. THAT'S WHY HE ENDED UP LOOKING LIKE THAT.
HE SOUNDS A BIT DUMB, DOESN'T HE?
BY THE WAY, WHAT'S YOUR SIGN?
MY SIGN REPRESENTS SUCH A DUMB CHARACTER.
CHEER UP, CAPRICORN BOY!
IT'S ONLY MYTHOLOGY...

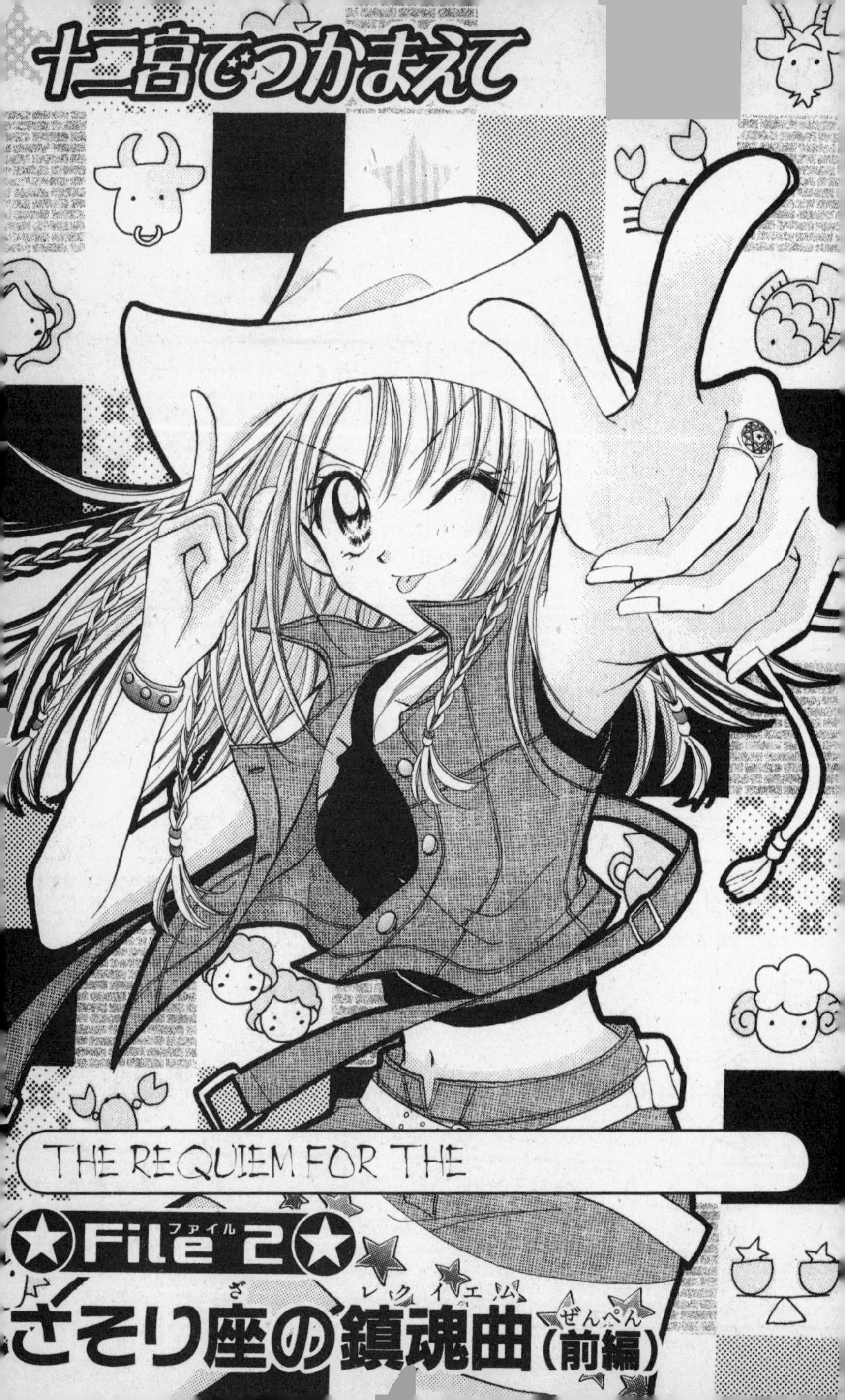
十二宮でつかまえて
THE REQUIEM FOR THE
★File 2★
さそり座の鎮魂曲（前編）

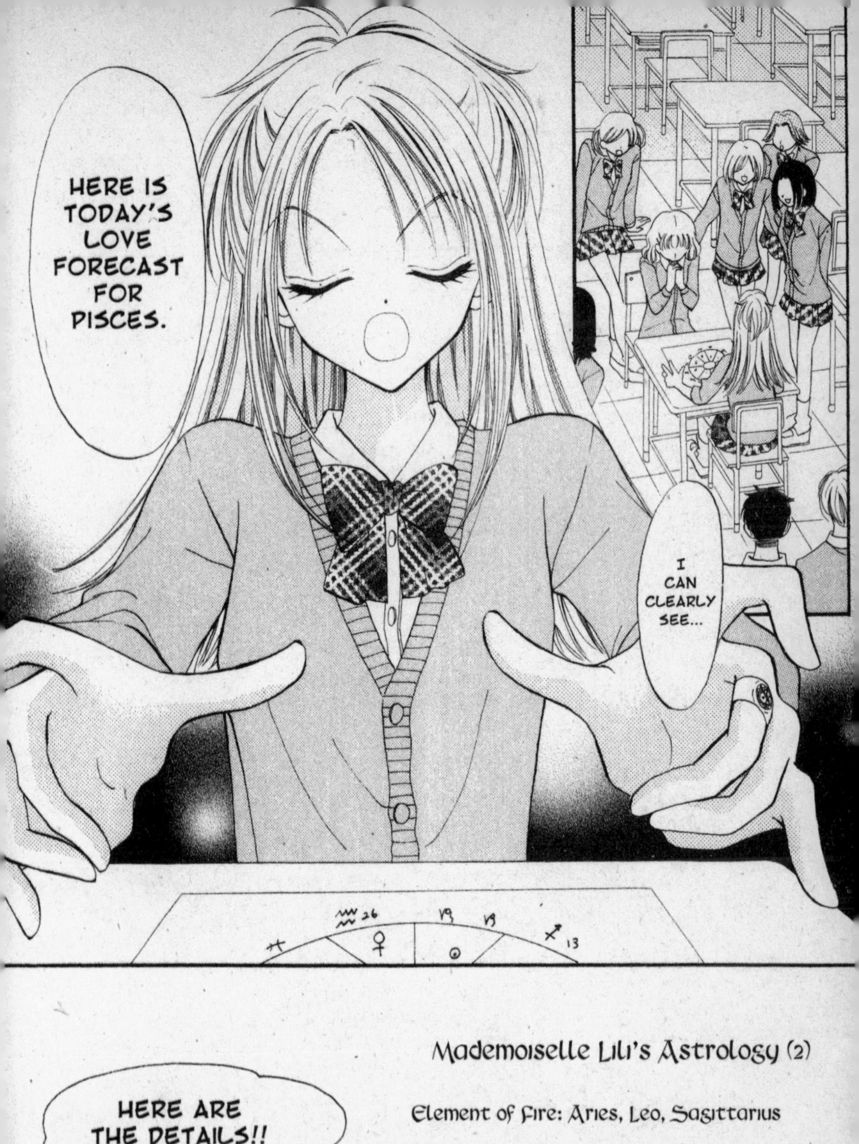
HERE IS TODAY'S LOVE FORECAST FOR PISCES.
I CAN CLEARLY SEE...

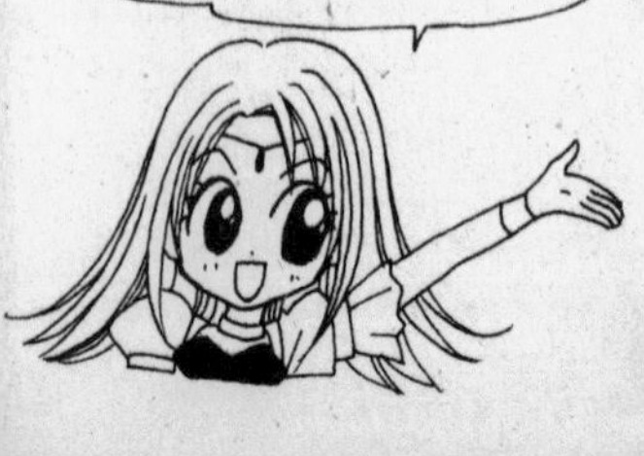
HERE ARE THE DETAILS!!

Mademoiselle Lili's Astrology (2)

Element of Fire: Aries, Leo, Sagittarius

Element of Earth: Capricorn, Virgo, Taurus

Element of Air: Aquarius, Gemini, Libra

Element of Water: Scorpio, Pisces, Cancer

Those who are not
compatible are
Fire signs with Water signs
Earth signs with Air signs

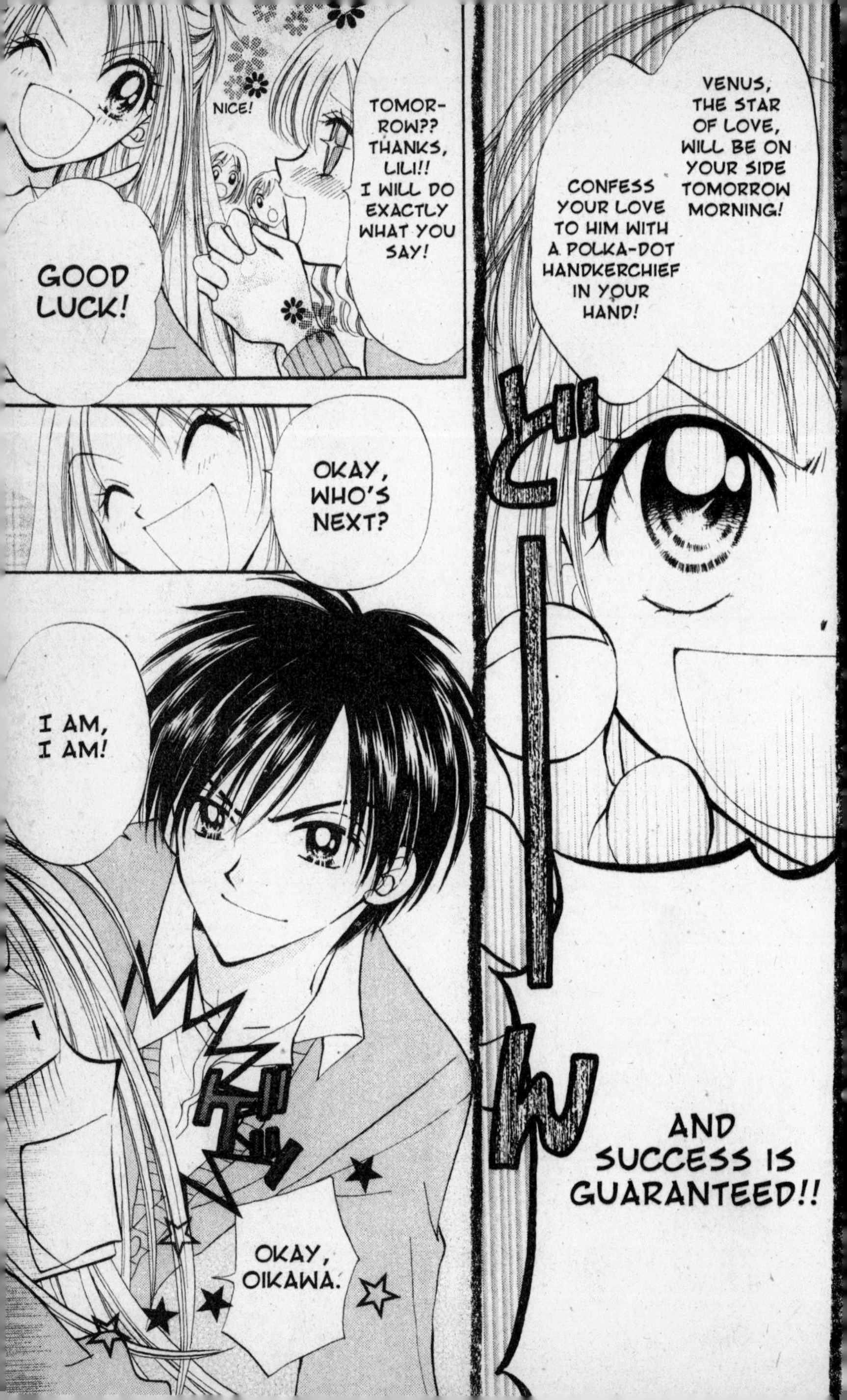
VENUS, THE STAR OF LOVE, WILL BE ON YOUR SIDE TOMORROW MORNING!
CONFESS YOUR LOVE TO HIM WITH A POLKA-DOT HANDKERCHIEF IN YOUR HAND!
AND SUCCESS IS GUARANTEED!!
TOMOR-ROW?? THANKS, LILI!! I WILL DO EXACTLY WHAT YOU SAY!
NICE!
GOOD LUCK!
OKAY, WHO'S NEXT?
I AM, I AM!
OKAY, OIKAWA.

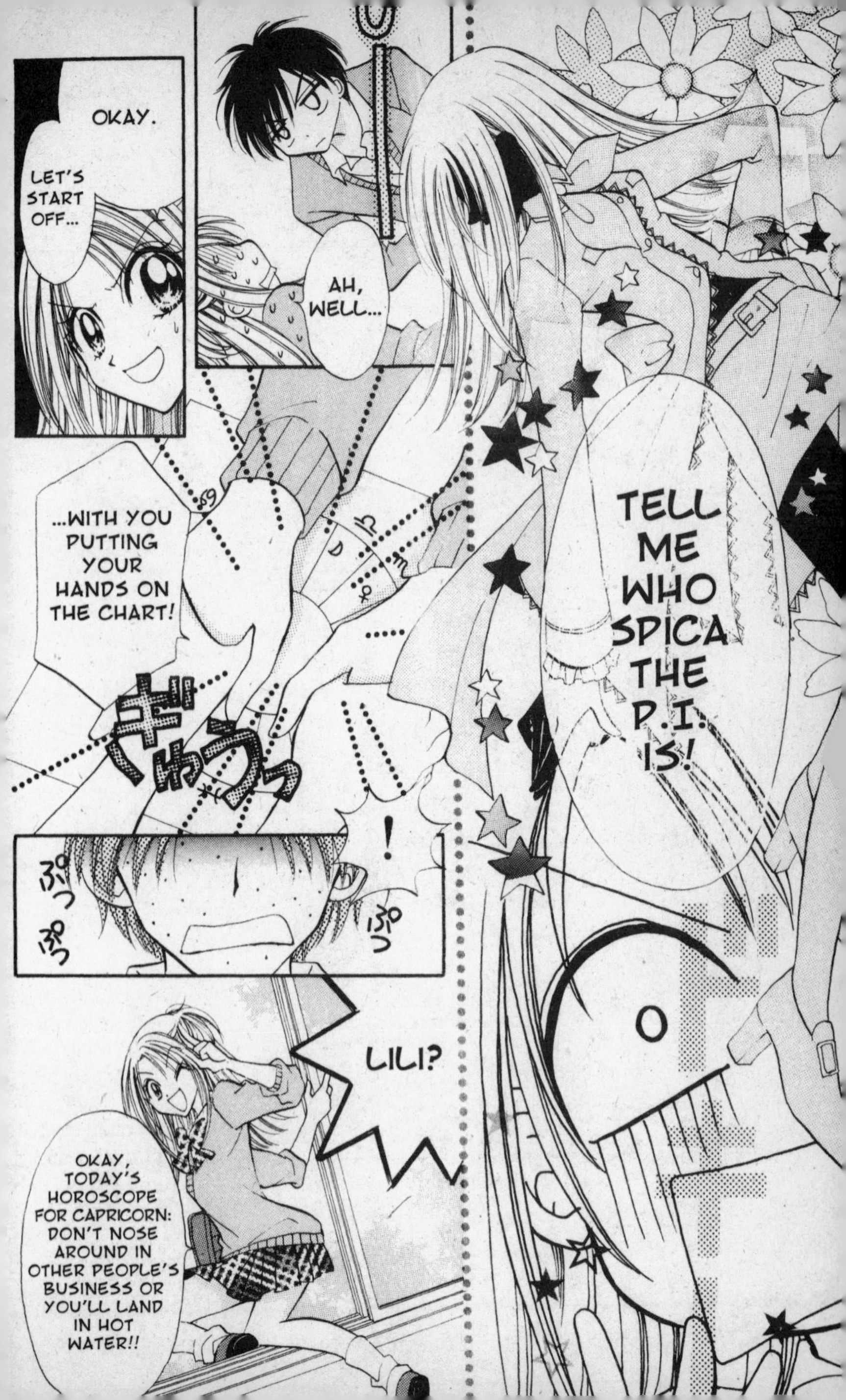

TELL ME WHO SPICA THE P.I. IS!
AH, WELL...
OKAY.
LET'S START OFF...
...WITH YOU PUTTING YOUR HANDS ON THE CHART!
.....
ぎゅうっ
!
ぷっ
ぷっ
ぷっ
LILI?
OKAY, TODAY'S HOROSCOPE FOR CAPRICORN: DON'T NOSE AROUND IN OTHER PEOPLE'S BUSINESS OR YOU'LL LAND IN HOT WATER!!

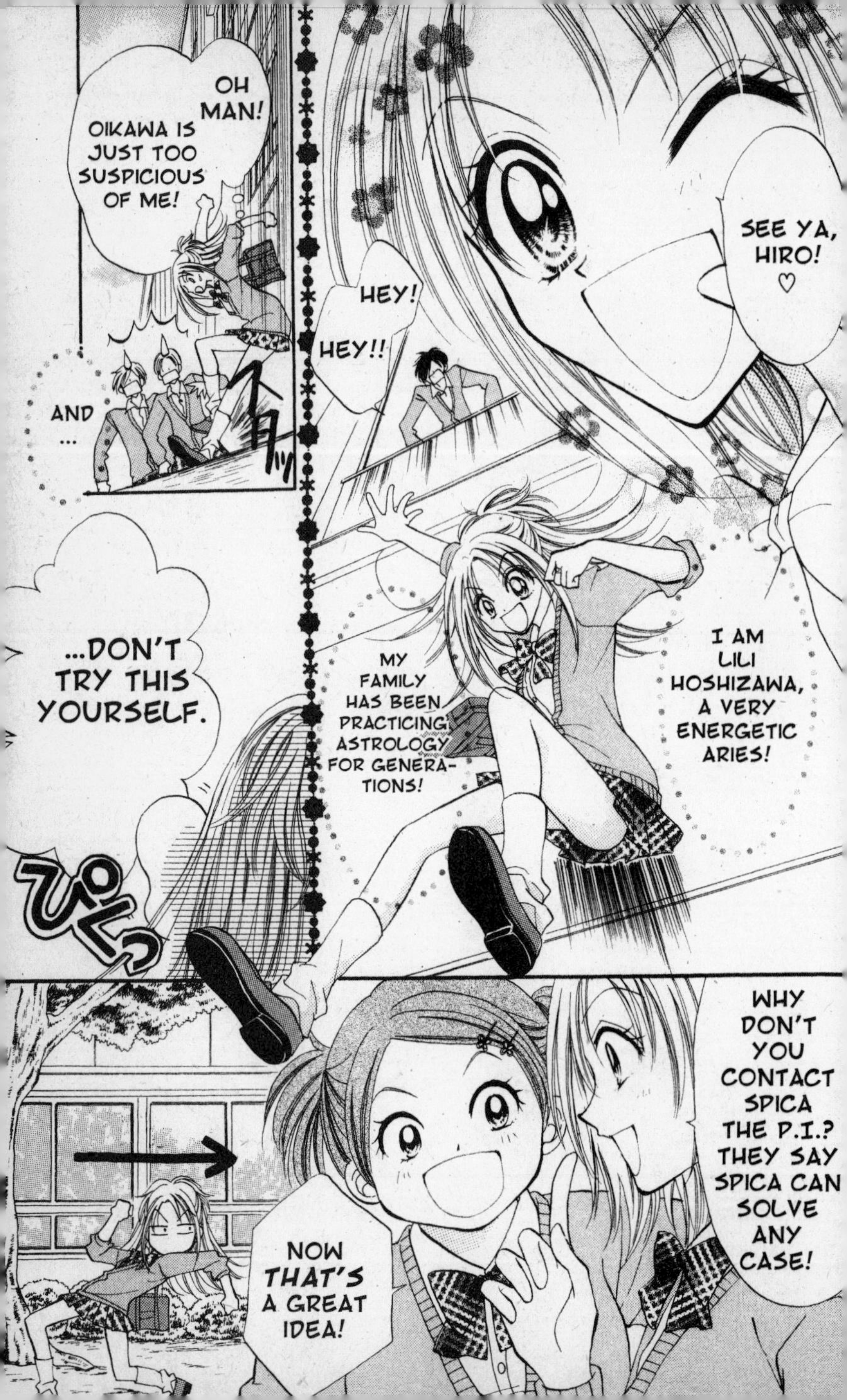
SEE YA, HIRO! ♡
HEY!
HEY!!
I AM LILI HOSHIZAWA, A VERY ENERGETIC ARIES!
MY FAMILY HAS BEEN PRACTICING ASTROLOGY FOR GENERATIONS!
OH MAN!
OIKAWA IS JUST TOO SUSPICIOUS OF ME!
AND ...
...DON'T TRY THIS YOURSELF.
WHY DON'T YOU CONTACT SPICA THE P.I.? THEY SAY SPICA CAN SOLVE ANY CASE!
NOW *THAT'S* A GREAT IDEA!

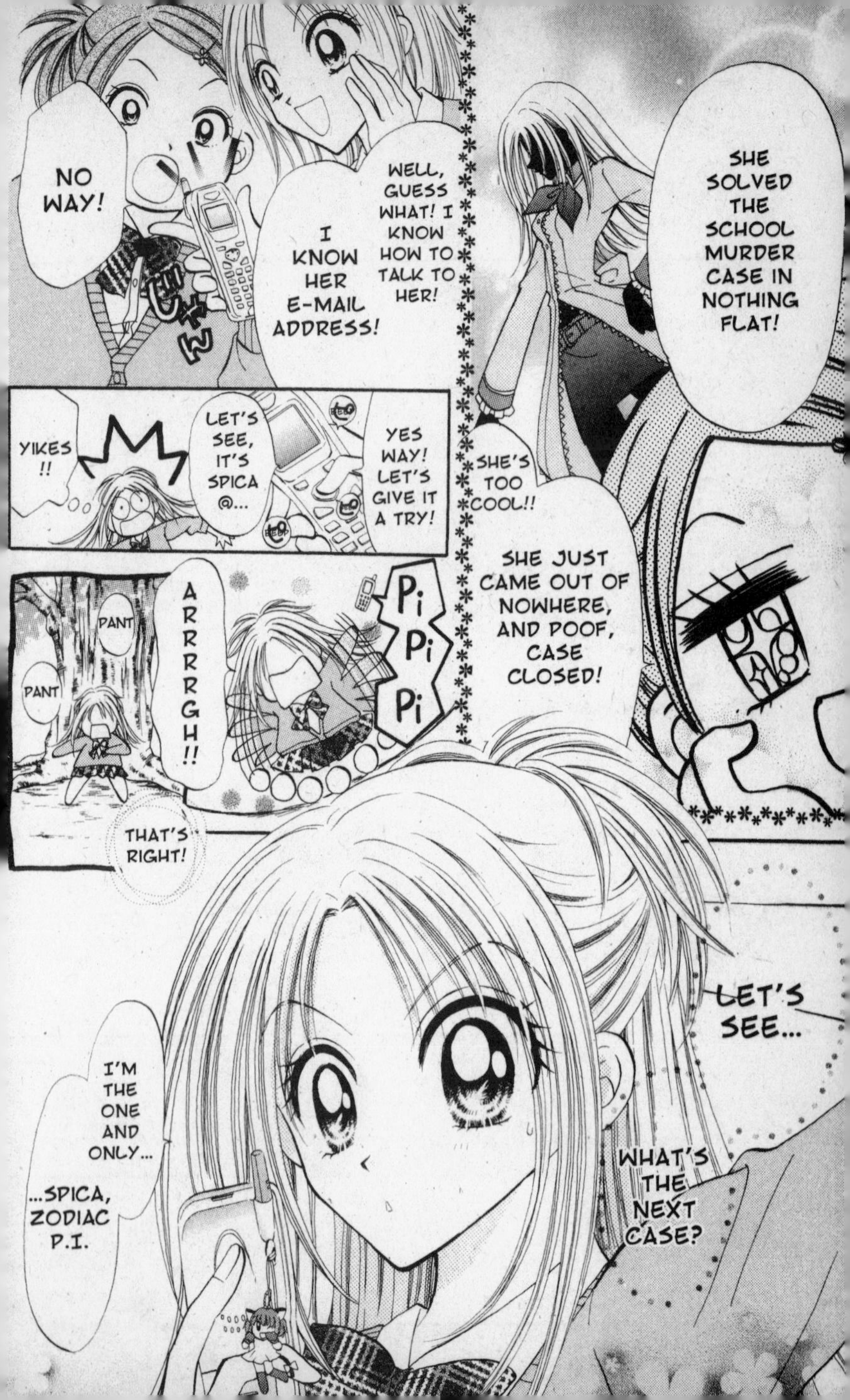
SHE SOLVED THE SCHOOL MURDER CASE IN NOTHING FLAT!
SHE'S TOO COOL!!
SHE JUST CAME OUT OF NOWHERE, AND POOF, CASE CLOSED!
WELL, GUESS WHAT! I KNOW HOW TO TALK TO HER!
I KNOW HER E-MAIL ADDRESS!
NO WAY!
YES WAY! LET'S GIVE IT A TRY!
LET'S SEE, IT'S SPICA @...
BEEP
BEEP
YIKES !!
Pi Pi Pi
ARRRRGH!!
PANT
PANT
THAT'S RIGHT!
LET'S SEE...
WHAT'S THE NEXT CASE?
I'M THE ONE AND ONLY...
...SPICA, ZODIAC P.I.

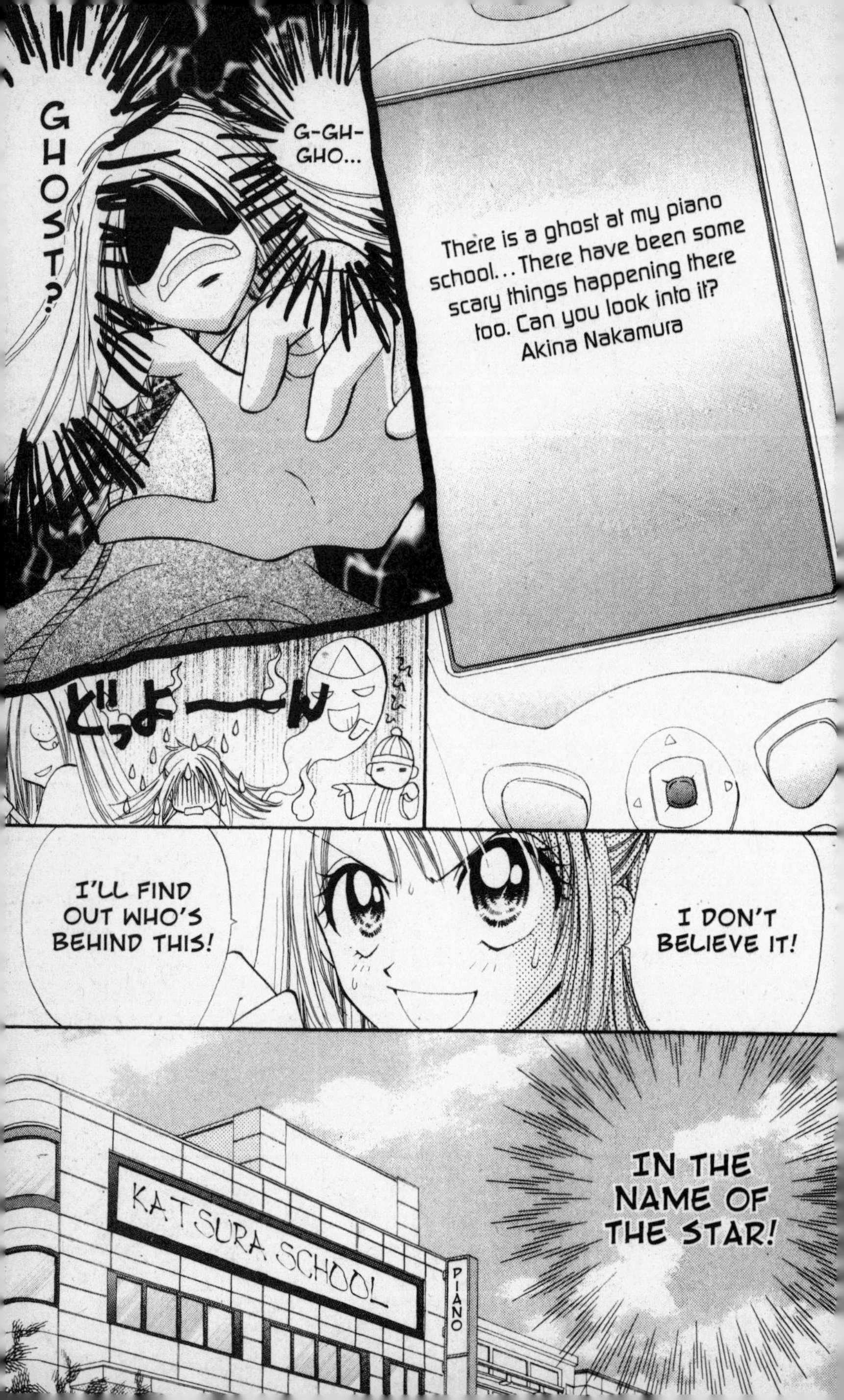
There is a ghost at my piano school... There have been some scary things happening there too. Can you look into it? Akina Nakamura
G-GH-GHO...
GHOST?
どっよーーん
I DON'T BELIEVE IT!
I'LL FIND OUT WHO'S BEHIND THIS!
IN THE NAME OF THE STAR!
KATSURA SCHOOL
PIANO

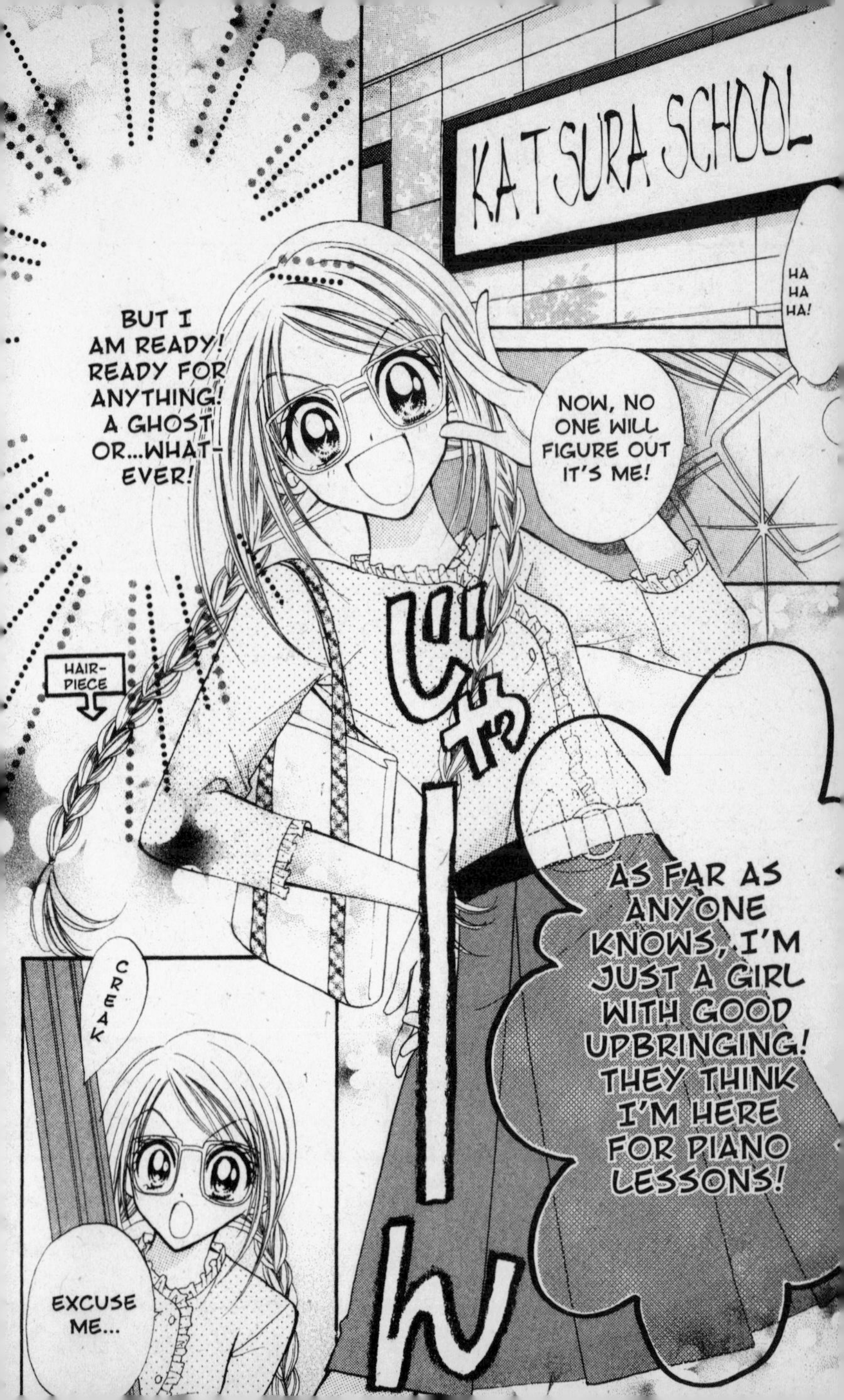
KATSURA SCHOOL
HA HA HA!
NOW, NO ONE WILL FIGURE OUT IT'S ME!
BUT I AM READY! READY FOR ANYTHING! A GHOST OR...WHAT-EVER!
じゃーん
HAIR-PIECE
AS FAR AS ANYONE KNOWS, I'M JUST A GIRL WITH GOOD UPBRINGING! THEY THINK I'M HERE FOR PIANO LESSONS!
CREAK
EXCUSE ME...

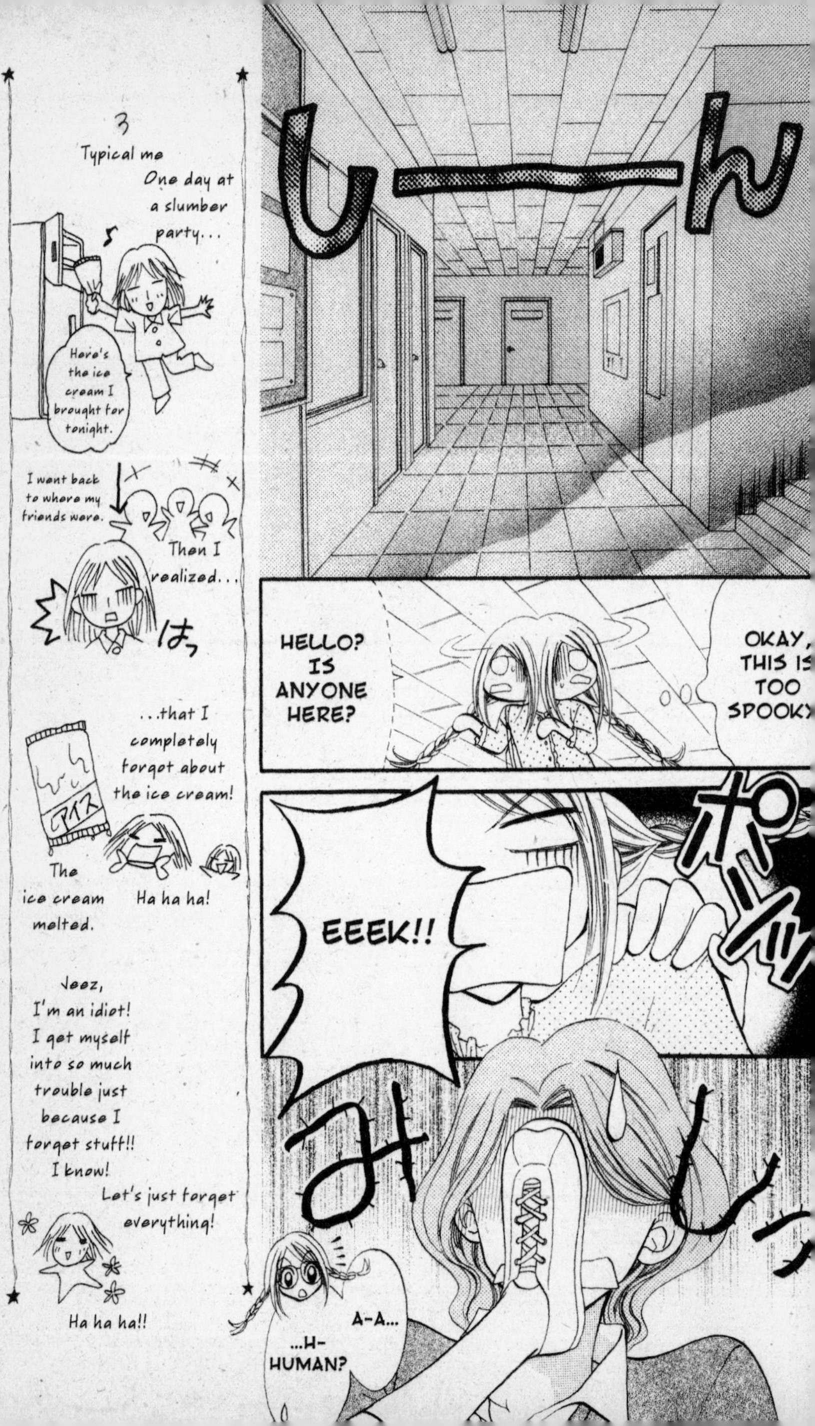
しーん
OKAY, THIS IS TOO SPOOKY
HELLO? IS ANYONE HERE?
ポーン
EEEK!!
みしっ
A-A...
...H-HUMAN?

3

Typical me

One day at a slumber party...

Here's the ice cream I brought for tonight.

I went back to where my friends were.

Then I realized...

はっ

...that I completely forgot about the ice cream!

アイス

The ice cream melted.

Ha ha ha!

Jeez, I'm an idiot! I get myself into so much trouble just because I forget stuff!! I know! Let's just forget everything!

Ha ha ha!!

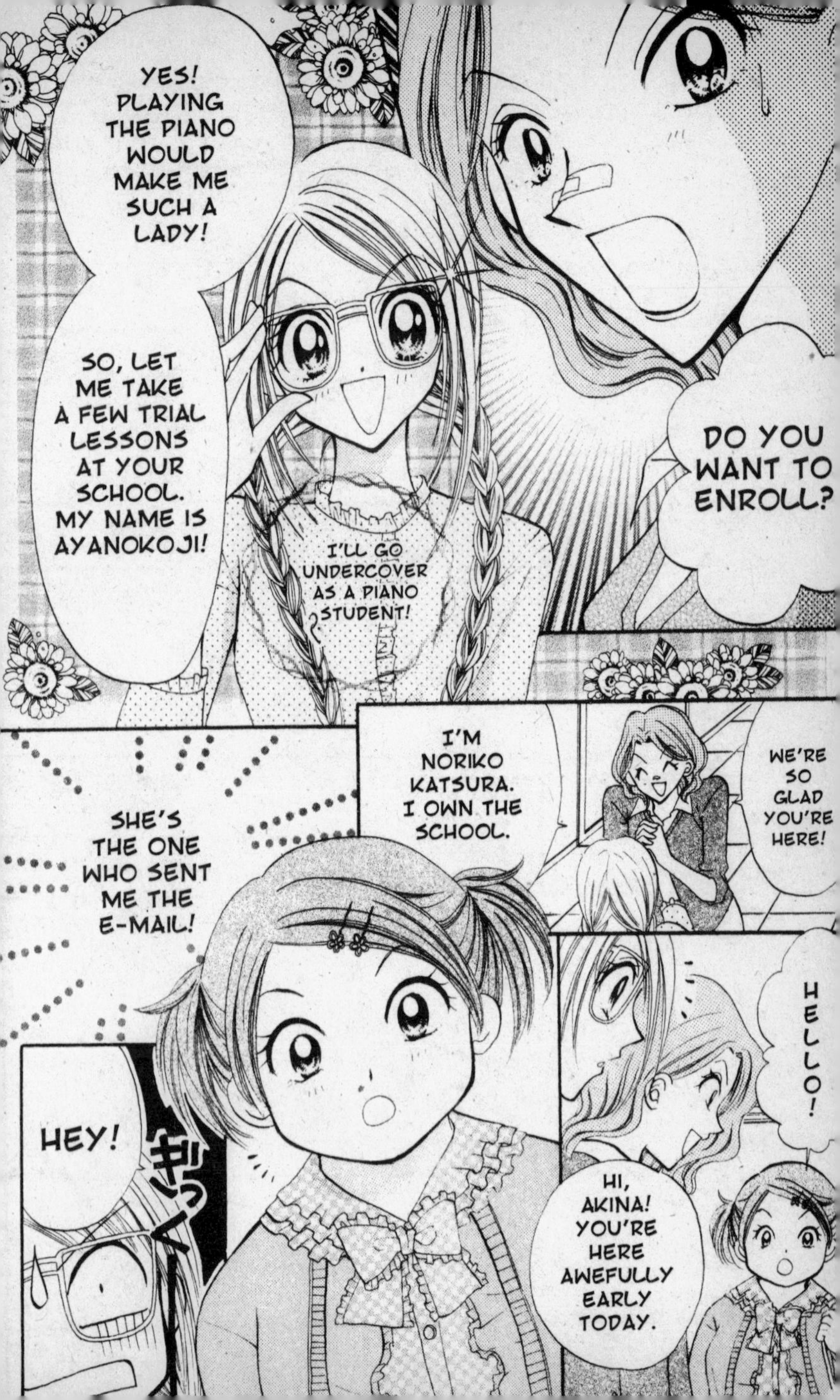
DO YOU WANT TO ENROLL?
YES! PLAYING THE PIANO WOULD MAKE ME SUCH A LADY!
SO, LET ME TAKE A FEW TRIAL LESSONS AT YOUR SCHOOL. MY NAME IS AYANOKOJI!
I'LL GO UNDERCOVER AS A PIANO STUDENT!
WE'RE SO GLAD YOU'RE HERE!
I'M NORIKO KATSURA. I OWN THE SCHOOL.
HELLO!
HI, AKINA! YOU'RE HERE AWEFULLY EARLY TODAY.
SHE'S THE ONE WHO SENT ME THE E-MAIL!
HEY!
ぎくっ

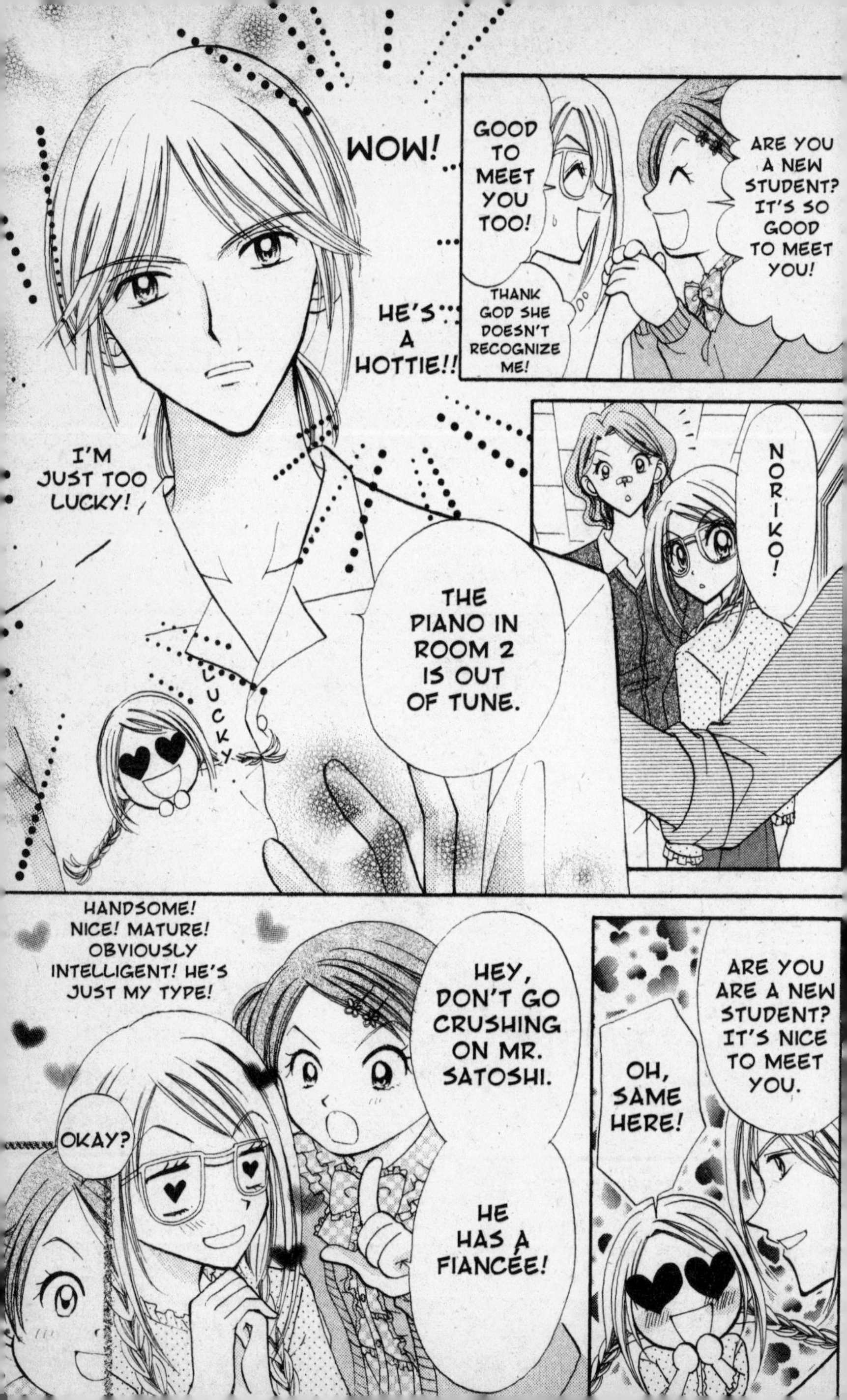
ARE YOU A NEW STUDENT? IT'S SO GOOD TO MEET YOU!
GOOD TO MEET YOU TOO!
THANK GOD SHE DOESN'T RECOGNIZE ME!
NORIKO!
WOW!
HE'S A HOTTIE!!
I'M JUST TOO LUCKY!
THE PIANO IN ROOM 2 IS OUT OF TUNE.
LUCKY
ARE YOU ARE A NEW STUDENT? IT'S NICE TO MEET YOU.
OH, SAME HERE!
HANDSOME! NICE! MATURE! OBVIOUSLY INTELLIGENT! HE'S JUST MY TYPE!
HEY, DON'T GO CRUSHING ON MR. SATOSHI.
HE HAS A FIANCÉE!
OKAY?

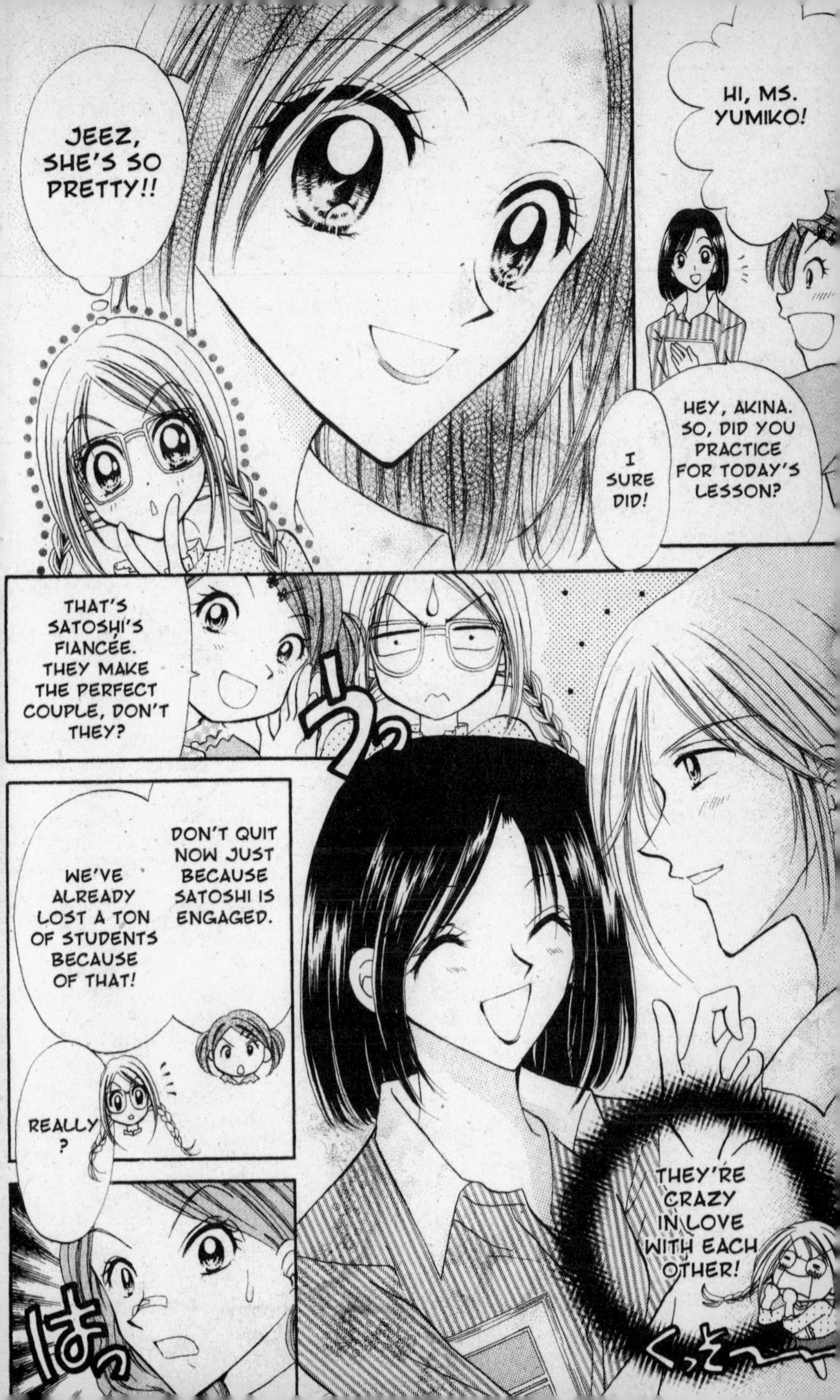

HI, MS. YUMIKO!
HEY, AKINA. SO, DID YOU PRACTICE FOR TODAY'S LESSON?
I SURE DID!
JEEZ, SHE'S SO PRETTY!!
THEY'RE CRAZY IN LOVE WITH EACH OTHER!
くそ〜
THAT'S SATOSHI'S FIANCÉE. THEY MAKE THE PERFECT COUPLE, DON'T THEY?
うっ
DON'T QUIT NOW JUST BECAUSE SATOSHI IS ENGAGED.
WE'VE ALREADY LOST A TON OF STUDENTS BECAUSE OF THAT!
REALLY?
はっ

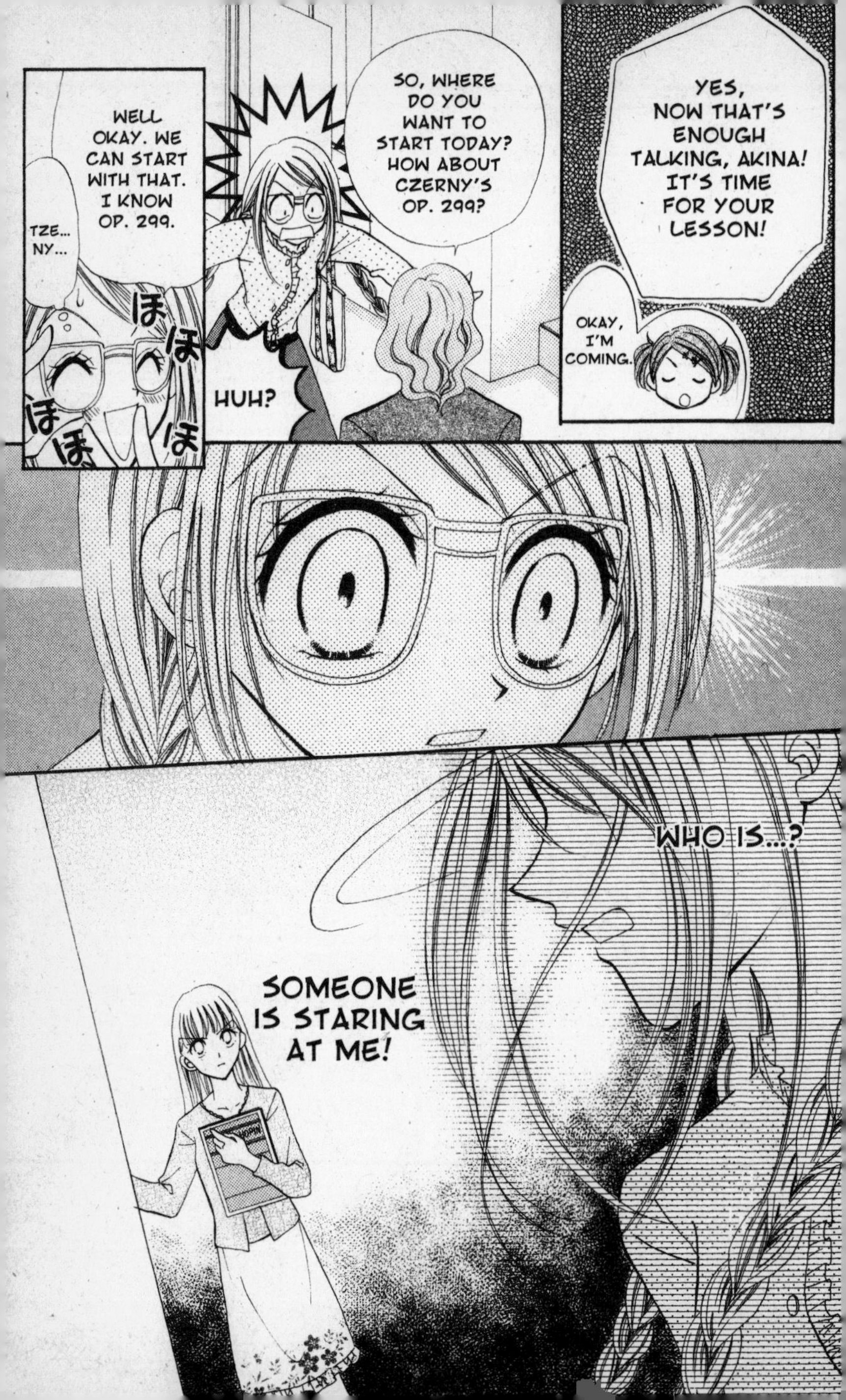
YES, NOW THAT'S ENOUGH TALKING, AKINA! IT'S TIME FOR YOUR LESSON!
OKAY, I'M COMING.
SO, WHERE DO YOU WANT TO START TODAY? HOW ABOUT CZERNY'S OP. 299?
HUH?
WELL OKAY. WE CAN START WITH THAT. I KNOW OP. 299.
TZE... NY...
ほほほほほ
WHO IS...?
SOMEONE IS STARING AT ME!

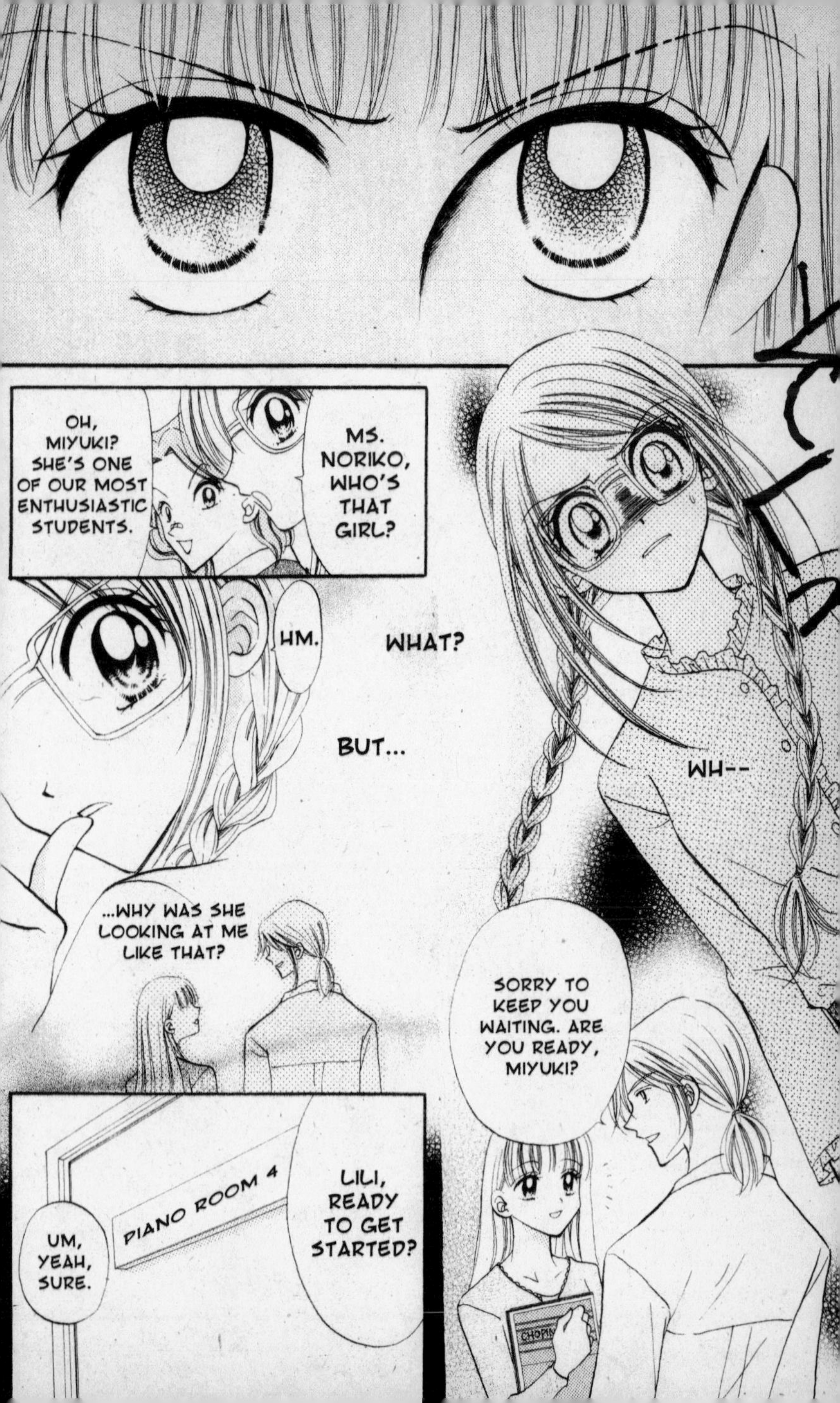
WH--
MS. NORIKO, WHO'S THAT GIRL?
OH, MIYUKI? SHE'S ONE OF OUR MOST ENTHUSIASTIC STUDENTS.
HM.
WHAT?
BUT...
...WHY WAS SHE LOOKING AT ME LIKE THAT?
SORRY TO KEEP YOU WAITING. ARE YOU READY, MIYUKI?
CHOPIN
PIANO ROOM 4
LILI, READY TO GET STARTED?
UM, YEAH, SURE.

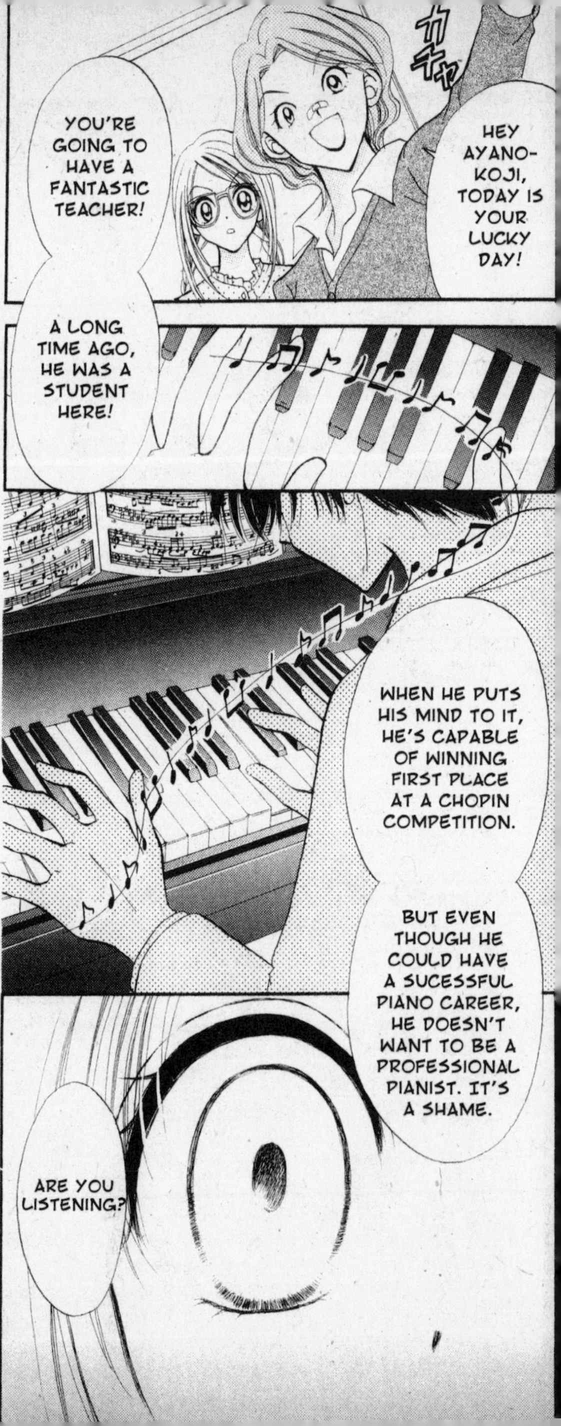
カチャ
HEY AYANO-KOJI, TODAY IS YOUR LUCKY DAY!
YOU'RE GOING TO HAVE A FANTASTIC TEACHER!
A LONG TIME AGO, HE WAS A STUDENT HERE!
WHEN HE PUTS HIS MIND TO IT, HE'S CAPABLE OF WINNING FIRST PLACE AT A CHOPIN COMPETITION.
BUT EVEN THOUGH HE COULD HAVE A SUCESSFUL PIANO CAREER, HE DOESN'T WANT TO BE A PROFESSIONAL PIANIST. IT'S A SHAME.
ARE YOU LISTENING?

4

About Piano

File 2 is a story about the piano. Even though I cant play a musical instrument, I can respect those who can!! It's amazing how they can move all ten fingers at the same time to make beautiful music. I played the flute at school, or at least I pretended to play it. I can't read music very well. Things like sharps and flats are too confusing for me. I do love to listen to music though. Chopin's Polonaise, Op. 53 in A-Flat Major, and Etudes Op. 10 are my favorites. Oh how I would love to be able to play the piano!! By the way, in order to write this episode, I had to sneak into a local piano school and take some pictures. Some people may have thought my behavior was a bit suspicious.

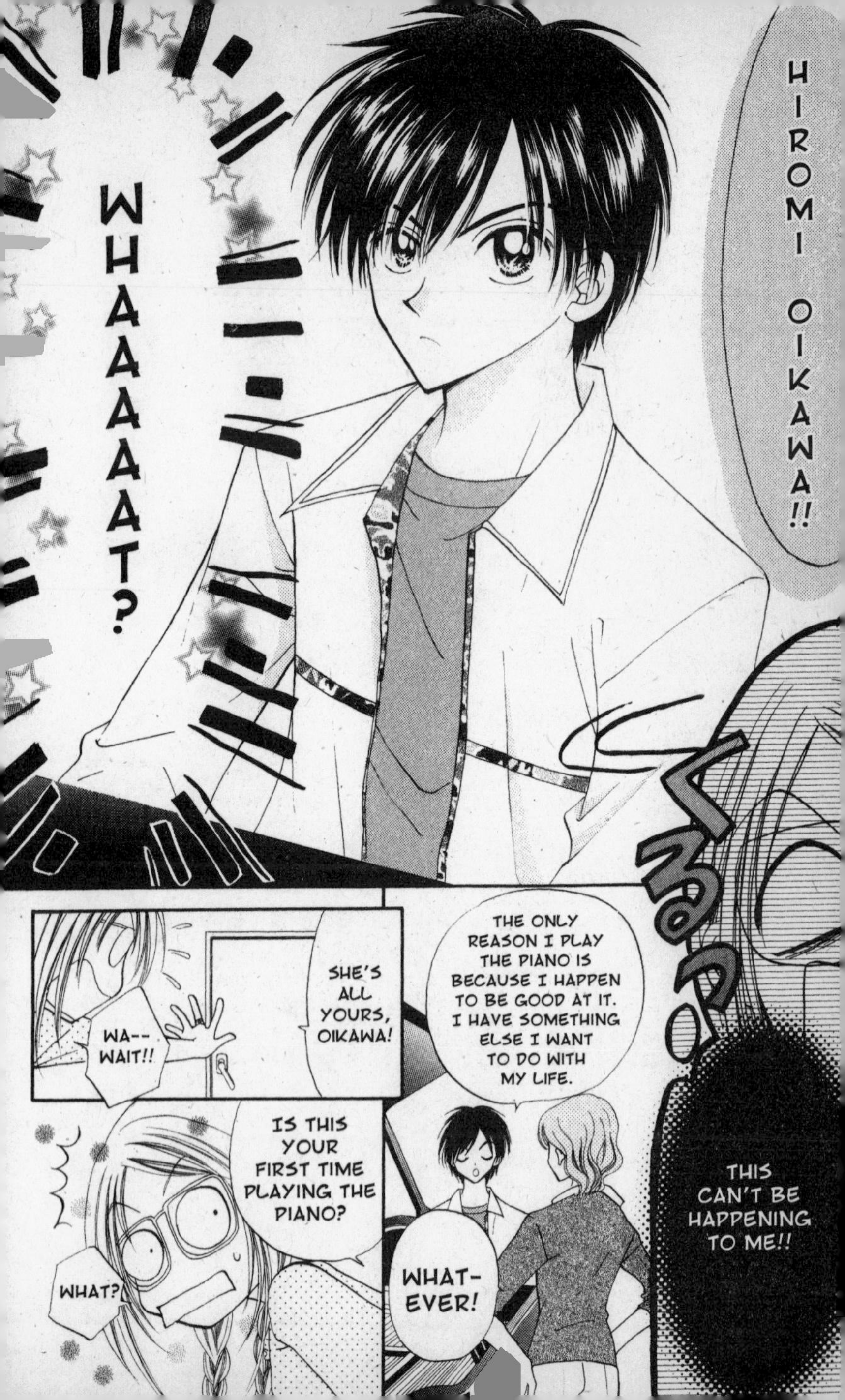
HIROMI OIKAWA!!
WHAAAAAT?
くるっ
THIS CAN'T BE HAPPENING TO ME!!
THE ONLY REASON I PLAY THE PIANO IS BECAUSE I HAPPEN TO BE GOOD AT IT. I HAVE SOMETHING ELSE I WANT TO DO WITH MY LIFE.
WHAT-EVER!
SHE'S ALL YOURS, OIKAWA!
WA--WAIT!!
IS THIS YOUR FIRST TIME PLAYING THE PIANO?
WHAT?

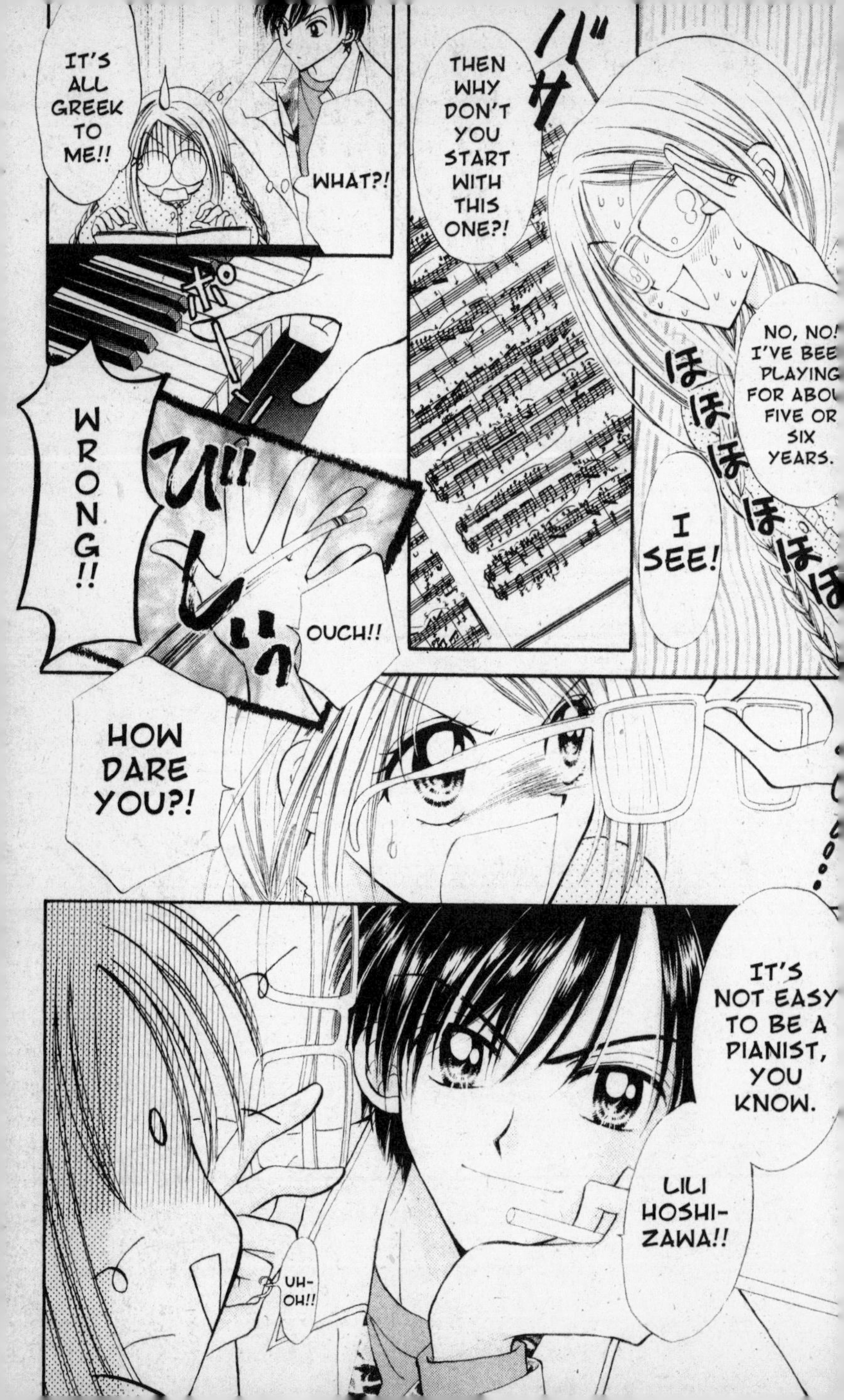

NO, NO! I'VE BEE PLAYING FOR ABOU FIVE OR SIX YEARS.
ほほほほほほ
I SEE!
バサ
THEN WHY DON'T YOU START WITH THIS ONE?!
IT'S ALL GREEK TO ME!!
WHAT?!
ポ
WRONG!!
びしぃっ
OUCH!!
...
HOW DARE YOU?!
IT'S NOT EASY TO BE A PIANIST, YOU KNOW.
LILI HOSHI-ZAWA!!
UH-OH!!

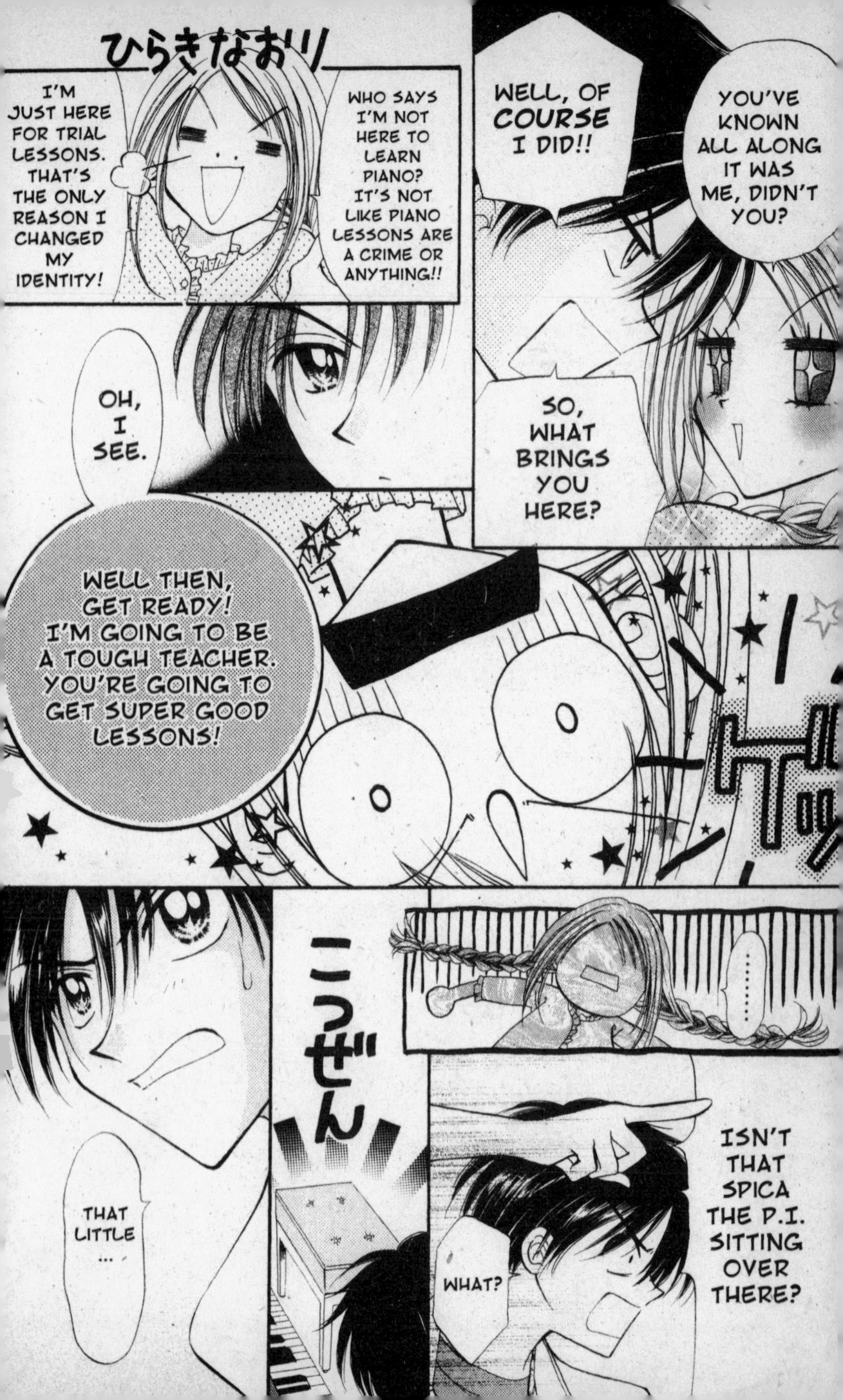

YOU'VE KNOWN ALL ALONG IT WAS ME, DIDN'T YOU?
WELL, OF COURSE I DID!!
ひらきなおり
WHO SAYS I'M NOT HERE TO LEARN PIANO? IT'S NOT LIKE PIANO LESSONS ARE A CRIME OR ANYTHING!!
I'M JUST HERE FOR TRIAL LESSONS. THAT'S THE ONLY REASON I CHANGED MY IDENTITY!
SO, WHAT BRINGS YOU HERE?
OH, I SEE.
WELL THEN, GET READY! I'M GOING TO BE A TOUGH TEACHER. YOU'RE GOING TO GET SUPER GOOD LESSONS!
……
ISN'T THAT SPICA THE P.I. SITTING OVER THERE?
WHAT?
こつぜん
THAT LITTLE ...

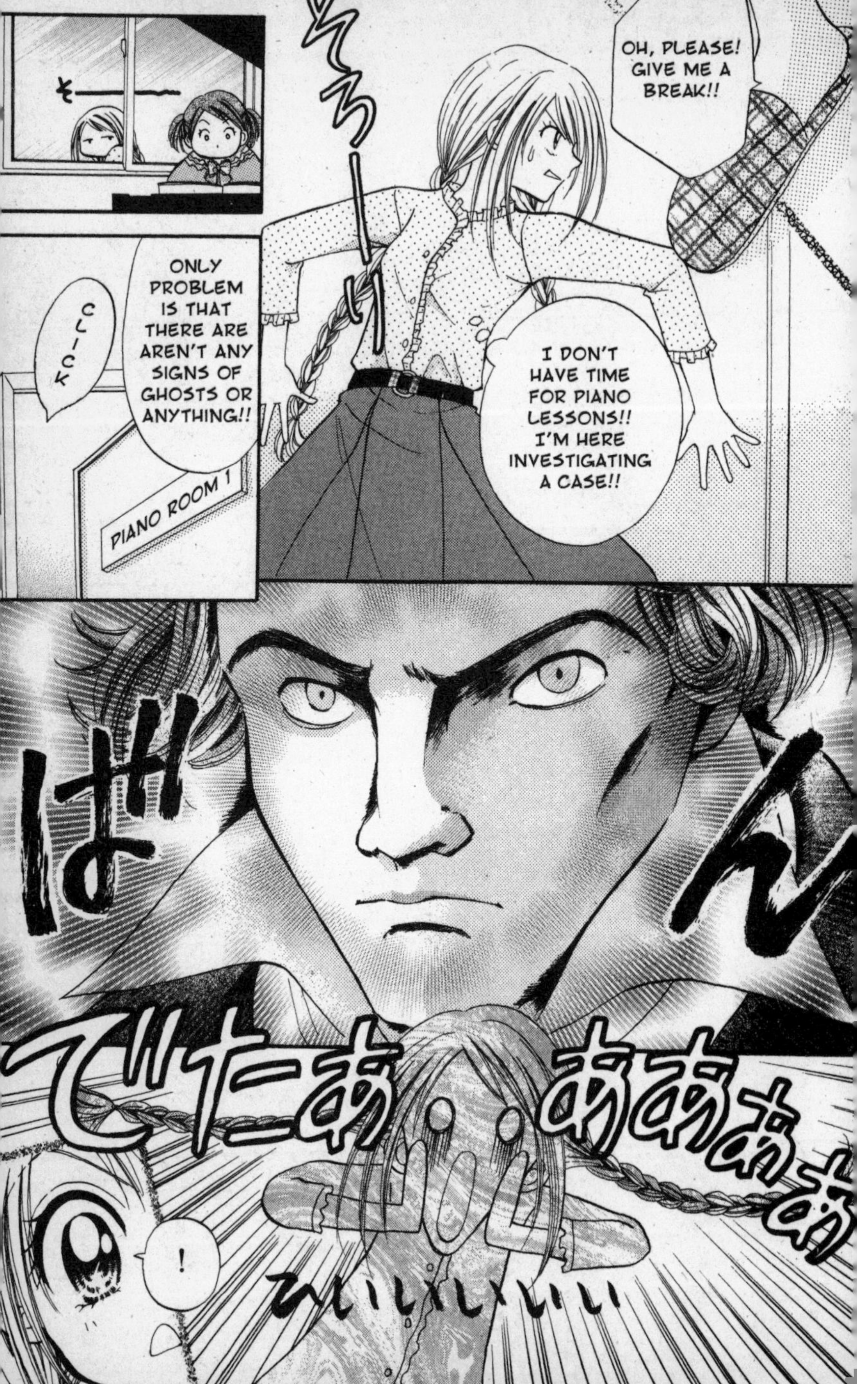

そろーーり
OH, PLEASE! GIVE ME A BREAK!!
I DON'T HAVE TIME FOR PIANO LESSONS!! I'M HERE INVESTIGATING A CASE!!
そ
ONLY PROBLEM IS THAT THERE ARE AREN'T ANY SIGNS OF GHOSTS OR ANYTHING!!
CLICK
PIANO ROOM 1
!

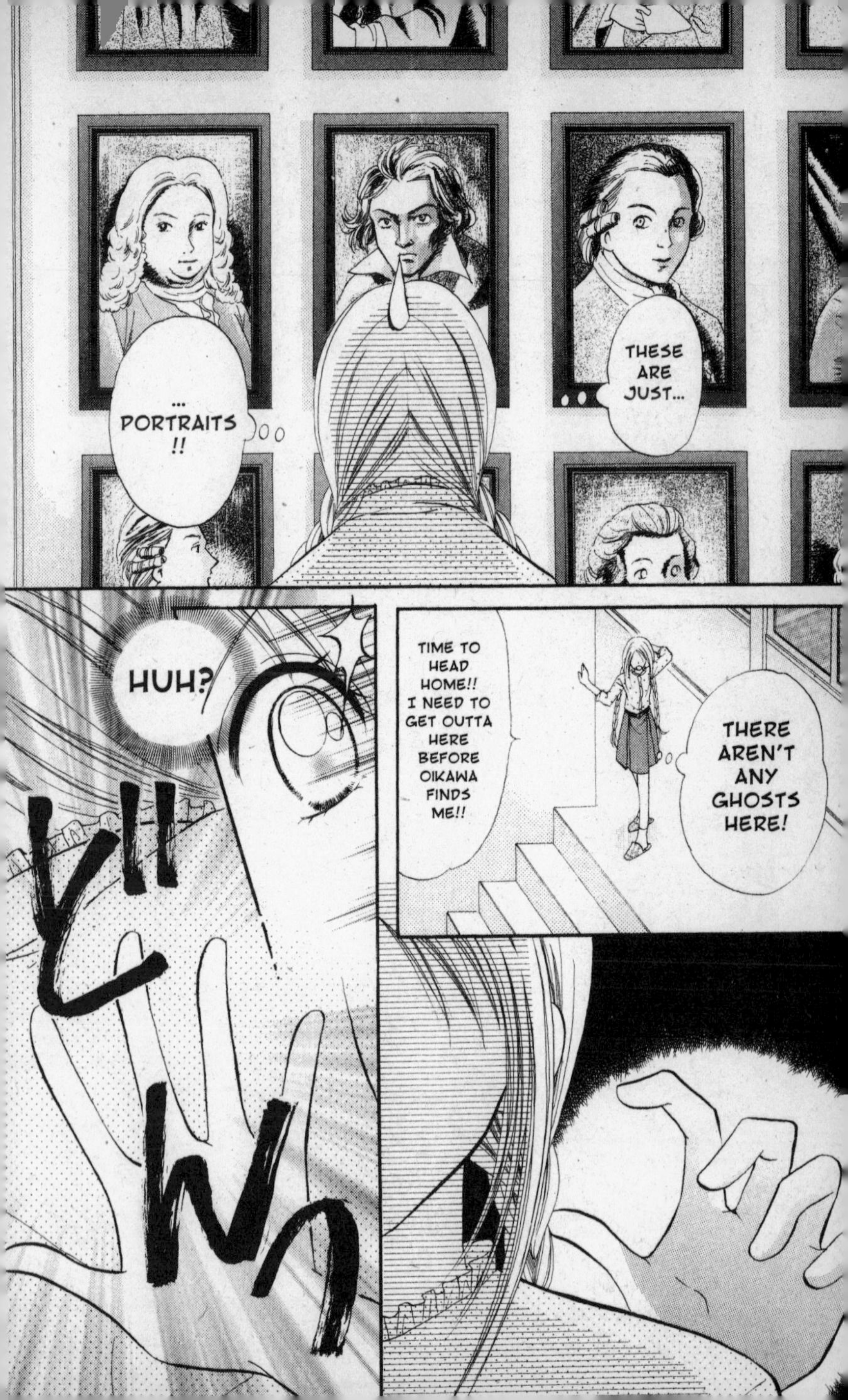
THESE ARE JUST...
...PORTRAITS!!
THERE AREN'T ANY GHOSTS HERE!
TIME TO HEAD HOME!! I NEED TO GET OUTTA HERE BEFORE OIKAWA FINDS ME!!
HUH?

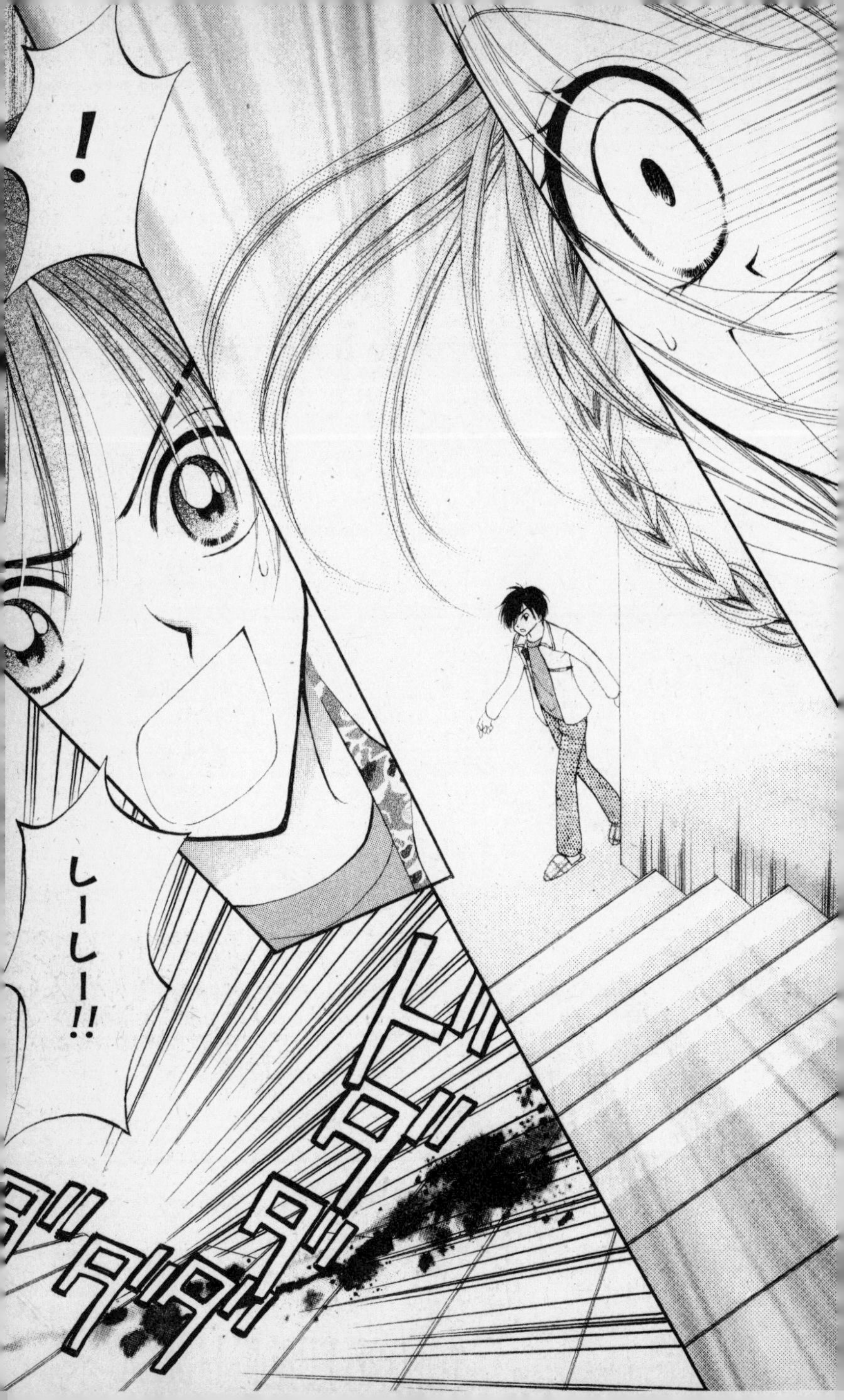
!
しーしー!!
ドダダダダダ

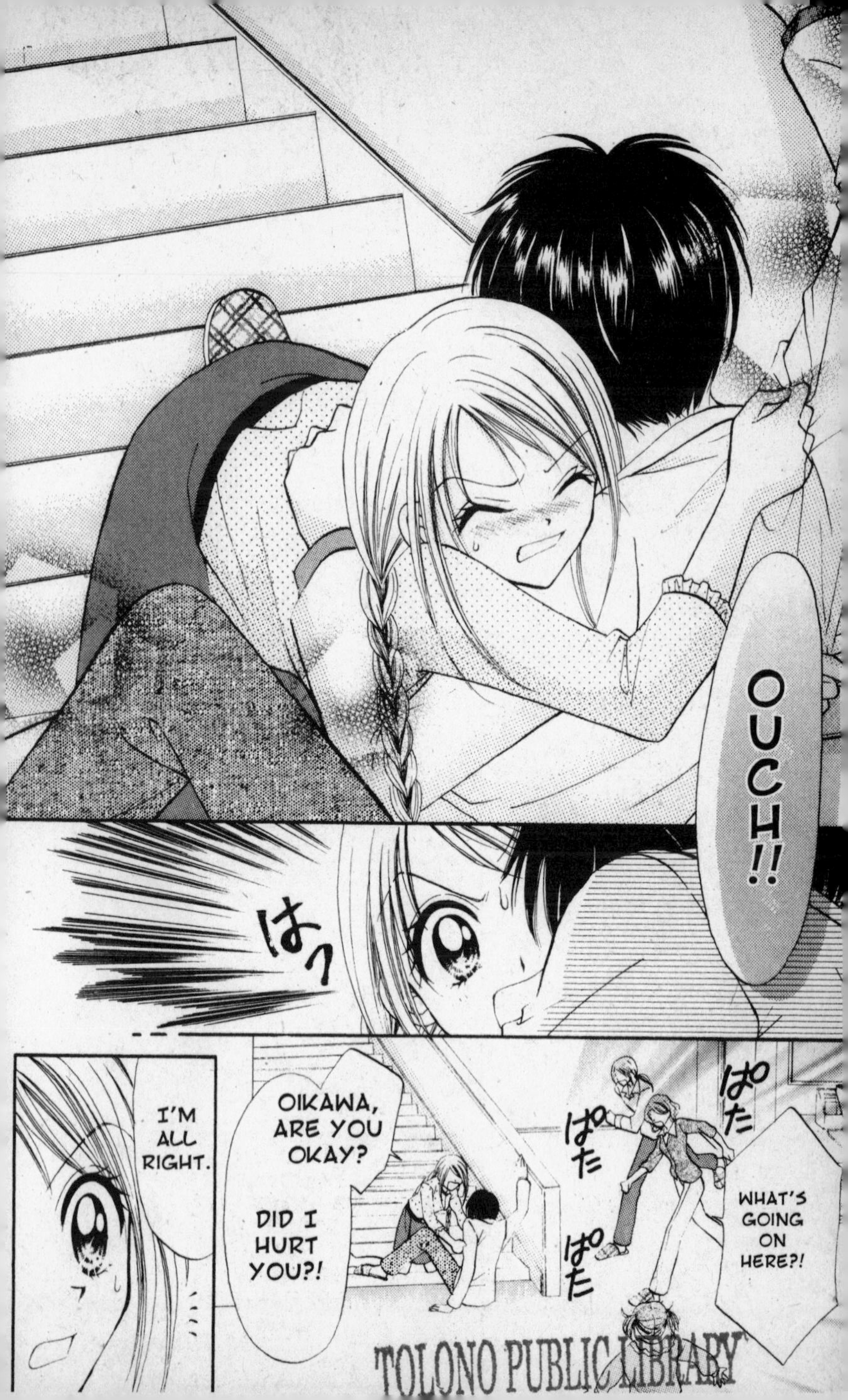
OUCH!!
はっ
ぱた
ぱた
WHAT'S GOING ON HERE?!
ぱた
OIKAWA, ARE YOU OKAY?
DID I HURT YOU?!
I'M ALL RIGHT.

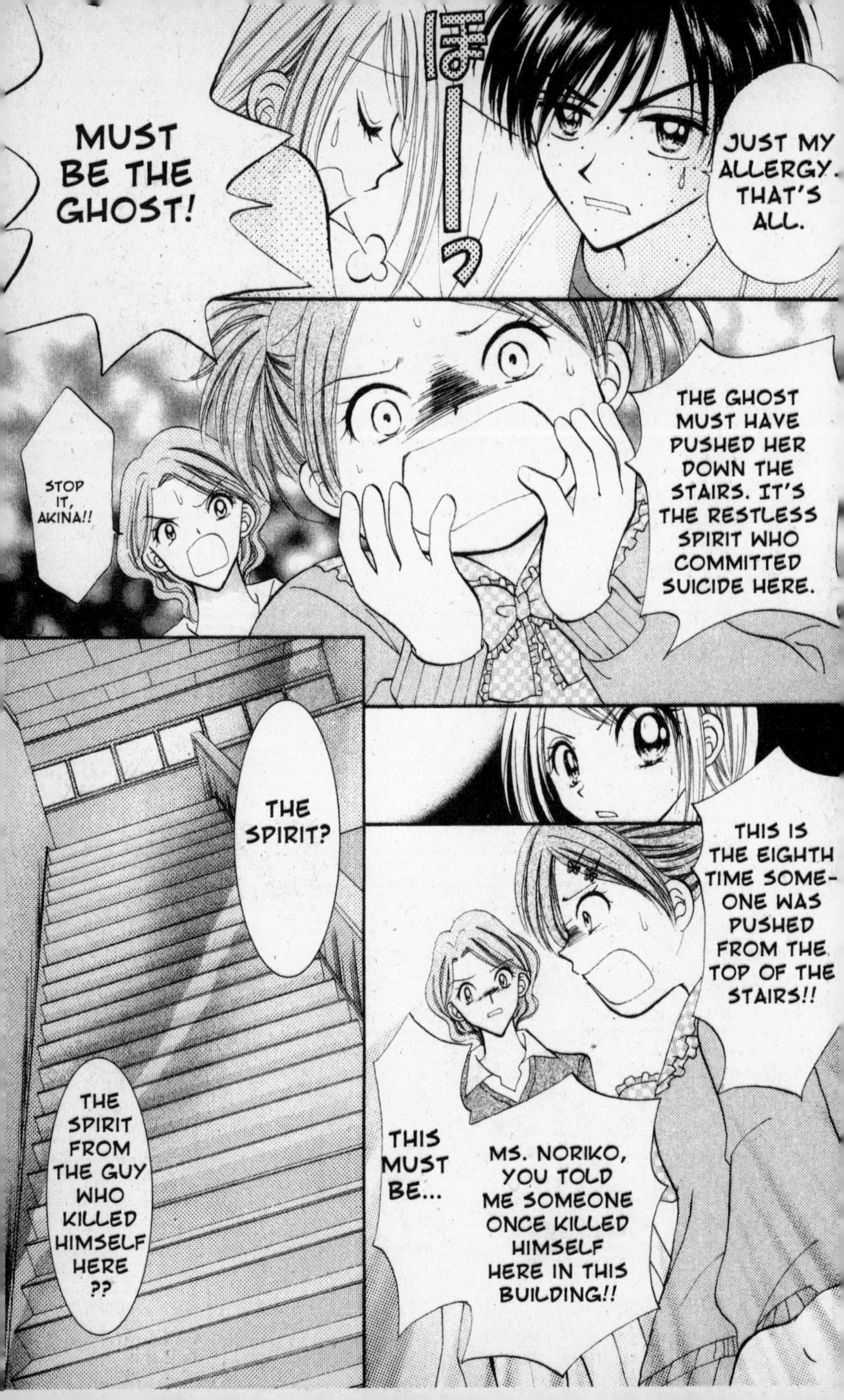
JUST MY ALLERGY. THAT'S ALL.
ぼーっ
MUST BE THE GHOST!
THE GHOST MUST HAVE PUSHED HER DOWN THE STAIRS. IT'S THE RESTLESS SPIRIT WHO COMMITTED SUICIDE HERE.
STOP IT, AKINA!!
THIS IS THE EIGHTH TIME SOME-ONE WAS PUSHED FROM THE TOP OF THE STAIRS!!
MS. NORIKO, YOU TOLD ME SOMEONE ONCE KILLED HIMSELF HERE IN THIS BUILDING!!
THIS MUST BE...
THE SPIRIT?
THE SPIRIT FROM THE GUY WHO KILLED HIMSELF HERE ??

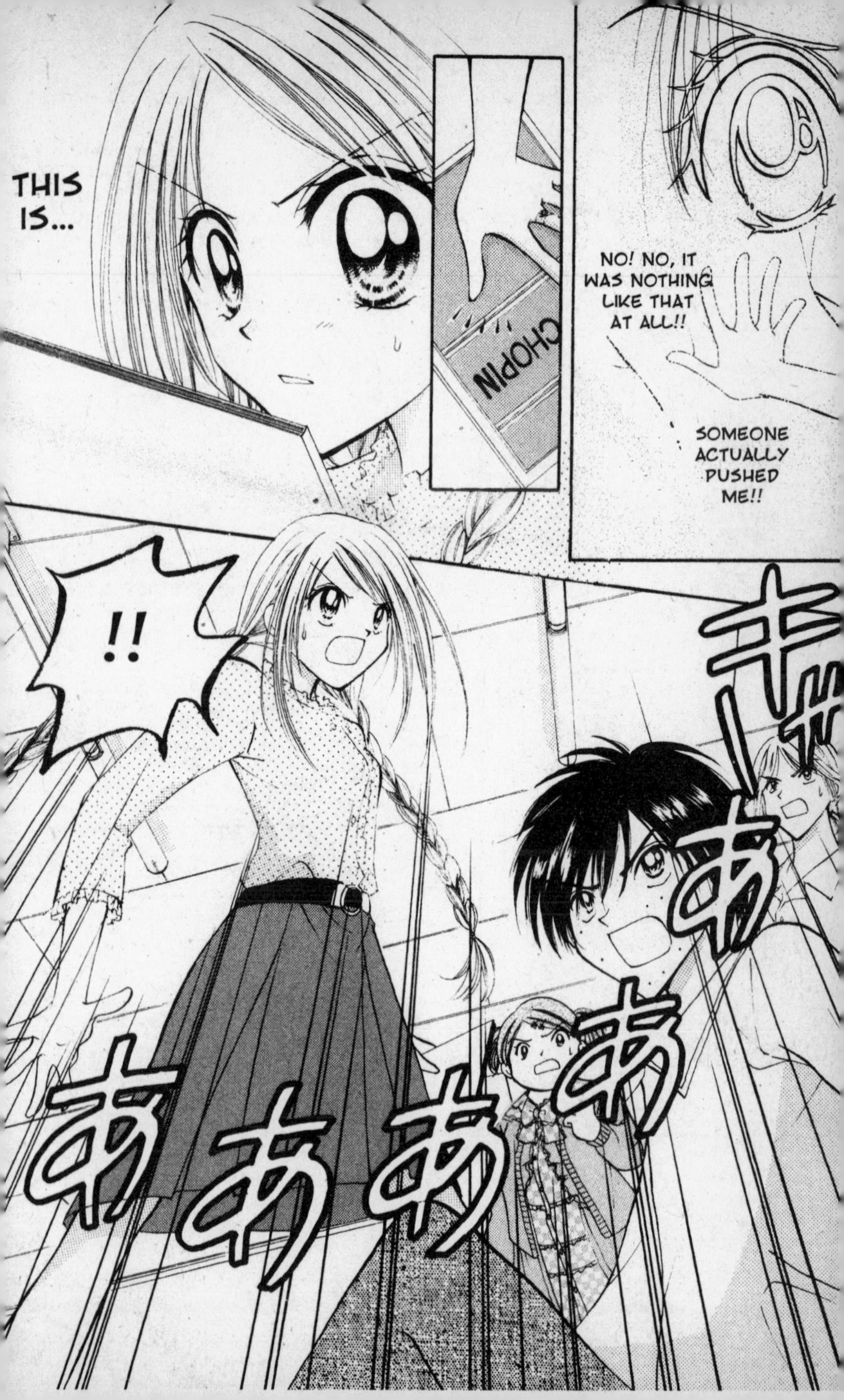
NO! NO, IT WAS NOTHING LIKE THAT AT ALL!!
SOMEONE ACTUALLY PUSHED ME!!
CHOPIN
THIS IS...
キャーああああああ
!!

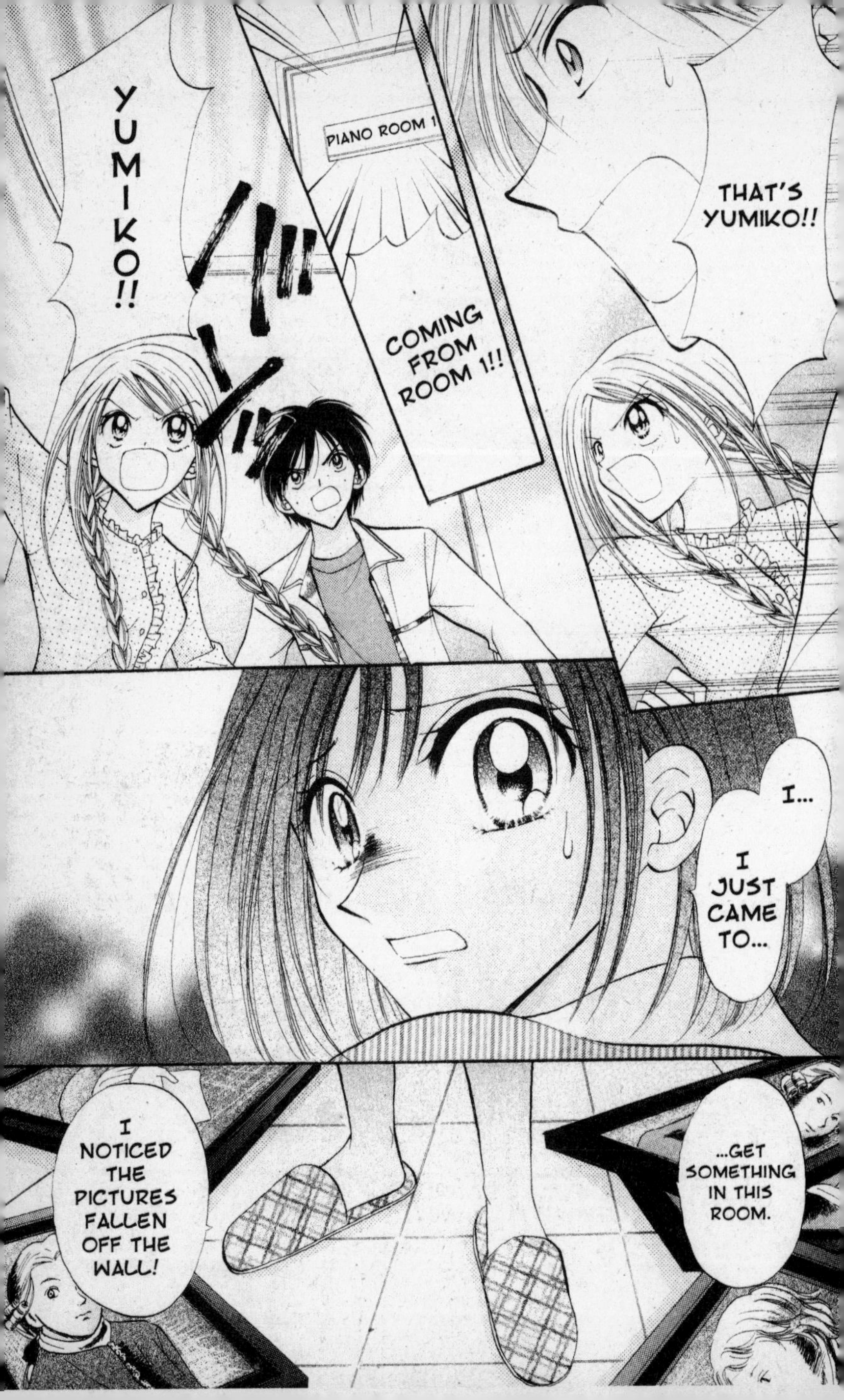
THAT'S YUMIKO!!
PIANO ROOM 1
COMING FROM ROOM 1!!
YUMIKO!!
I...
I JUST CAME TO...
...GET SOMETHING IN THIS ROOM.
I NOTICED THE PICTURES FALLEN OFF THE WALL!

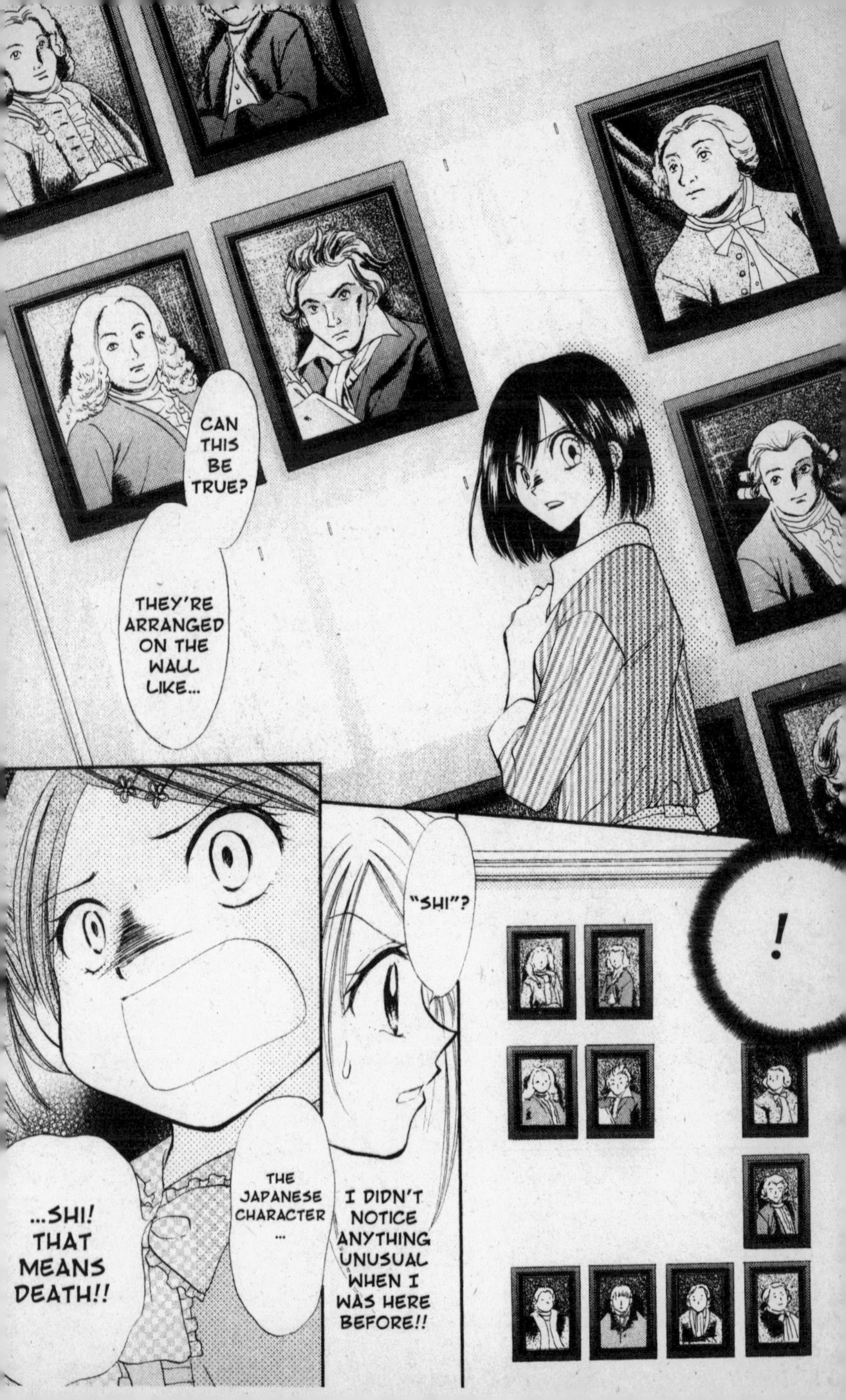
CAN THIS BE TRUE?
THEY'RE ARRANGED ON THE WALL LIKE...
!
"SHI"?
I DIDN'T NOTICE ANYTHING UNUSUAL WHEN I WAS HERE BEFORE!!
THE JAPANESE CHARACTER...
...SHI! THAT MEANS DEATH!!

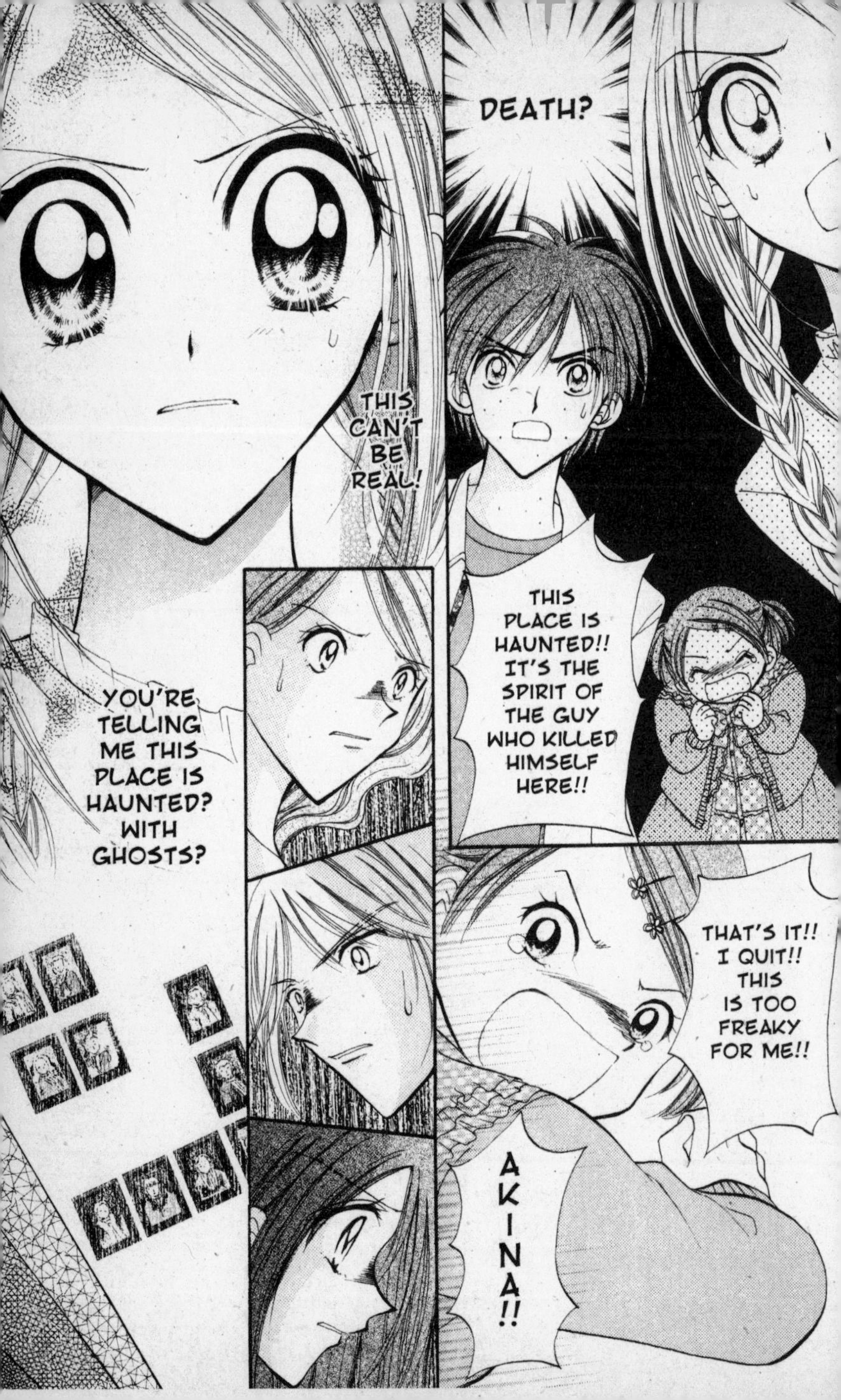
DEATH?
THIS PLACE IS HAUNTED!! IT'S THE SPIRIT OF THE GUY WHO KILLED HIMSELF HERE!!
THIS CAN'T BE REAL!
YOU'RE TELLING ME THIS PLACE IS HAUNTED? WITH GHOSTS?
THAT'S IT!! I QUIT!! THIS IS TOO FREAKY FOR ME!!
AKINA!!

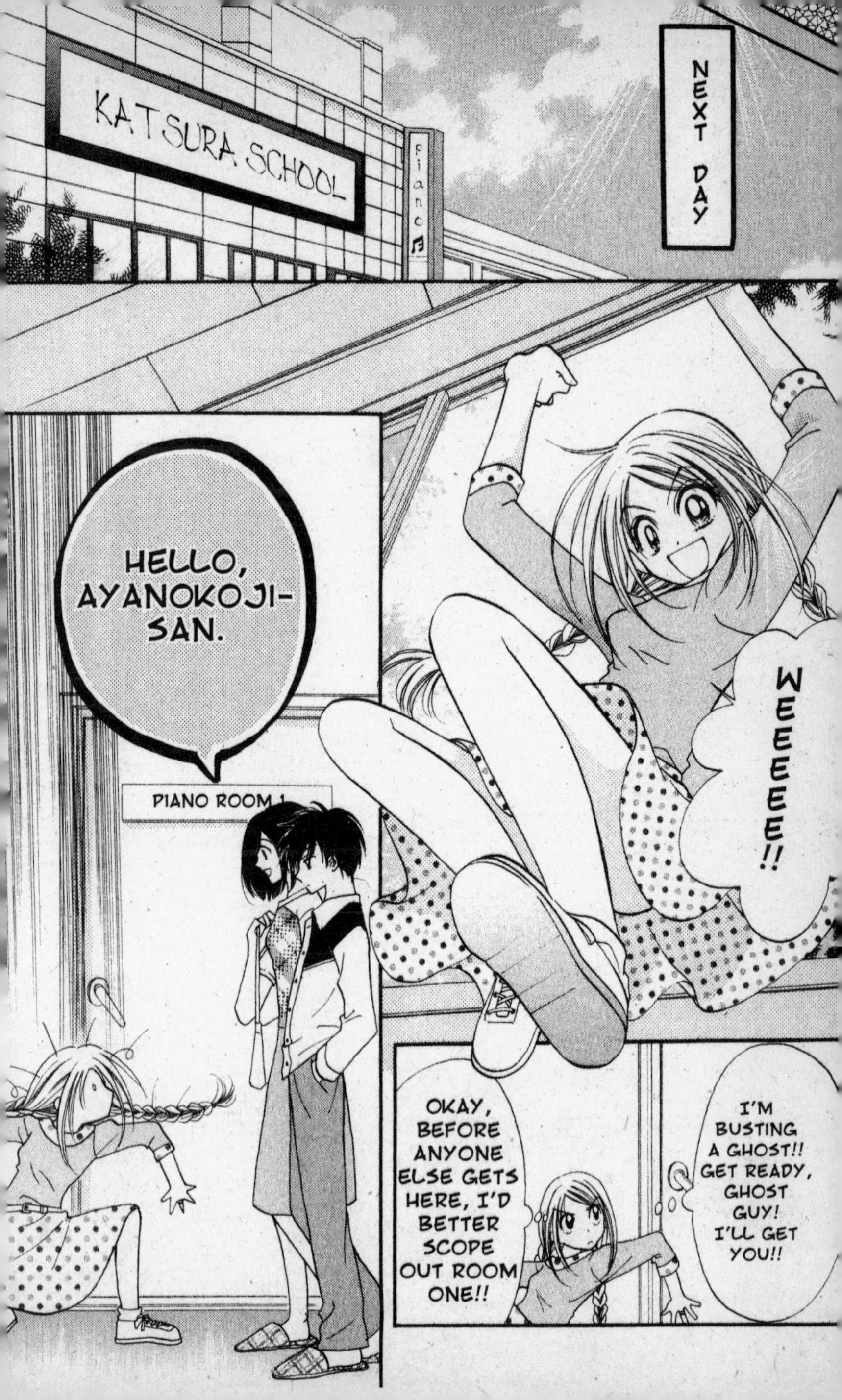
NEXT DAY
KATSURA SCHOOL
piano
WEEEEEE!!
I'M BUSTING A GHOST!! GET READY, GHOST GUY! I'LL GET YOU!!
OKAY, BEFORE ANYONE ELSE GETS HERE, I'D BETTER SCOPE OUT ROOM ONE!!
HELLO, AYANOKOJI-SAN.
PIANO ROOM 1

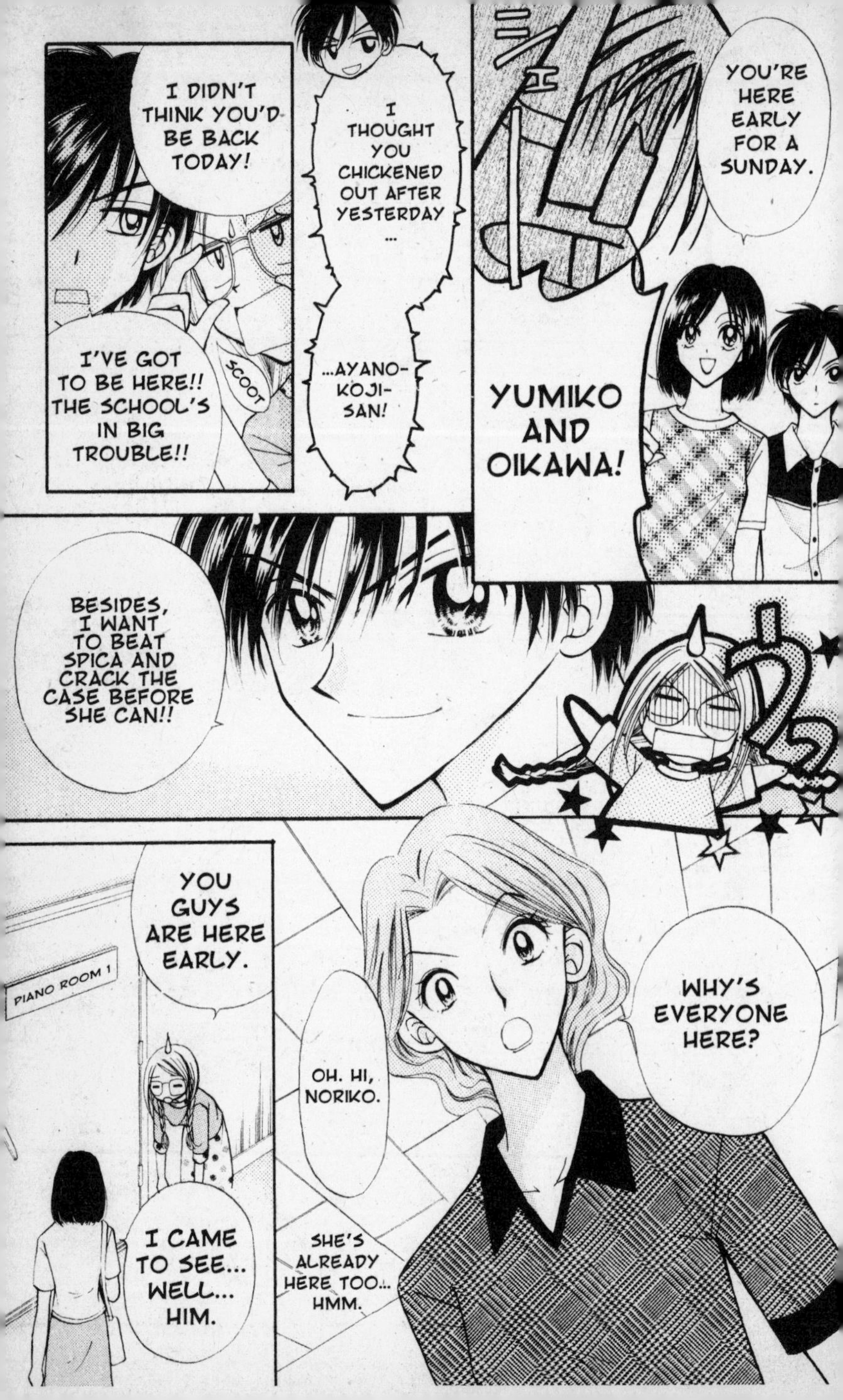

YOU'RE HERE EARLY FOR A SUNDAY.
YUMIKO AND OIKAWA!
I THOUGHT YOU CHICKENED OUT AFTER YESTERDAY...
...AYANO-KOJI-SAN!
I DIDN'T THINK YOU'D BE BACK TODAY!
SCOOT
I'VE GOT TO BE HERE!! THE SCHOOL'S IN BIG TROUBLE!!
BESIDES, I WANT TO BEAT SPICA AND CRACK THE CASE BEFORE SHE CAN!!
WHY'S EVERYONE HERE?
OH. HI, NORIKO.
YOU GUYS ARE HERE EARLY.
PIANO ROOM 1
SHE'S ALREADY HERE TOO... HMM.
I CAME TO SEE... WELL... HIM.

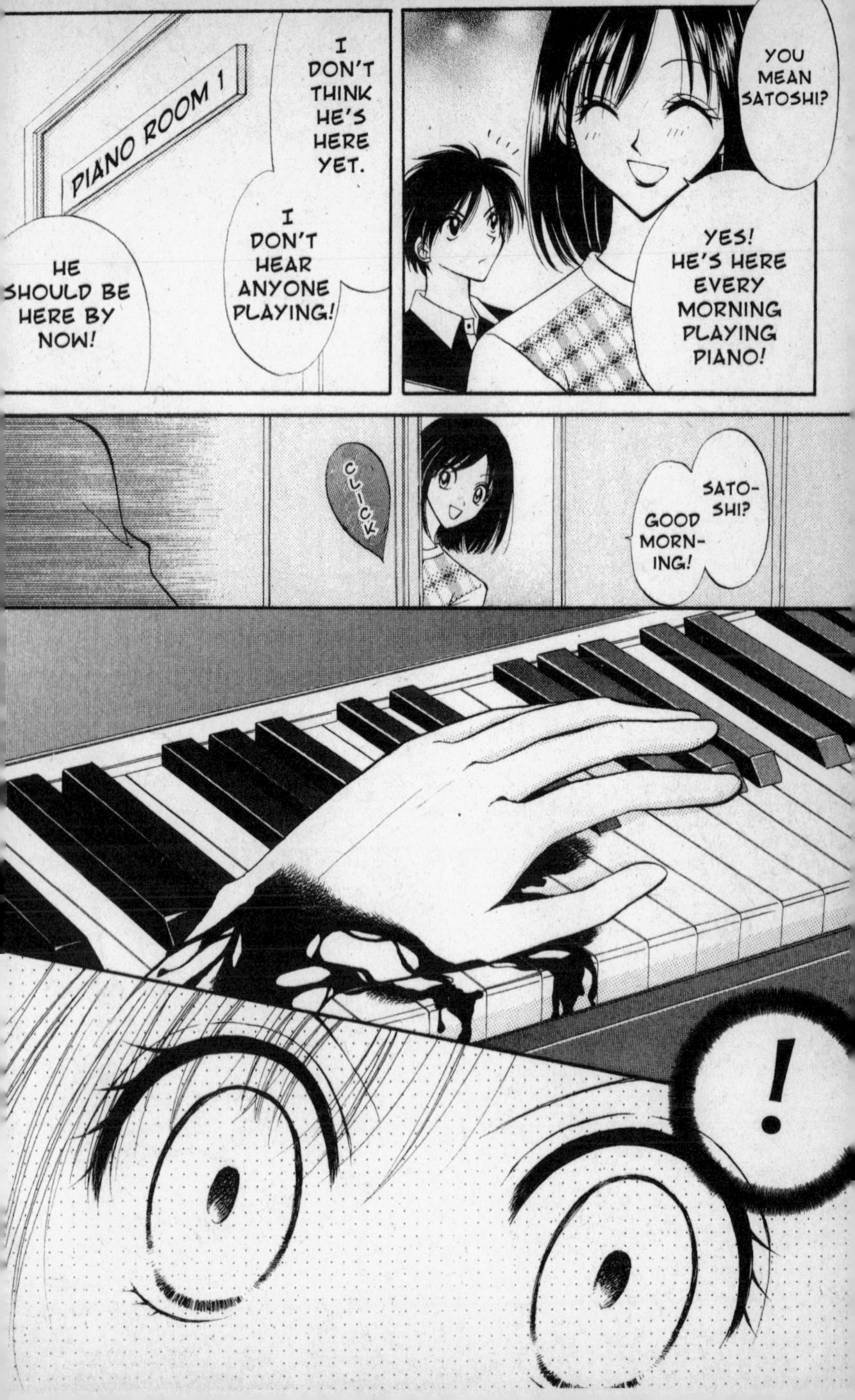
YOU MEAN SATOSHI?
YES! HE'S HERE EVERY MORNING PLAYING PIANO!
I DON'T THINK HE'S HERE YET.
I DON'T HEAR ANYONE PLAYING!
PIANO ROOM 1
HE SHOULD BE HERE BY NOW!
SATO-SHI? GOOD MORN-ING!
CLICK
!

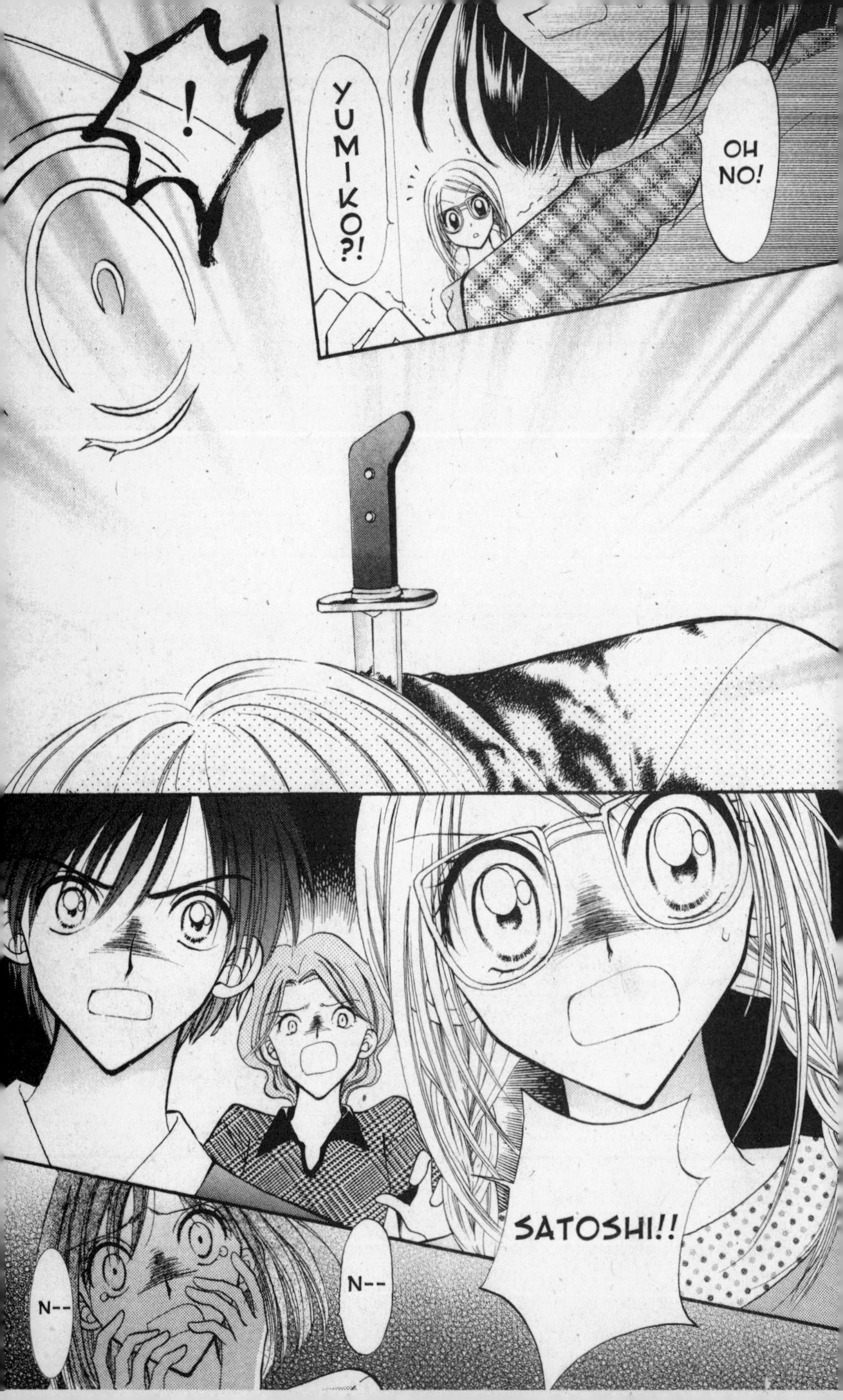
OH NO!
YUMIKO?!
!
SATOSHI!!
N--
N--

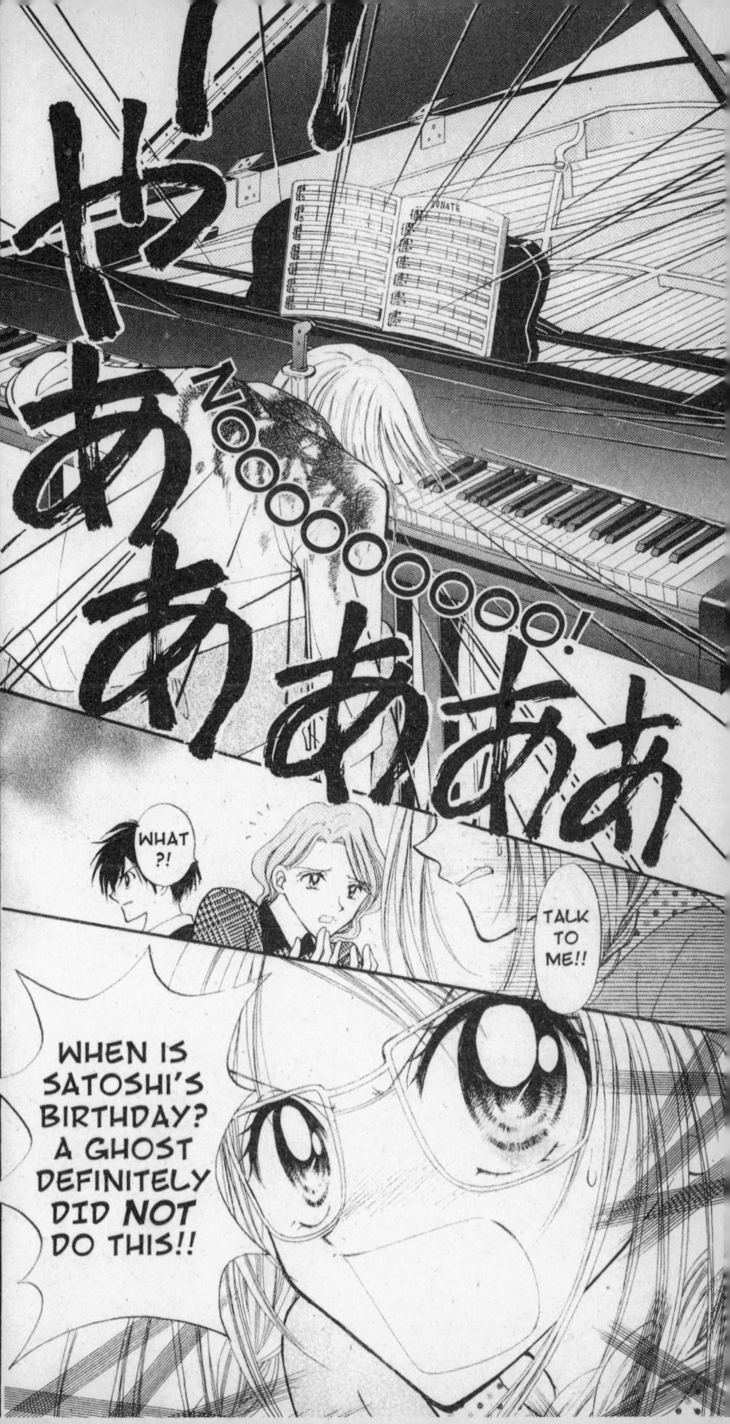

や!あああああ
NOOOOOOOOOOO!
SONATE
TALK TO ME!!
WHAT?!
WHEN IS SATOSHI'S BIRTHDAY? A GHOST DEFINITELY DID **NOT** DO THIS!!

☆ CHARACTER PROFILE ☆

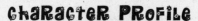

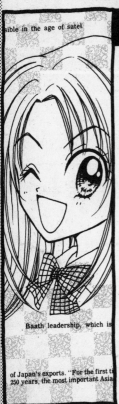

sible in the age of satel
Baath leadership, which is
of Japan's exports. "For the first ti
250 years, the most important Asia

Lili Hoshizawa

☆Birthday	April 16th
☆Sign	Aries
☆Blood Type	B
☆Favorite food	Grilled Beef
☆Favorite subject	P.E.
☆Least Favorite subject(s)	Anything other than P.E.
☆Favorite color	Red
☆Hobby	Wearing disguises
☆Special skills	Astrology, humor
☆Someone she respects	Her mother

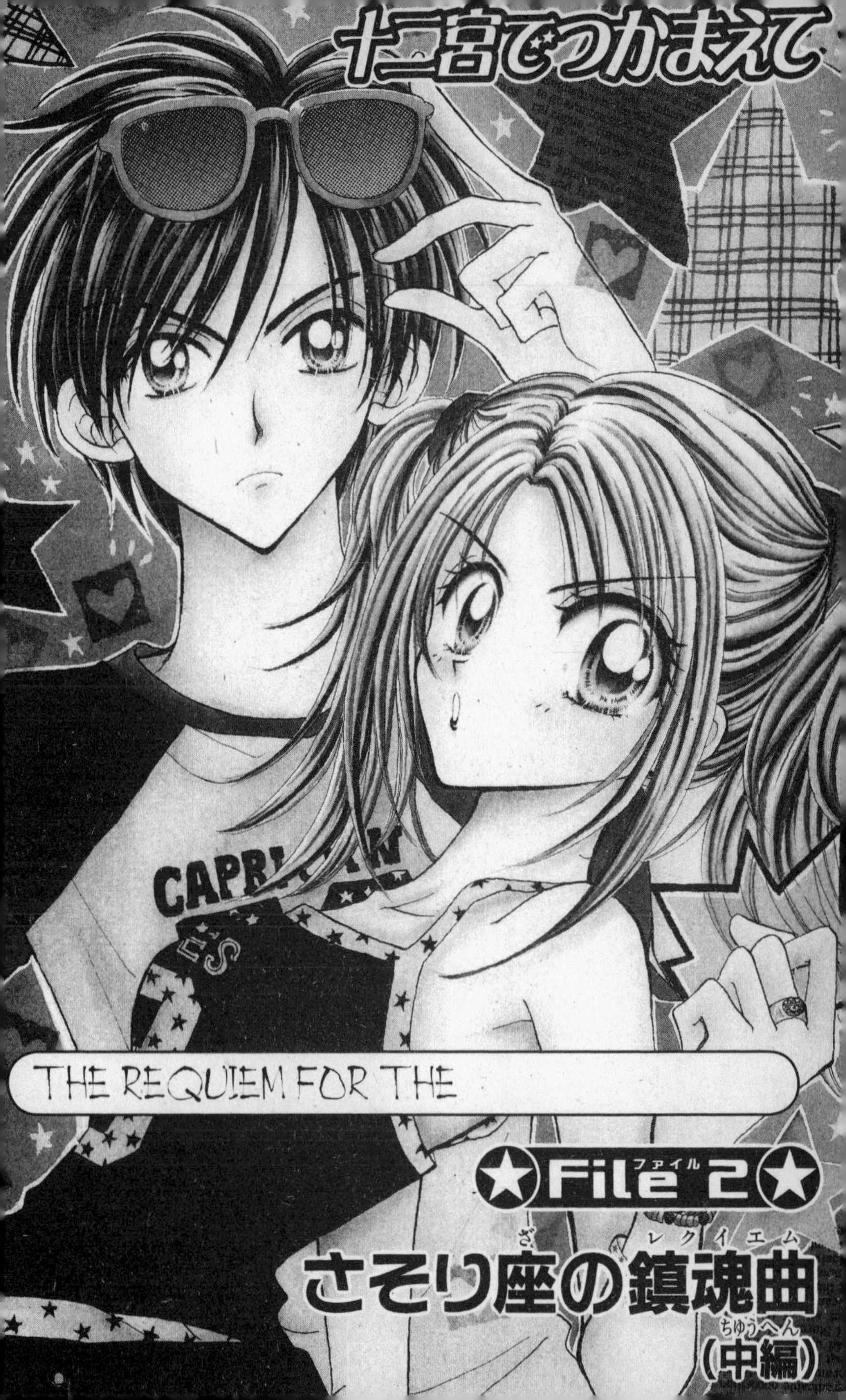
十二宮でつかまえて
THE REQUIEM FOR THE
★File 2★
さそり座の鎮魂曲
（中編）

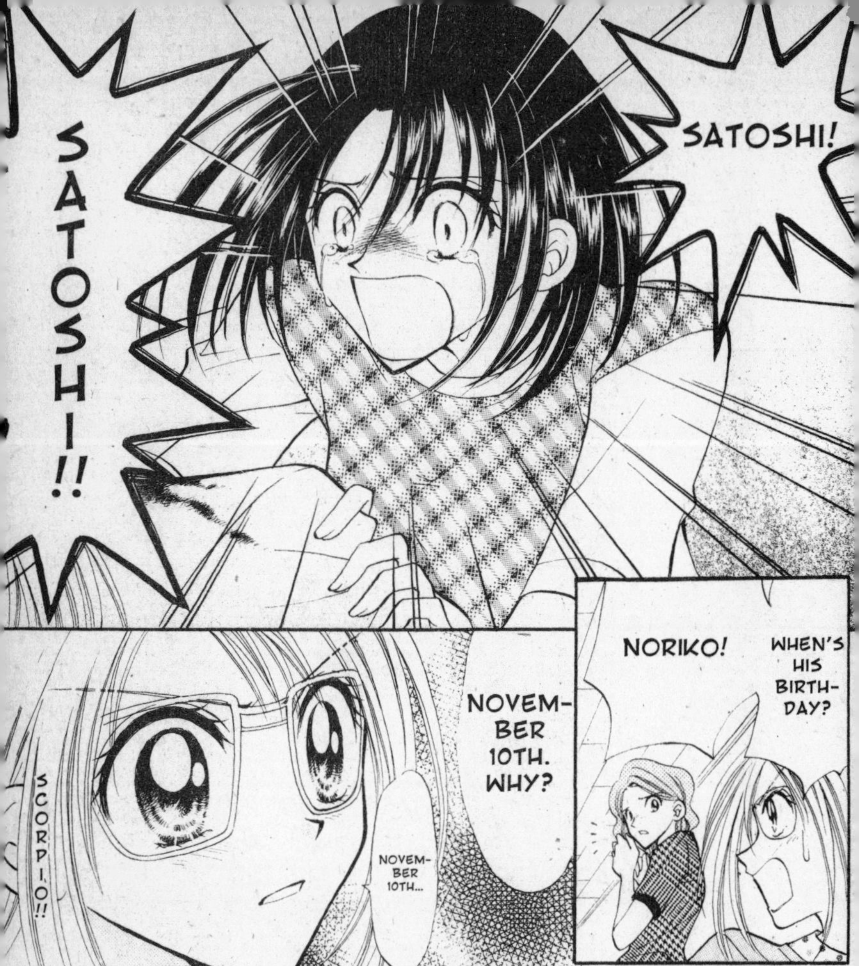
SATOSHI!
SATOSHI!!
WHEN'S HIS BIRTHDAY?
NORIKO!
NOVEMBER 10TH. WHY?
NOVEMBER 10TH...
SCORPIO!!

Mademoiselle Lili's Astrology (3)

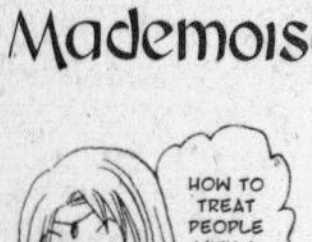
HOW TO TREAT PEOPLE WITH A PARTICULAR SIGN!

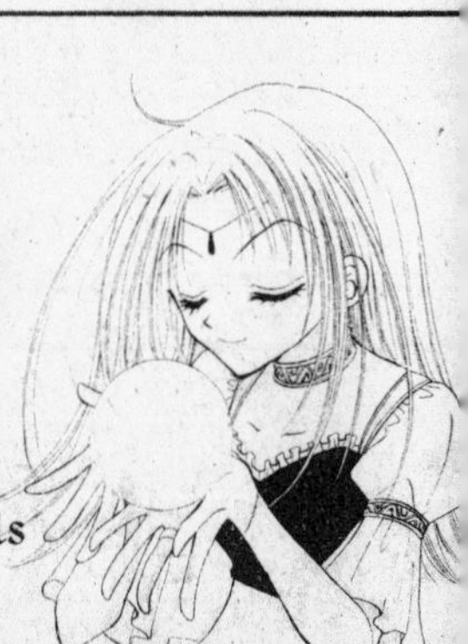

Virgo (Sign of Virgo) Demeter
I named her after Demeter, the Greek goddess of agriculture. The Virgo constellation is believed to take the shape of this goddess. Virgos are delicate and intelligent. They have great organizational skills and are great workers. To be good friends with a Virgo, watch your language! Girls, you must act like a lady if you're going to snag a Virgo for yourself.

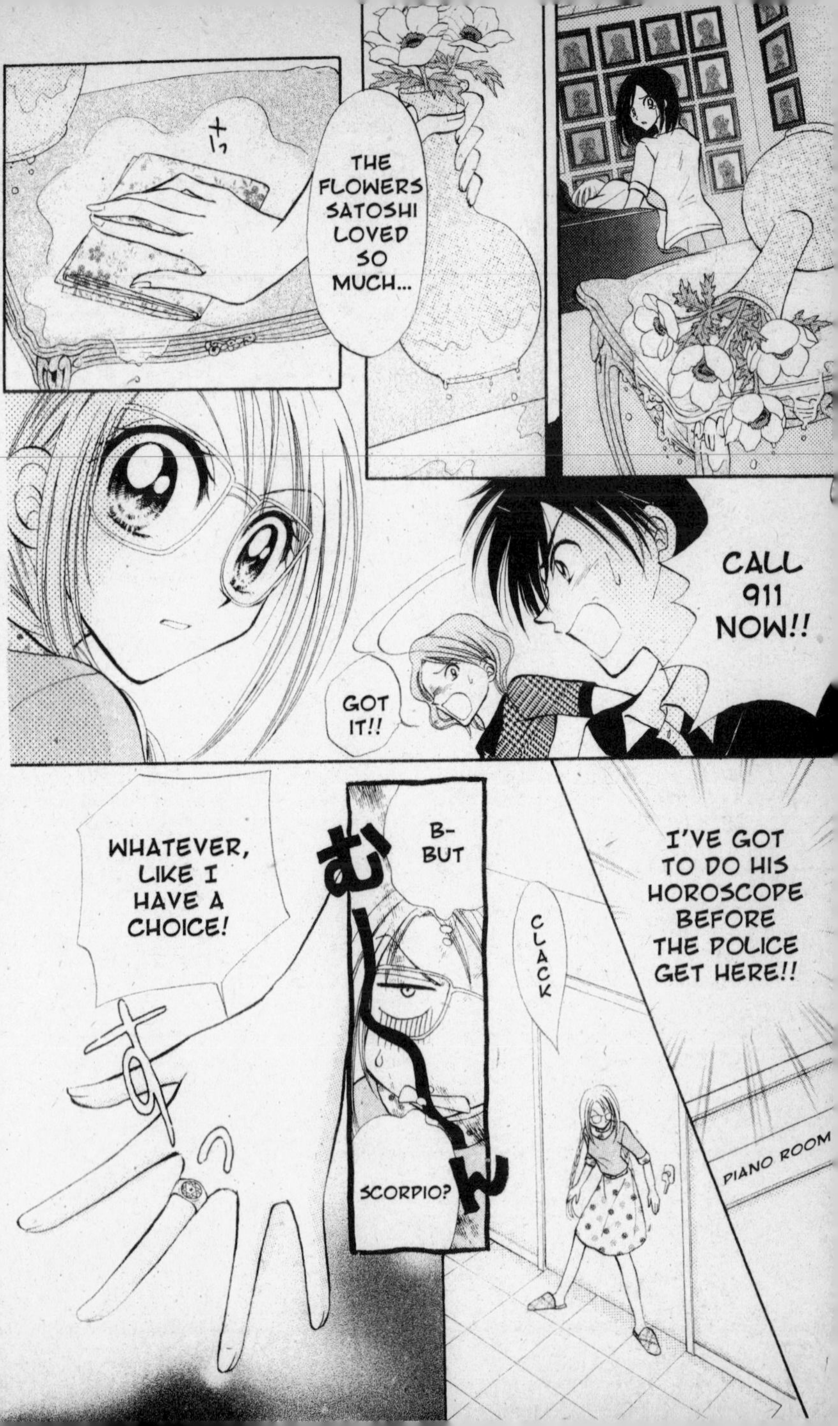
THE FLOWERS SATOSHI LOVED SO MUCH...
CALL 911 NOW!!
GOT IT!!
I'VE GOT TO DO HIS HOROSCOPE BEFORE THE POLICE GET HERE!!
CLACK
PIANO ROOM
B-BUT
SCORPIO?
WHATEVER, LIKE I HAVE A CHOICE!

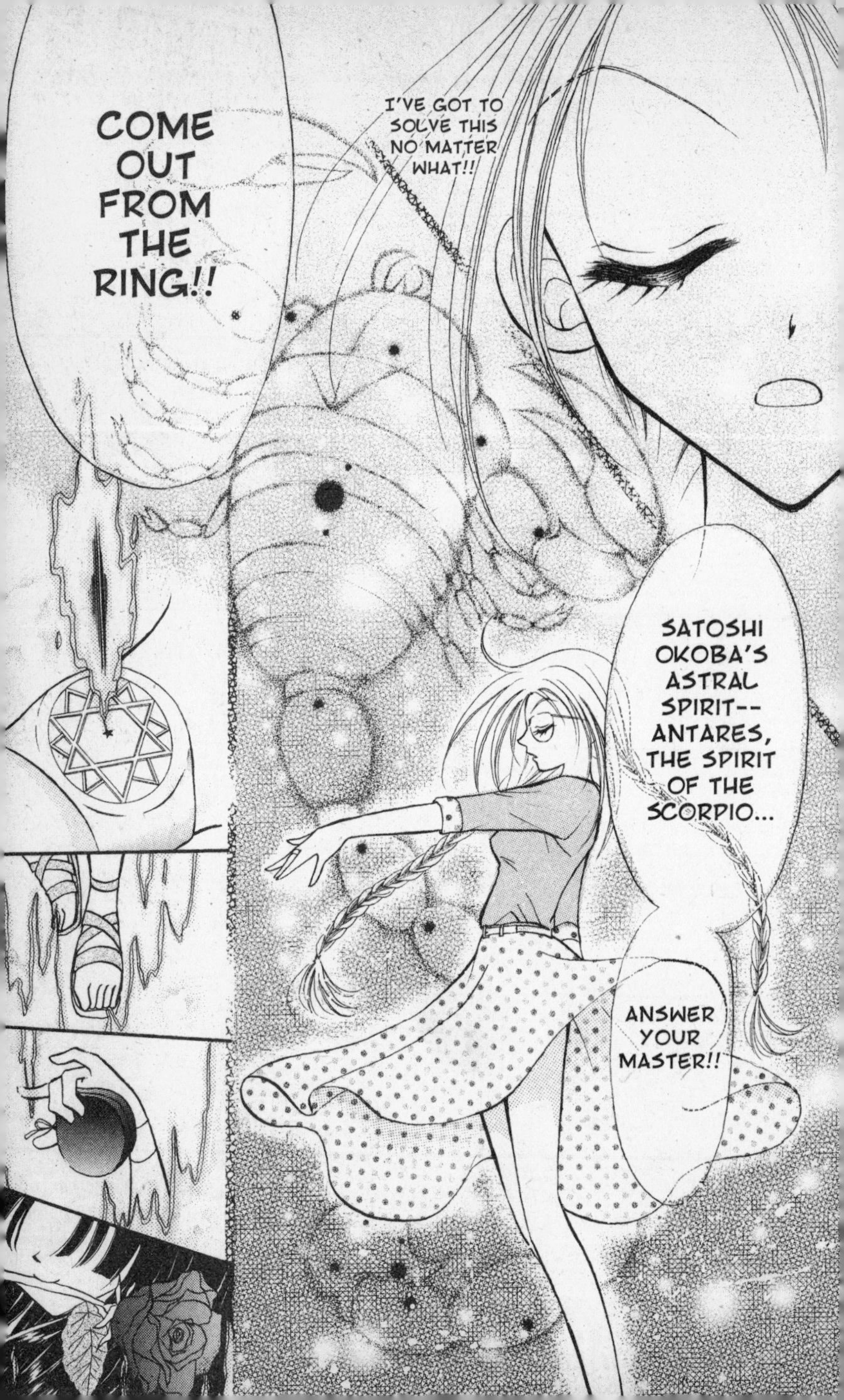
I'VE GOT TO SOLVE THIS NO MATTER WHAT!!
SATOSHI OKOBA'S ASTRAL SPIRIT-- ANTARES, THE SPIRIT OF THE SCORPIO...
ANSWER YOUR MASTER!!
COME OUT FROM THE RING!!

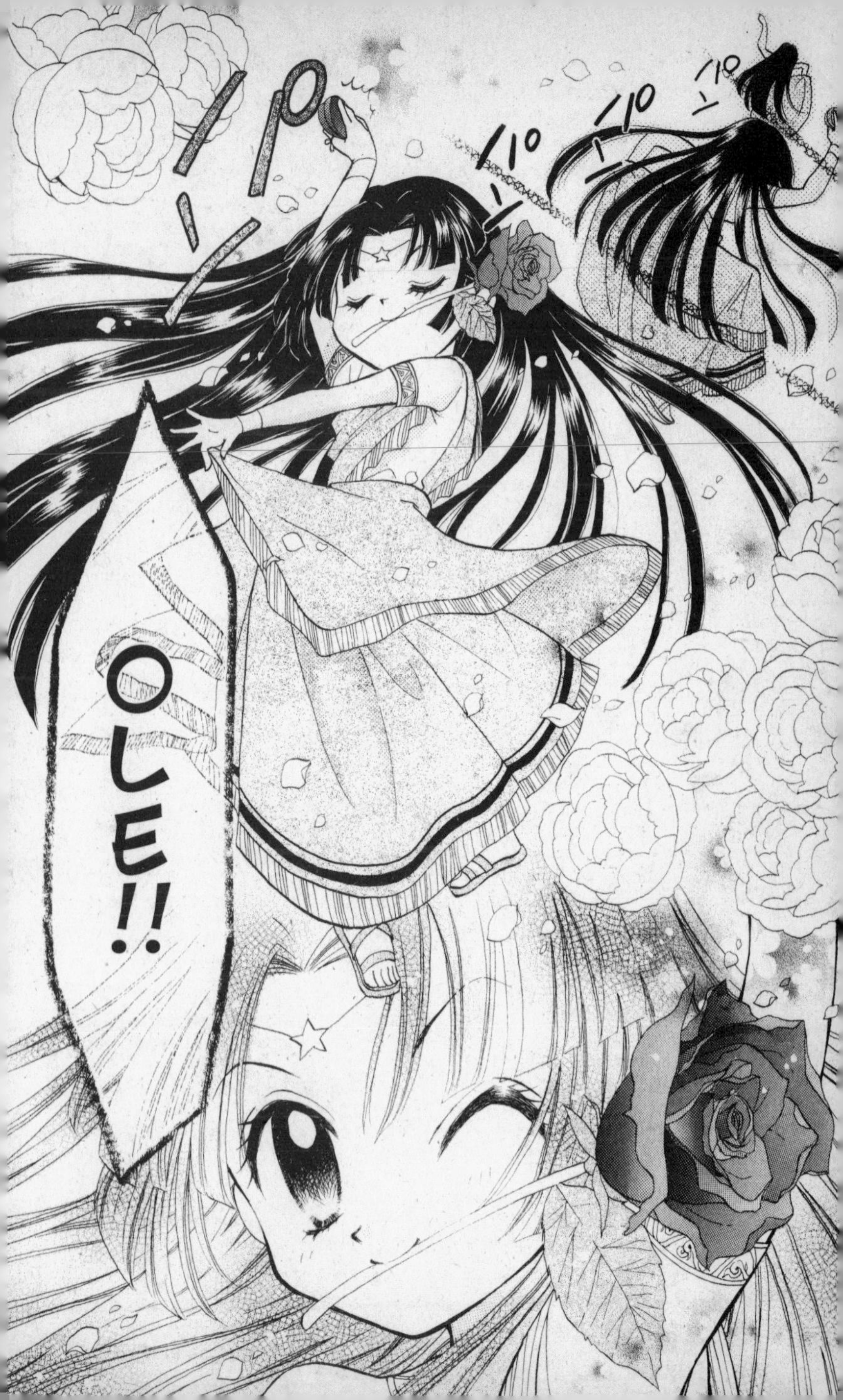
OLE!!

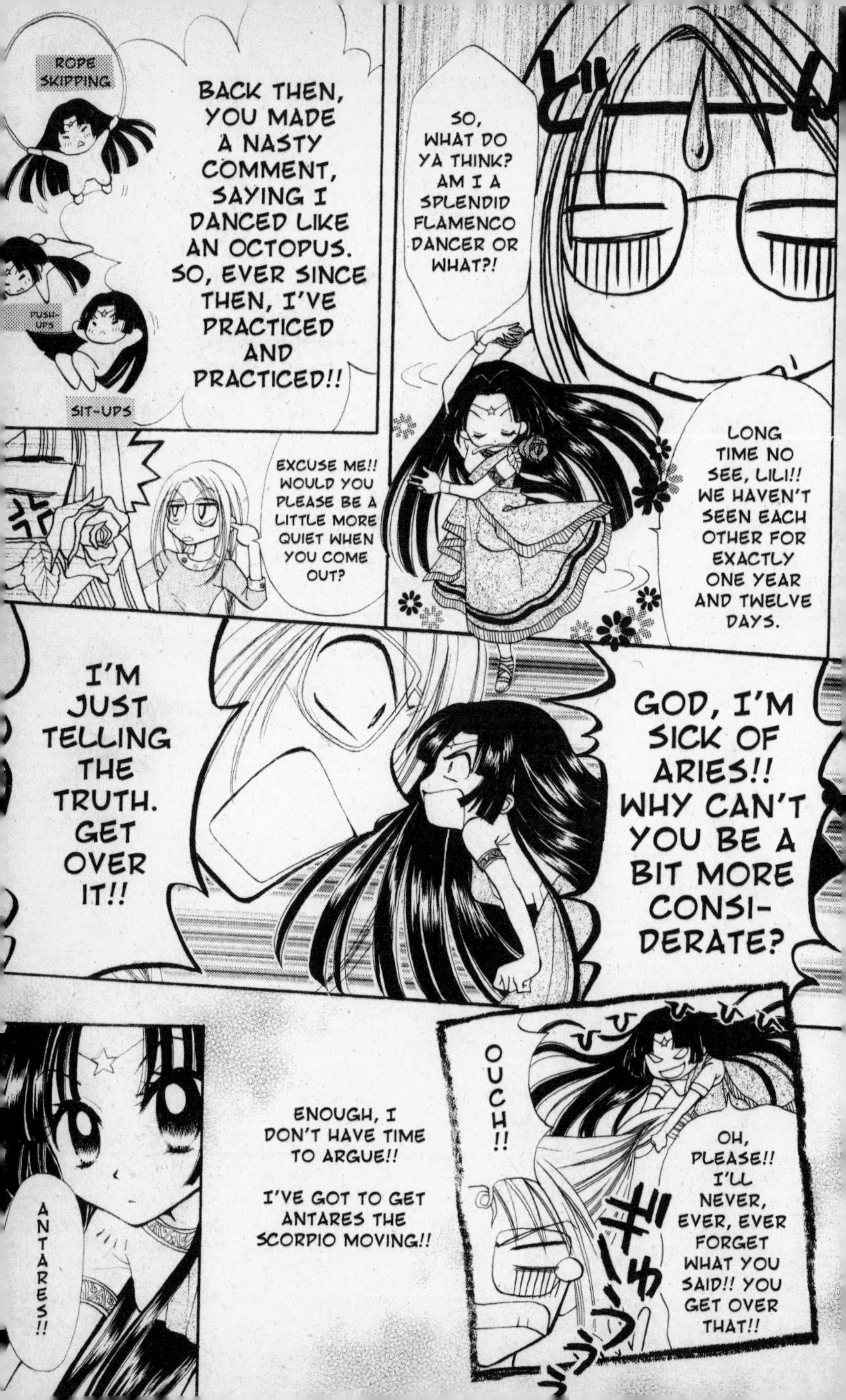
SO, WHAT DO YA THINK? AM I A SPLENDID FLAMENCO DANCER OR WHAT?!
LONG TIME NO SEE, LILI!! WE HAVEN'T SEEN EACH OTHER FOR EXACTLY ONE YEAR AND TWELVE DAYS.
BACK THEN, YOU MADE A NASTY COMMENT, SAYING I DANCED LIKE AN OCTOPUS. SO, EVER SINCE THEN, I'VE PRACTICED AND PRACTICED!!
ROPE SKIPPING
PUSH-UPS
SIT-UPS
EXCUSE ME!! WOULD YOU PLEASE BE A LITTLE MORE QUIET WHEN YOU COME OUT?
GOD, I'M SICK OF ARIES!! WHY CAN'T YOU BE A BIT MORE CONSI-DERATE?
I'M JUST TELLING THE TRUTH. GET OVER IT!!
OUCH!!
OH, PLEASE!! I'LL NEVER, EVER, EVER FORGET WHAT YOU SAID!! YOU GET OVER THAT!!
ENOUGH, I DON'T HAVE TIME TO ARGUE!!
I'VE GOT TO GET ANTARES THE SCORPIO MOVING!!
ANTARES!!

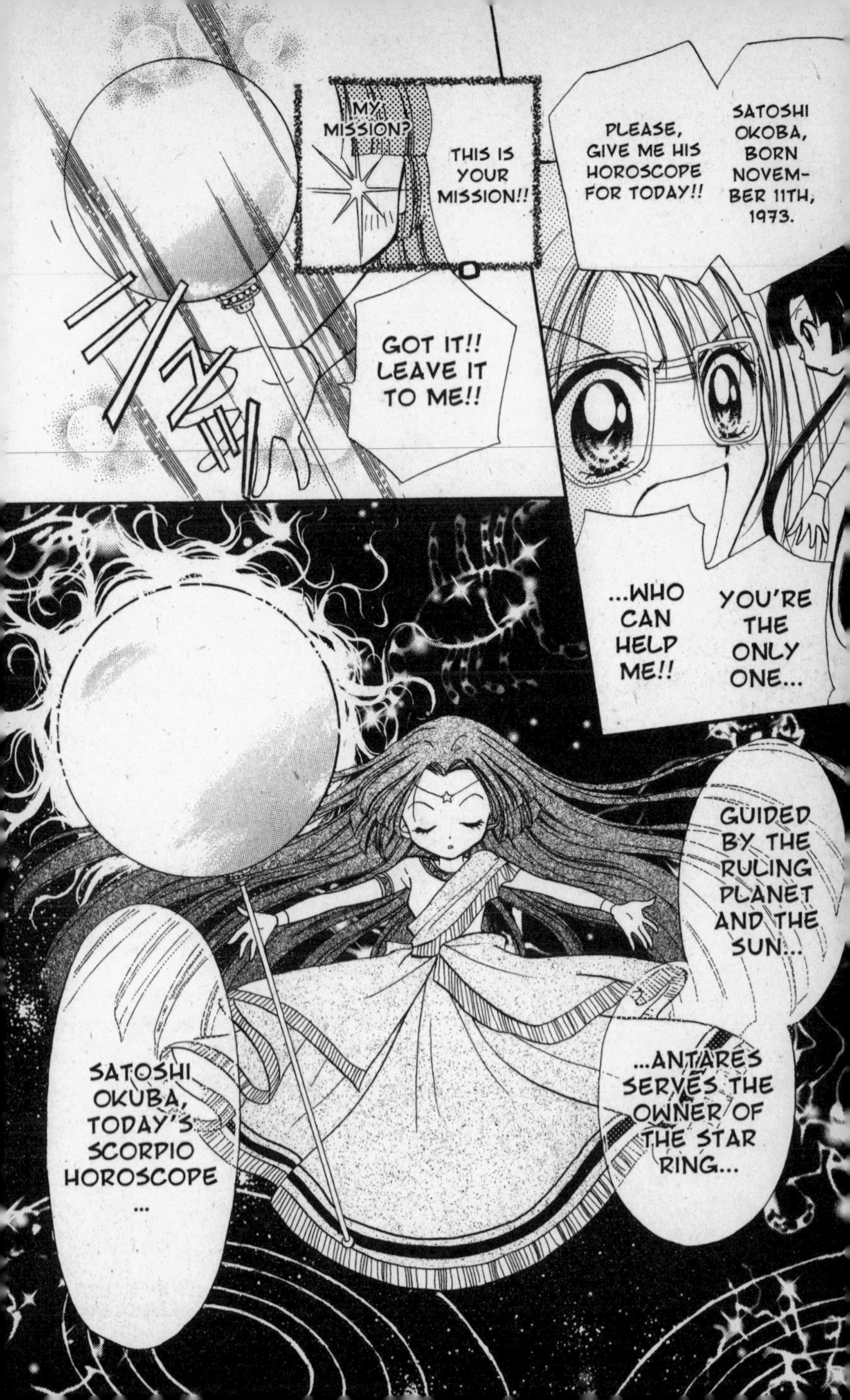
SATOSHI OKOBA, BORN NOVEMBER 11TH, 1973.
PLEASE, GIVE ME HIS HOROSCOPE FOR TODAY!!
YOU'RE THE ONLY ONE...
...WHO CAN HELP ME!!
MY MISSION?
THIS IS YOUR MISSION!!
GOT IT!! LEAVE IT TO ME!!
GUIDED BY THE RULING PLANET AND THE SUN...
...ANTARES SERVES THE OWNER OF THE STAR RING...
SATOSHI OKUBA, TODAY'S SCORPIO HOROSCOPE ...

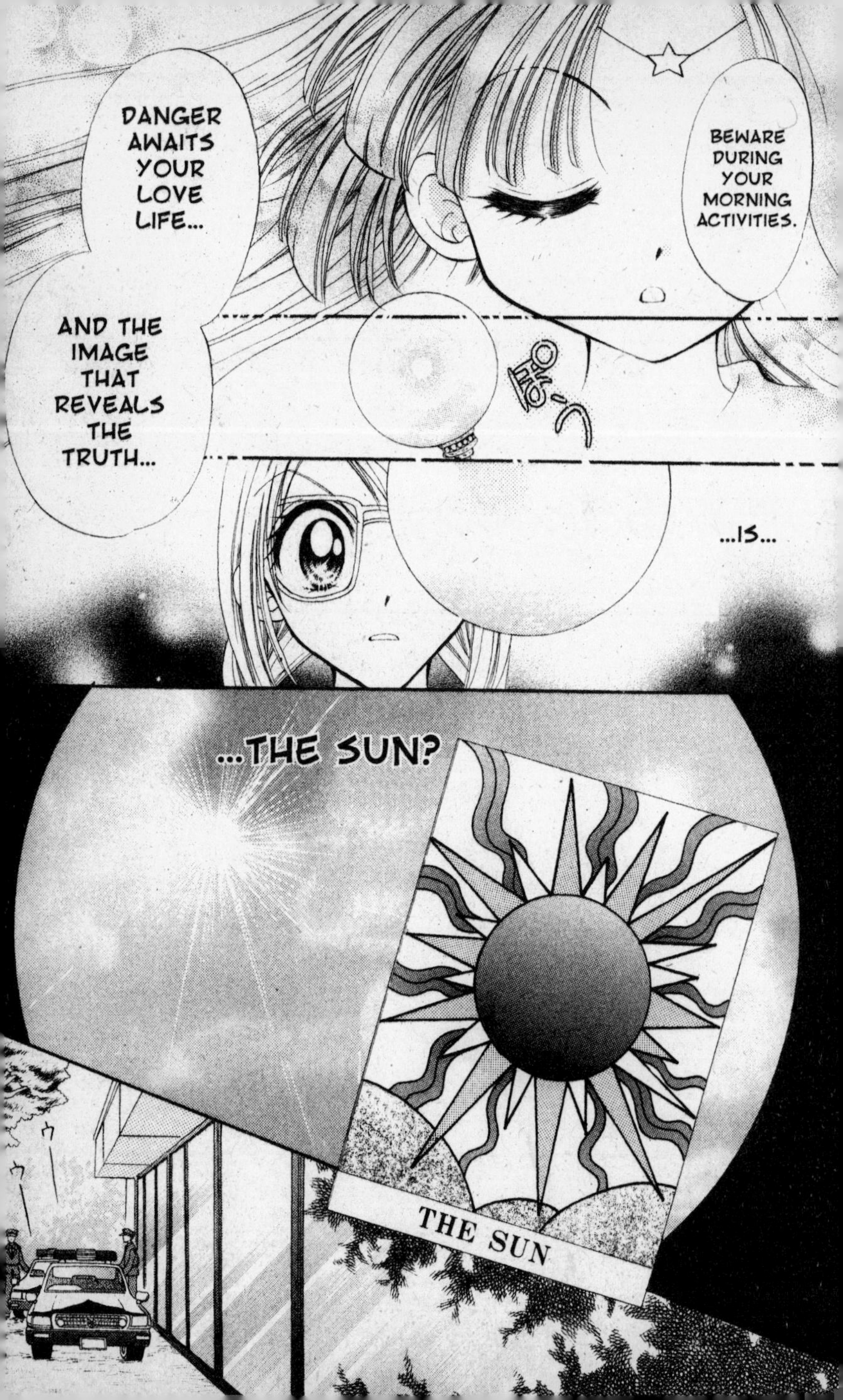
BEWARE DURING YOUR MORNING ACTIVITIES.
DANGER AWAITS YOUR LOVE LIFE...
AND THE IMAGE THAT REVEALS THE TRUTH...
...IS...
...THE SUN?
THE SUN

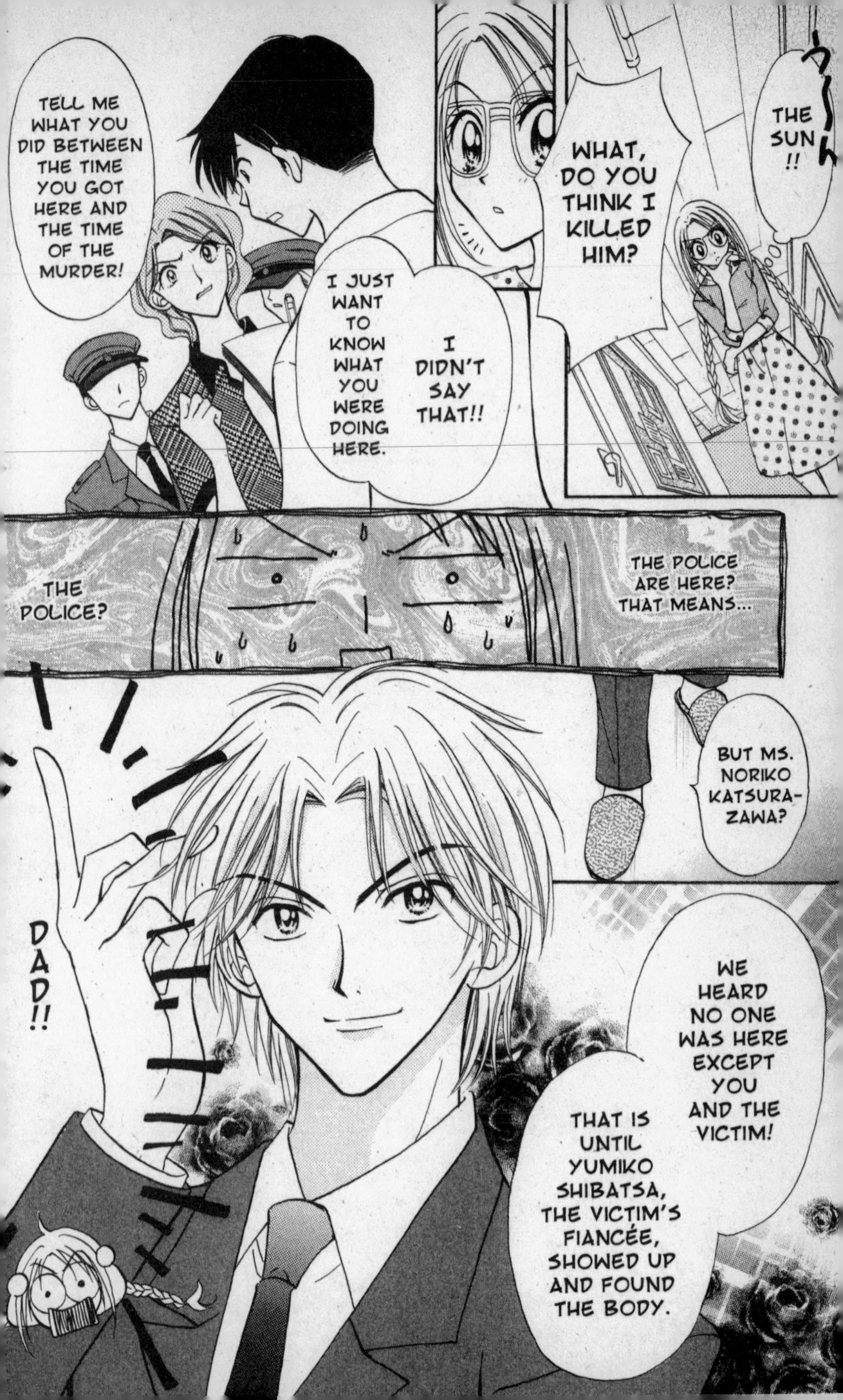

う～ん
THE SUN!!
WHAT, DO YOU THINK I KILLED HIM?
TELL ME WHAT YOU DID BETWEEN THE TIME YOU GOT HERE AND THE TIME OF THE MURDER!
I DIDN'T SAY THAT!!
I JUST WANT TO KNOW WHAT YOU WERE DOING HERE.
THE POLICE ARE HERE? THAT MEANS...
THE POLICE?
BUT MS. NORIKO KATSURA-ZAWA?
WE HEARD NO ONE WAS HERE EXCEPT YOU AND THE VICTIM!
THAT IS UNTIL YUMIKO SHIBATSA, THE VICTIM'S FIANCÉE, SHOWED UP AND FOUND THE BODY.
DAD!!

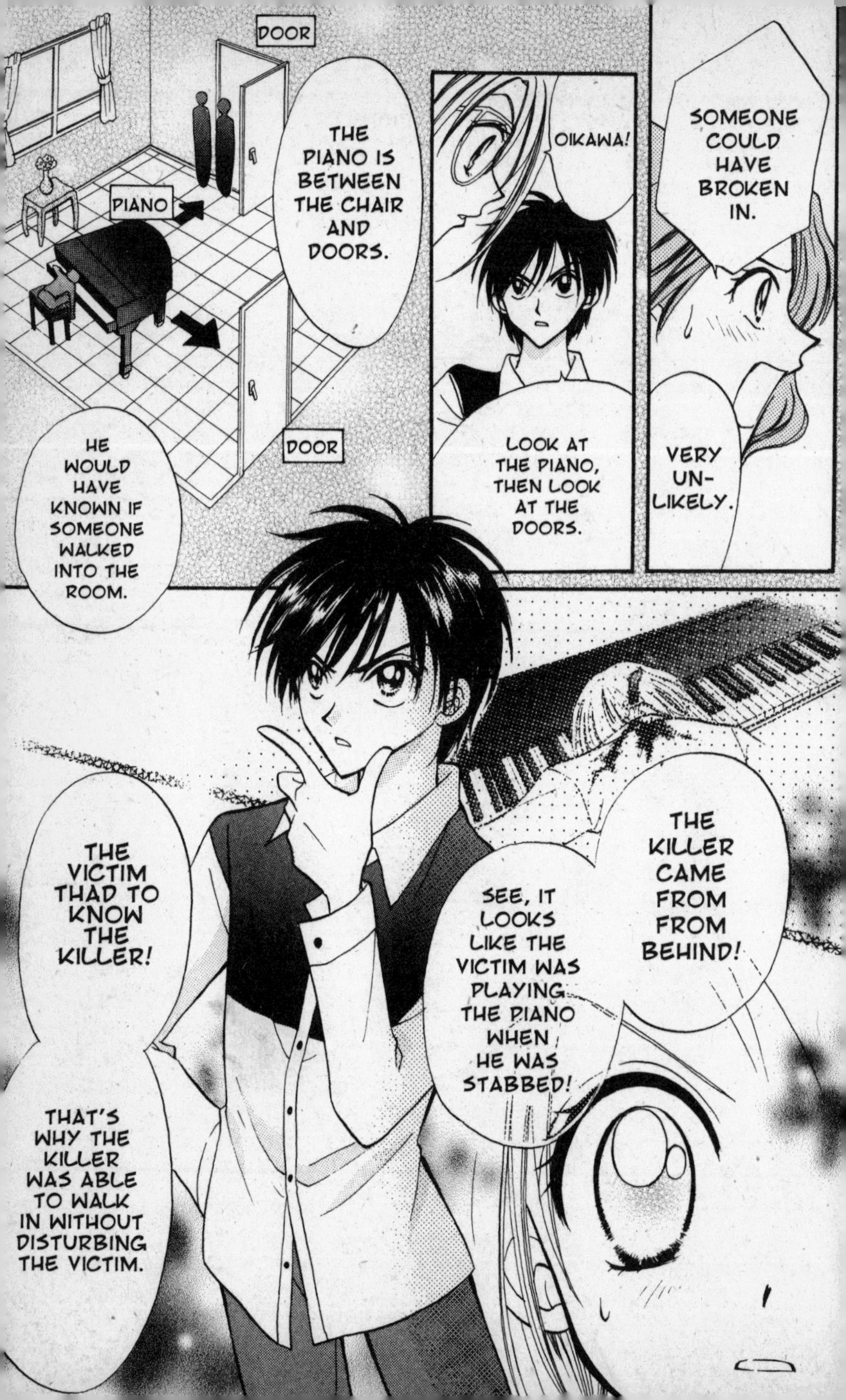
SOMEONE COULD HAVE BROKEN IN.
VERY UN-LIKELY.
OIKAWA!
LOOK AT THE PIANO, THEN LOOK AT THE DOORS.
THE PIANO IS BETWEEN THE CHAIR AND DOORS.
DOOR
PIANO
DOOR
HE WOULD HAVE KNOWN IF SOMEONE WALKED INTO THE ROOM.
THE KILLER CAME FROM FROM BEHIND!
SEE, IT LOOKS LIKE THE VICTIM WAS PLAYING THE PIANO WHEN HE WAS STABBED!
THE VICTIM THAD TO KNOW THE KILLER!
THAT'S WHY THE KILLER WAS ABLE TO WALK IN WITHOUT DISTURBING THE VICTIM.

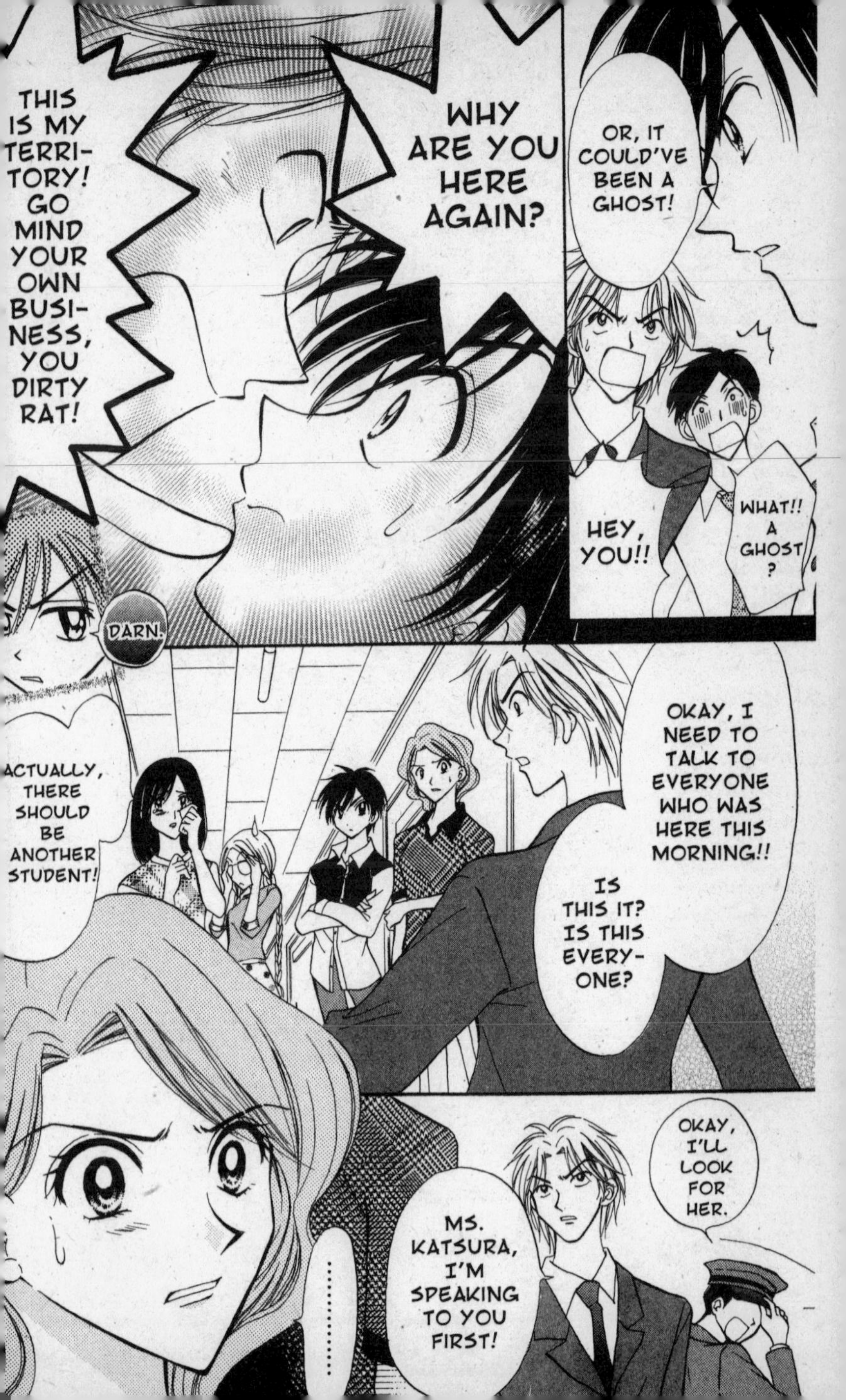
OR, IT COULD'VE BEEN A GHOST!
WHAT!! A GHOST?
HEY, YOU!!
WHY ARE YOU HERE AGAIN?
THIS IS MY TERRITORY! GO MIND YOUR OWN BUSINESS, YOU DIRTY RAT!
DARN.
OKAY, I NEED TO TALK TO EVERYONE WHO WAS HERE THIS MORNING!!
IS THIS IT? IS THIS EVERYONE?
ACTUALLY, THERE SHOULD BE ANOTHER STUDENT!
OKAY, I'LL LOOK FOR HER.
MS. KATSURA, I'M SPEAKING TO YOU FIRST!
......

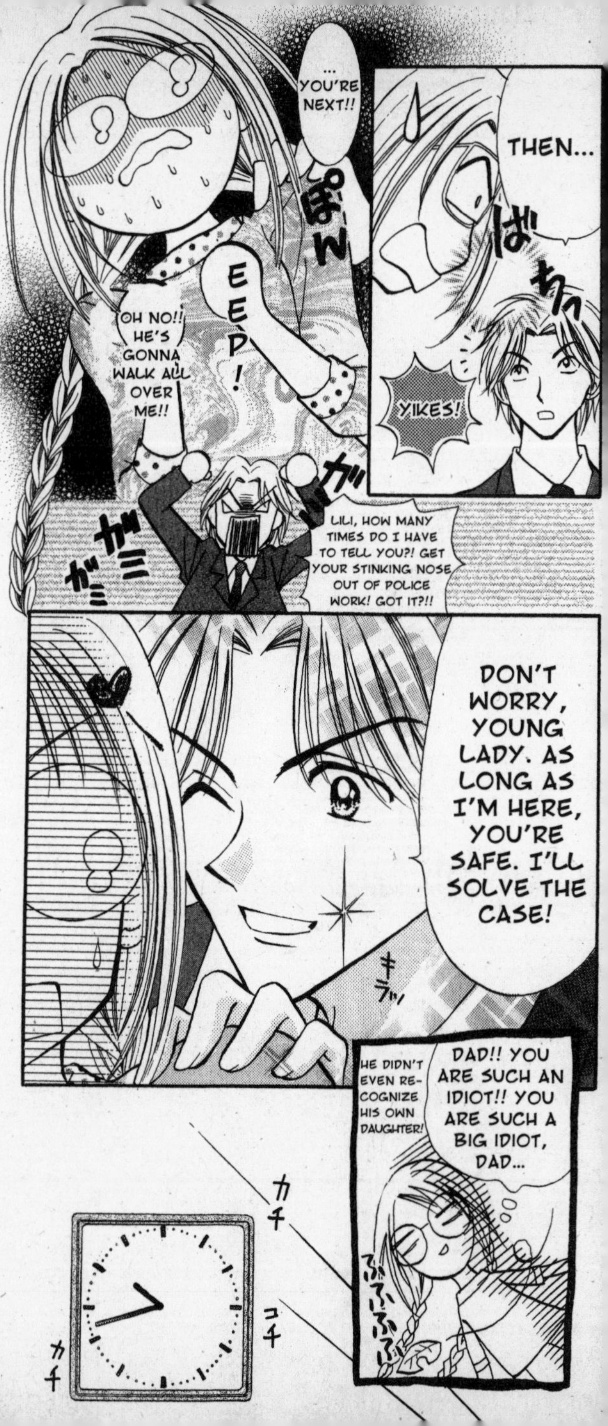
THEN...
ばちっ
YIKES!
... YOU'RE NEXT!!
ぽん
EEP!
OH NO!! HE'S GONNA WALK ALL OVER ME!!
ガッ
LILI, HOW MANY TIMES DO I HAVE TO TELL YOU?! GET YOUR STINKING NOSE OUT OF POLICE WORK! GOT IT?!!
ガミガミ
DON'T WORRY, YOUNG LADY. AS LONG AS I'M HERE, YOU'RE SAFE. I'LL SOLVE THE CASE!
キラッ
DAD!! YOU ARE SUCH AN IDIOT!! YOU ARE SUCH A BIG IDIOT, DAD...
HE DIDN'T EVEN RE-COGNIZE HIS OWN DAUGHTER!
ふふふふふ
カチ
コチ
カチ

Kobe

I went to Kobe for vacation. I've been there before, but last time I went, I almost freaked out! I wanted to see the city skyline at night. You can see it if you take the cablecar. So that's what I did. But there was one itty, bitty problem: I'm terrified of heights!! I just about wet my pants before I calmed down enough to look out the window. I couldnt look long, but I could tell the lights were beautiful, glittering like little gemstones.

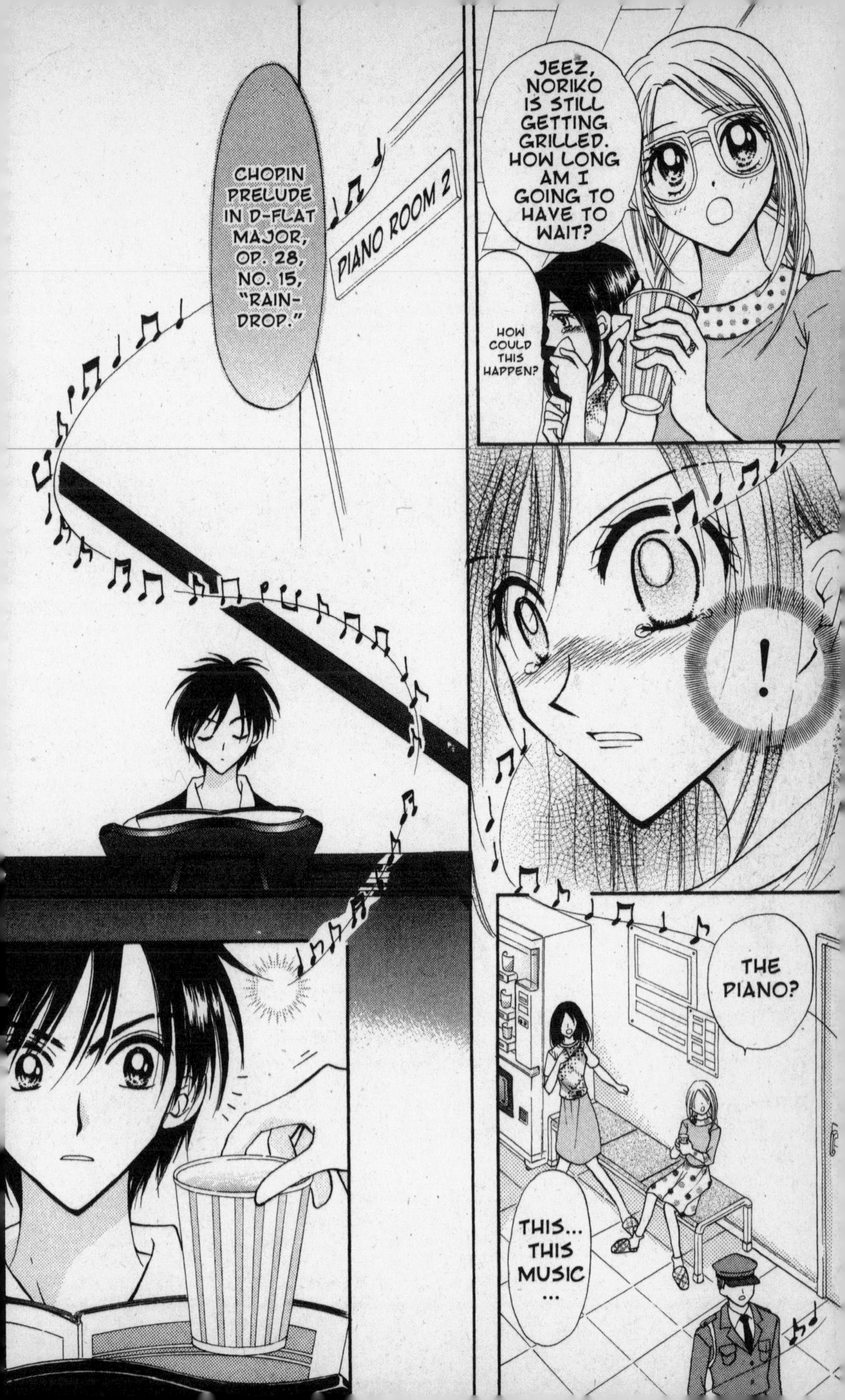
JEEZ, NORIKO IS STILL GETTING GRILLED. HOW LONG AM I GOING TO HAVE TO WAIT?
HOW COULD THIS HAPPEN?
!
THE PIANO?
THIS... THIS MUSIC...
CHOPIN PRELUDE IN D-FLAT MAJOR, OP. 28, NO. 15, "RAIN-DROP."
PIANO ROOM 2

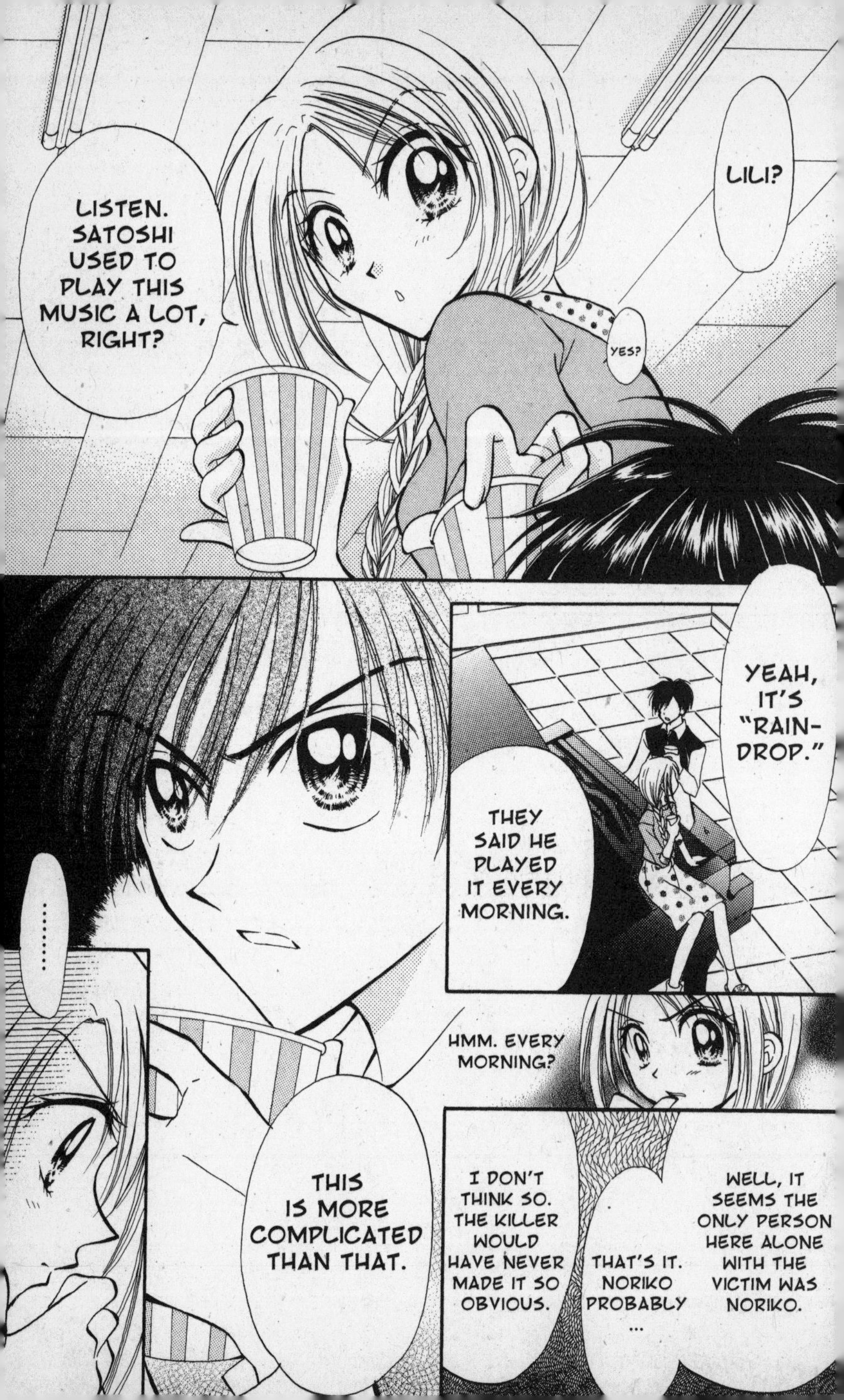
LILI?
YES?
LISTEN. SATOSHI USED TO PLAY THIS MUSIC A LOT, RIGHT?
YEAH, IT'S "RAIN-DROP."
THEY SAID HE PLAYED IT EVERY MORNING.
......
HMM. EVERY MORNING?
WELL, IT SEEMS THE ONLY PERSON HERE ALONE WITH THE VICTIM WAS NORIKO.
THAT'S IT. NORIKO PROBABLY ...
I DON'T THINK SO. THE KILLER WOULD HAVE NEVER MADE IT SO OBVIOUS.
THIS IS MORE COMPLICATED THAN THAT.

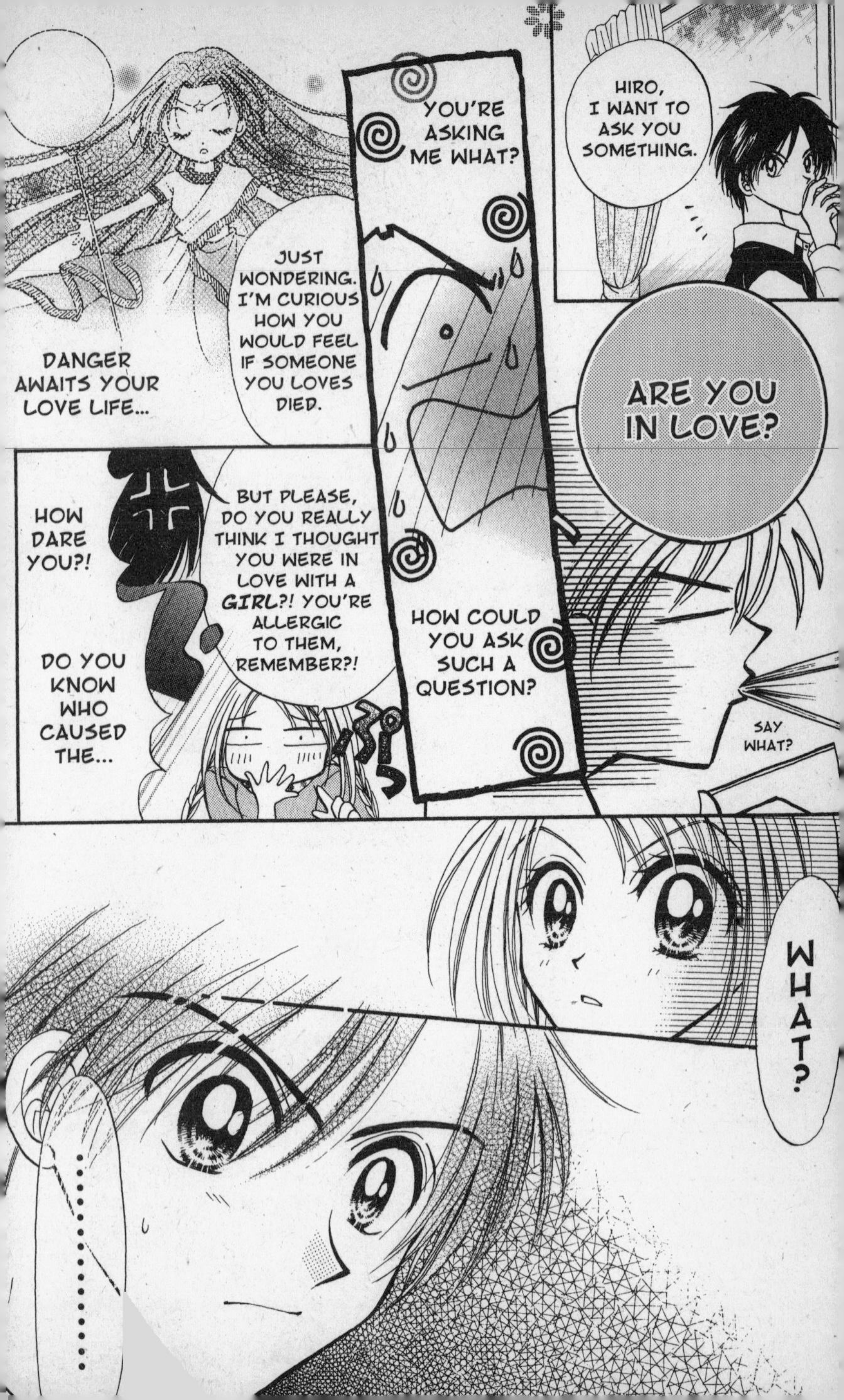
HIRO, I WANT TO ASK YOU SOMETHING.
ARE YOU IN LOVE?
SAY WHAT?
YOU'RE ASKING ME WHAT?
HOW COULD YOU ASK SUCH A QUESTION?
JUST WONDERING. I'M CURIOUS HOW YOU WOULD FEEL IF SOMEONE YOU LOVES DIED.
DANGER AWAITS YOUR LOVE LIFE...
BUT PLEASE, DO YOU REALLY THINK I THOUGHT YOU WERE IN LOVE WITH A GIRL?! YOU'RE ALLERGIC TO THEM, REMEMBER?!
HOW DARE YOU?!
DO YOU KNOW WHO CAUSED THE...
WHAT?
......

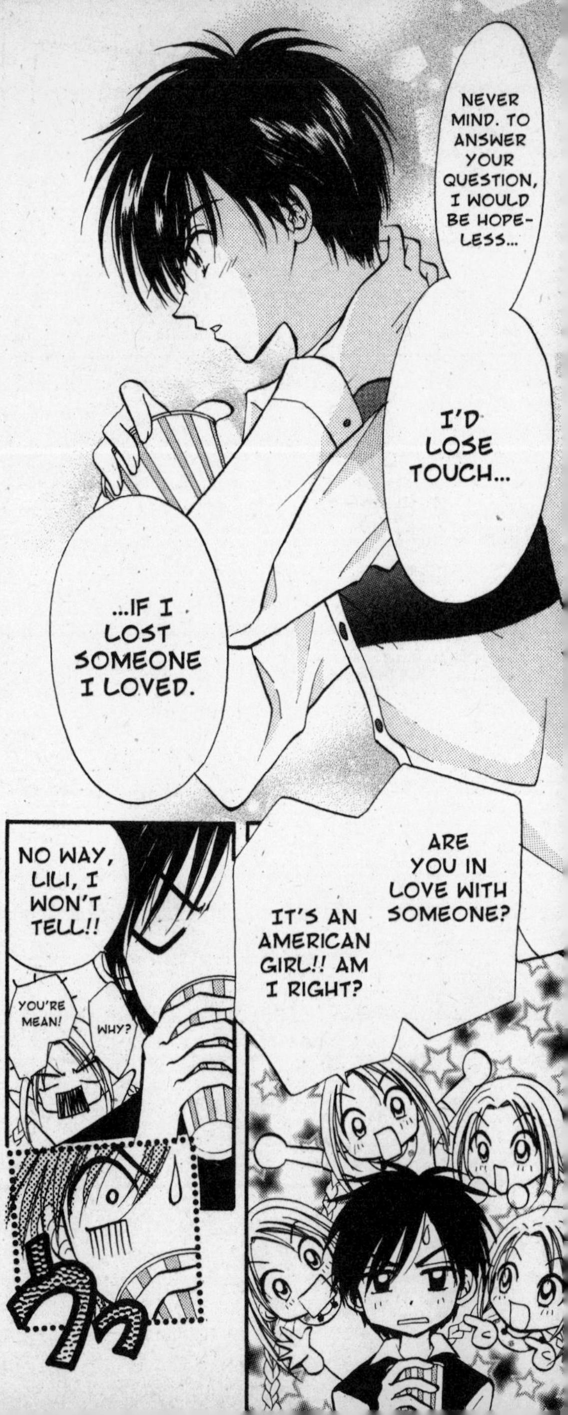
NEVER MIND. TO ANSWER YOUR QUESTION, I WOULD BE HOPE-LESS...
I'D LOSE TOUCH...
...IF I LOST SOMEONE I LOVED.
ARE YOU IN LOVE WITH SOMEONE?
IT'S AN AMERICAN GIRL!! AM I RIGHT?
NO WAY, LILI, I WON'T TELL!!
WHY?
YOU'RE MEAN!
うっ

Letters

The last time I wrote a letter, I said you could send me a self-addressed, stamped envelope, and I would send you something special. That something special is a thank you note. But some fans write to me and forget to give me their name and address. Without that info, I can't send you a thank you note. Also, some of you want me to fill out a biography sheet, with all of my important stats. In Japan, those profiles are called sign cho papers. I'm sorry, they take so long to fill out, I can't possibly do those.

One thing I do enjoy doing: purikuras. You know, those are photobooths that print your picture on a sticker. You can choose your background, and I love the cute little backgrounds.

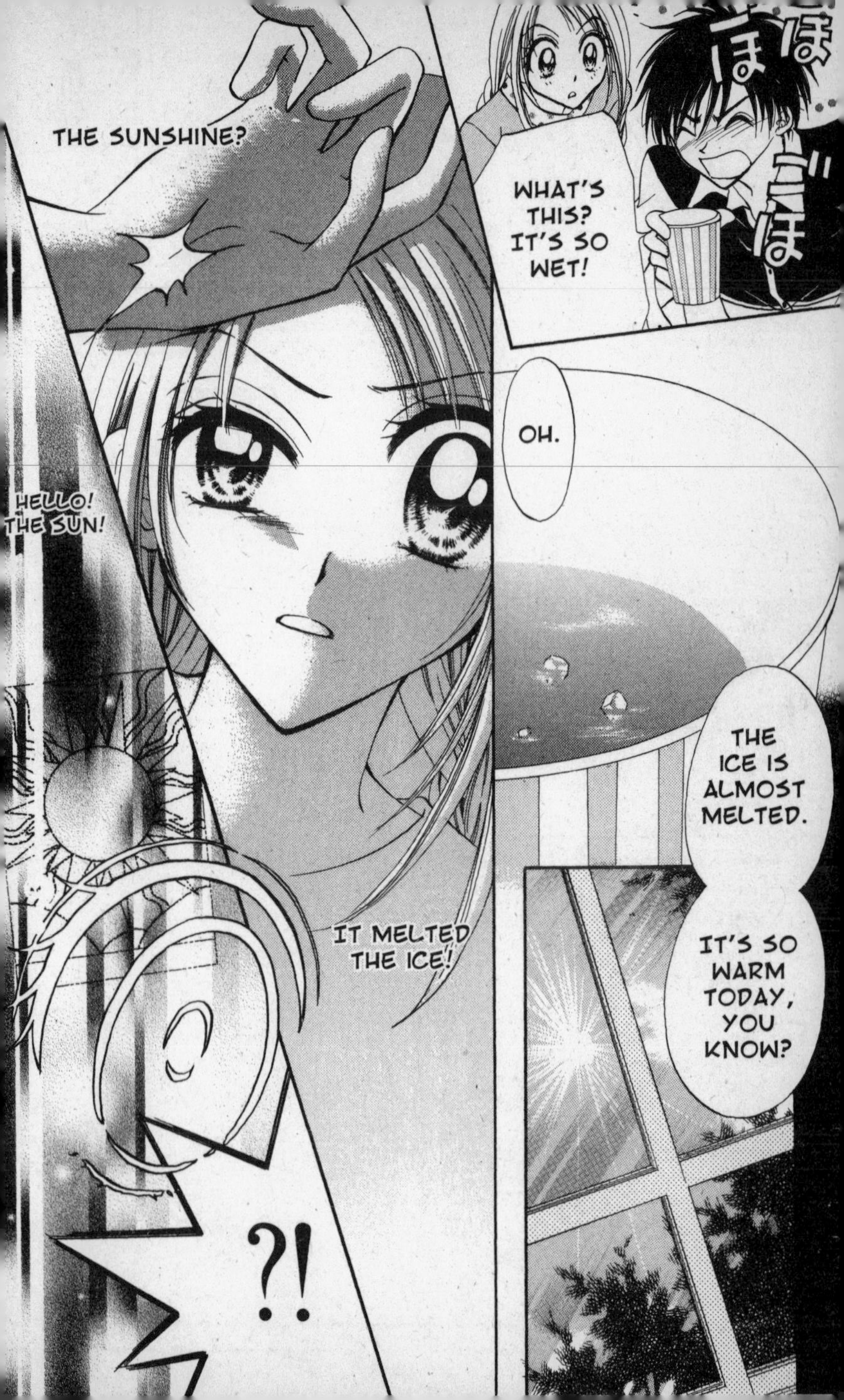
WHAT'S THIS? IT'S SO WET!
OH.
THE ICE IS ALMOST MELTED.
IT'S SO WARM TODAY, YOU KNOW?
THE SUNSHINE?
HELLO! THE SUN!
IT MELTED THE ICE!
?!

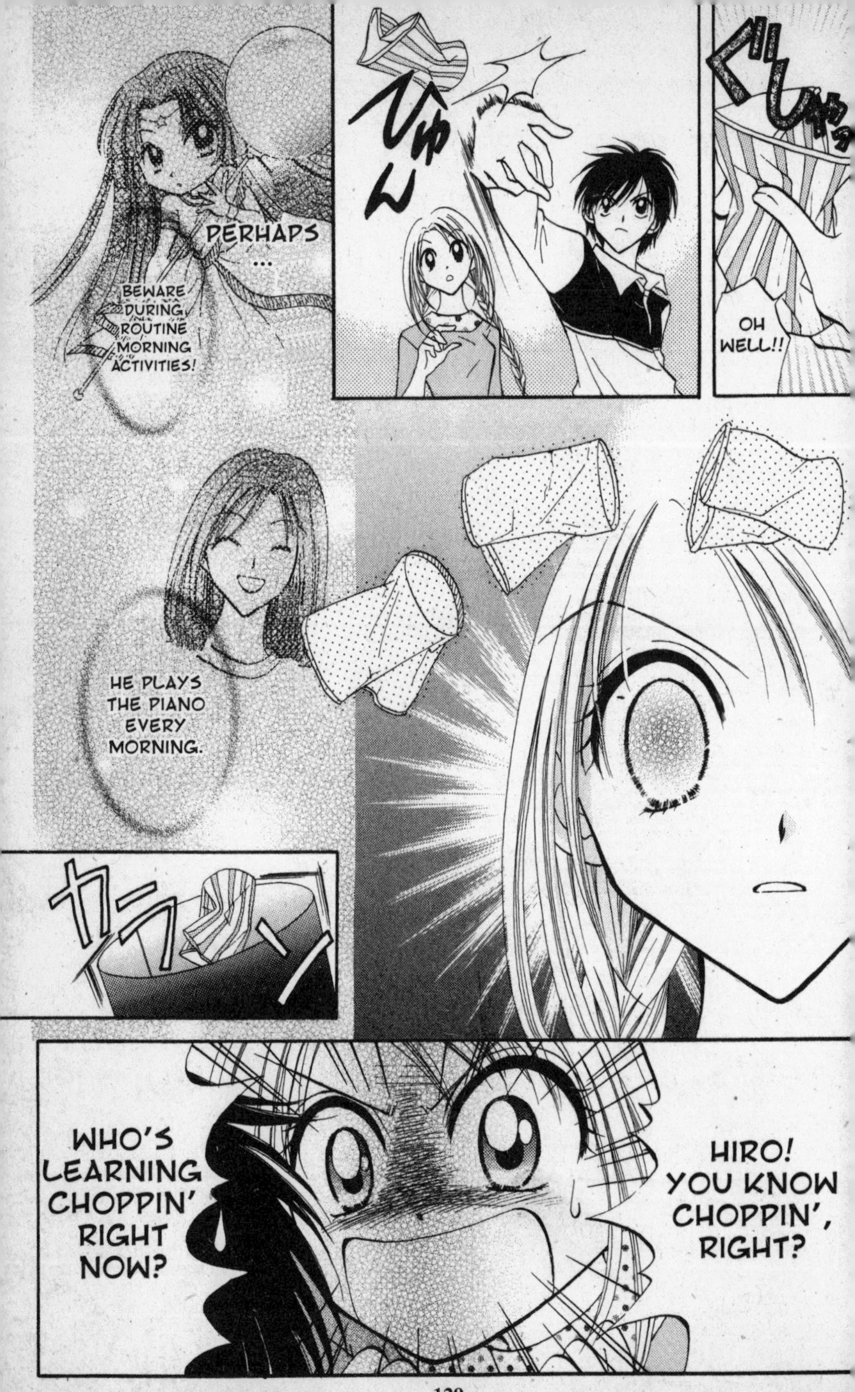
くしゃっ
OH WELL!!
ひゅん
PERHAPS...
BEWARE DURING ROUTINE MORNING ACTIVITIES!
HE PLAYS THE PIANO EVERY MORNING.
カラーン
HIRO! YOU KNOW CHOPPIN', RIGHT?
WHO'S LEARNING CHOPPIN' RIGHT NOW?

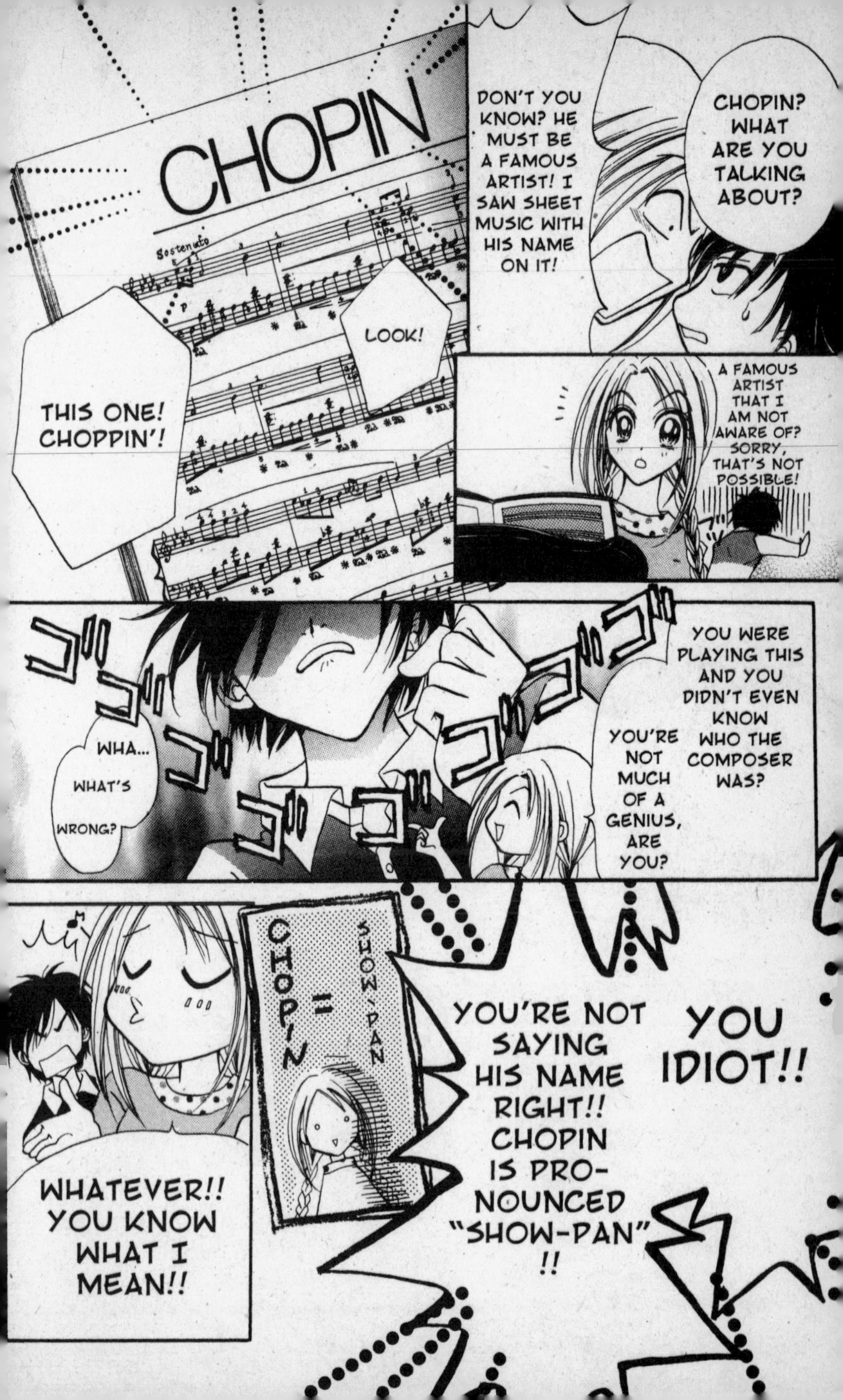
CHOPIN? WHAT ARE YOU TALKING ABOUT?
DON'T YOU KNOW? HE MUST BE A FAMOUS ARTIST! I SAW SHEET MUSIC WITH HIS NAME ON IT!
A FAMOUS ARTIST THAT I AM NOT AWARE OF? SORRY, THAT'S NOT POSSIBLE!
LOOK!
CHOPIN
Sostenuto
THIS ONE! CHOPPIN'!
ゴゴゴ
YOU WERE PLAYING THIS AND YOU DIDN'T EVEN KNOW WHO THE COMPOSER WAS?
YOU'RE NOT MUCH OF A GENIUS, ARE YOU?
WHA... WHAT'S WRONG?
YOU IDIOT!!
YOU'RE NOT SAYING HIS NAME RIGHT!! CHOPIN IS PRO-NOUNCED "SHOW-PAN"!!
CHOPIN = SHOW-PAN
WHATEVER!! YOU KNOW WHAT I MEAN!!

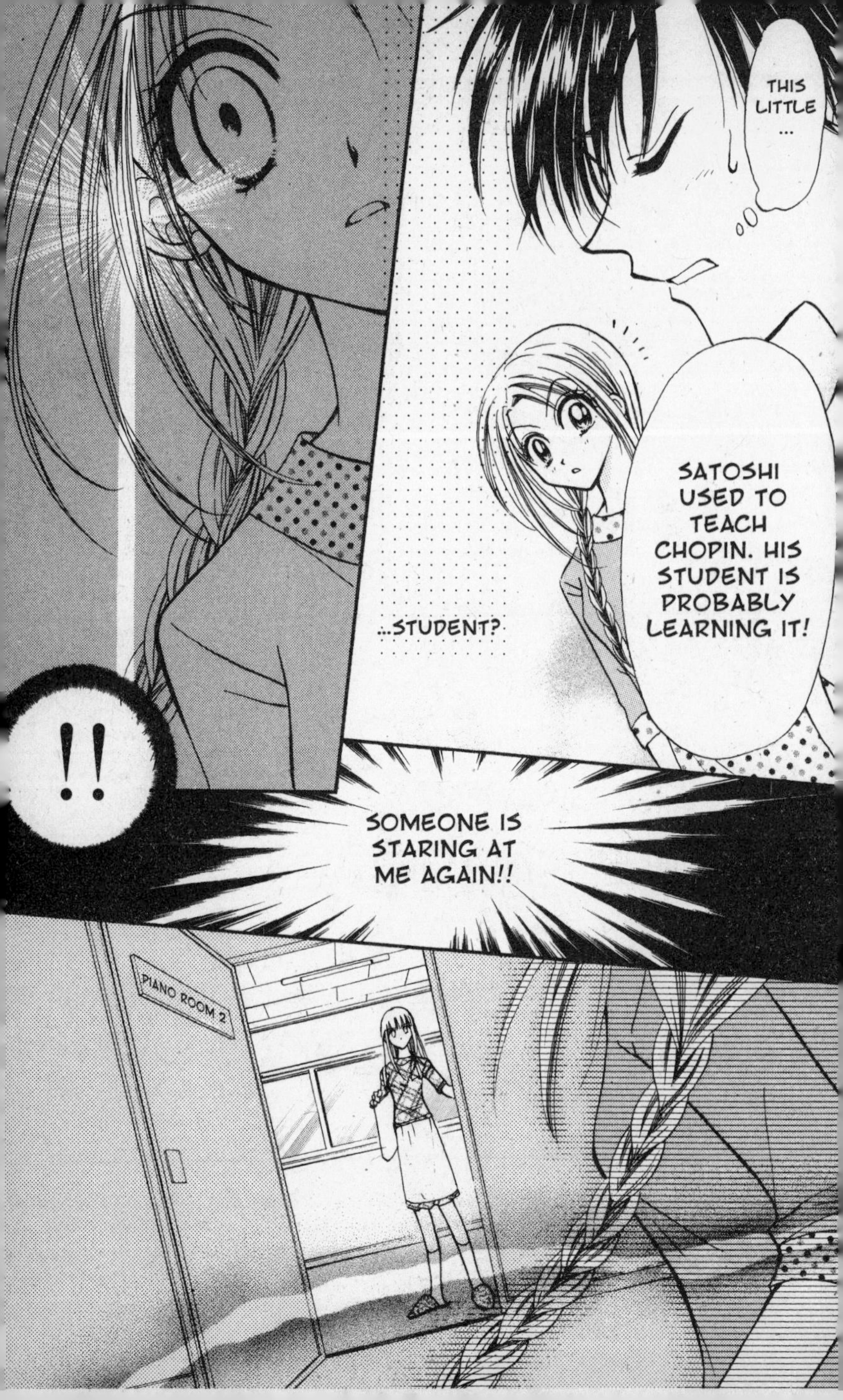
THIS LITTLE ...
SATOSHI USED TO TEACH CHOPIN. HIS STUDENT IS PROBABLY LEARNING IT!
...STUDENT?
!!
SOMEONE IS STARING AT ME AGAIN!!
PIANO ROOM 2

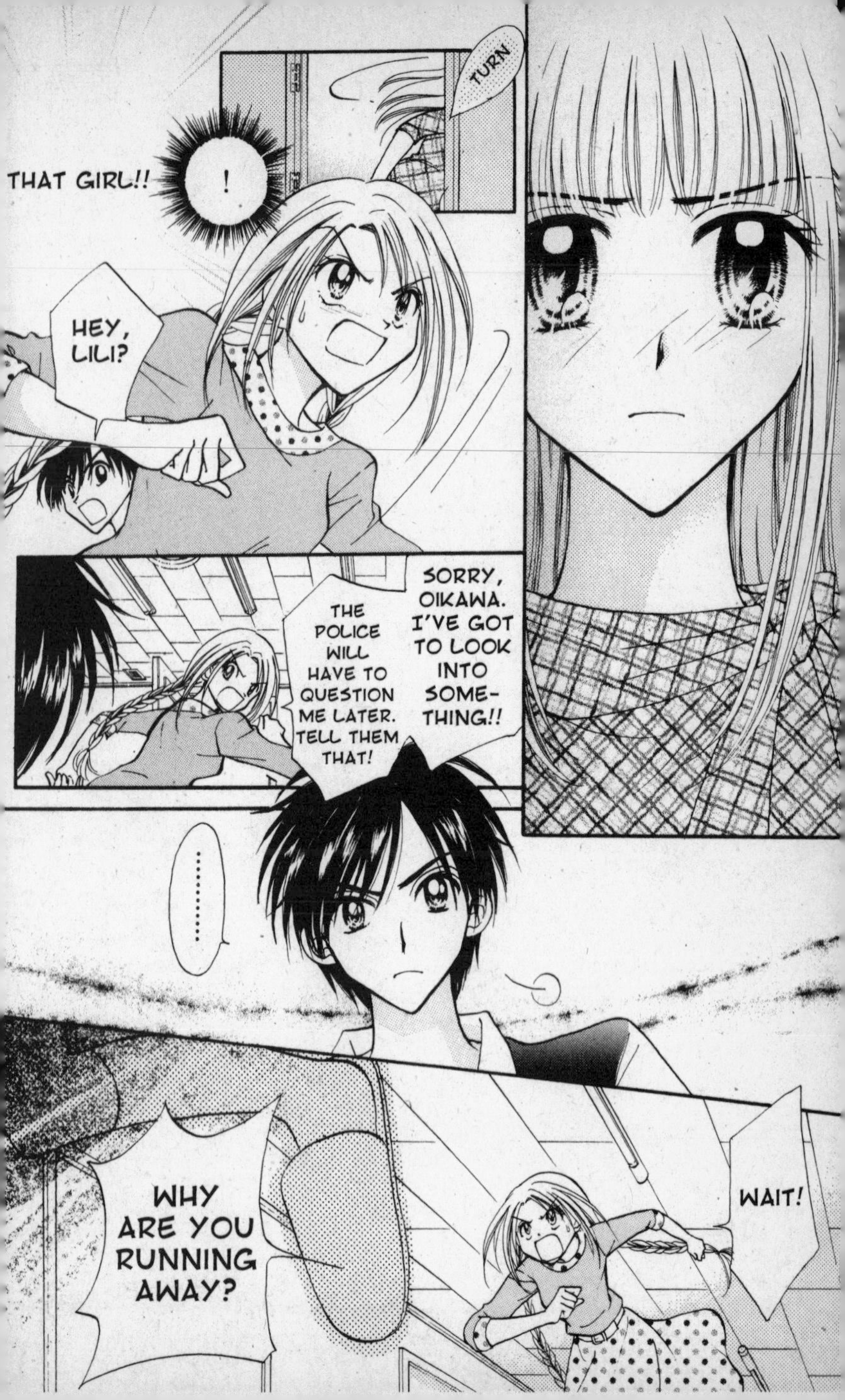
TURN
!
THAT GIRL!!
HEY, LILI?
SORRY, OIKAWA. I'VE GOT TO LOOK INTO SOME-THING!!
THE POLICE WILL HAVE TO QUESTION ME LATER. TELL THEM THAT!
......
WAIT!
WHY ARE YOU RUNNING AWAY?

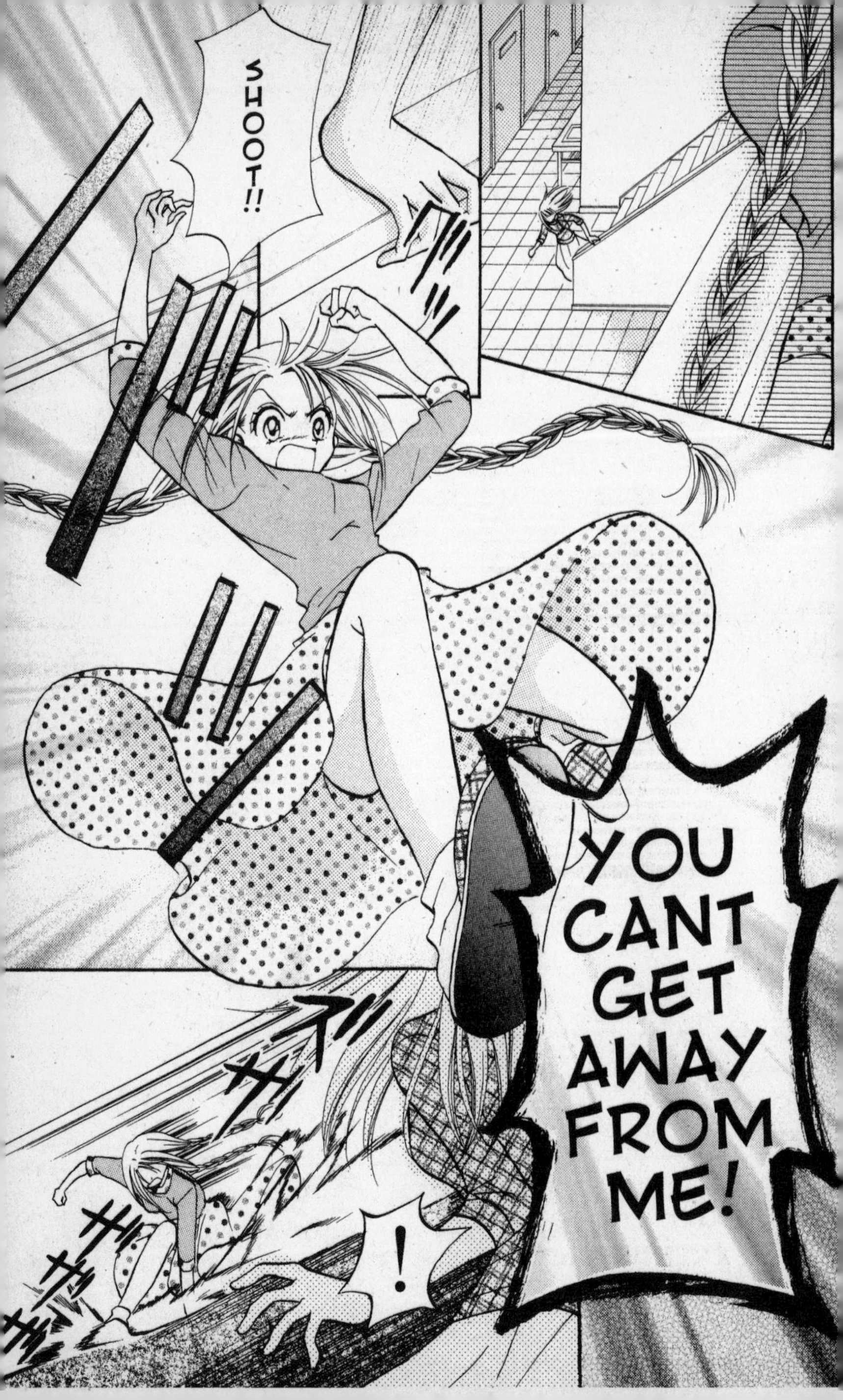
SHOOT!!
YOU CANT GET AWAY FROM ME!
!

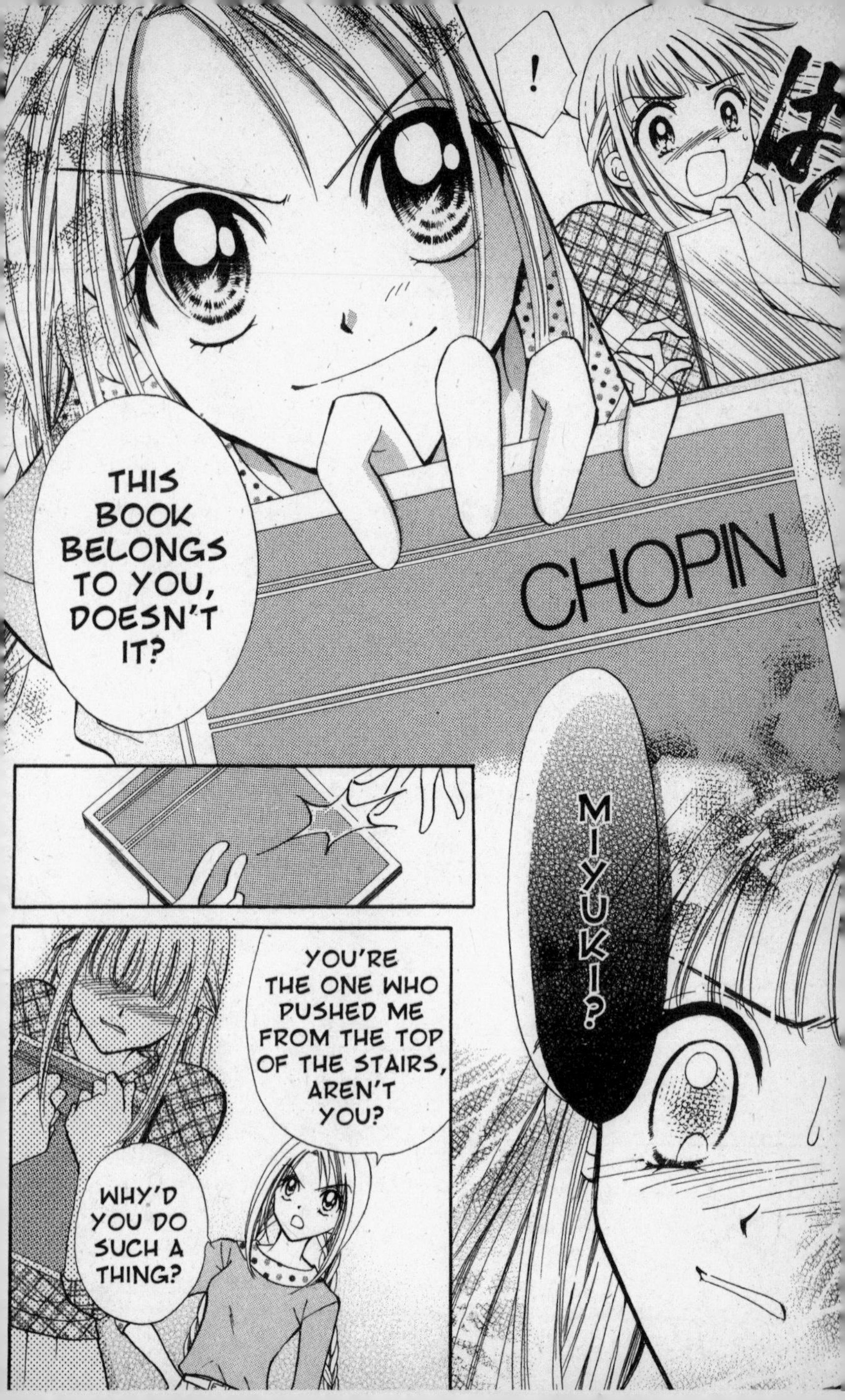
!
CHOPIN
THIS BOOK BELONGS TO YOU, DOESN'T IT?
MIYUKI?
YOU'RE THE ONE WHO PUSHED ME FROM THE TOP OF THE STAIRS, AREN'T YOU?
WHY'D YOU DO SUCH A THING?

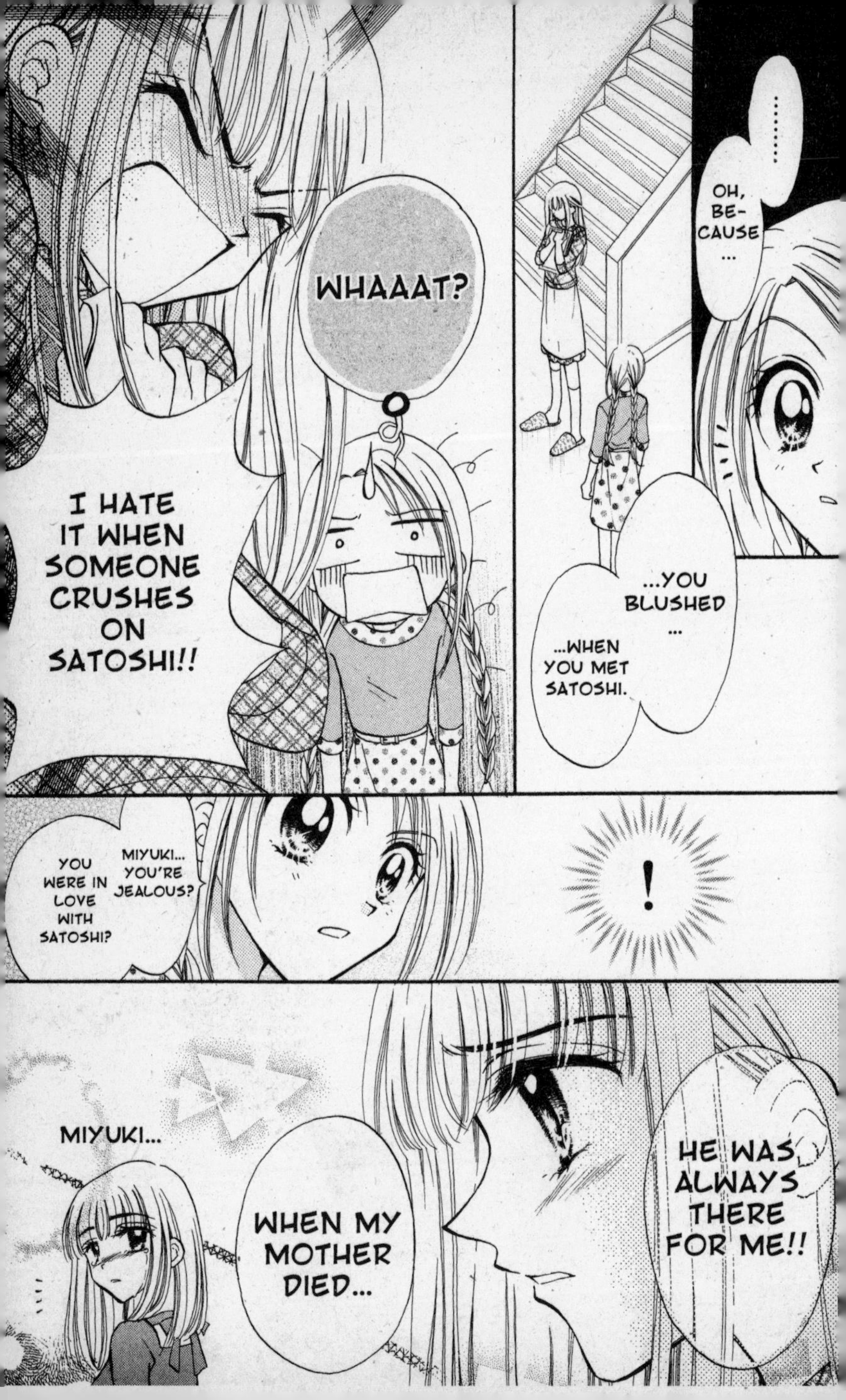
......
OH, BECAUSE...
...YOU BLUSHED...
...WHEN YOU MET SATOSHI.
WHAAAT?
I HATE IT WHEN SOMEONE CRUSHES ON SATOSHI!!
!
MIYUKI... YOU'RE JEALOUS?
YOU WERE IN LOVE WITH SATOSHI?
HE WAS ALWAYS THERE FOR ME!!
WHEN MY MOTHER DIED...
MIYUKI...

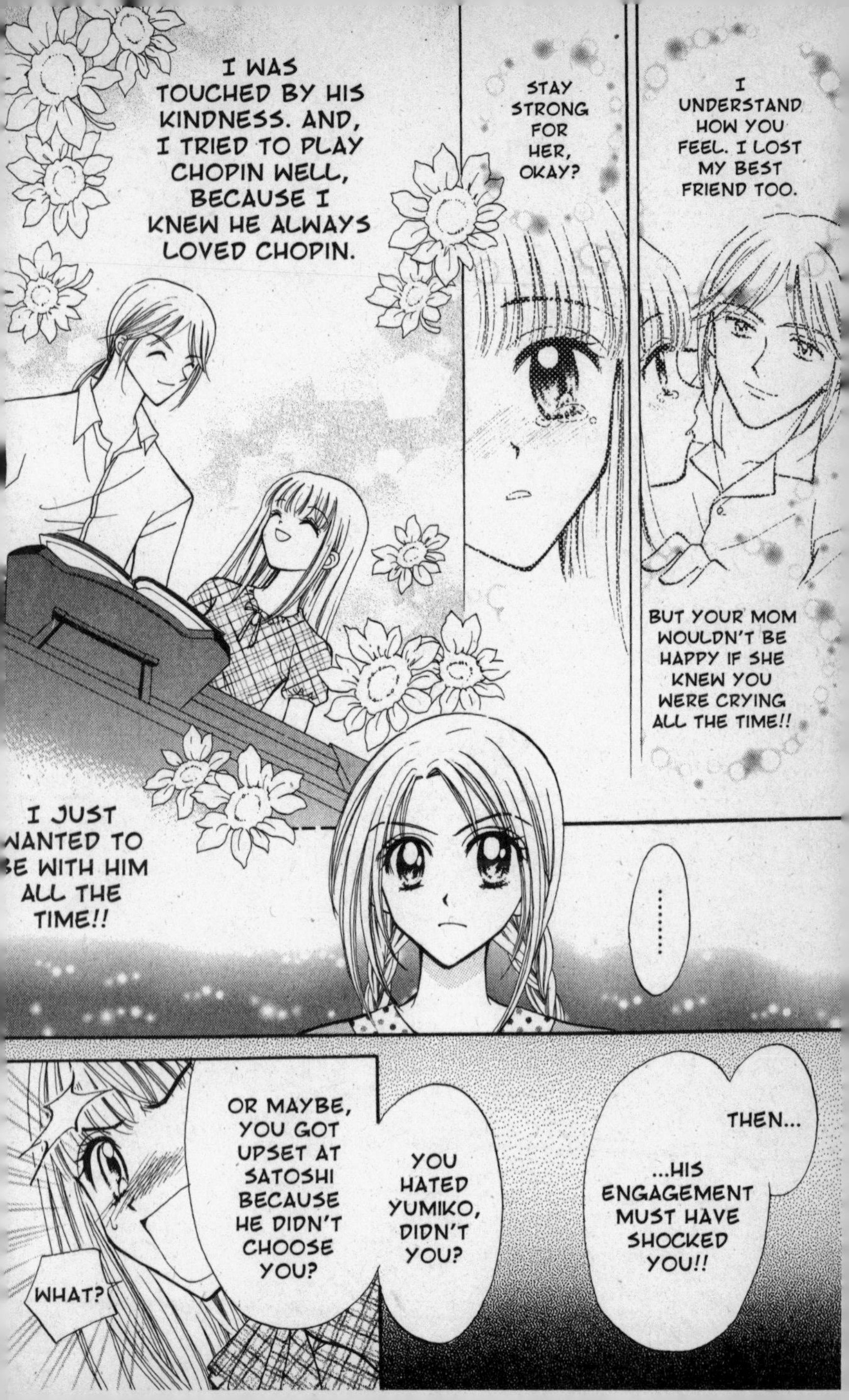
I UNDERSTAND HOW YOU FEEL. I LOST MY BEST FRIEND TOO.
BUT YOUR MOM WOULDN'T BE HAPPY IF SHE KNEW YOU WERE CRYING ALL THE TIME!!
STAY STRONG FOR HER, OKAY?
......
I WAS TOUCHED BY HIS KINDNESS. AND, I TRIED TO PLAY CHOPIN WELL, BECAUSE I KNEW HE ALWAYS LOVED CHOPIN.
I JUST WANTED TO BE WITH HIM ALL THE TIME!!
THEN...
...HIS ENGAGEMENT MUST HAVE SHOCKED YOU!!
YOU HATED YUMIKO, DIDN'T YOU?
OR MAYBE, YOU GOT UPSET AT SATOSHI BECAUSE HE DIDN'T CHOOSE YOU?
WHAT?

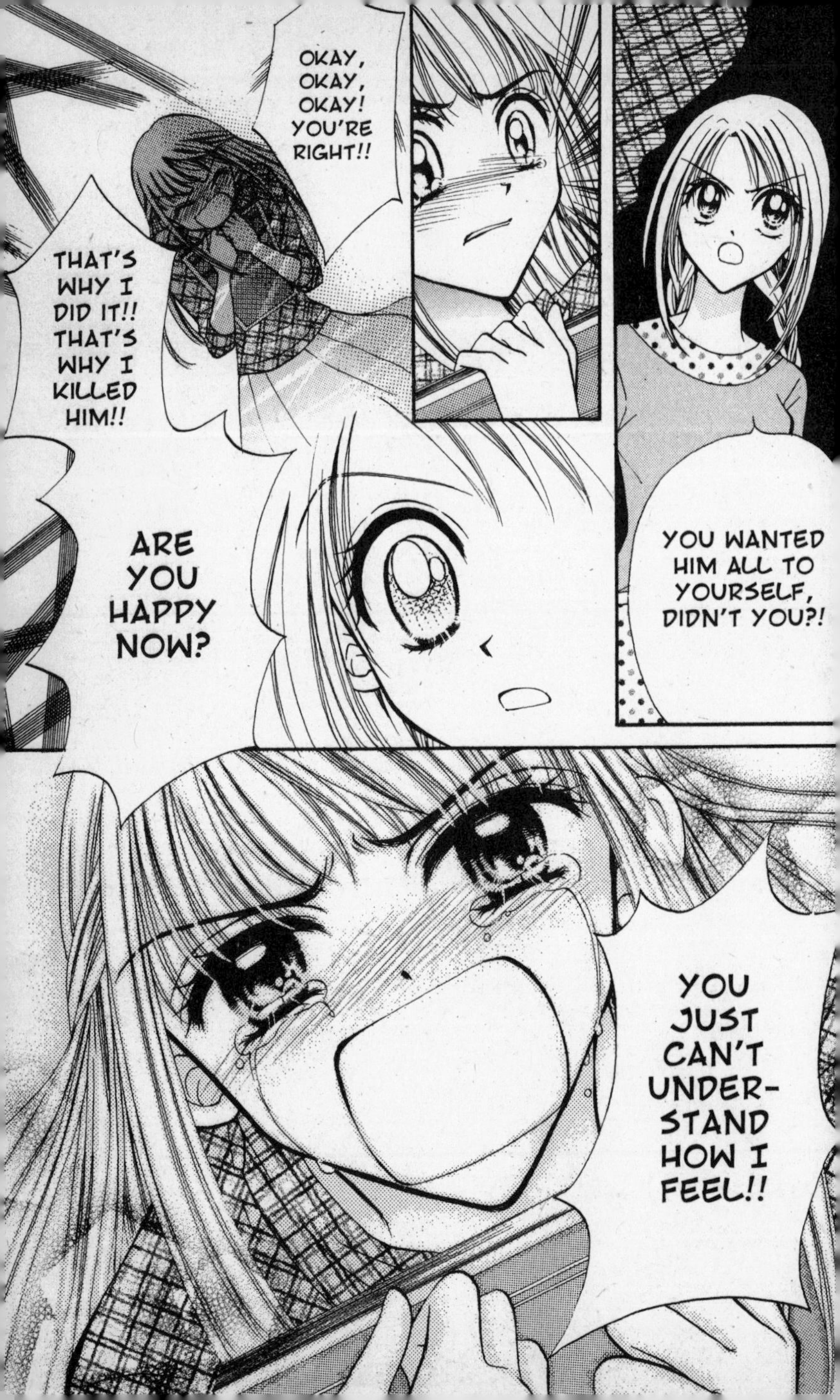
YOU WANTED HIM ALL TO YOURSELF, DIDN'T YOU?!
OKAY, OKAY, OKAY! YOU'RE RIGHT!!
THAT'S WHY I DID IT!! THAT'S WHY I KILLED HIM!!
ARE YOU HAPPY NOW?
YOU JUST CAN'T UNDER-STAND HOW I FEEL!!

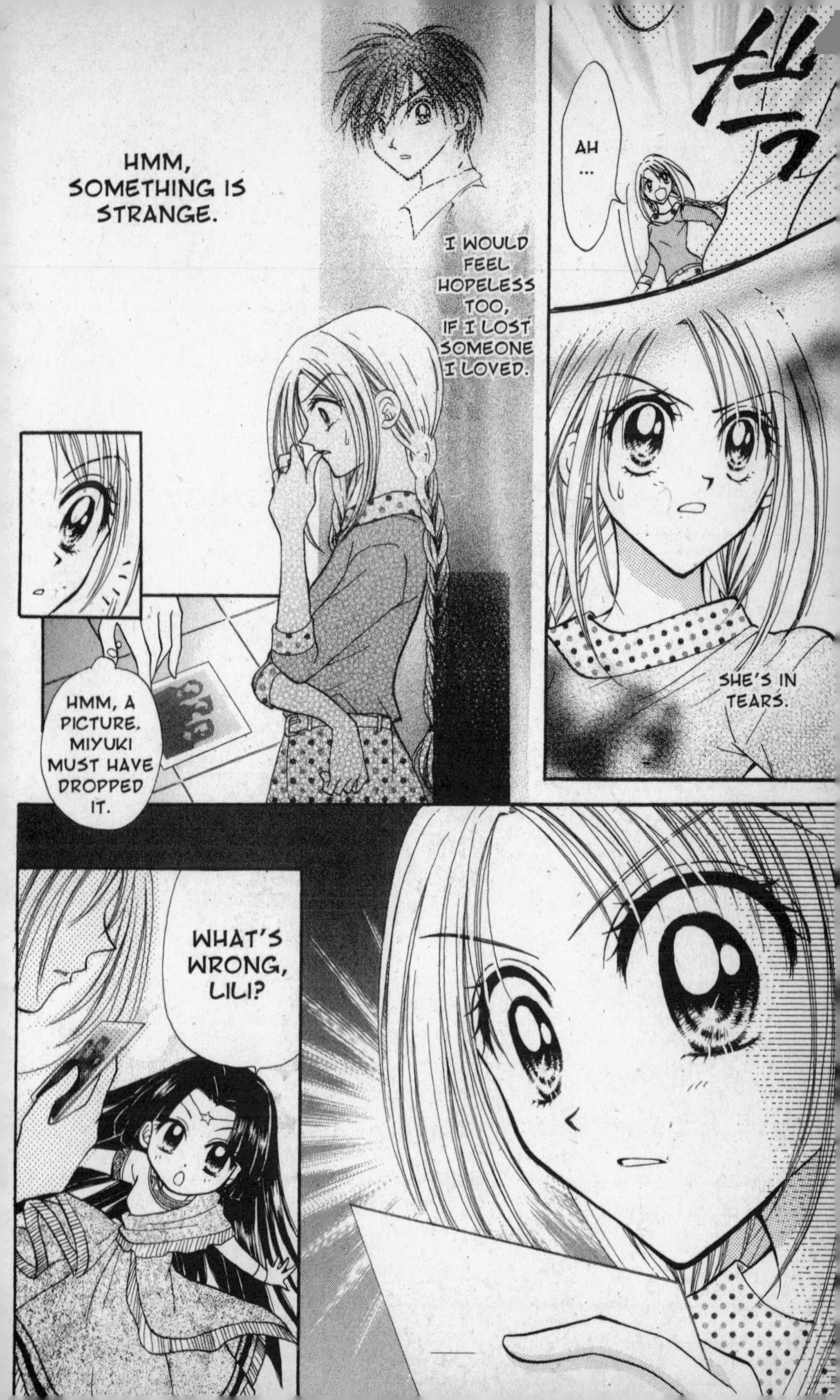
AH ...
SHE'S IN TEARS.
I WOULD FEEL HOPELESS TOO, IF I LOST SOMEONE I LOVED.
HMM, SOMETHING IS STRANGE.
HMM, A PICTURE. MIYUKI MUST HAVE DROPPED IT.
WHAT'S WRONG, LILI?

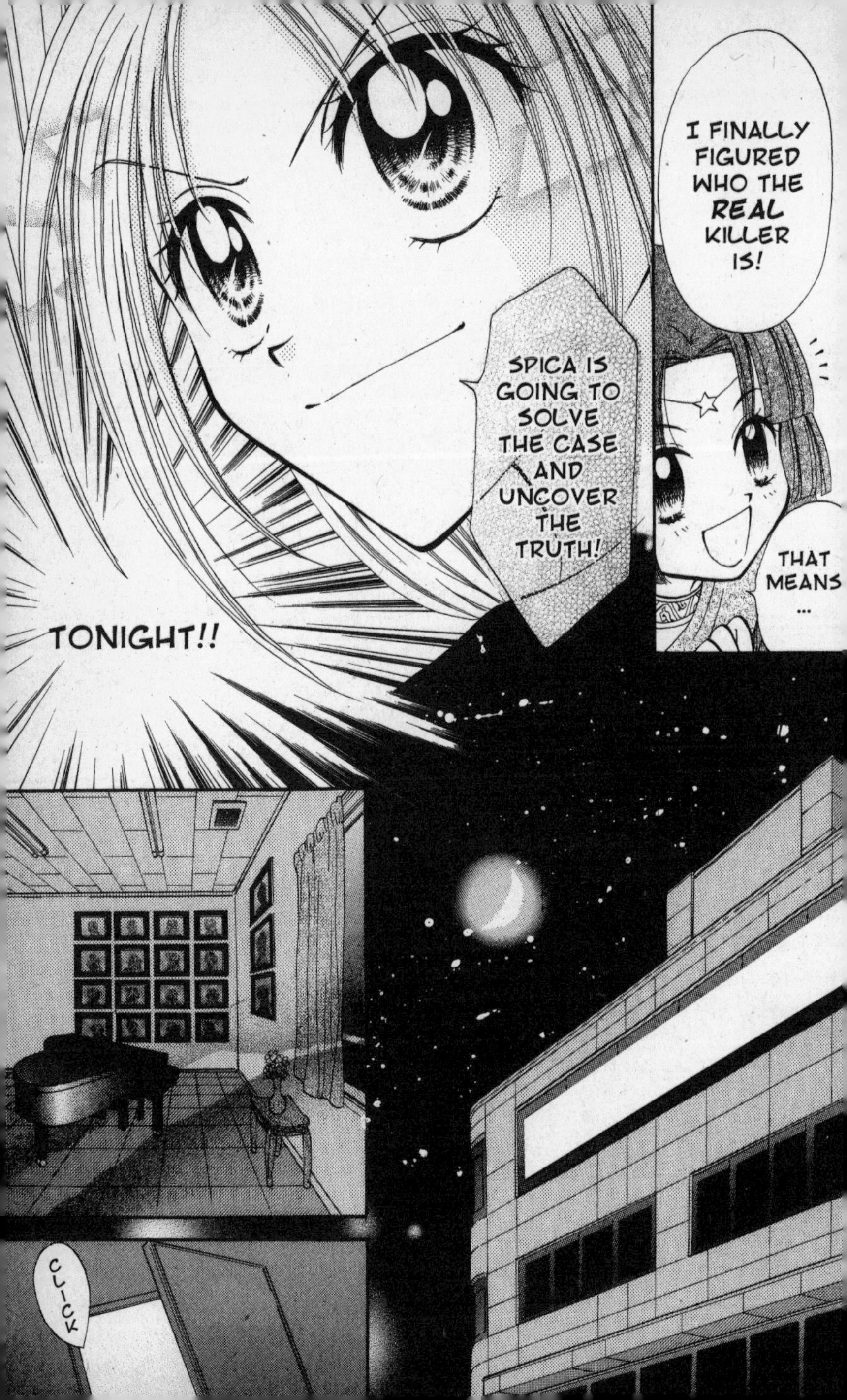
I FINALLY FIGURED WHO THE **REAL** KILLER IS!
THAT MEANS ...
SPICA IS GOING TO SOLVE THE CASE AND UNCOVER THE TRUTH!
TONIGHT!!
CLICK

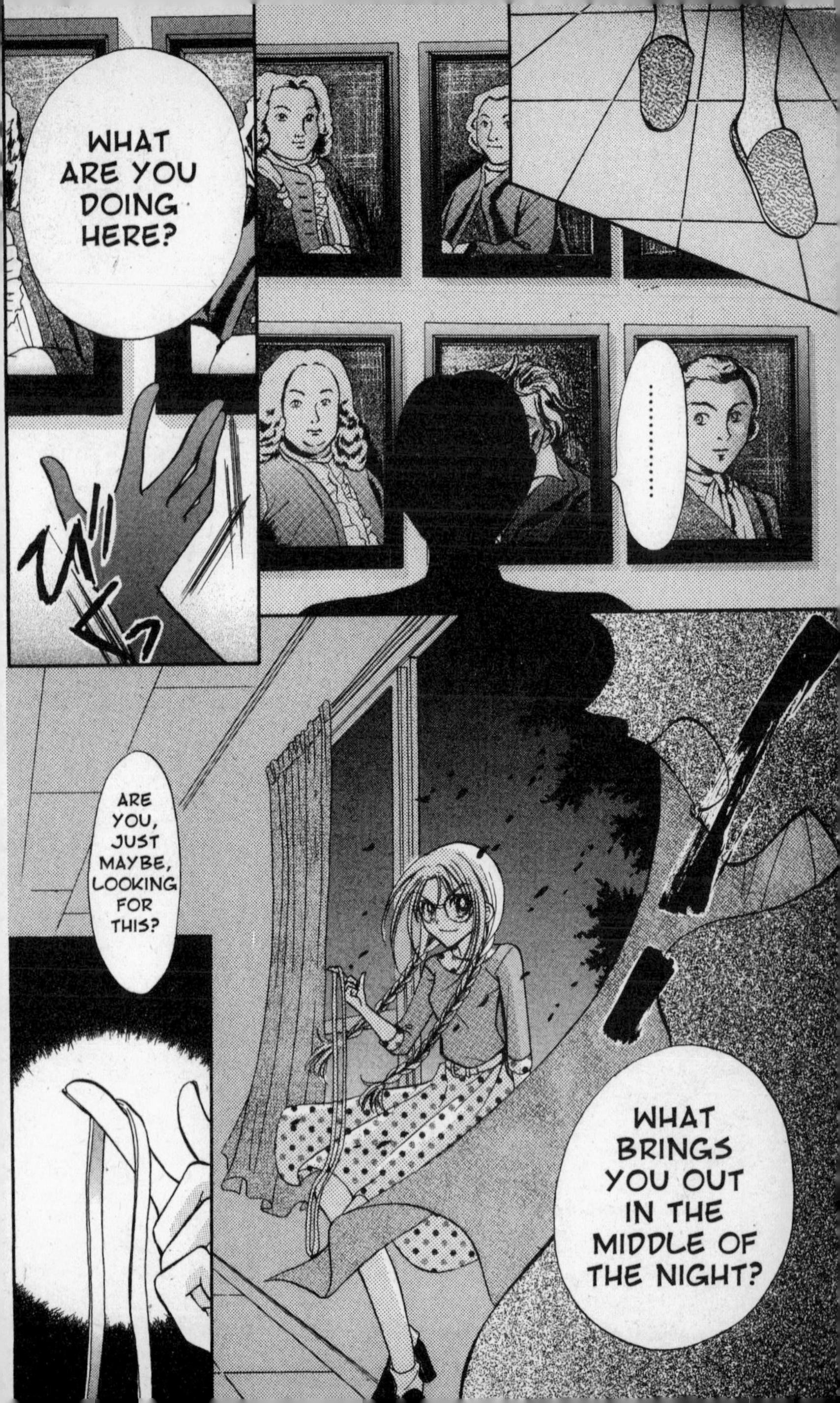
......
WHAT ARE YOU DOING HERE?
WHAT BRINGS YOU OUT IN THE MIDDLE OF THE NIGHT?
ARE YOU, JUST MAYBE, LOOKING FOR THIS?

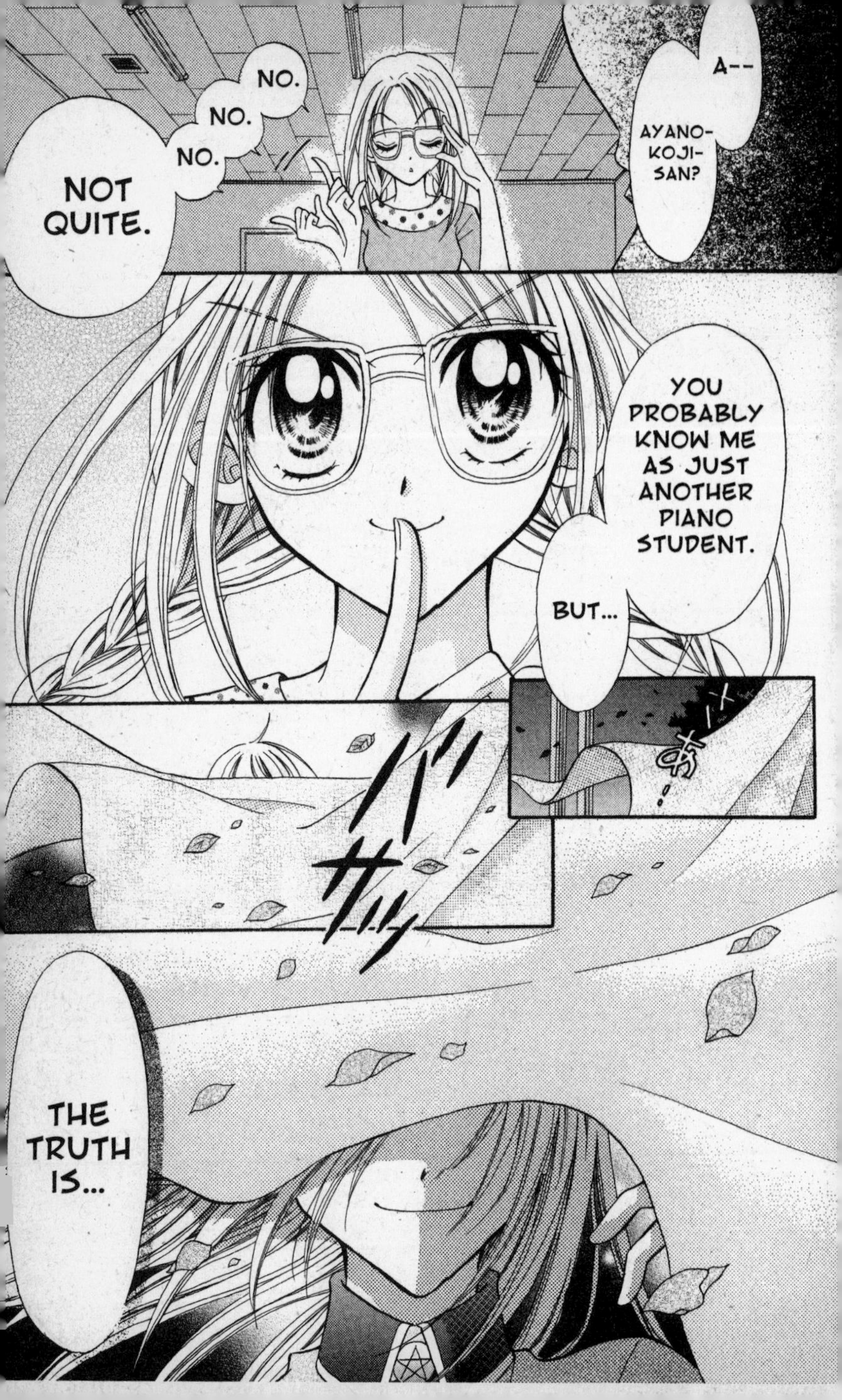
A--
AYANO-KOJI-SAN?
NO.
NO.
NO.
NOT QUITE.
YOU PROBABLY KNOW ME AS JUST ANOTHER PIANO STUDENT.
BUT...
THE TRUTH IS...

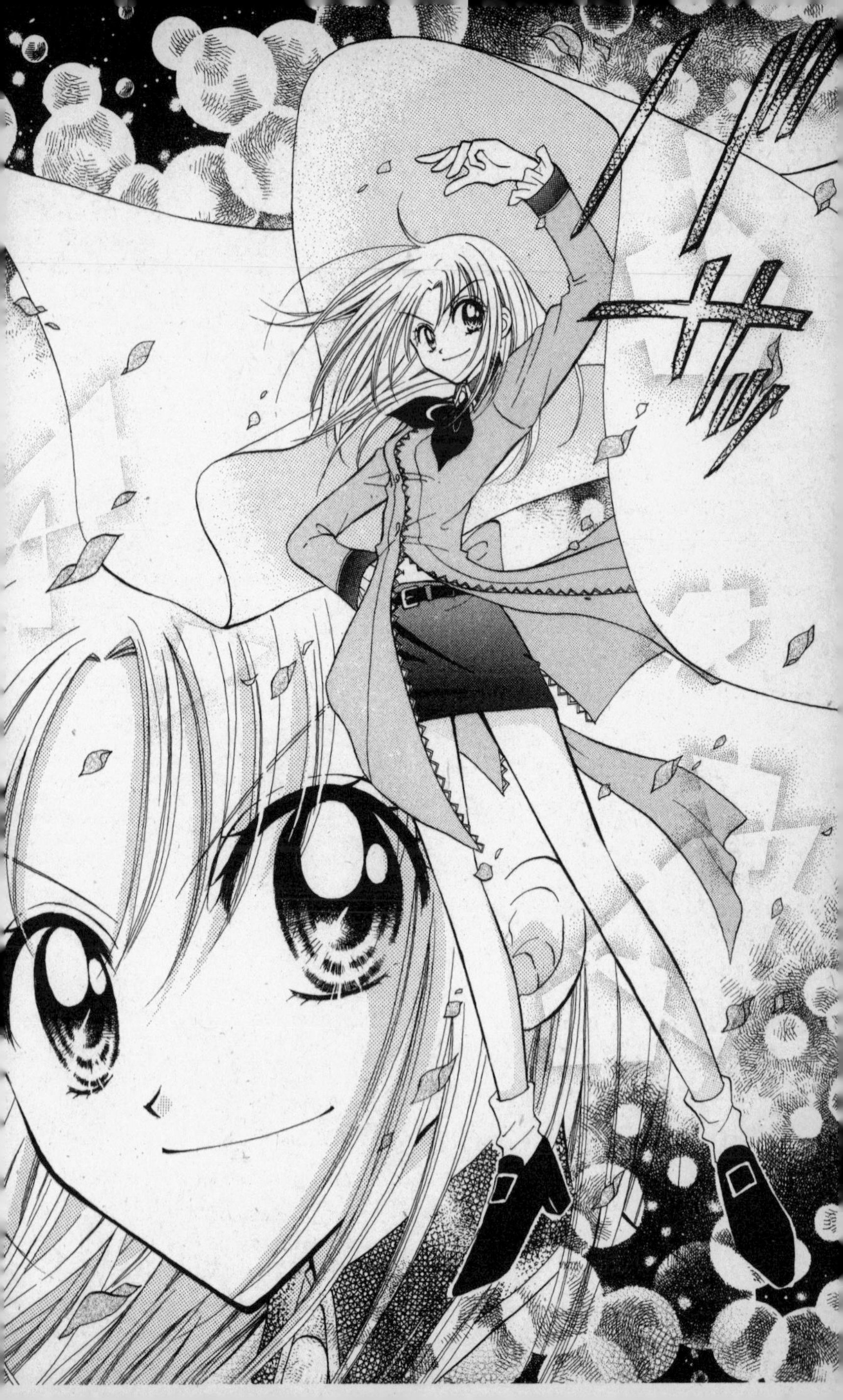

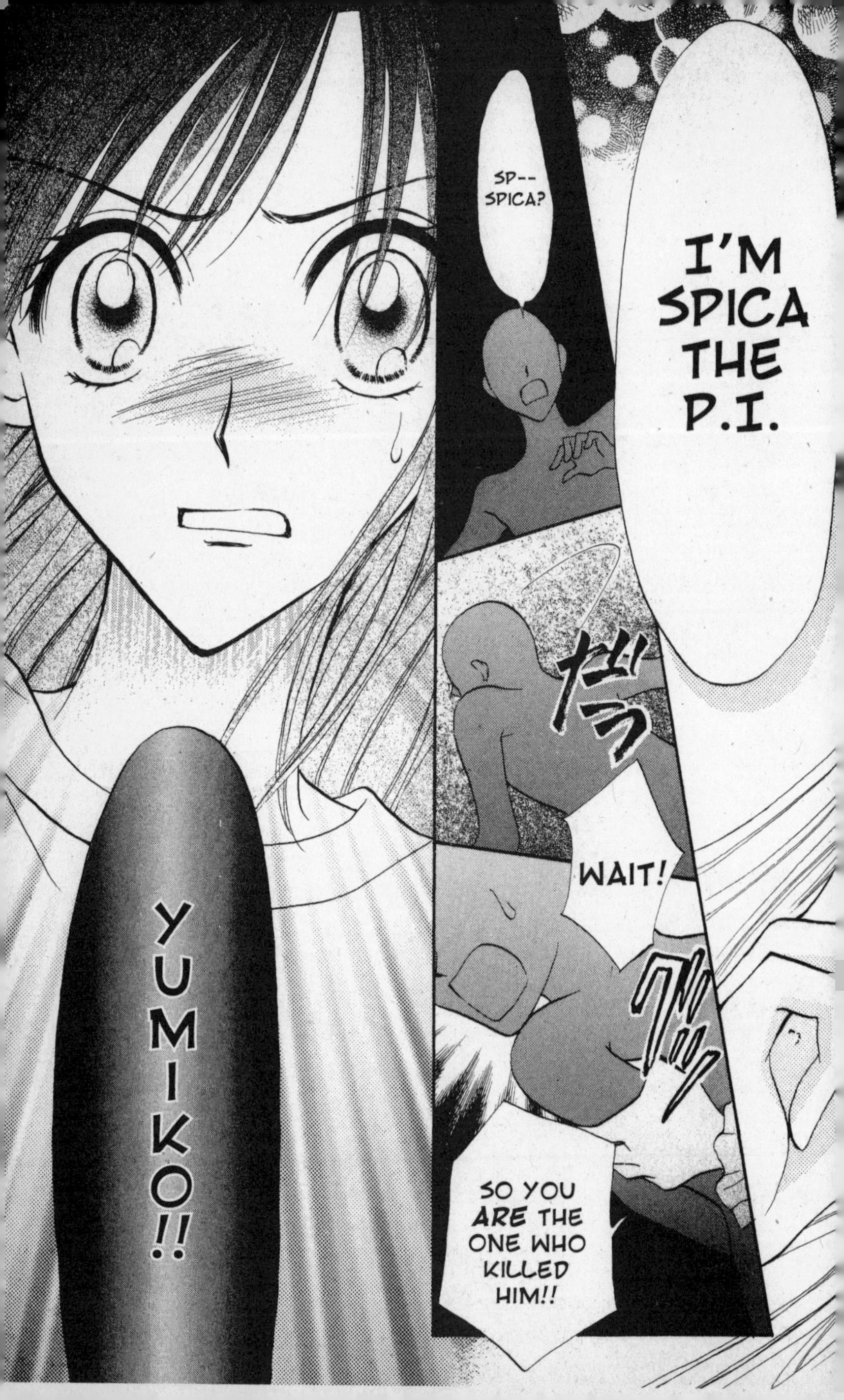
I'M SPICA THE P.I.
SP-- SPICA?
WAIT!
SO YOU ARE THE ONE WHO KILLED HIM!!
YUMIKO!!

☆ Character Profile ☆

ations for an imperial dem
Summerville forecasts that by th
of the decade Asia will absorb 45 pe

Hiromi Oikawa

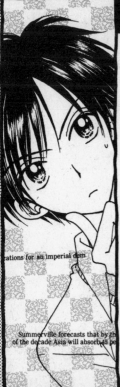

☆Birthday	January 1st
☆Sign	Capricorn
☆Blood Type	AB-
☆Favorite food	The Japanese delicacy, Natto
☆Least favorite food	Sweets and meat
☆Favorite subject(s)	All subjects
☆Favorite color	Navy blue
☆Hobby	Reading
☆Special skills and qualifications	Calligraphy, Japanese Kanji, weather forecasting, hazardous material inspection, accounting. (I'm good at everything!!)

Hiromi is allergic to girls! And strong-minded girls are always showing him up, especially Lili!! Let's hope he improves as a hero. So cheer him on!! I love drawing characters with black hair.

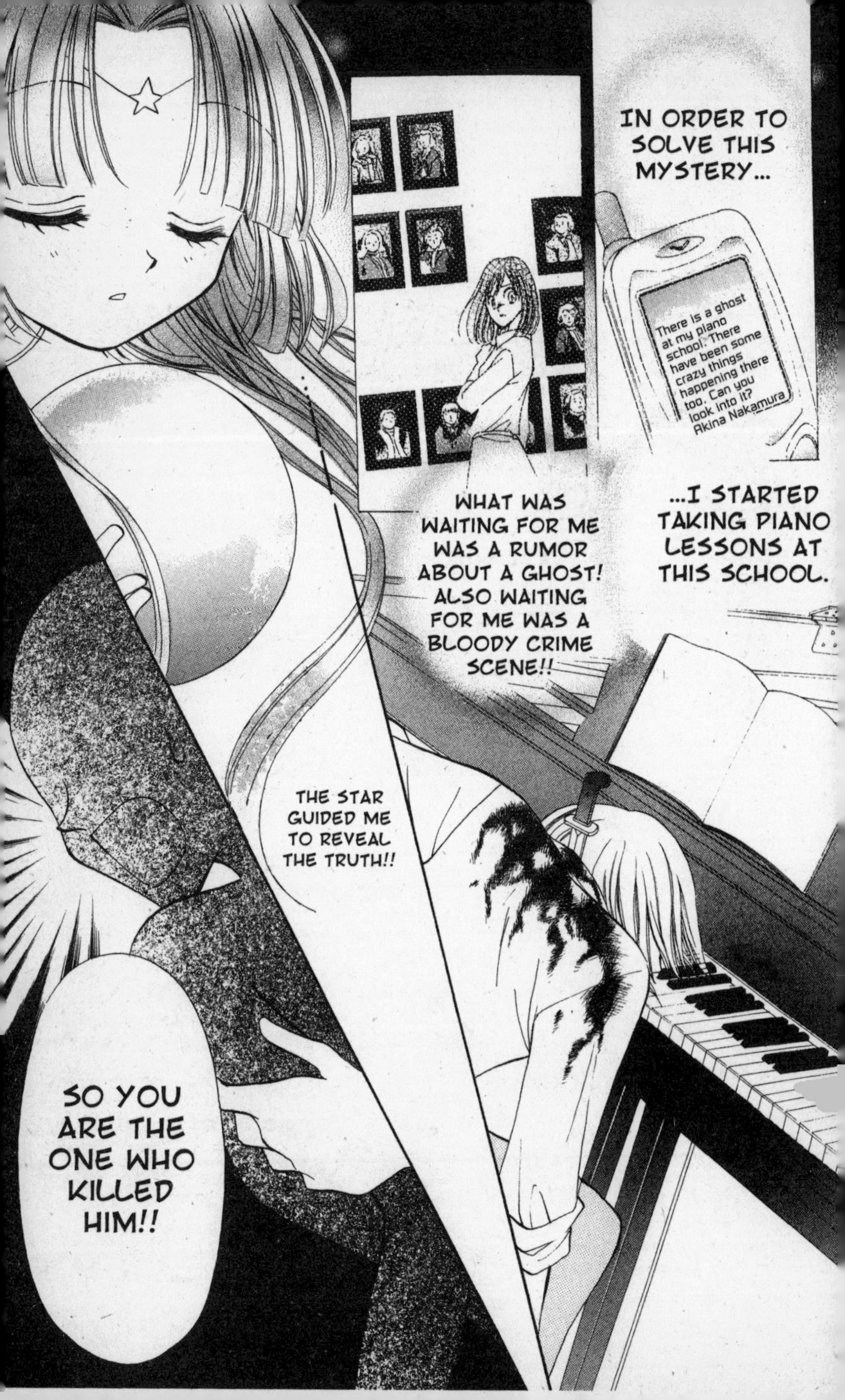
IN ORDER TO SOLVE THIS MYSTERY...
There is a ghost at my piano school. There have been some crazy things happening there too. Can you look into it? Akina Nakamura
...I STARTED TAKING PIANO LESSONS AT THIS SCHOOL.
WHAT WAS WAITING FOR ME WAS A RUMOR ABOUT A GHOST! ALSO WAITING FOR ME WAS A BLOODY CRIME SCENE!!
THE STAR GUIDED ME TO REVEAL THE TRUTH!!
SO YOU ARE THE ONE WHO KILLED HIM!!

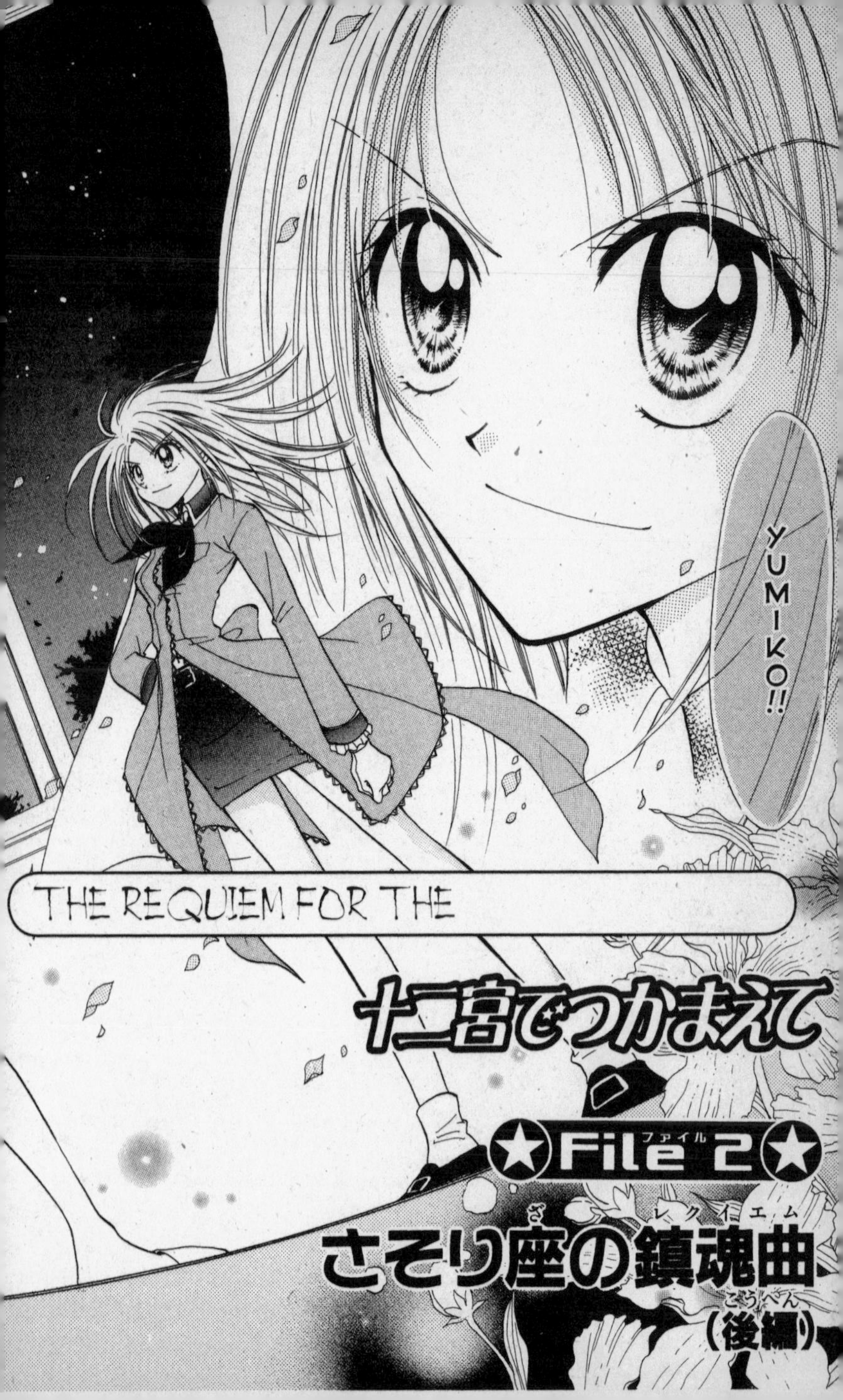
YUMIKO!!
THE REQUIEM FOR THE
十二宮でつかまえて
★File 2★
さそり座の鎮魂曲
（後編）

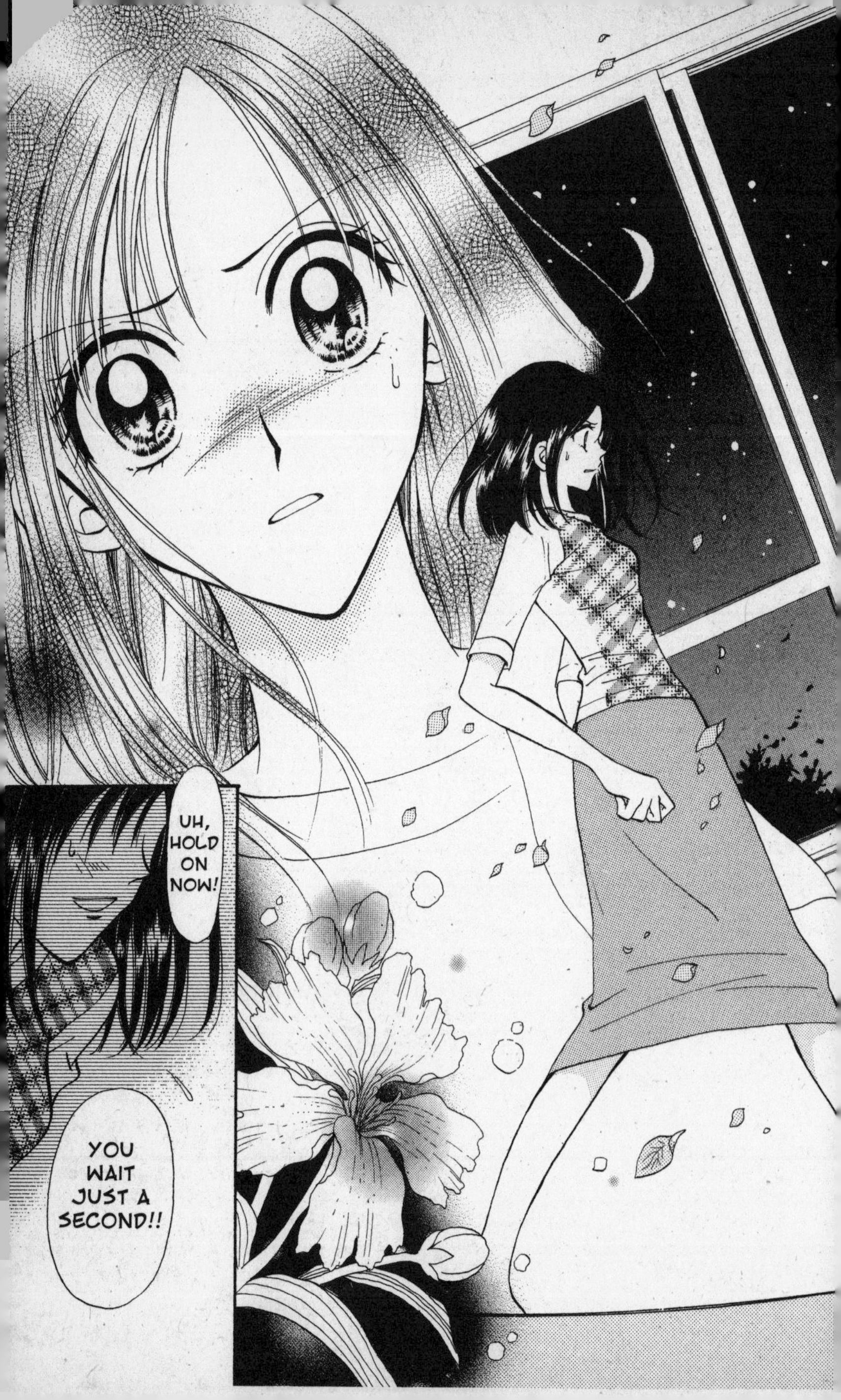
UH, HOLD ON NOW!
YOU WAIT JUST A SECOND!!

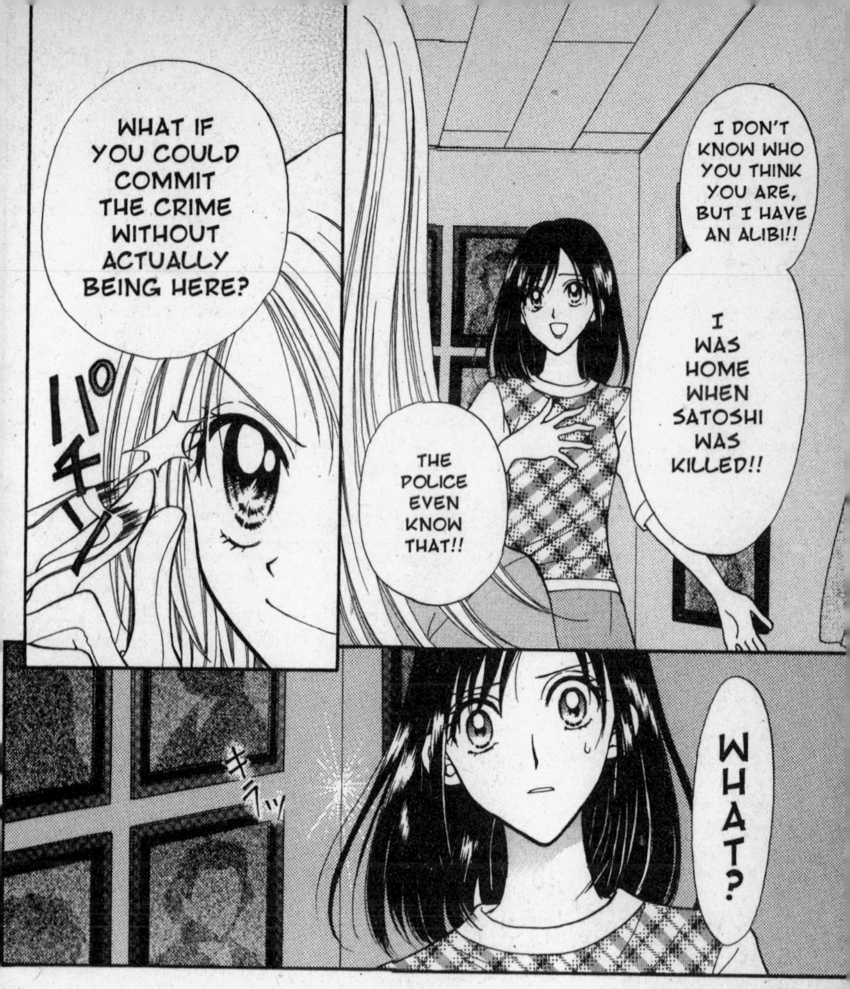
I DON'T KNOW WHO YOU THINK YOU ARE, BUT I HAVE AN ALIBI!!
I WAS HOME WHEN SATOSHI WAS KILLED!!
THE POLICE EVEN KNOW THAT!!
WHAT IF YOU COULD COMMIT THE CRIME WITHOUT ACTUALLY BEING HERE?
WHAT?

Mademoiselle Lili's Astrology (4)

How to treat people with a particular sign

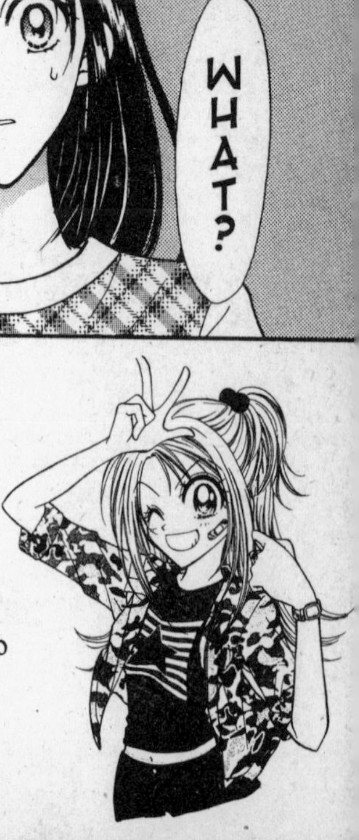

Scorpio (Sign of Scorpio) Antares
Antares is a star of the first magnitude in the Scorpio constellation. The Scorpion looks calm and cool. They can be very passionate, but they can also be vengeful. So they need a trustworthy partner. Scorpio boys tend to be home-loving and caring.

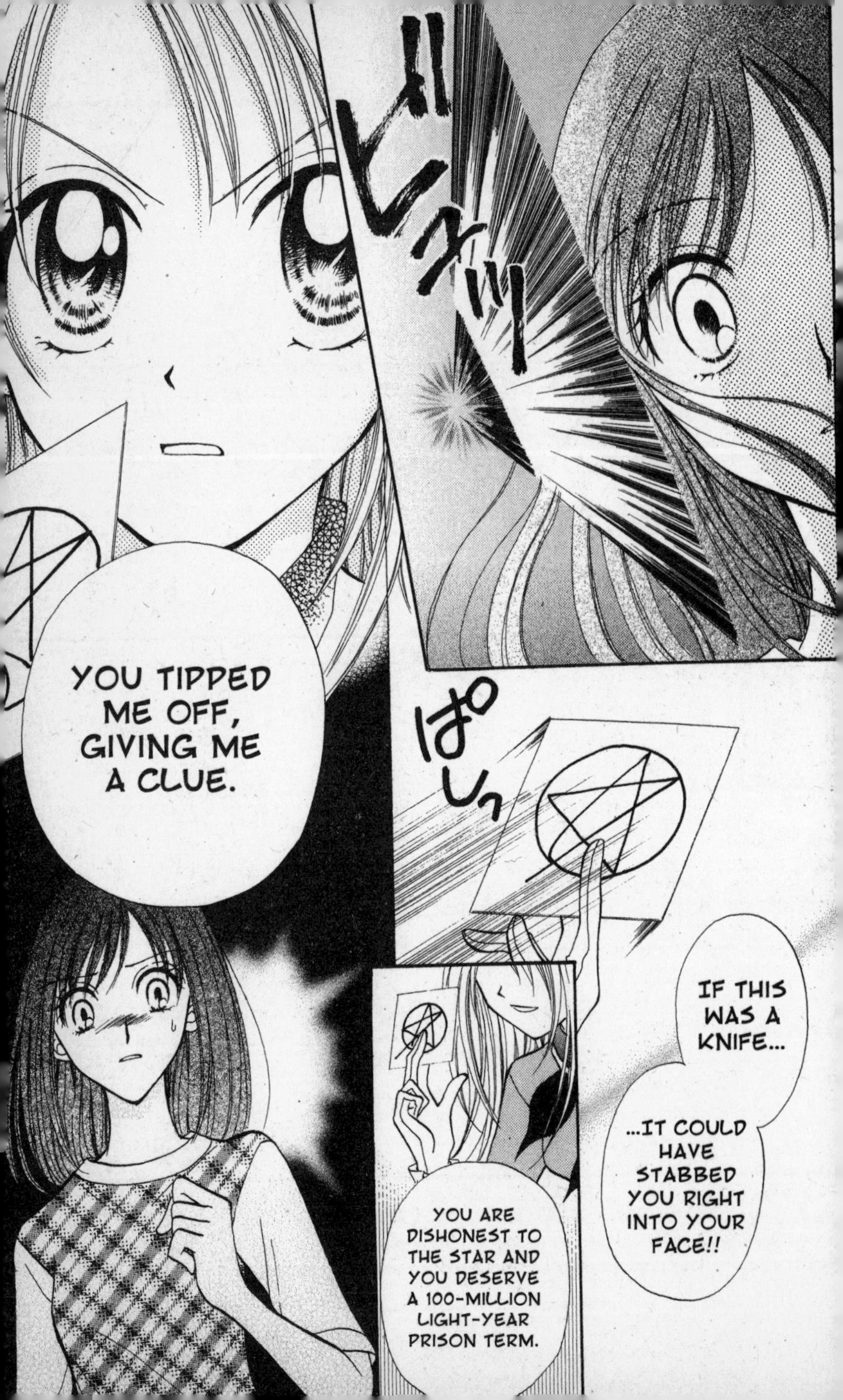
YOU TIPPED ME OFF, GIVING ME A CLUE.
ぱしっ
IF THIS WAS A KNIFE...
...IT COULD HAVE STABBED YOU RIGHT INTO YOUR FACE!!
YOU ARE DISHONEST TO THE STAR AND YOU DESERVE A 100-MILLION LIGHT-YEAR PRISON TERM.

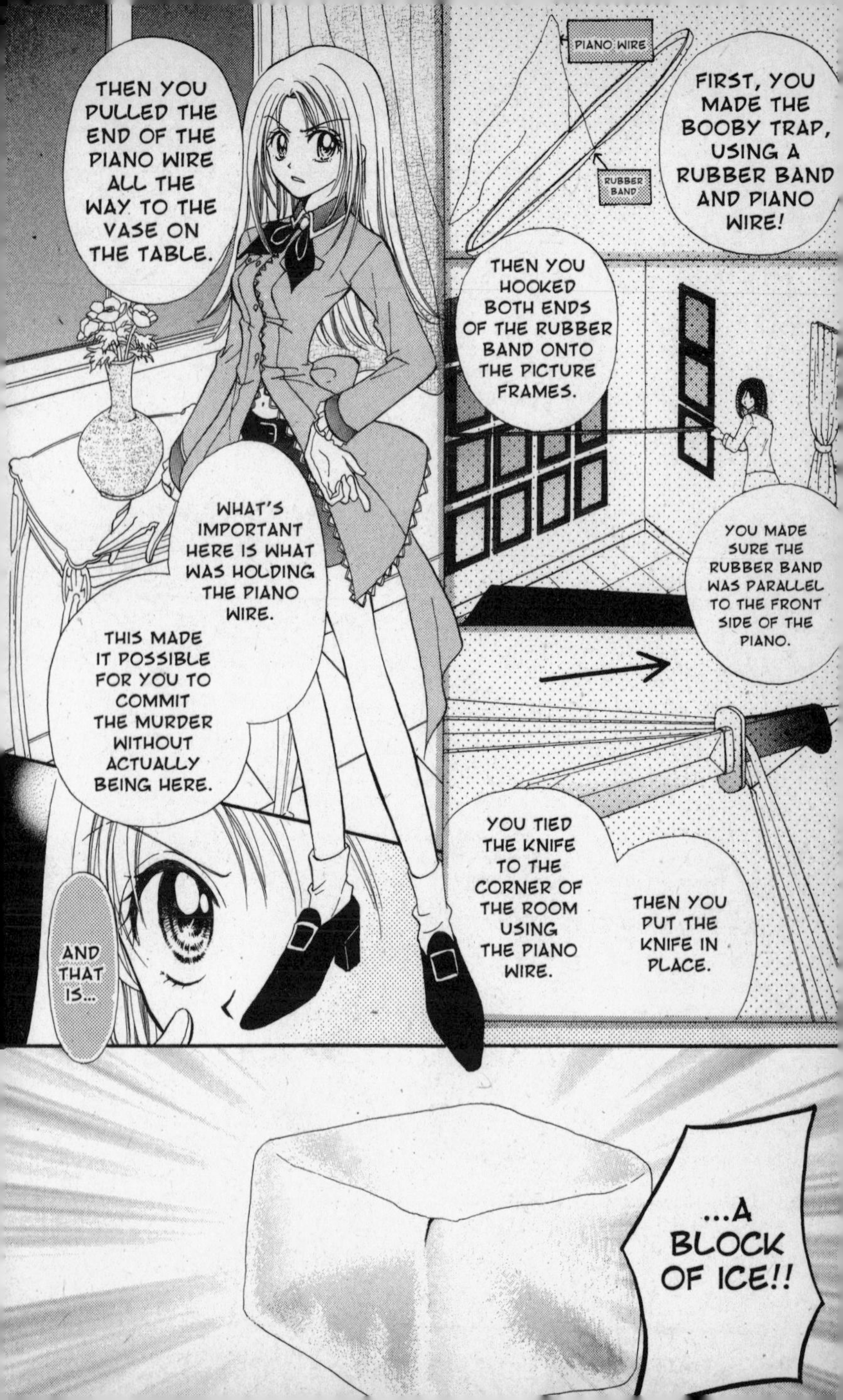
PIANO WIRE
RUBBER BAND
FIRST, YOU MADE THE BOOBY TRAP, USING A RUBBER BAND AND PIANO WIRE!
THEN YOU HOOKED BOTH ENDS OF THE RUBBER BAND ONTO THE PICTURE FRAMES.
YOU MADE SURE THE RUBBER BAND WAS PARALLEL TO THE FRONT SIDE OF THE PIANO.
YOU TIED THE KNIFE TO THE CORNER OF THE ROOM USING THE PIANO WIRE.
THEN YOU PUT THE KNIFE IN PLACE.
THEN YOU PULLED THE END OF THE PIANO WIRE ALL THE WAY TO THE VASE ON THE TABLE.
WHAT'S IMPORTANT HERE IS WHAT WAS HOLDING THE PIANO WIRE.
THIS MADE IT POSSIBLE FOR YOU TO COMMIT THE MURDER WITHOUT ACTUALLY BEING HERE.
AND THAT IS...
...A BLOCK OF ICE!!

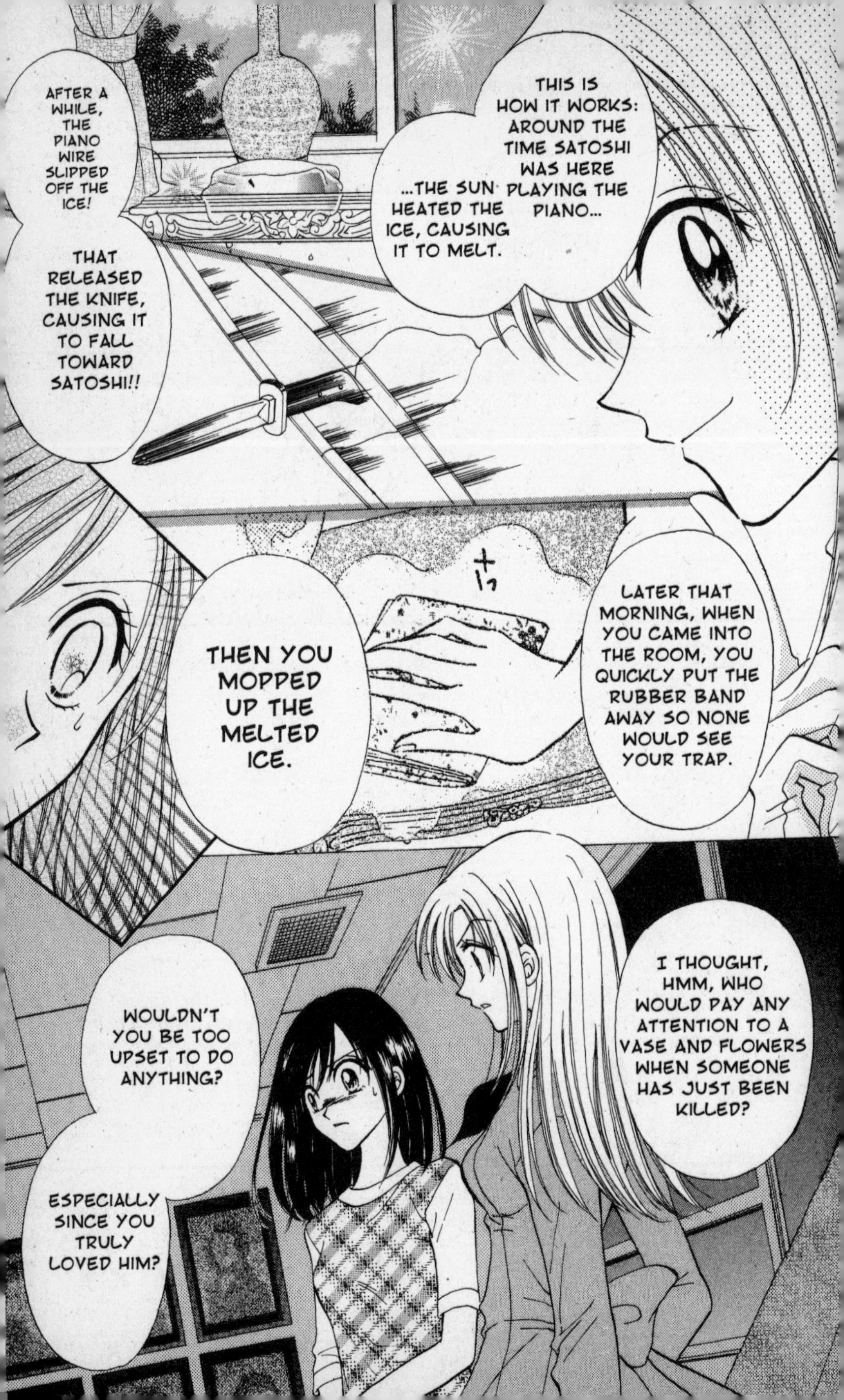
THIS IS HOW IT WORKS: AROUND THE TIME SATOSHI WAS HERE PLAYING THE PIANO...
...THE SUN HEATED THE ICE, CAUSING IT TO MELT.
AFTER A WHILE, THE PIANO WIRE SLIPPED OFF THE ICE!
THAT RELEASED THE KNIFE, CAUSING IT TO FALL TOWARD SATOSHI!!
LATER THAT MORNING, WHEN YOU CAME INTO THE ROOM, YOU QUICKLY PUT THE RUBBER BAND AWAY SO NONE WOULD SEE YOUR TRAP.
THEN YOU MOPPED UP THE MELTED ICE.
I THOUGHT, HMM, WHO WOULD PAY ANY ATTENTION TO A VASE AND FLOWERS WHEN SOMEONE HAS JUST BEEN KILLED?
WOULDN'T YOU BE TOO UPSET TO DO ANYTHING?
ESPECIALLY SINCE YOU TRULY LOVED HIM?

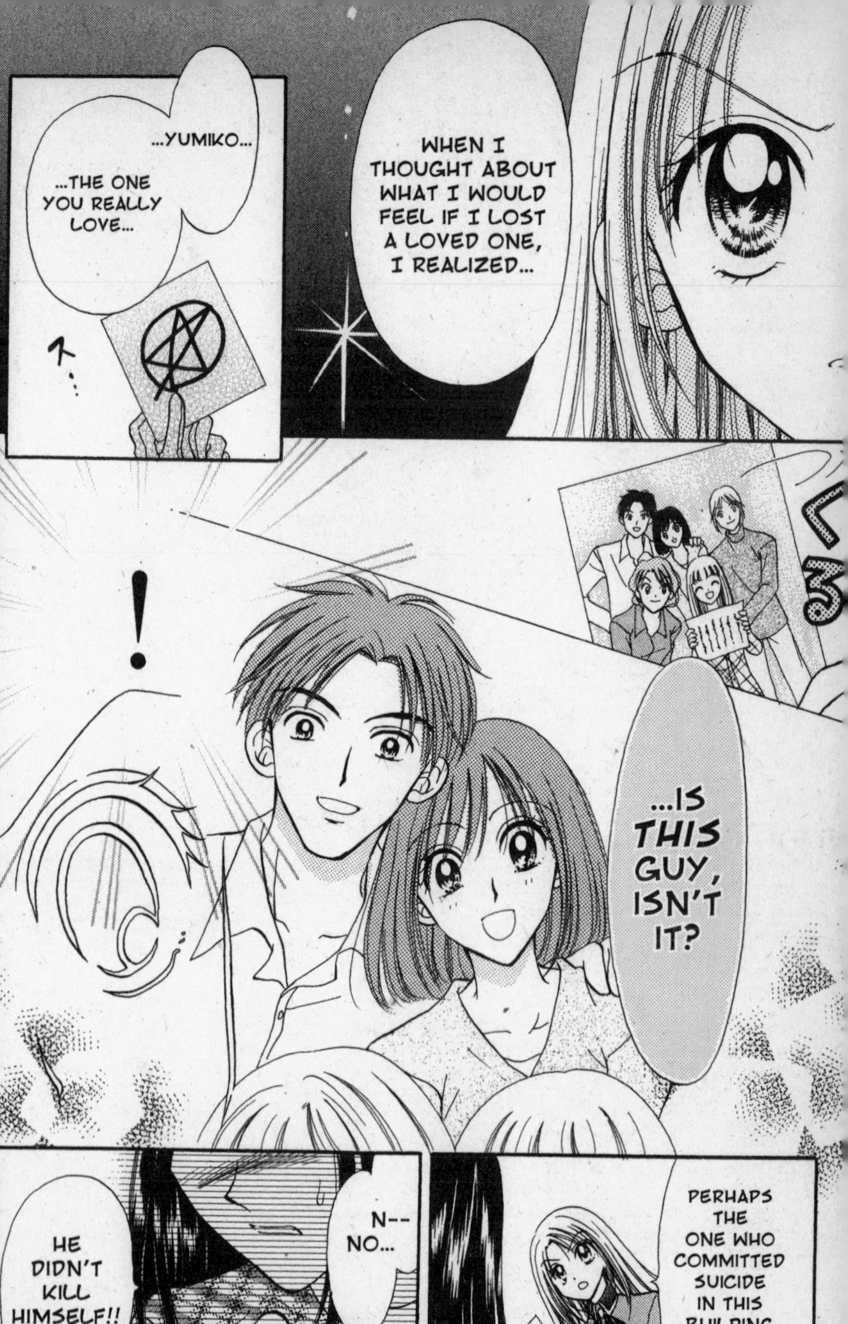
WHEN I THOUGHT ABOUT WHAT I WOULD FEEL IF I LOST A LOVED ONE, I REALIZED...
...YUMIKO...
...THE ONE YOU REALLY LOVE...
!
...IS *THIS* GUY, ISN'T IT?
PERHAPS THE ONE WHO COMMITTED SUICIDE IN THIS BUILDING IS...
N-- NO...
HE DIDN'T KILL HIMSELF!!

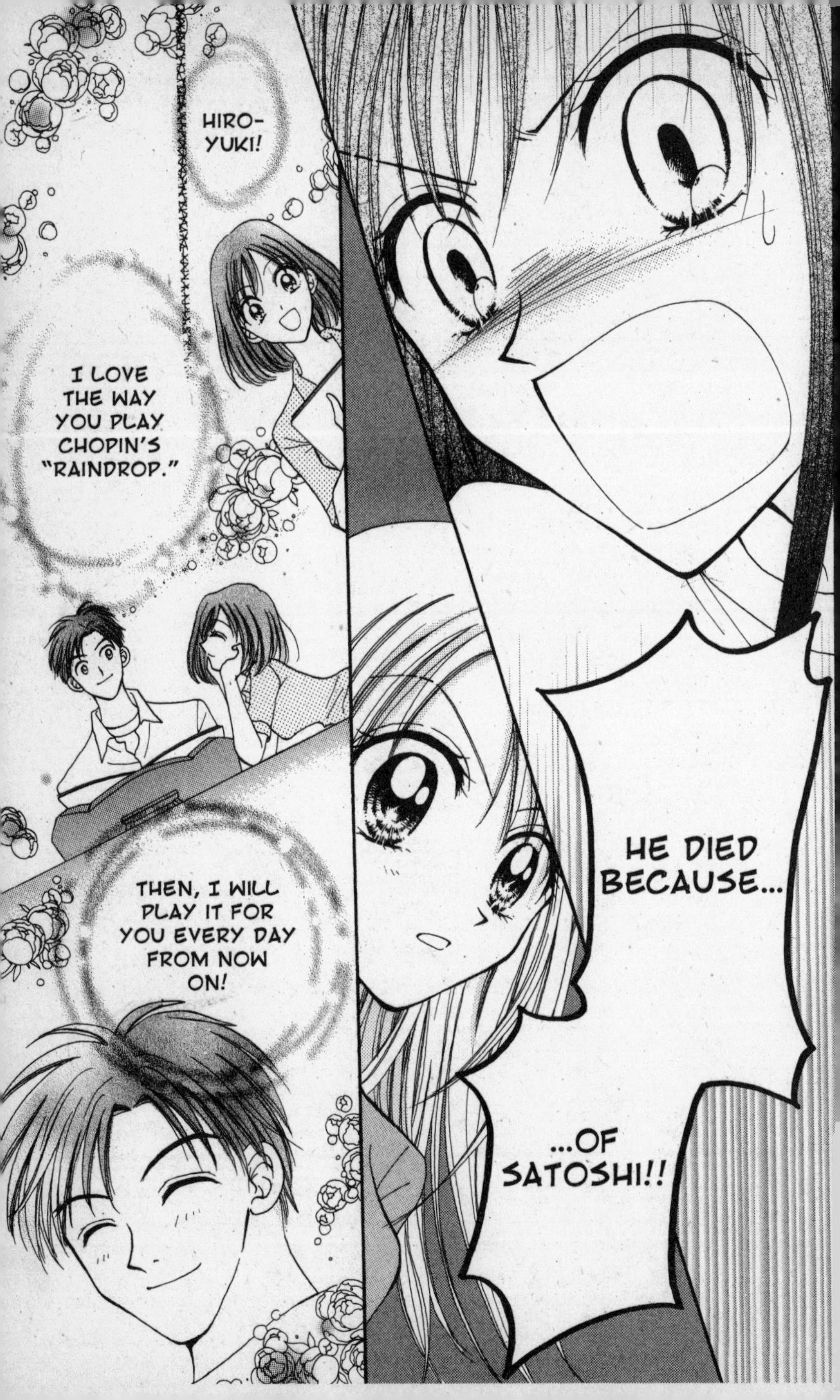
HE DIED BECAUSE...
...OF SATOSHI!!
HIRO-YUKI!
I LOVE THE WAY YOU PLAY CHOPIN'S "RAINDROP."
THEN, I WILL PLAY IT FOR YOU EVERY DAY FROM NOW ON!

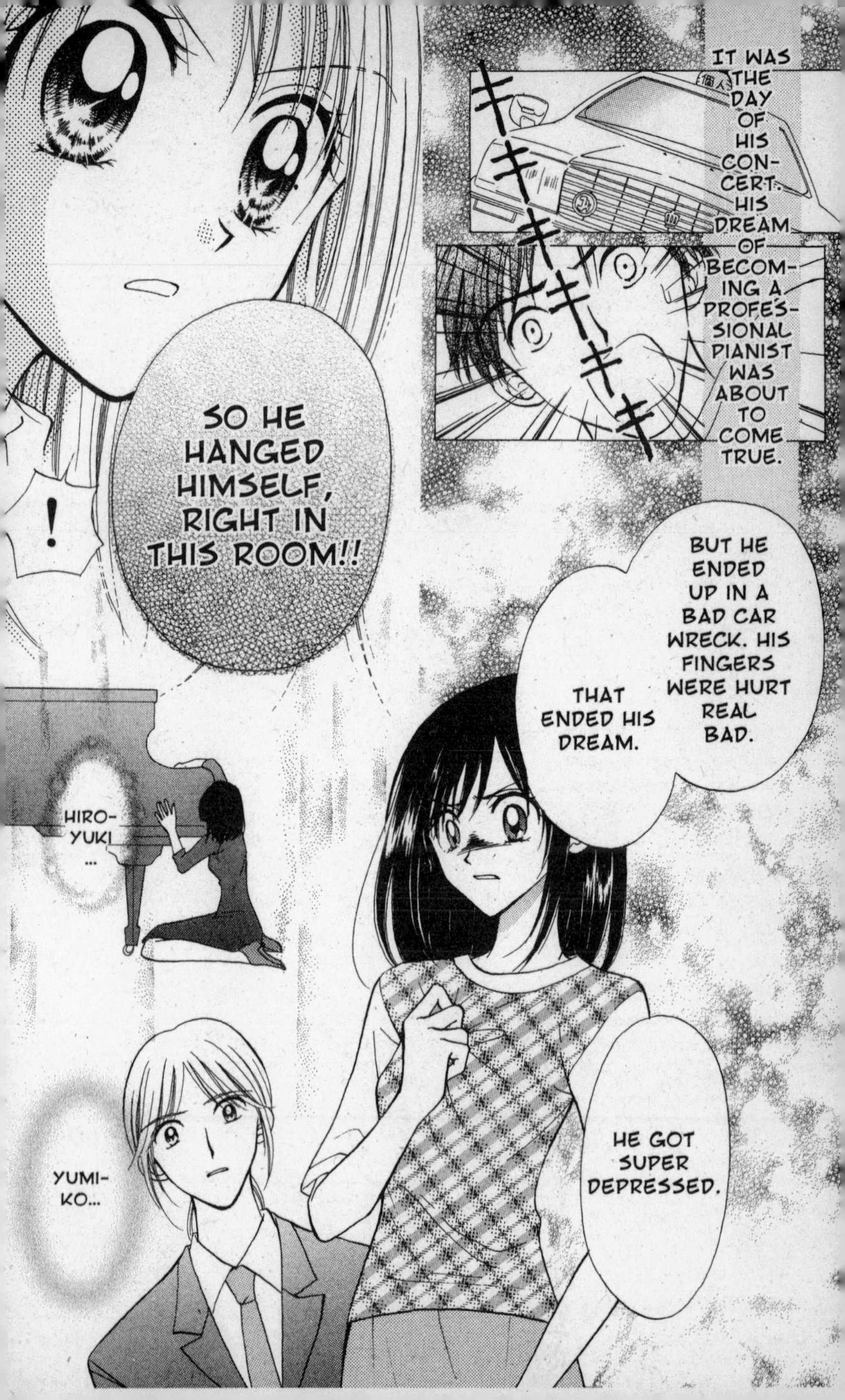

IT WAS THE DAY OF HIS CONCERT. HIS DREAM OF BECOMING A PROFESSIONAL PIANIST WAS ABOUT TO COME TRUE.
BUT HE ENDED UP IN A BAD CAR WRECK. HIS FINGERS WERE HURT REAL BAD.
THAT ENDED HIS DREAM.
HIROYUKI...
HE GOT SUPER DEPRESSED.
YUMIKO...
SO HE HANGED HIMSELF, RIGHT IN THIS ROOM!!
!

Thank you

I receive letters from fans telling how they think the mysteries will turn out. There was one reader who was right about Chihiro's killer, the victim in File 1. I was so impressed that I felt like giving her some kind of a prize!! Ha ha!! Bravo!! I would like to express special thanks to the wonderful people who make my life easier: Mika Murase, thanks for bringing me tasty treats. Sachiyo Murase, thanks for helping me work. Marimo Shirasawa, thanks for visiting us. Aiko Tsunoda, Thanks for taking time to edit my work during your leave. Also thanks to Gomi and Zushi!! Finally, thank to you all, the readers !! Write any comments to me at:

Natsumi Ando
Nakayoshi
Editorial Office
PO BOX 91
Akasaka Post Office
Tokyo, Japan
1078652

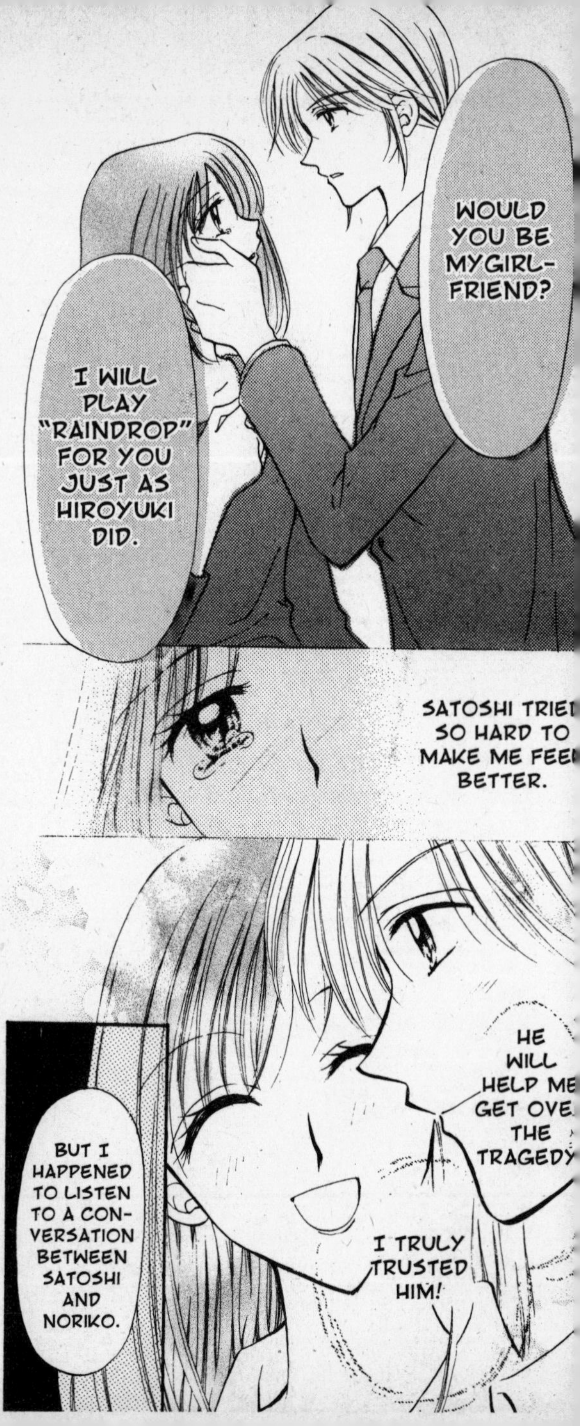
WOULD YOU BE MY GIRL-FRIEND?
I WILL PLAY "RAINDROP" FOR YOU JUST AS HIROYUKI DID.
SATOSHI TRIE SO HARD TO MAKE ME FEE BETTER.
HE WILL HELP ME GET OVE THE TRAGEDY
I TRULY TRUSTED HIM!
BUT I HAPPENED TO LISTEN TO A CON-VERSATION BETWEEN SATOSHI AND NORIKO.

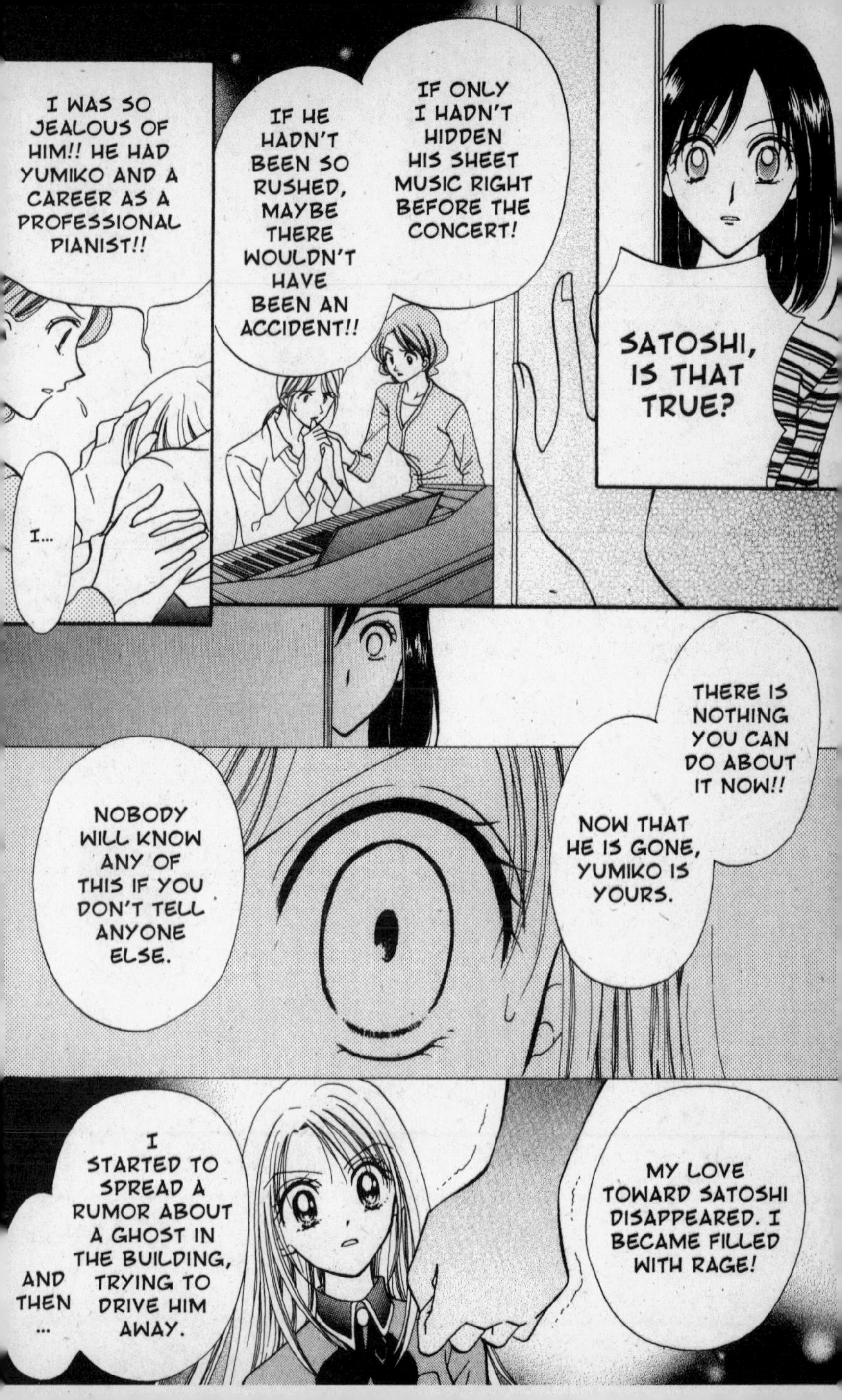
SATOSHI, IS THAT TRUE?
IF ONLY I HADN'T HIDDEN HIS SHEET MUSIC RIGHT BEFORE THE CONCERT!
IF HE HADN'T BEEN SO RUSHED, MAYBE THERE WOULDN'T HAVE BEEN AN ACCIDENT!!
I WAS SO JEALOUS OF HIM!! HE HAD YUMIKO AND A CAREER AS A PROFESSIONAL PIANIST!!
I...
THERE IS NOTHING YOU CAN DO ABOUT IT NOW!!
NOW THAT HE IS GONE, YUMIKO IS YOURS.
NOBODY WILL KNOW ANY OF THIS IF YOU DON'T TELL ANYONE ELSE.
MY LOVE TOWARD SATOSHI DISAPPEARED. I BECAME FILLED WITH RAGE!
I STARTED TO SPREAD A RUMOR ABOUT A GHOST IN THE BUILDING, TRYING TO DRIVE HIM AWAY.
AND THEN ...

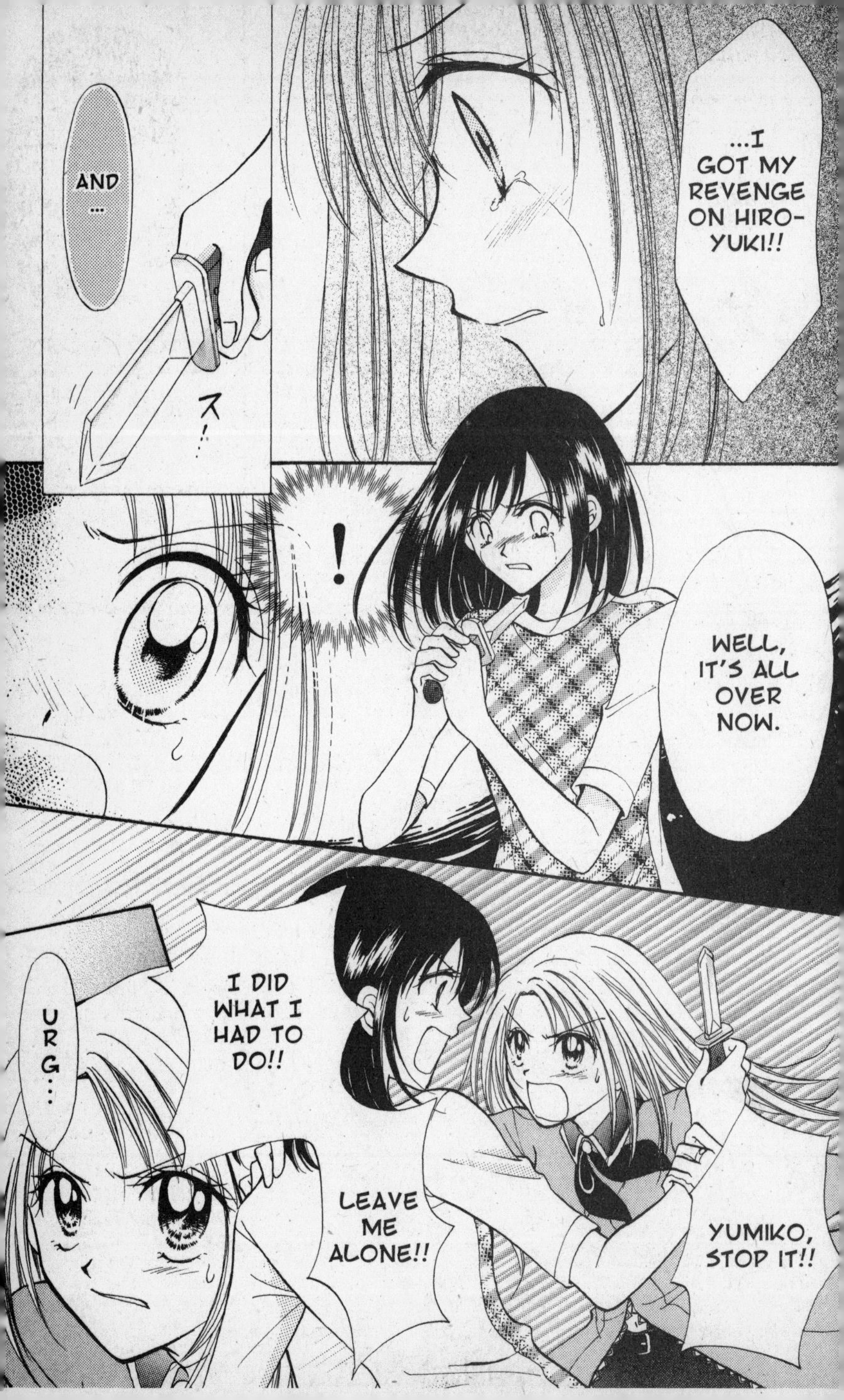
...I GOT MY REVENGE ON HIRO-YUKI!!
AND ...
ス‥
WELL, IT'S ALL OVER NOW.
!
YUMIKO, STOP IT!!
LEAVE ME ALONE!!
I DID WHAT I HAD TO DO!!
URG...

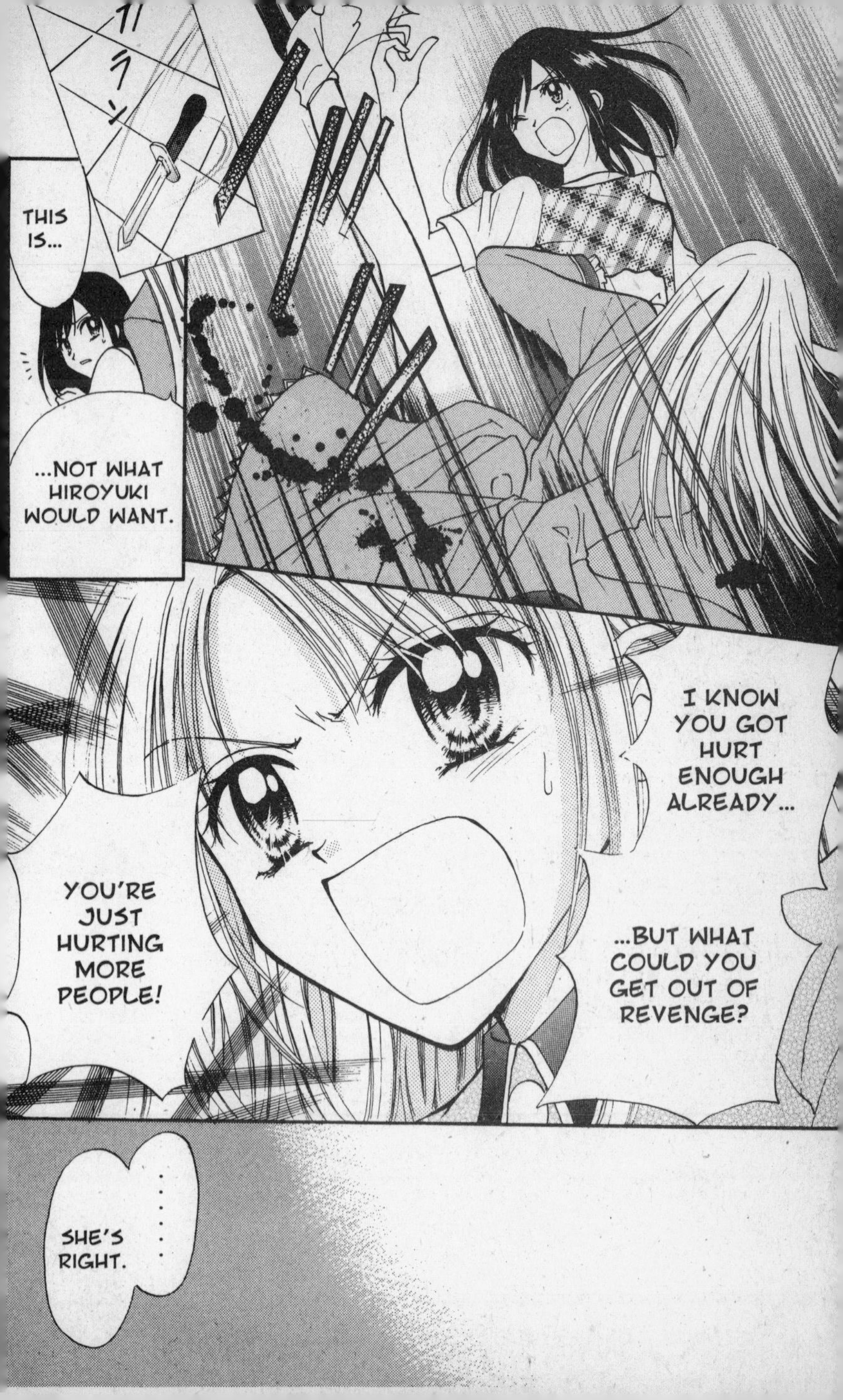

ギラン
THIS IS...
...NOT WHAT HIROYUKI WOULD WANT.
I KNOW YOU GOT HURT ENOUGH ALREADY...
...BUT WHAT COULD YOU GET OUT OF REVENGE?
YOU'RE JUST HURTING MORE PEOPLE!
......
SHE'S RIGHT.

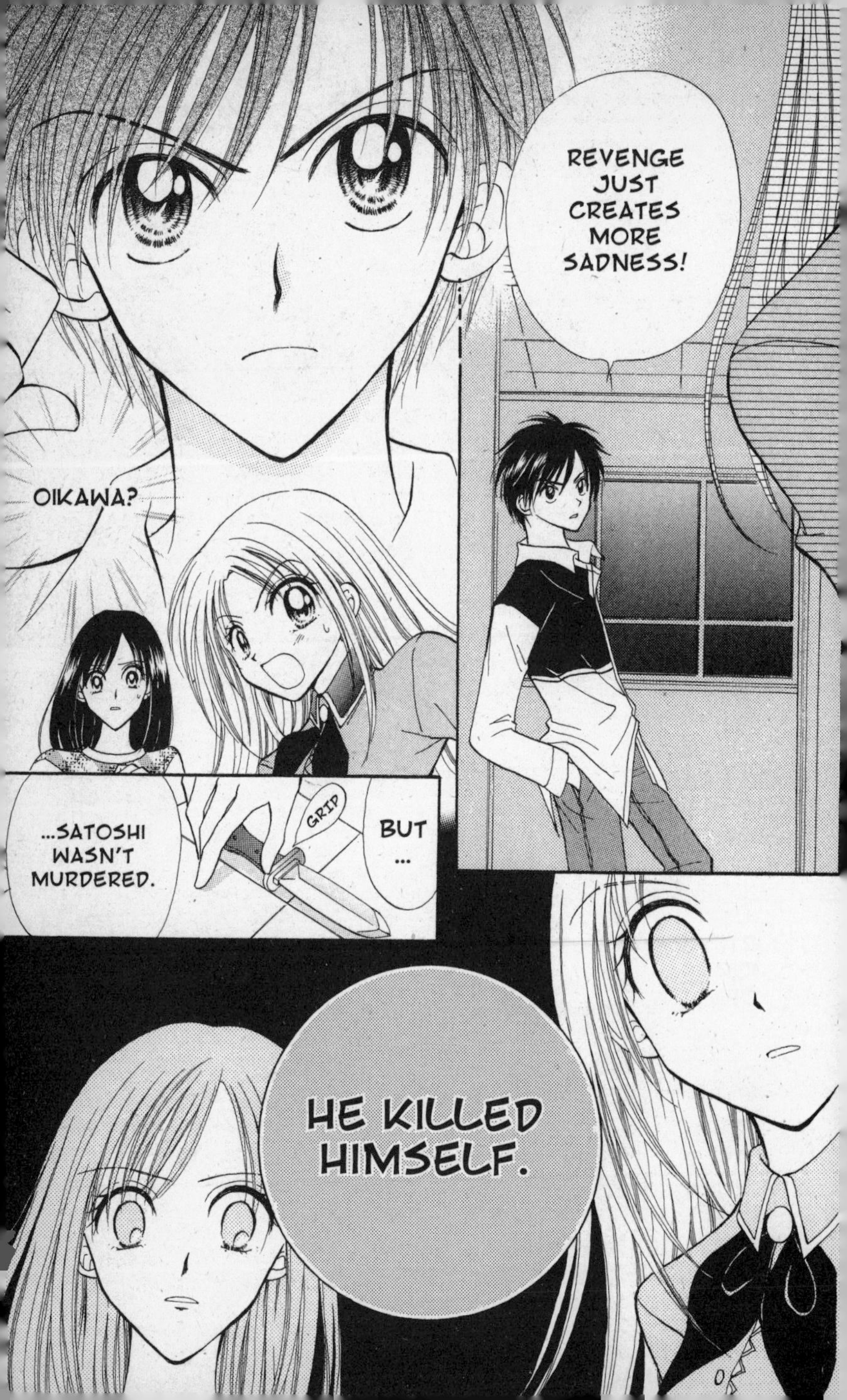
REVENGE JUST CREATES MORE SADNESS!
OIKAWA?
BUT ...
GRIP
...SATOSHI WASN'T MURDERED.
HE KILLED HIMSELF.

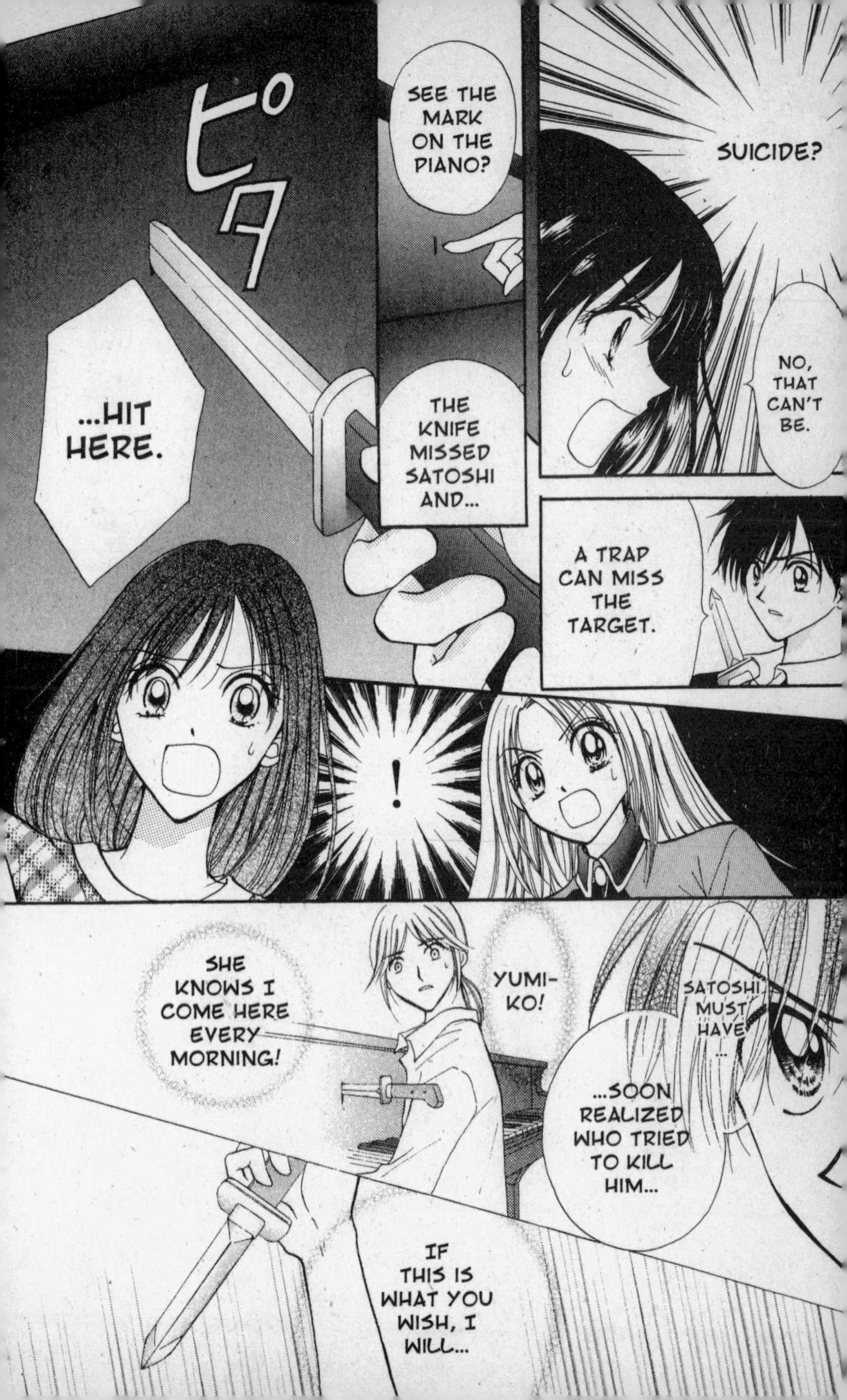
SUICIDE?
NO, THAT CAN'T BE.
A TRAP CAN MISS THE TARGET.
SEE THE MARK ON THE PIANO?
THE KNIFE MISSED SATOSHI AND...
ピタ
...HIT HERE.
!
SATOSHI MUST HAVE...
...SOON REALIZED WHO TRIED TO KILL HIM...
YUMI-KO!
SHE KNOWS I COME HERE EVERY MORNING!
IF THIS IS WHAT YOU WISH, I WILL...

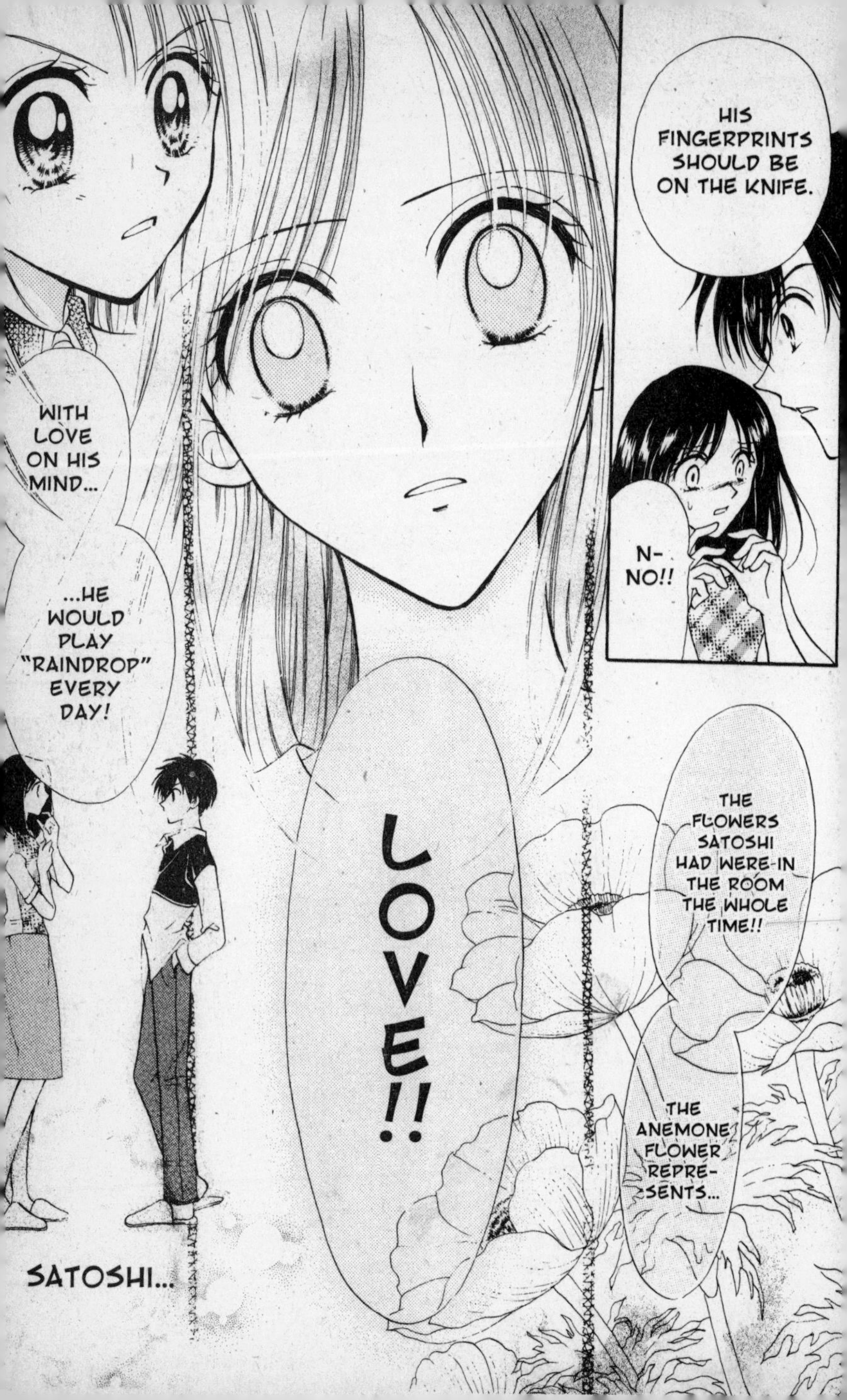
HIS FINGERPRINTS SHOULD BE ON THE KNIFE.
N-NO!!
THE FLOWERS SATOSHI HAD WERE IN THE ROOM THE WHOLE TIME!!
THE ANEMONE FLOWER REPRE-SENTS...
LOVE!!
WITH LOVE ON HIS MIND...
...HE WOULD PLAY "RAINDROP" EVERY DAY!
SATOSHI...

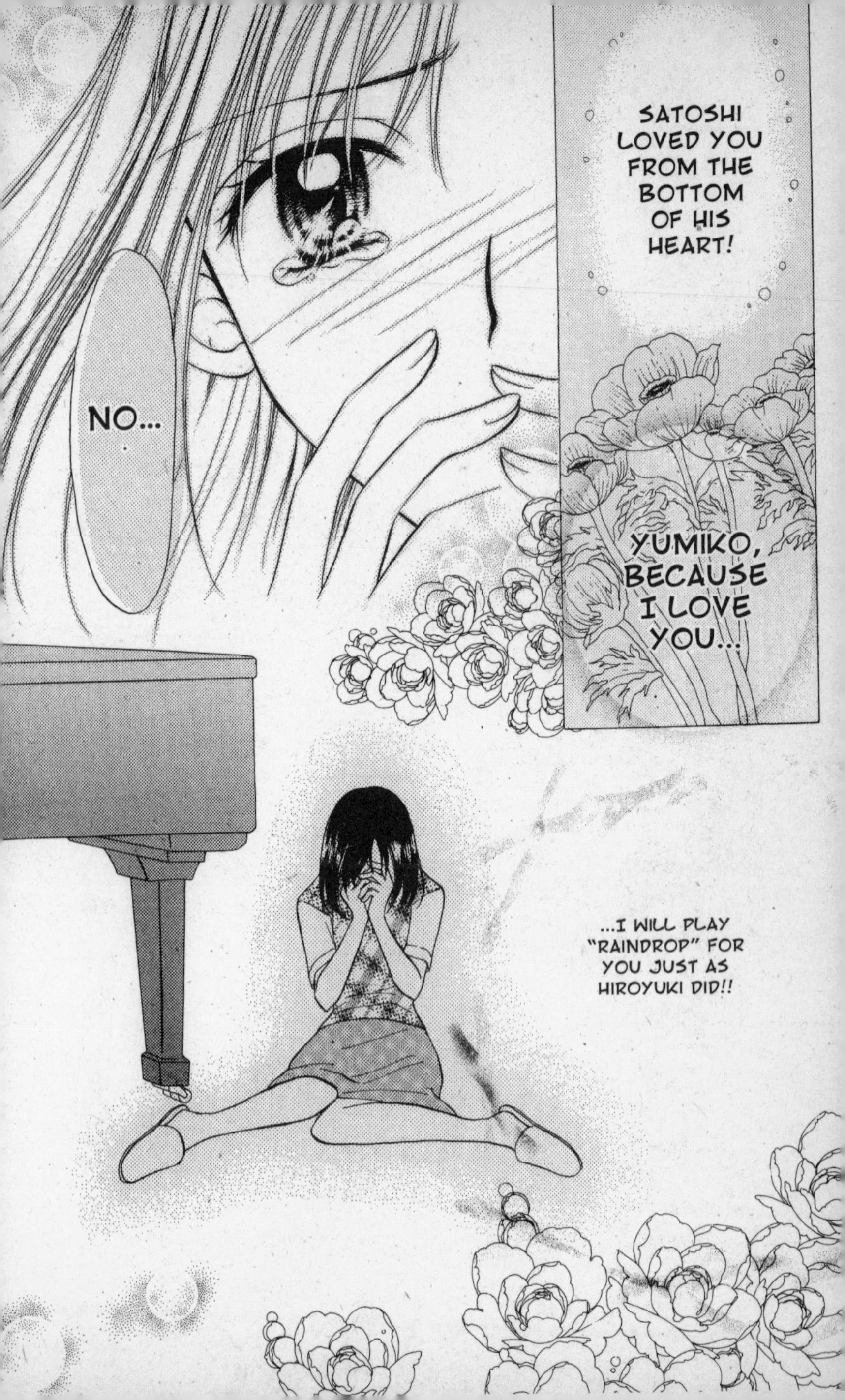
SATOSHI LOVED YOU FROM THE BOTTOM OF HIS HEART!
YUMIKO, BECAUSE I LOVE YOU...
NO...
...I WILL PLAY "RAINDROP" FOR YOU JUST AS HIROYUKI DID!!

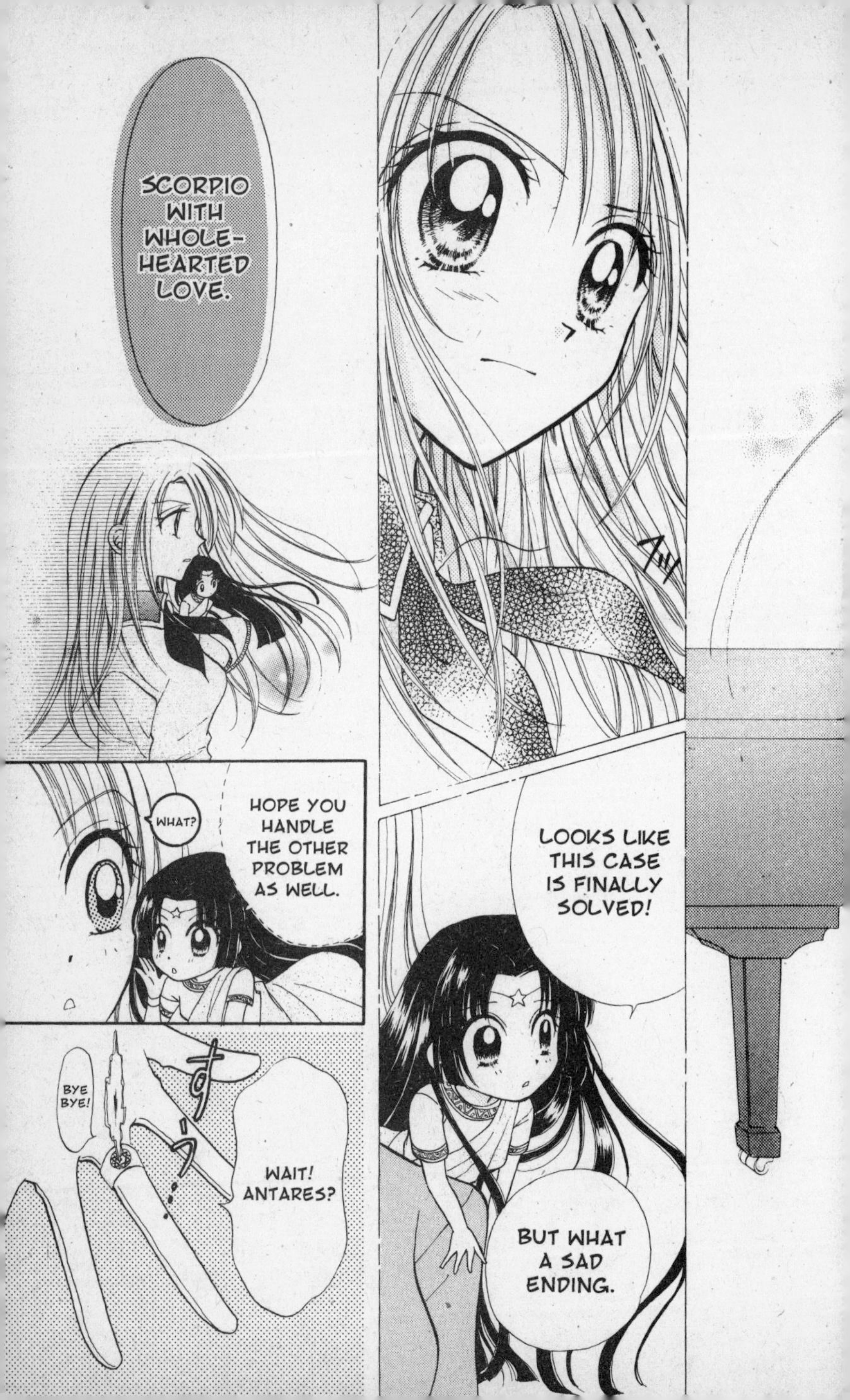

LOOKS LIKE THIS CASE IS FINALLY SOLVED!
BUT WHAT A SAD ENDING.
SCORPIO WITH WHOLE-HEARTED LOVE.
HOPE YOU HANDLE THE OTHER PROBLEM AS WELL.
WHAT?
BYE BYE!
WAIT! ANTARES?

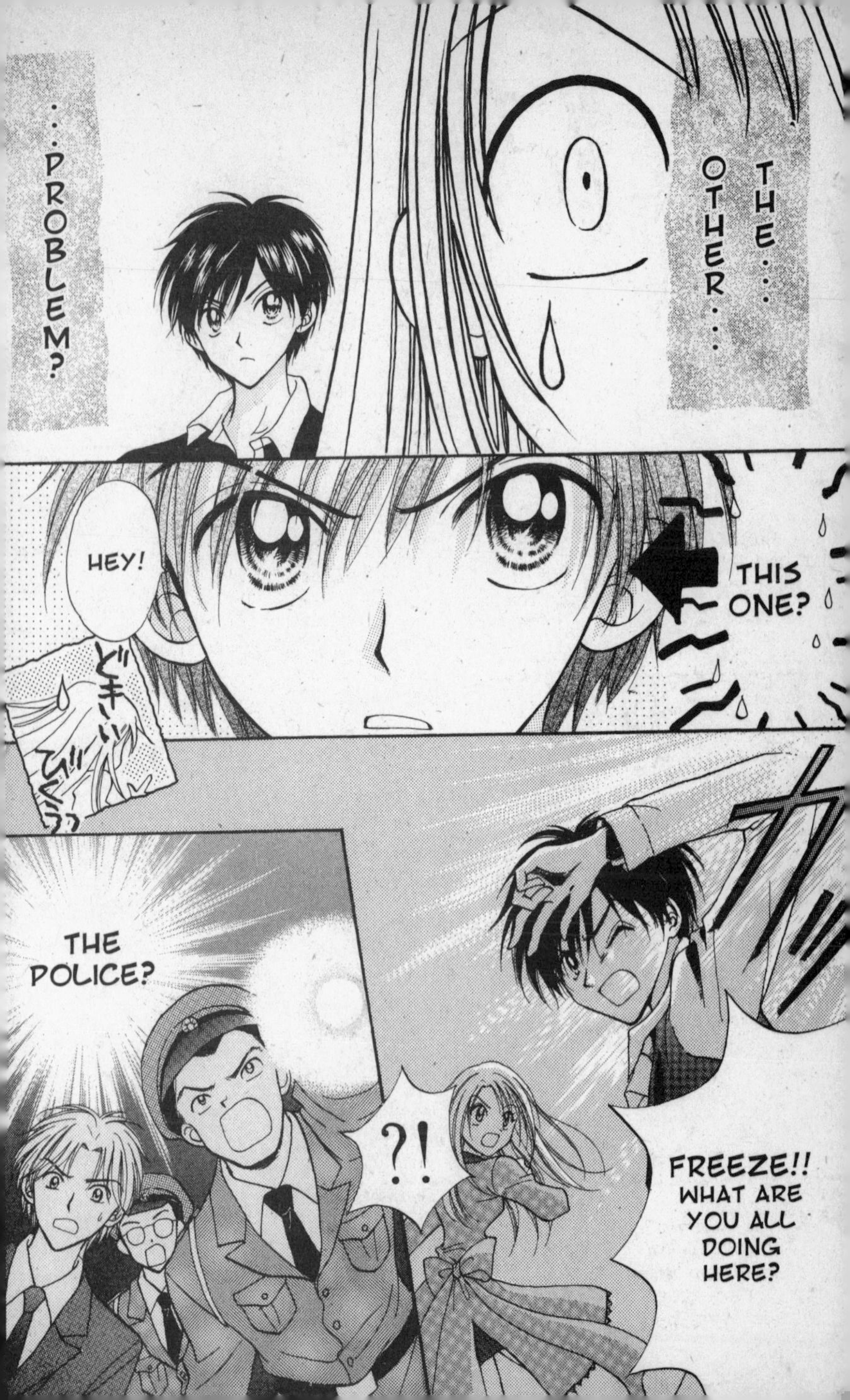
THE... OTHER...
...PROBLEM?
THIS ONE?
HEY!
FREEZE!! WHAT ARE YOU ALL DOING HERE?
?!
THE POLICE?

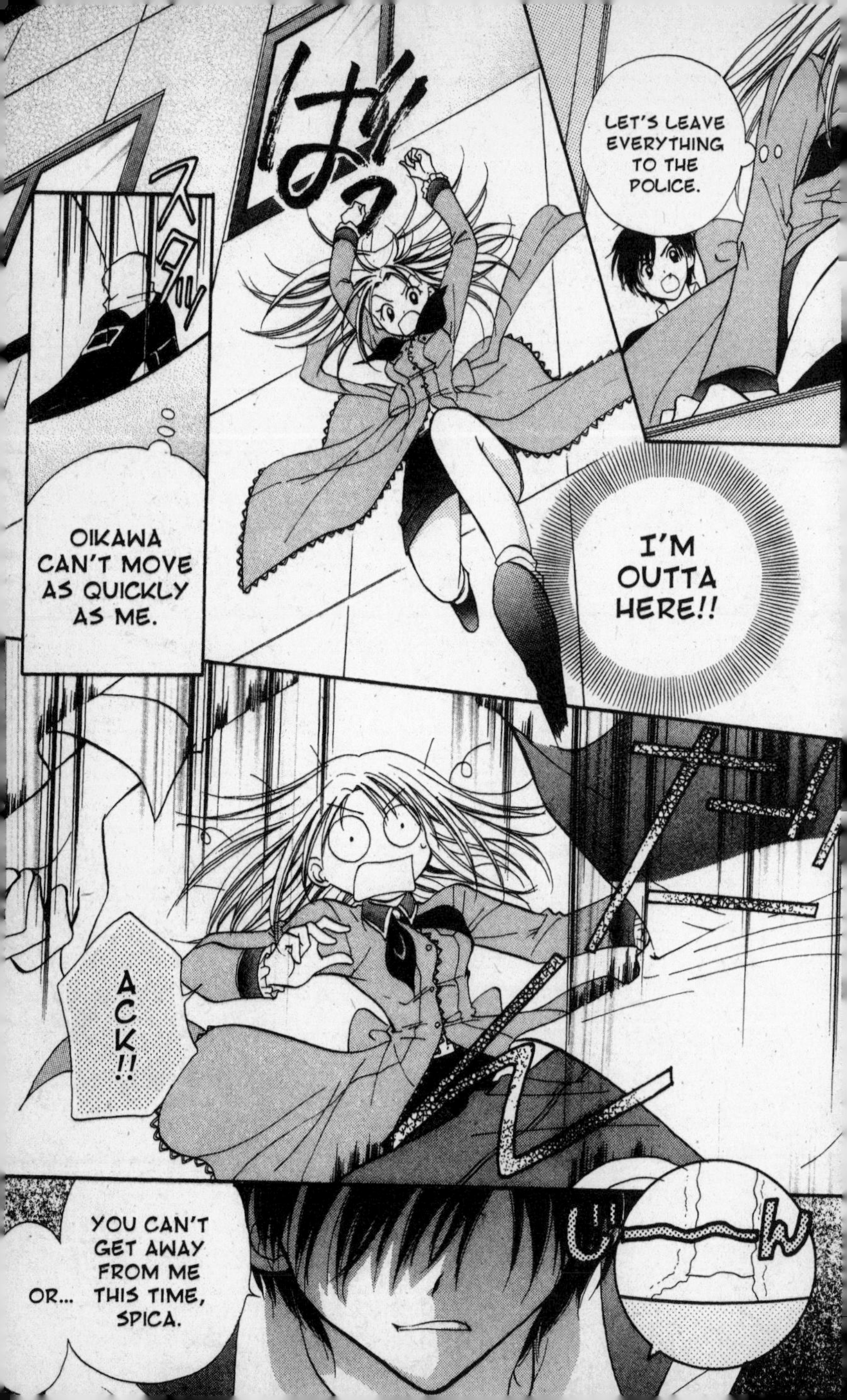
LET'S LEAVE EVERYTHING TO THE POLICE.
ばっ
I'M OUTTA HERE!!
スタッ
OIKAWA CAN'T MOVE AS QUICKLY AS ME.
ACK!!
YOU CAN'T GET AWAY FROM ME THIS TIME, SPICA.
OR...

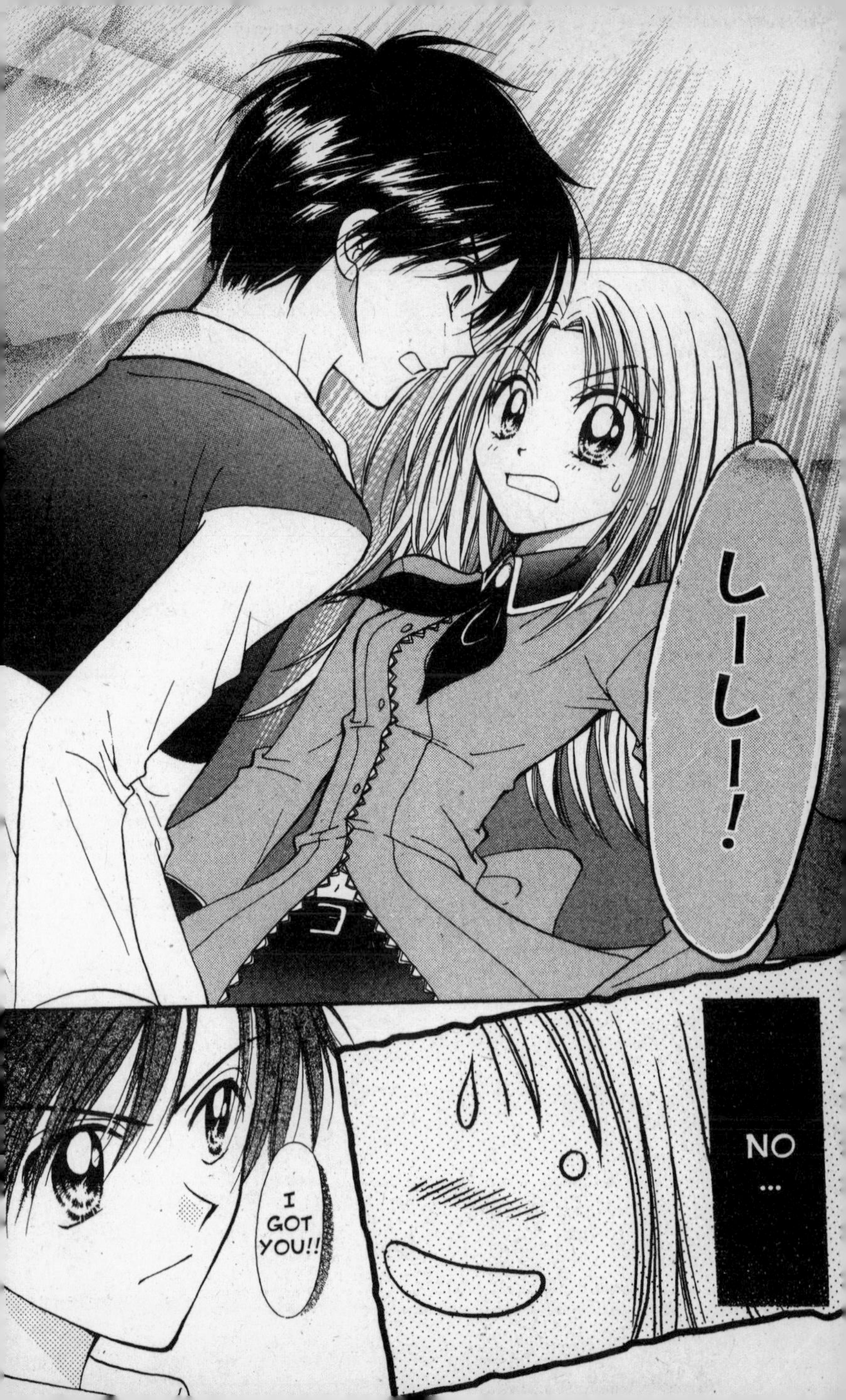
しーしー!
NO ...
I GOT YOU!!

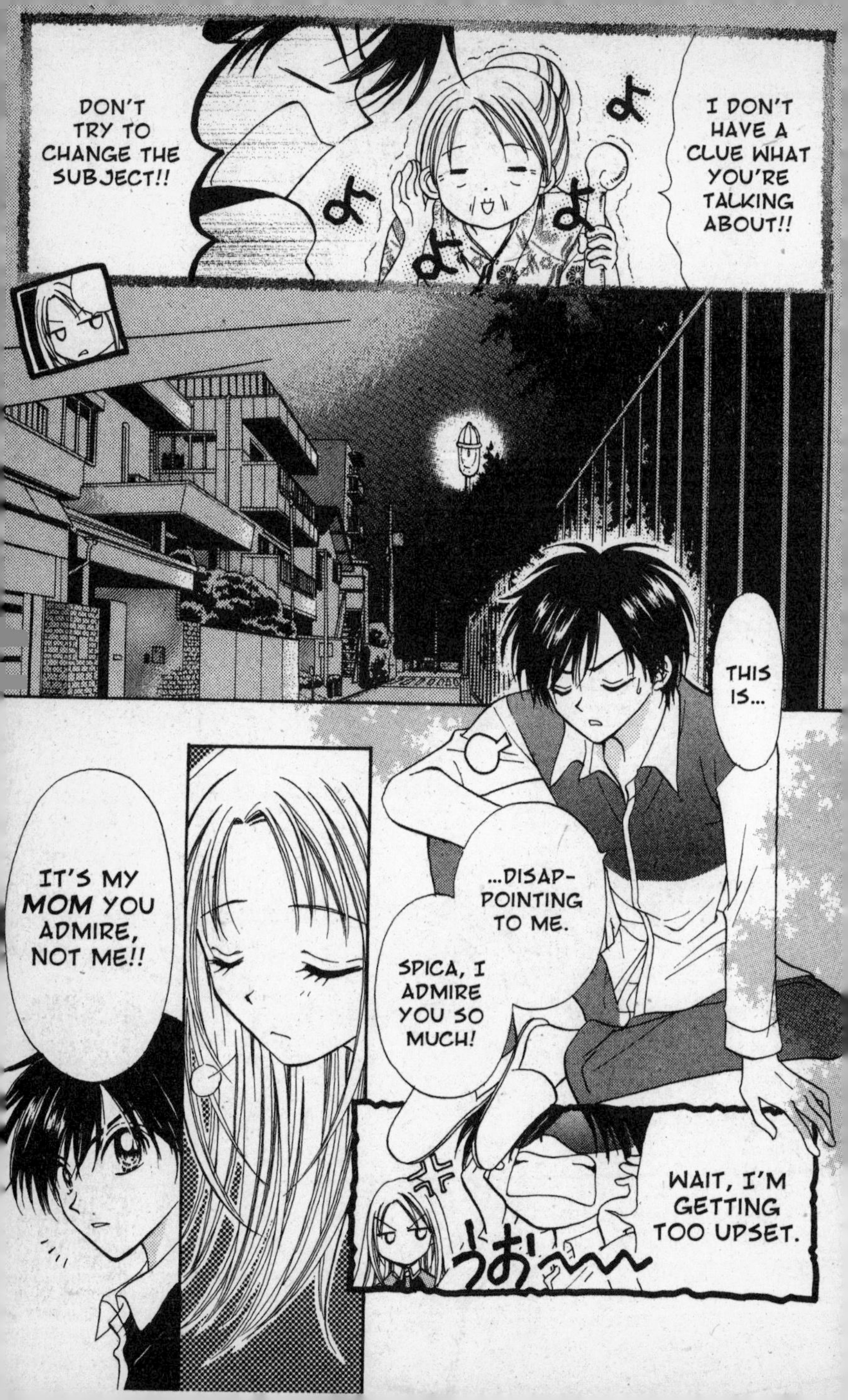
I DON'T HAVE A CLUE WHAT YOU'RE TALKING ABOUT!!
よ よ よ よ よ
DON'T TRY TO CHANGE THE SUBJECT!!
THIS IS...
...DISAP-POINTING TO ME.
SPICA, I ADMIRE YOU SO MUCH!
WAIT, I'M GETTING TOO UPSET.
うおっ〜〜
IT'S MY **MOM** YOU ADMIRE, NOT ME!!

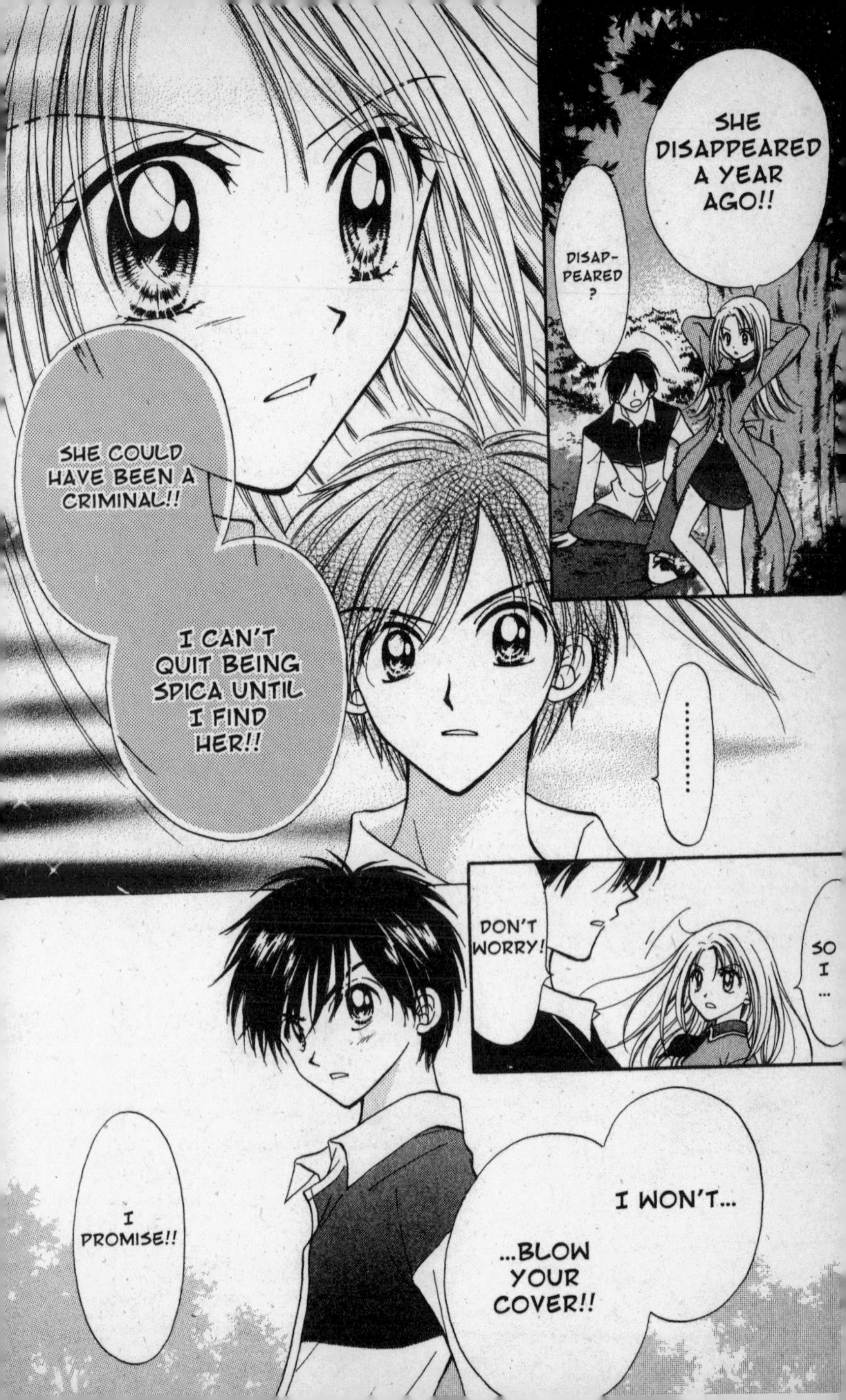
SHE DISAPPEARED A YEAR AGO!!
DISAP-PEARED?
SHE COULD HAVE BEEN A CRIMINAL!!
I CAN'T QUIT BEING SPICA UNTIL I FIND HER!!
......
SO I ...
DON'T WORRY!
I WON'T...
...BLOW YOUR COVER!!
I PROMISE!!

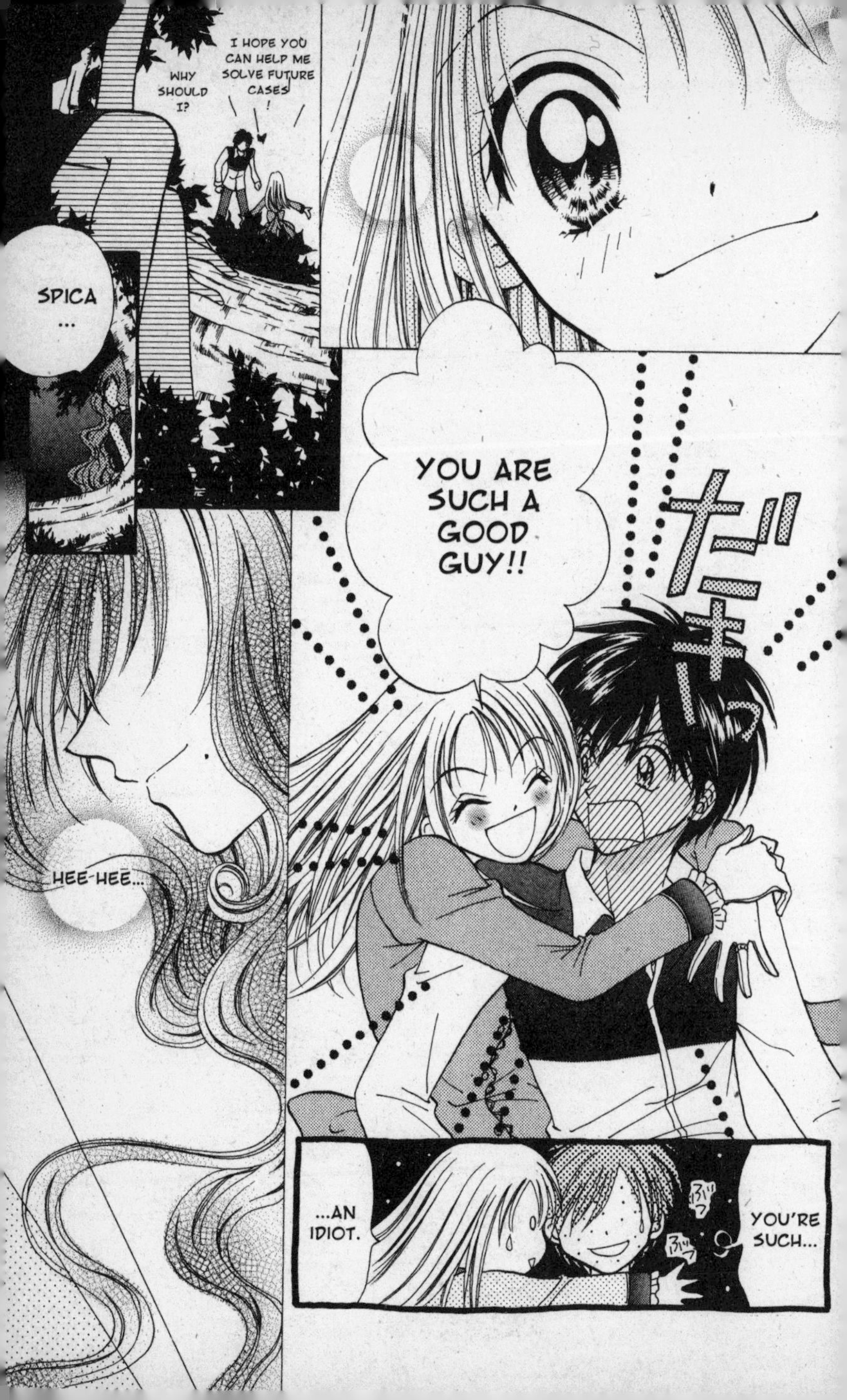
I HOPE YOU CAN HELP ME SOLVE FUTURE CASES!
WHY SHOULD I?
SPICA...
YOU ARE SUCH A GOOD GUY!!
だきっ
YOU'RE SUCH...
ふっ
ふっ
...AN IDIOT.
HEE-HEE...

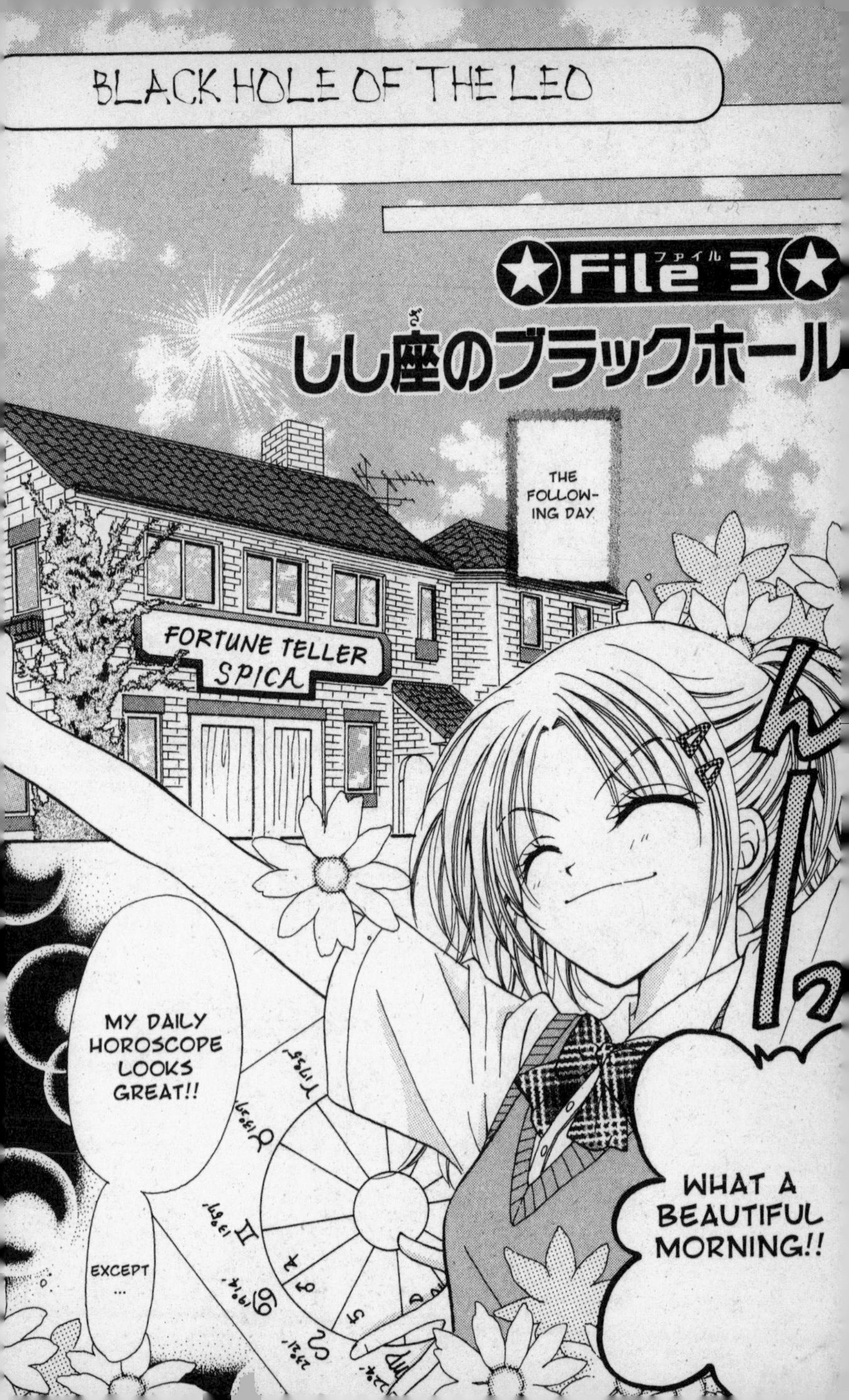
BLACK HOLE OF THE LEO
☆File 3☆
ファイル
しし座のブラックホール
THE FOLLOWING DAY
FORTUNE TELLER SPICA
んーっ
WHAT A BEAUTIFUL MORNING!!
MY DAILY HOROSCOPE LOOKS GREAT!!
EXCEPT ...

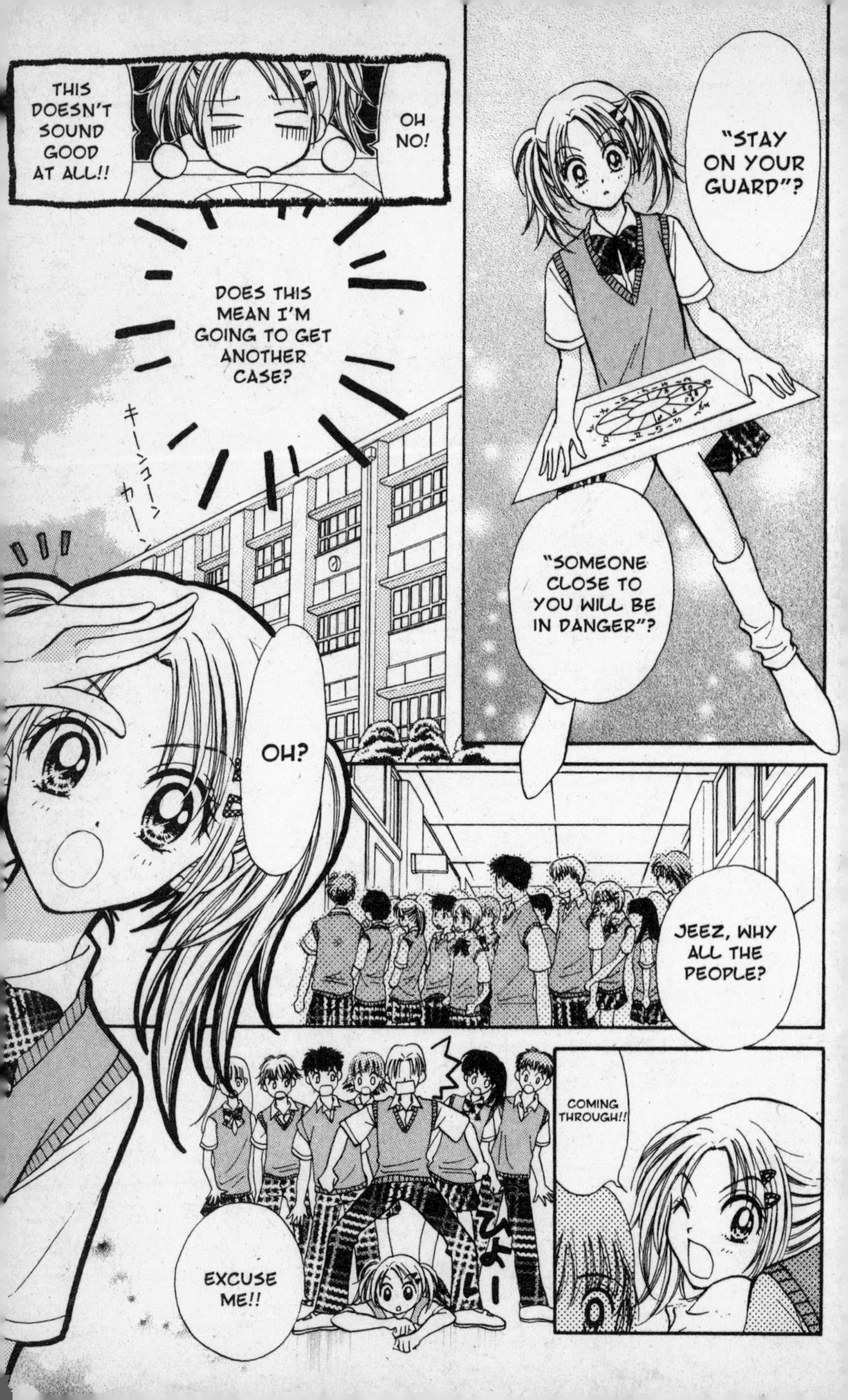

"STAY ON YOUR GUARD"?
"SOMEONE CLOSE TO YOU WILL BE IN DANGER"?
OH NO!
THIS DOESN'T SOUND GOOD AT ALL!!
DOES THIS MEAN I'M GOING TO GET ANOTHER CASE?
キーンコーン カーン
OH?
JEEZ, WHY ALL THE PEOPLE?
COMING THROUGH!!
EXCUSE ME!!

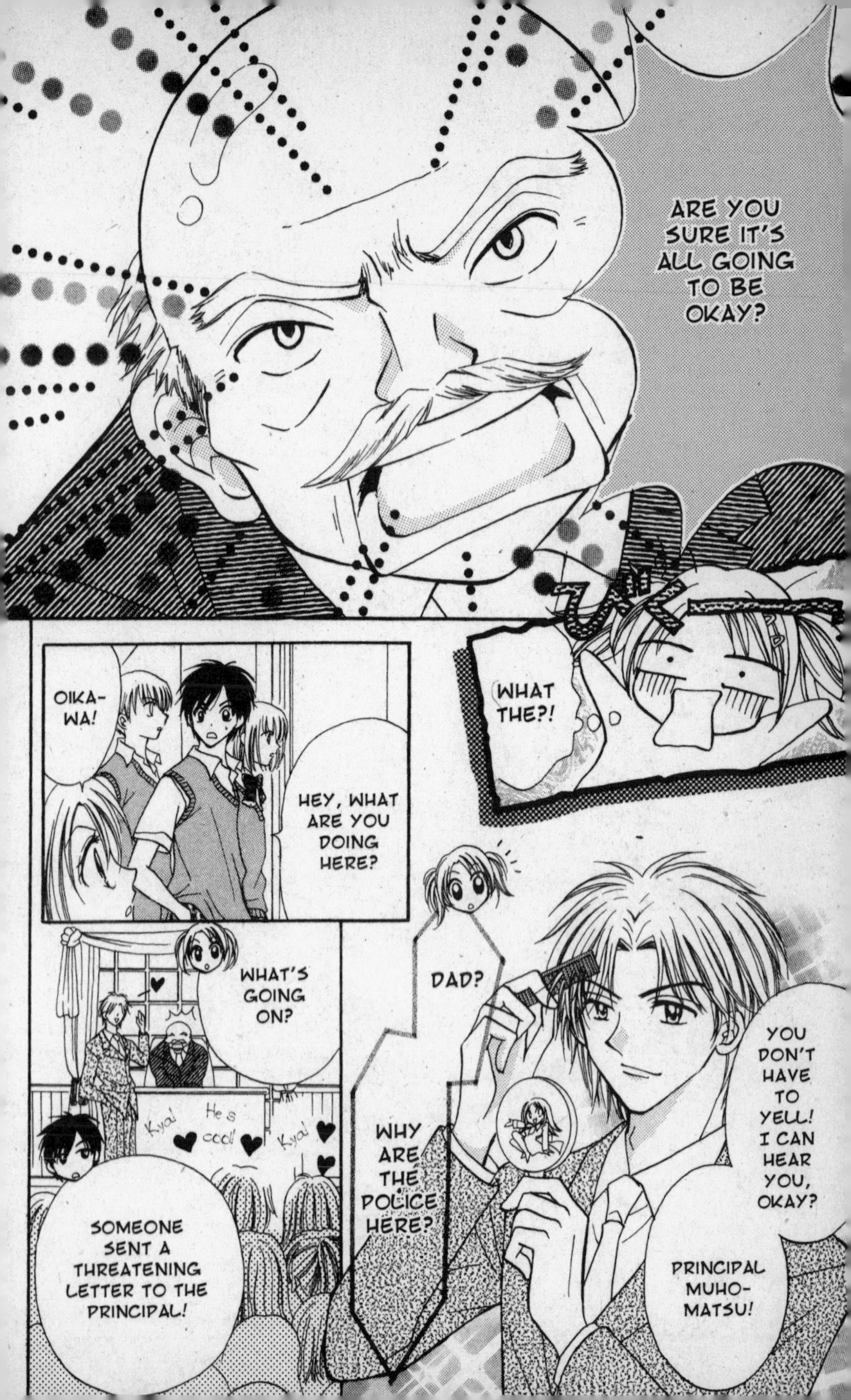
ARE YOU SURE IT'S ALL GOING TO BE OKAY?
WHAT THE?!
OIKA-WA!
HEY, WHAT ARE YOU DOING HERE?
DAD?
YOU DON'T HAVE TO YELL! I CAN HEAR YOU, OKAY?
PRINCIPAL MUHO-MATSU!
WHY ARE THE POLICE HERE?
WHAT'S GOING ON?
Kya!
He's cool!
Kya!
SOMEONE SENT A THREATENING LETTER TO THE PRINCIPAL!

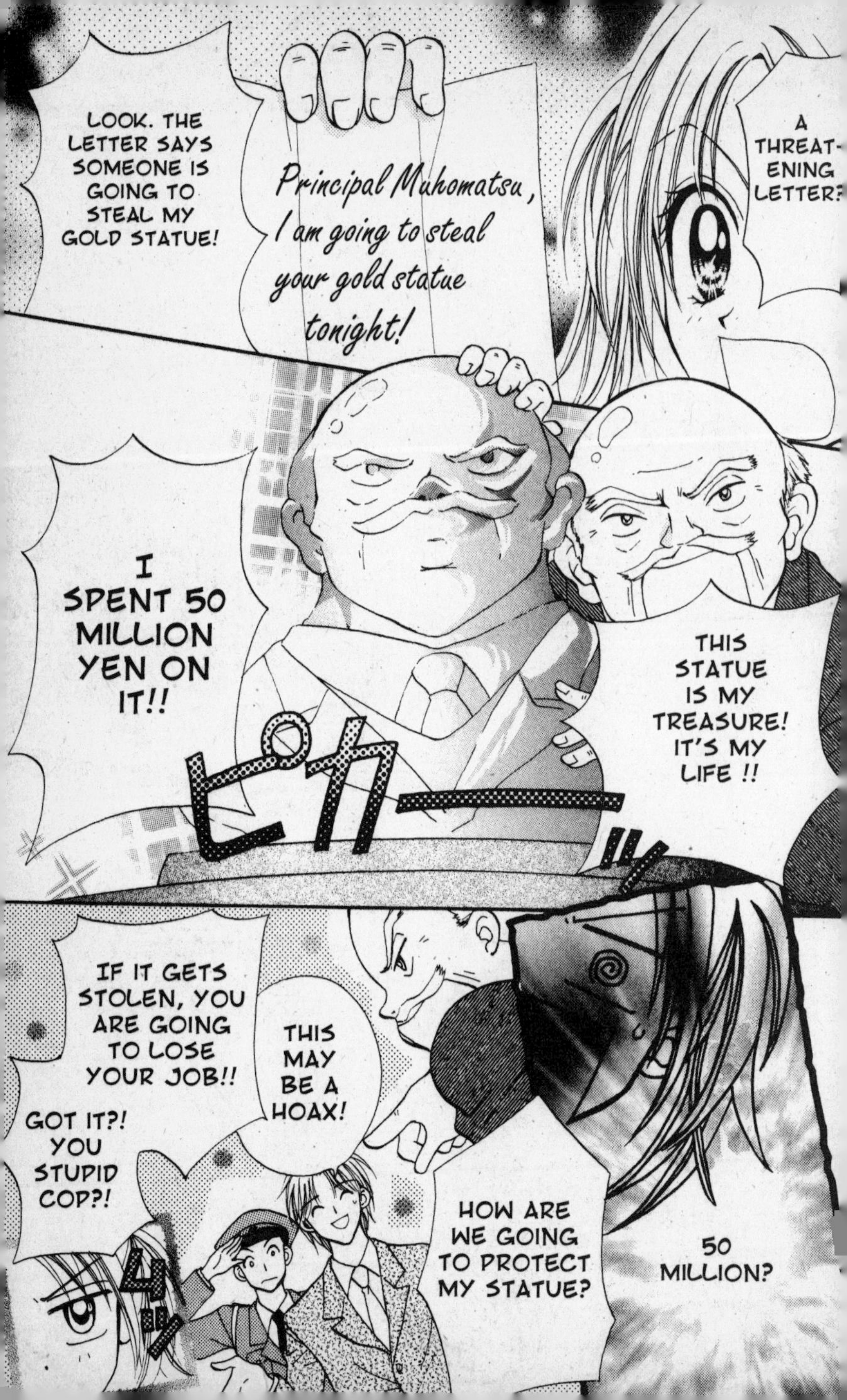
A THREAT-ENING LETTER?
Principal Muhomatsu, I am going to steal your gold statue tonight!
LOOK. THE LETTER SAYS SOMEONE IS GOING TO STEAL MY GOLD STATUE!
THIS STATUE IS MY TREASURE! IT'S MY LIFE !!
I SPENT 50 MILLION YEN ON IT!!
ピカー
50 MILLION?
HOW ARE WE GOING TO PROTECT MY STATUE?
THIS MAY BE A HOAX!
IF IT GETS STOLEN, YOU ARE GOING TO LOSE YOUR JOB!!
GOT IT?! YOU STUPID COP?!

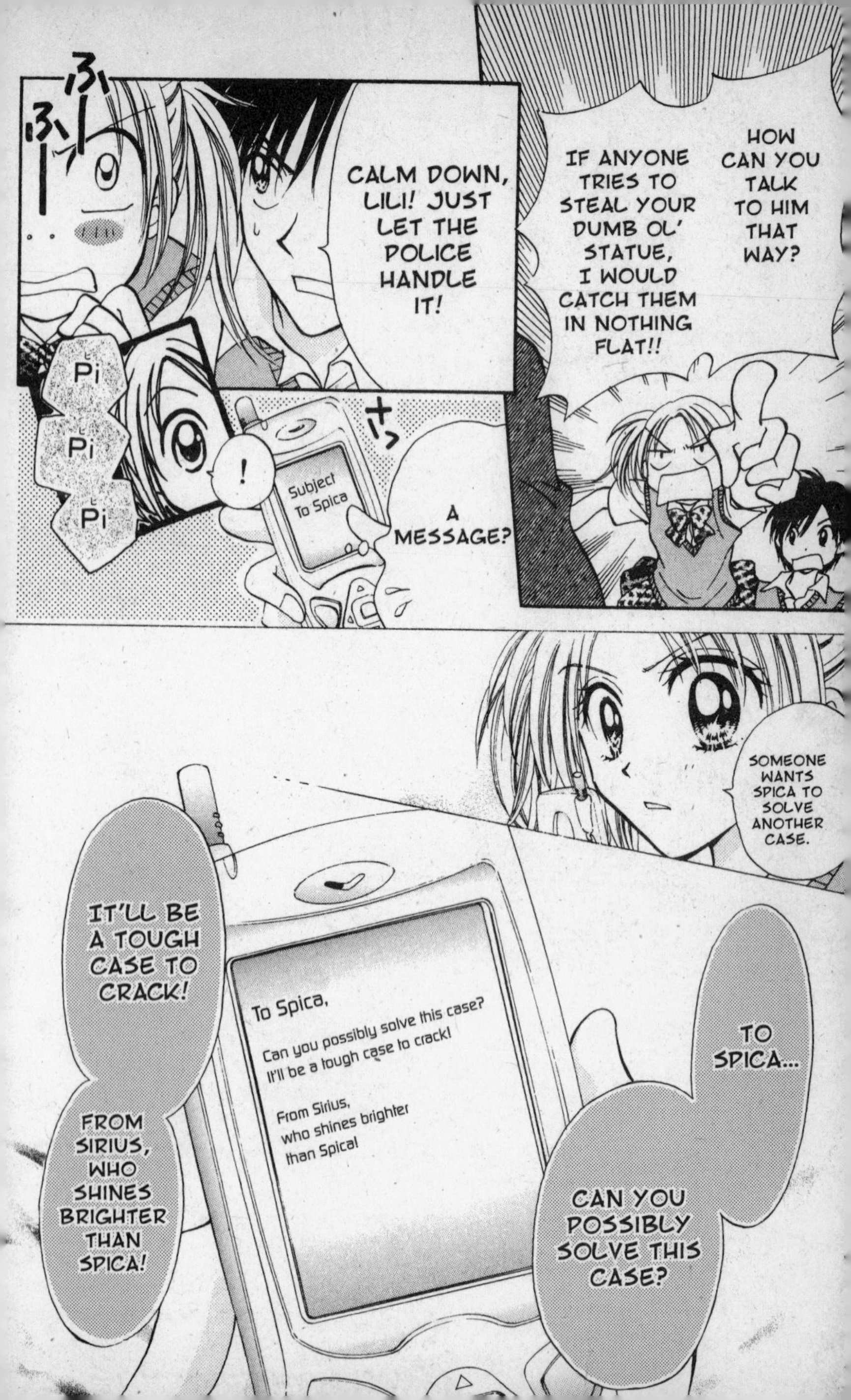
HOW CAN YOU TALK TO HIM THAT WAY?
IF ANYONE TRIES TO STEAL YOUR DUMB OL' STATUE, I WOULD CATCH THEM IN NOTHING FLAT!!
ふーふー
CALM DOWN, LILI! JUST LET THE POLICE HANDLE IT!
Pi
Pi
Pi
!
Subject To Spica
A MESSAGE?
SOMEONE WANTS SPICA TO SOLVE ANOTHER CASE.
To Spica,
Can you possibly solve this case? It'll be a tough case to crack!
From Sirius, who shines brighter than Spica!
TO SPICA...
CAN YOU POSSIBLY SOLVE THIS CASE?
IT'LL BE A TOUGH CASE TO CRACK!
FROM SIRIUS, WHO SHINES BRIGHTER THAN SPICA!

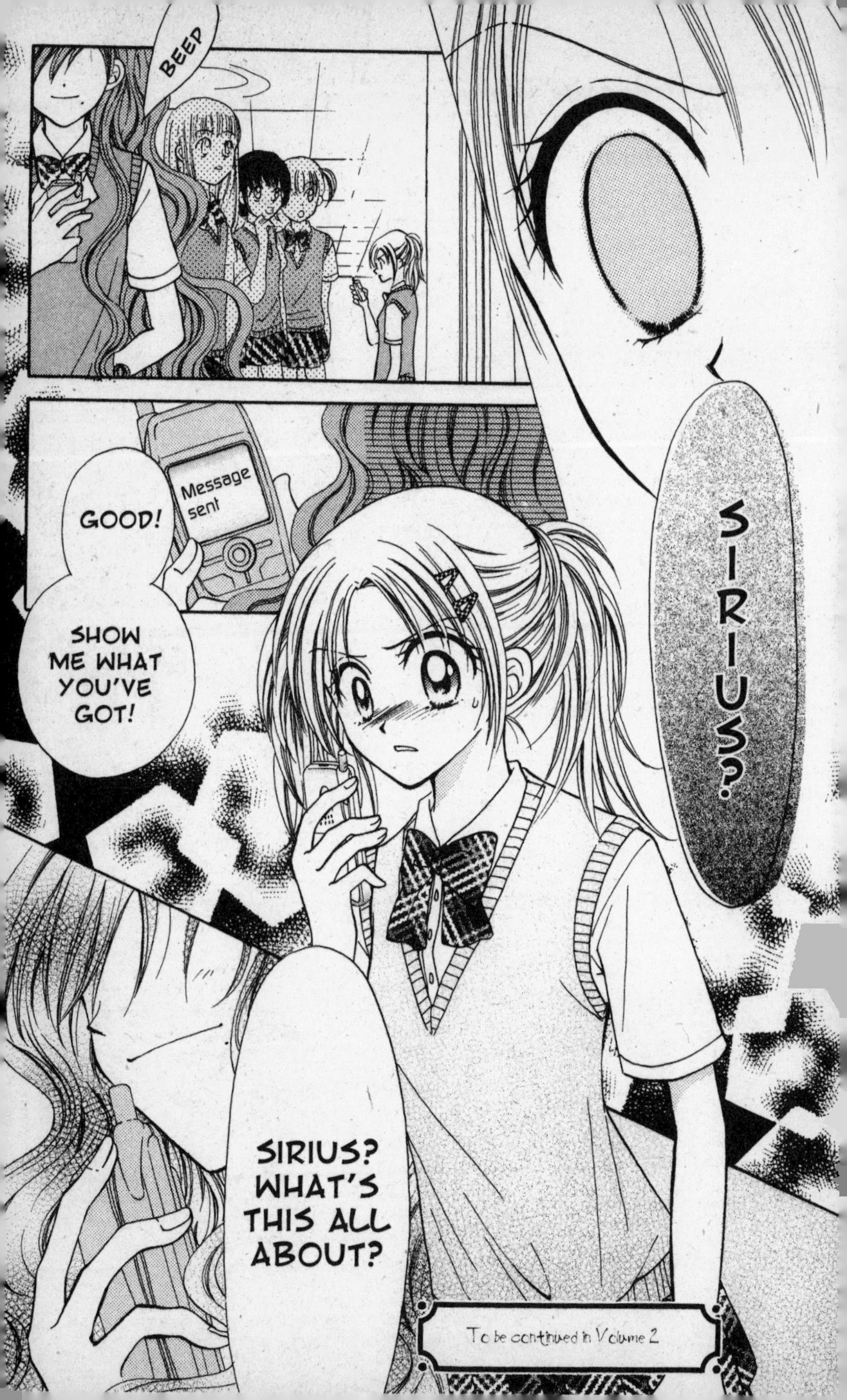

SIRIUS?
BEEP
Message sent
GOOD!
SHOW ME WHAT YOU'VE GOT!
SIRIUS? WHAT'S THIS ALL ABOUT?
To be continued in Volume 2

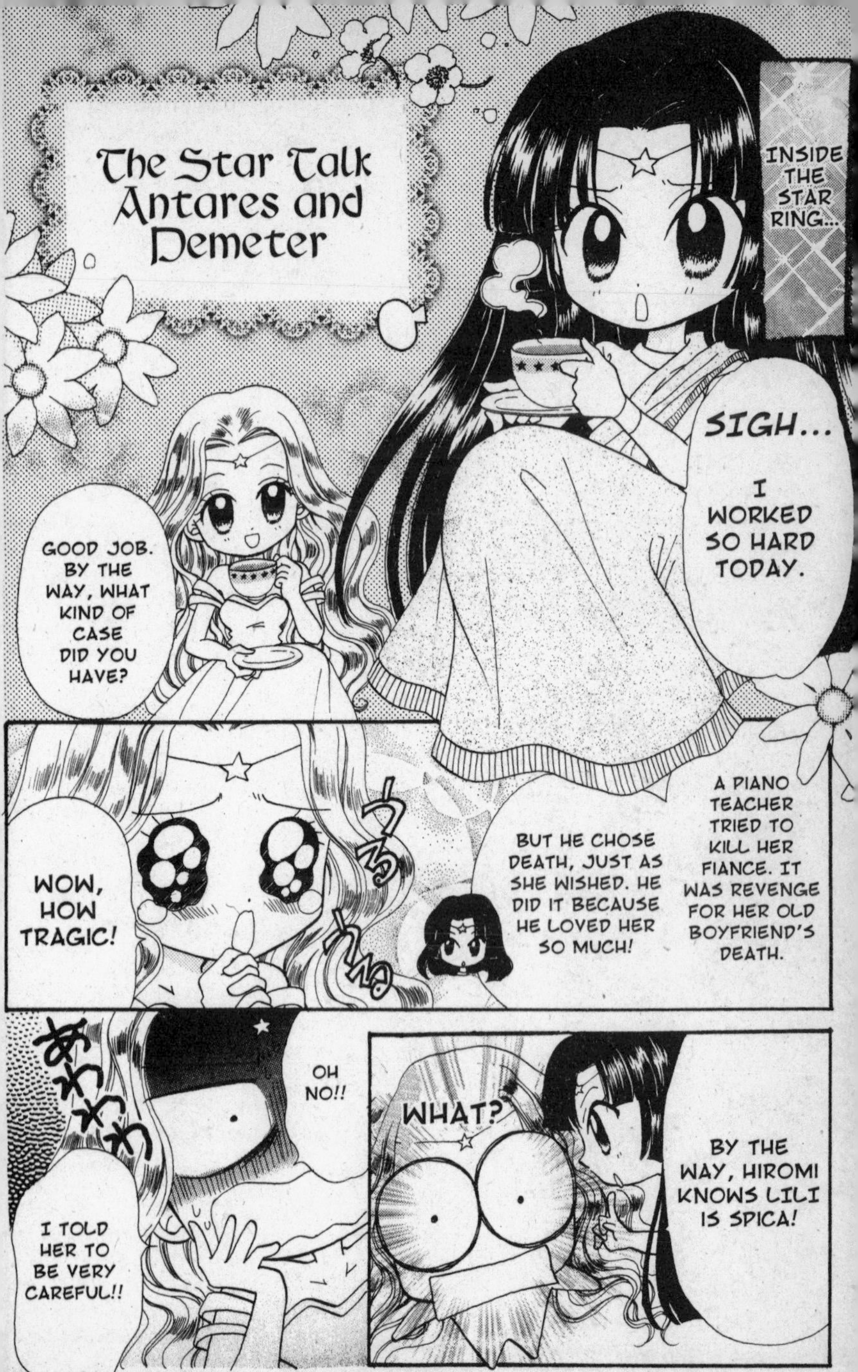
The Star Talk Antares and Demeter
INSIDE THE STAR RING...
SIGH...
I WORKED SO HARD TODAY.
GOOD JOB. BY THE WAY, WHAT KIND OF CASE DID YOU HAVE?
A PIANO TEACHER TRIED TO KILL HER FIANCE. IT WAS REVENGE FOR HER OLD BOYFRIEND'S DEATH.
BUT HE CHOSE DEATH, JUST AS SHE WISHED. HE DID IT BECAUSE HE LOVED HER SO MUCH!
うるうる
WOW, HOW TRAGIC!
BY THE WAY, HIROMI KNOWS LILI IS SPICA!
WHAT?
OH NO!!
あわわわ
I TOLD HER TO BE VERY CAREFUL!!

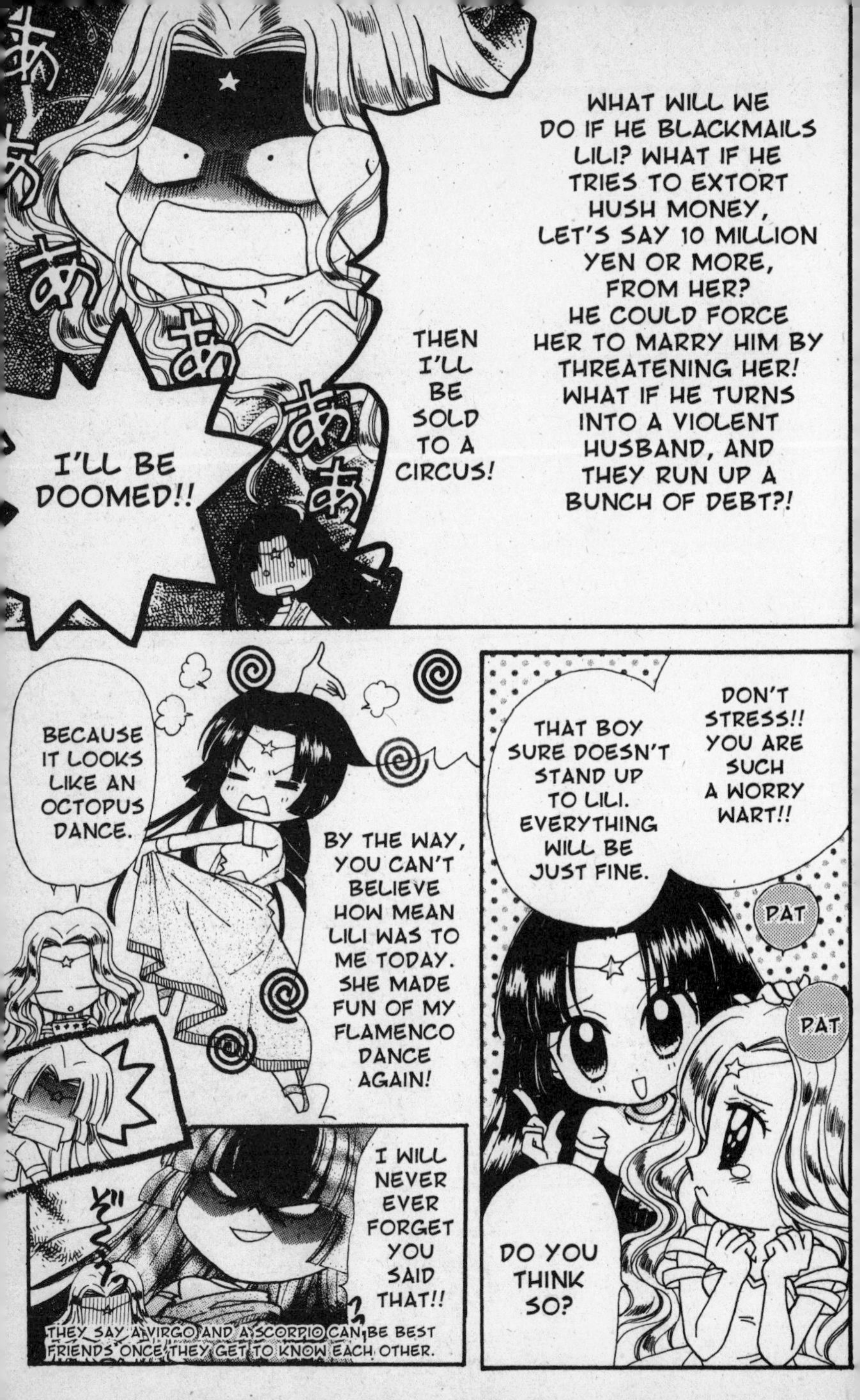

WHAT WILL WE DO IF HE BLACKMAILS LILI? WHAT IF HE TRIES TO EXTORT HUSH MONEY, LET'S SAY 10 MILLION YEN OR MORE, FROM HER? HE COULD FORCE HER TO MARRY HIM BY THREATENING HER! WHAT IF HE TURNS INTO A VIOLENT HUSBAND, AND THEY RUN UP A BUNCH OF DEBT?!
THEN I'LL BE SOLD TO A CIRCUS!
I'LL BE DOOMED!!
DON'T STRESS!! YOU ARE SUCH A WORRY WART!!
THAT BOY SURE DOESN'T STAND UP TO LILI. EVERYTHING WILL BE JUST FINE.
PAT
PAT
DO YOU THINK SO?
BY THE WAY, YOU CAN'T BELIEVE HOW MEAN LILI WAS TO ME TODAY. SHE MADE FUN OF MY FLAMENCO DANCE AGAIN!
BECAUSE IT LOOKS LIKE AN OCTOPUS DANCE.
I WILL NEVER EVER FORGET YOU SAID THAT!!
THEY SAY A VIRGO AND A SCORPIO CAN BE BEST FRIENDS ONCE THEY GET TO KNOW EACH OTHER.

Q&A

Using the couple of extra pages, I would like to answer frequently asked questions from the readers. Hope you enjoy!

★ How can I become a better artist?

I get a ton of questions like this. I want to improve my drawing too!! In my opinion, you have to keep practicing. Make it a habit of drawing something everyday. Try to draw people in different poses and various facial expressions. You wont perfect the art of drawing overnight. It takes time. When I see drawings that I did many years ago, I can appreciate how much I've improved!

★ What are you into these days?

I am into collecting rings. Two of my favorites are:

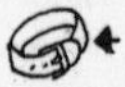

A band that's made of leather. It looks like a belt.

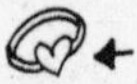

The other, a ring with a heart-shaped stone. The stone changes colors. It has up to seven different colors! I also enjoy bathing with bath gels! I especially like the milky ones. Conditioning ones aren't bad either. I've tried vanilla, strawberry, and mudbath gels too. I didn't like the muddy one!

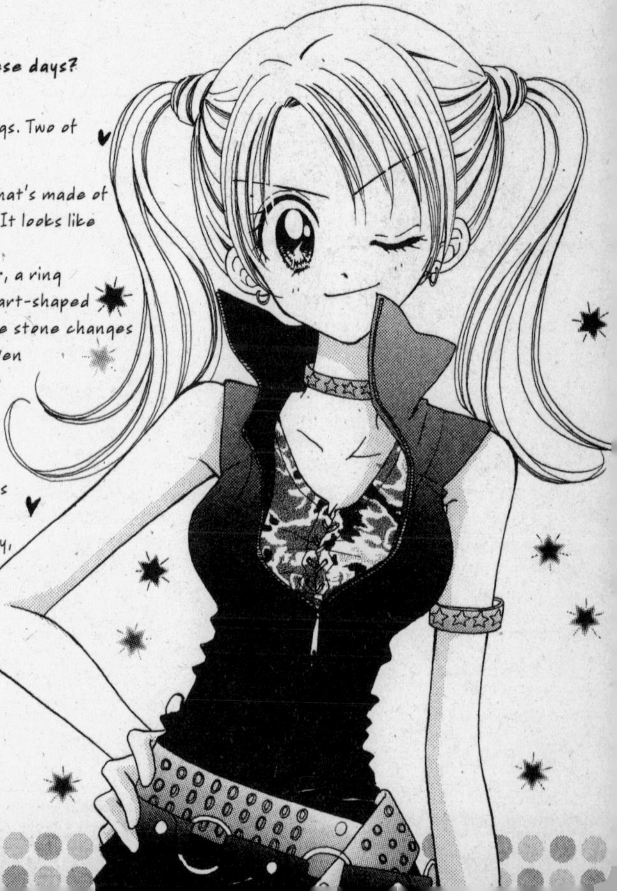

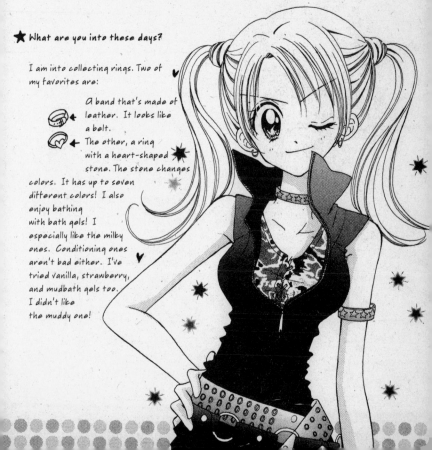

How can I become a manga artist?

Many readers tell me they want to be manga artists. Many ask if they can learn it in school. I don't think many schools offer courses on manga. The best way to do it is to go ahead and create your art. Then send it to a publisher every few months.

How do you name your characters?

To create a character, I first decide on her face and personality. After that, I try to brainstorm, hoping to come up with the perfect name. If that doesn't work, I might use my friends' names. I like names with meaning, so sometimes I make u a name. For example, Lili was named after Rin Rinto. That's a star on a Japanese soap opera. Rinr means brave and heroic. Brave girls cool!! So, this story's heroine got her name from the words "brave" and "heroic."

I am in charge of the Astral Spirit Design Contest for Nakayoshi. I always dreamed of having suc a project. I haven't seen all the works submitted, but many of them are very impressive. I'm havin the toughest time choosing the winner. Thanks to all who participated in the contest. I will let you know more about the contest in volume 2.

Thanks for sticking around! I hope to talk to you all soon!

Next Time in

Zodiac P.I.

Volume 2

Lili is flooded with cases involving
some people who are near and dear to
her heart, but she somehow manages
to go on with her life. However, her
appearance on an astrology TV show
may proove to be out of her league when
an astrologist is poisoned. It's her first
high-profile case and it's up to Lili to
solve the case before the public court!

Bonus Lab Experiment

Kat & mouse

1 teacher torture

Story: Alex de Campi
Art: Federica Manfredi

SPECIAL LOW MANGA PRICE: $5.99

When Kat moves to a posh private school, things seem perfect--that is, until a clique of rich, popular kids frame Kat's science teacher dad for stealing school property. Can Kat and her new friend, rebellious computer nerd Mouse, prove who the real culprits are before Kat's dad loses his job?

Y YOUTH AGE 10+

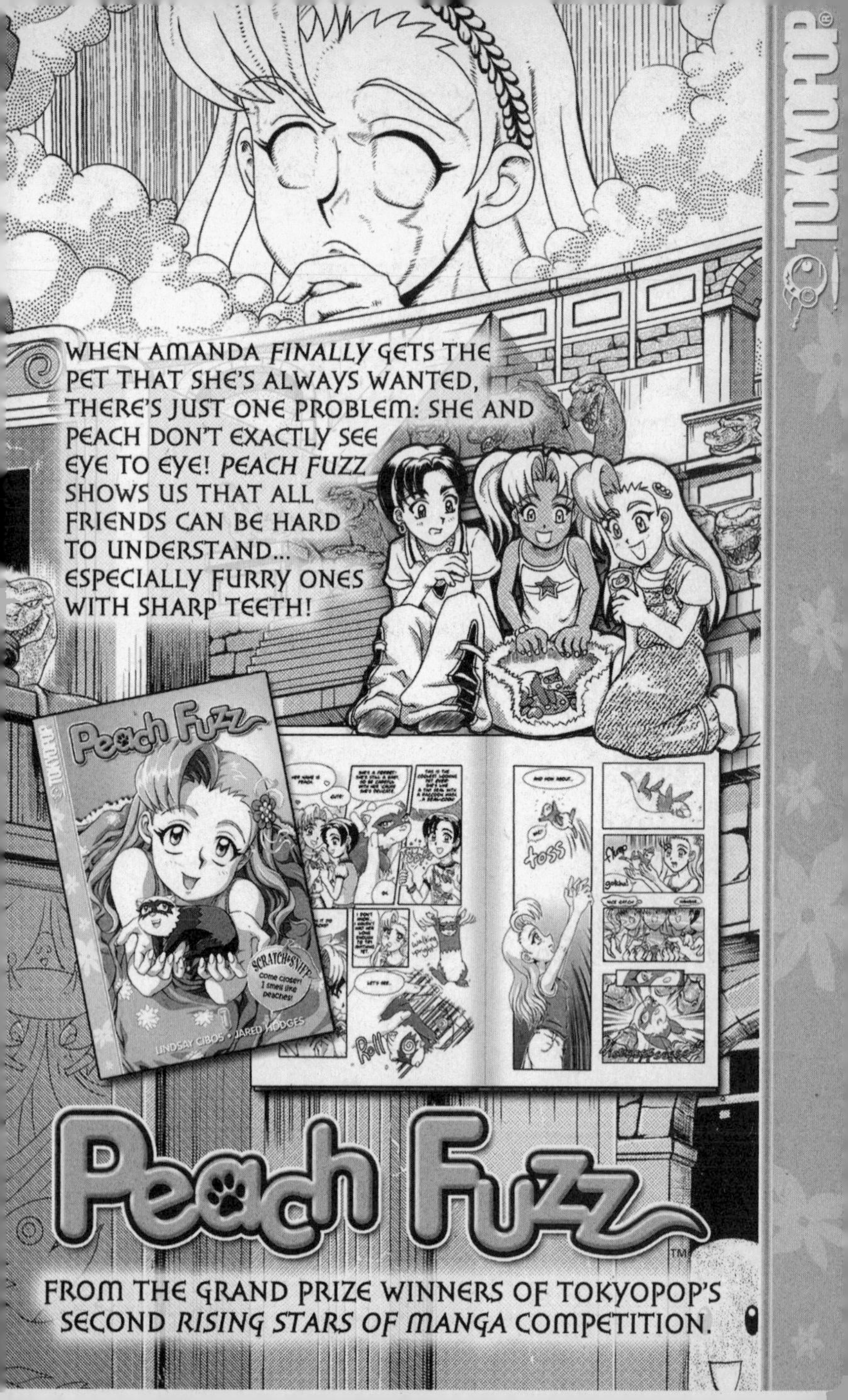
TOKYOPOP®
WHEN AMANDA *FINALLY* GETS THE PET THAT SHE'S ALWAYS WANTED, THERE'S JUST ONE PROBLEM: SHE AND PEACH DON'T EXACTLY SEE EYE TO EYE! *PEACH FUZZ* SHOWS US THAT ALL FRIENDS CAN BE HARD TO UNDERSTAND... ESPECIALLY FURRY ONES WITH SHARP TEETH!
Peach Fuzz
SCRATCH & SNIFF
Come closer! I smell like peaches!
LINDSAY CIBOS • JARED HODGES
Peach Fuzz™
FROM THE GRAND PRIZE WINNERS OF TOKYOPOP'S SECOND *RISING STARS OF MANGA* COMPETITION.

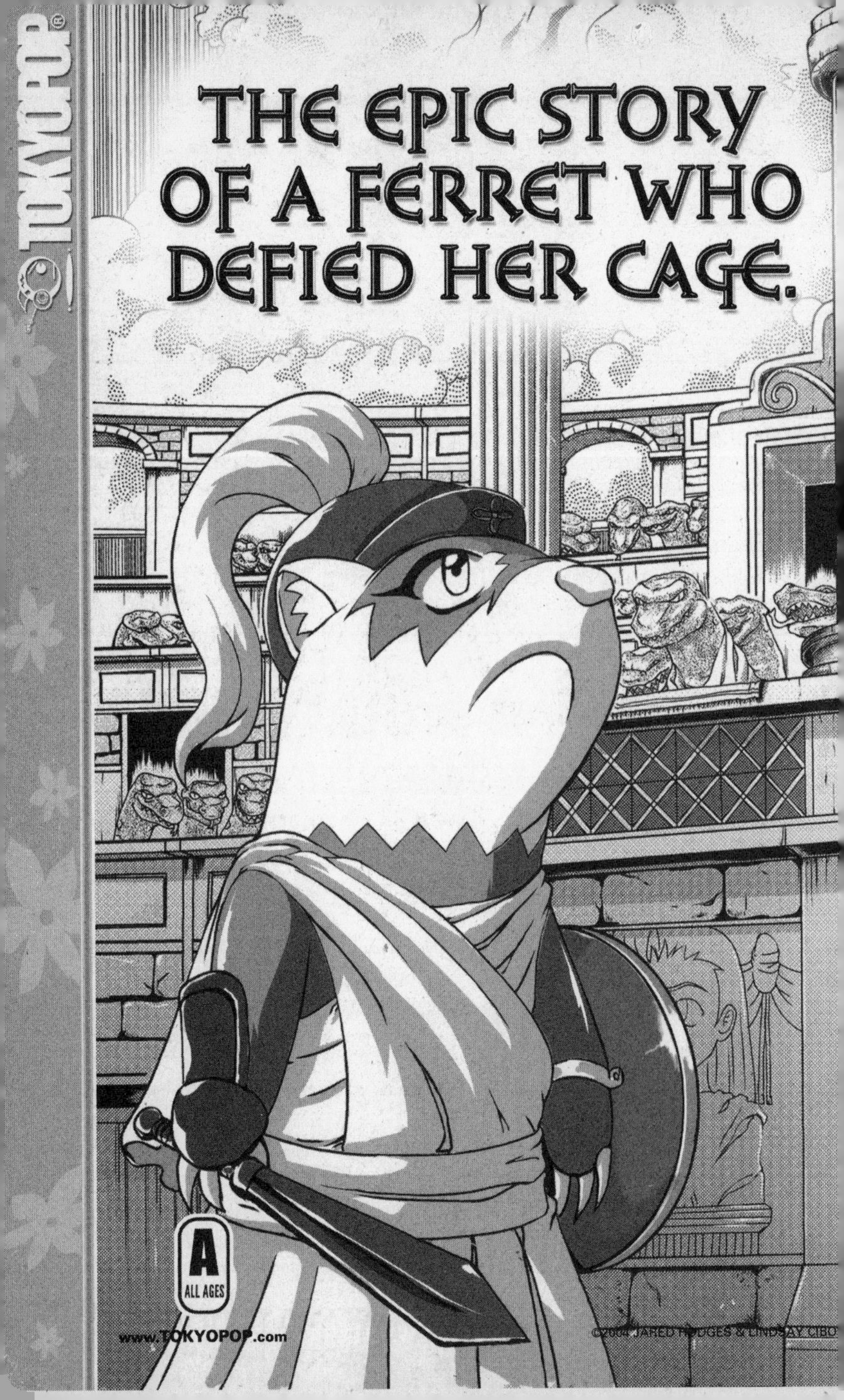
TOKYOPOP
THE EPIC STORY OF A FERRET WHO DEFIED HER CAGE.
A
ALL AGES
www.TOKYOPOP.com
©2004 JARED HODGES & LINDSAY CIBO

STOP!

This is the back of the book.
You wouldn't want to spoil a great ending!

his book is printed "manga-style," in the authentic Japanese right-to-left ormat. Since none of the artwork has been flipped or altered, readers et to experience the story just as the creator intended. You've been sking for it, so TOKYOPOP® delivered: authentic, hot-off-the-press, nd far more fun!

right panel and follow the numbers. Have fun, and look for more 100% authentic manga from TOKYOPOP®!